The Acquisition of Heritage Languages

Heritage speakers are native speakers of a minority language they learn at home, but, due to socio-political pressure from the majority language spoken in their community, their heritage language does not fully develop. In the last decade, the acquisition of heritage languages has become a central focus of study within linguistics and applied linguistics. This work centers on the grammatical development of the heritage language and the language learning trajectory of heritage speakers, synthesizing recent experimental research. *The Acquisition of Heritage Languages* offers a global perspective, with a wealth of examples from heritage languages around the world. Written in an accessible style, this authoritative and up-to-date text is essential reading for professionals, students, and researchers of all levels working in the fields of sociolinguistics, psycholinguistics, education, language policies, and language teaching.

- Discusses examples and studies from heritage languages all over the world
- Provides accessible explanations of linguistic terms
- Explores the theories and research methods applied to heritage language acquisition.

SILVINA MONTRUL is Professor of Spanish and Linguistics at the University of Illinois at Urbana-Champaign, and directs the University Language Academy for Children and the Second Language Acquisition and Bilingualism Lab.

The Acquisition of Heritage Languages

Silvina Montrul

CAMBRIDGE
UNIVERSITY PRESS

Shaftesbury Road, Cambridge CB2 8EA, United Kingdom

One Liberty Plaza, 20th Floor, New York, NY 10006, USA

477 Williamstown Road, Port Melbourne, VIC 3207, Australia

314–321, 3rd Floor, Plot 3, Splendor Forum, Jasola District Centre, New Delhi – 110025, India

103 Penang Road, #05–06/07, Visioncrest Commercial, Singapore 238467

Cambridge University Press is part of Cambridge University Press & Assessment, a department of the University of Cambridge.

We share the University's mission to contribute to society through the pursuit of education, learning and research at the highest international levels of excellence.

www.cambridge.org
Information on this title: www.cambridge.org/9781009346238

© Silvina Montrul 2016

First published 2016
First paperback edition 2022

A catalogue record for this publication is available from the British Library

Library of Congress Cataloging-in-Publication data
Montrul, Silvina.
The acquisition of heritage languages / Silvina Montrul.
    pages   cm
Includes bibliographical references and index.
ISBN 978-1-107-00724-6 (hbk)
1. Linguistic minorities–Social aspects   2. Language acquisition–Social
aspects.   3. Language and languages–Study and teaching–Foreign
speakers.   4. Sociolinguistics.   I. Title.
P40.5.L56M66   2015
418.0071–dc23   2015023044

ISBN   978-1-107-00724-6   Hardback
ISBN   978-1-009-34623-8   Paperback

Contents

Figures

Tables

Acknowledgments

I want to start by thanking deeply all the heritage speakers who have participated in my classes and in my studies, and who continue to inspire my work. My interest and amazement with heritage language acquisition dates back to 1998, when I took a position as Assistant Professor of Spanish at the University at Albany, SUNY. Although my stay at Albany was brief, the experience made an indelible mark on my research. The opportunity to work with a large number of Hispanic students in my classes redirected and expanded the thinking about second language acquisition and bilingualism that I had developed as a PhD student at McGill University in Montreal. When I left Canada, I was convinced that native language ability was achievable by any typically developing individual, that bilingual children are not cognitively confused when they learn two languages at the same time, and that growing up bilingually from childhood leads to highly proficient command of the two languages. But the Hispanic students I had the privilege to work with in the United States and their Spanish language abilities told me a very different story. By learning more about these students' personal histories as language learners in the United States and observing their uneven command of Spanish, I realized that the high level of achievement in the two languages obtained by many French-English Canadians in Quebec was not generalizable to Hispanic students in the United States. I became convinced that attitudinal and political factors were related to the overall lack of educational support heritage languages receive in the United States, which prevented these bilingual speakers from reaching their full potential in their native language.

The language of Hispanic children and the Hispanic population has been widely studied in education and sociolinguistics, but had not been approached from the psycholinguistic and theoretical linguistic perspective in which I had been trained. It was my sense at that time that this population could contribute powerful data to theories of language in general, as well as to theories of language acquisition and our notions of bilingualism. As I was developing studies on tense and aspect in the second language acquisition of Spanish in collaboration with Roumyana Slabakova, I decided to also collect data with bilingual Spanish speakers in the United States. In 2002 and 2004 I had my first two articles on language loss and incomplete acquisition among these bilingual heritage speakers published in *Bilingualism: Language and Cognition*. Around the same time I came across Masha Polinsky's writings on American Russian and William O'Grady's studies on Korean in America, which have since inspired me and convinced me of the urgency of unraveling the linguistic systems of heritage speakers.

Determined to pursue this goal, in 2004 I launched a major-scale research program to investigate key linguistic differences between second language learners and heritage speakers so that we would be better able to inform pedagogical practices that address their different linguistic and cultural needs. The project also tackled issues of theoretical significance. The "critical period hypothesis" had long been invoked to explain why postpuberty second language learners rarely reach the level of linguistic ability of native speakers. I put this hypothesis to the test by looking at the flip side of second language acquisition: bilinguals who had been exposed to two languages early in childhood or later and were losing their first language. The main results of this research project and the ideas I uncovered about age effects in language loss were published in *Incomplete Acquisition in Bilingualism: Reexamining the Age Factor* (2008), my first book on heritage speakers.

Even before I published *Incomplete Acquisition in Bilingualism*, interest in heritage languages and heritage speakers from different perspectives was already soaring in North America and other parts of the world, and the last two decades has seen a voluminous spurt of research using different methodologies. From 2007 and until 2013, I had the honor and pleasure to participate in the seven Heritage Language Summer Institutes organized by Olga Kagan, Director of the National Heritage Language Resource Center at UCLA, and Masha Polinsky (Director of Research). These week-long institutes were aimed at fostering and stimulating discussion of theoretical and practical issues dealing with heritage language and heritage language education, and brought together teachers, researchers, administrators, students, and community organizers of all types of heritage languages from the United States and other parts of the world. I have also had the honor and opportunity to share my work with colleagues and students in different parts of the United States and the world, all of whom share similar concerns about the education of heritage speakers. I learned a lot about the heritage speakers and minority language speakers in Canada, Ireland, Sweden, Germany, the Netherlands, Japan, and Australia. Many of the ideas and the extensive body of work I cover in this book found inspiration in all these meetings and interactions with colleagues around the world. For that reason, the target audience I had in mind when writing this book is students, researchers, and heritage language educators from different academic backgrounds and disciplinary orientations. The book focuses on the grammatical development of heritage languages, and is intended for readers with an introductory background in linguistics, or language acquisition, soci-olinguistics, psycholinguistics, education, language policies, and language teaching who have little background in the field of language acquisition.

In the present book heritage speakers and the heritage language acquisi-tion process take center stage. The main ideas on incomplete acquisition and attrition in heritage speakers that I advanced in *Incomplete Acquisition in Bilingualism* are present in this book as well, but these have evolved with new findings and have been refined since then. Not only does the present book represent my own thinking on heritage languages and their acquisition, but it does so in the context of the copious research that has appeared in the last two decades. Because heritage languages include indigenous languages, national/regional minority languages, and immigrant languages, I made every effort to cover representative classic and current research from different parts of the world, such as North America, Europe, and Australia.

I would like to thank all the people who have inspired me and helped me in bringing this work to completion. Chief among them are my colleagues from Illinois, graduate students, and co-authors in many of the studies cited in this book: James Yoon, Rakesh Bhatt, Elabbas Benmamoun, Roxana Girju, Tania Ionin, Melissa Bowles, Rebecca Foote, Jill Jegerski, Pam Hadley, Matt Rispoli, Eman Saadah, Archna Bhatia, Abdulkafi Albirini, Noelia Sánchez-Walker, Eunice Chung, Elias Shakkour, and Itxaso Rodríguez. I want to thank Masha Polinsky and Olga Kagan in particular, for inviting me to be part of the seven Heritage Language Summer Institutes they organ-ized from 2007 to 2013. Their outstanding leadership, dedication, inclu-siveness, and enthusiasm to promote heritage languages are a blessing and an inspiration for all of us working in this field. During these years, I have had stimulating dialogue with several colleagues who have challenged me and, undeniably, enriched me and my work. They are: William O'Grady, Maria Carreira, Kim Potowski, Julio Torres, Cristina Sanz, Oksana Laleko, Anna Mikhaylova, Agnes He, Maria Luisa Parra, Cecilia Colombi, Carmen Silva-Corvalán, Gabriela Zapata, Carol Klee, Irina Sekerina, Tom Roeper, Luiz Amaral, Barbara Pearson, Conchúr Ó Giollagáin, Rakel Österberg, Lars Fant, Kenneth Hyltenstam, Pieter Muysken, Shanley Allen, Sharon Unsworth, Elma Blom, Tanja Kupisch, Bernhard Brehmer, Jason Rothman, Diego Pascual y Cabo, Virginia Valian, Ricardo Otheguy, and Janet Fodor, among many others. Without the enthusiasm from Cambridge University Press, this project would not have been possible and I am grateful to Helen Barton for encouraging me to pursue it. I am most grateful to the readers who evaluated the proposal and the manuscript for their useful feedback and suggestions. Writing can be a lonely pursuit, and can only be improved with the help of attentive readers. I owe a huge thank you to Sara Mason, Abdulkafi Albirini, Roumyana Slabakova, Jill Jegerski, and Masha Polinsky for agreeing to read the manuscript at different stages and giving me substantive feedback. Any errors that remain are my responsibility, of course.

As with every book I have written, I would not have been able to do it without the patience, support, and understanding from my family. I owe tremendous debt to my husband Marc and to the two Spanish heritage speakers in my life, Lea (17 years old) and Olivia (11 years old).

1 Introduction

Language acquisition is the growth of language – and, more specifically, growth of a grammatical and communicative system – in the mind of a speaker. Human beings are biologically programmed with a faculty for language, but a key ingredient for language to develop or grow is input. Input consists of actual samples of language use or naturally occurring written/oral discourse, preferably experienced in the context of social interaction.

As children move spontaneously from babbling to first words, phrases, and sentences in what many consider a relatively short time, the study of language acquisition by monolingual children has fascinated many parents and scholars for years. Because learning the grammar of a language is a process with a beginning followed by a period of development that spans several years, the study of language acquisition is concerned with describing the typical courses of development of different aspects of vocabulary and grammar, and explaining why they follow the sequence they do and not any other logically possible ones. Another concern of the study of language acquisition is the outcome of the process – what the end state looks like – and identifying the cognitive, social, and environmental factors that contribute to reaching and shaping the linguistic properties of the end state. The typical, normal outcome of first language acquisition is reaching adult native speaker knowledge and use of language within their speech community. Although it seems trivially true that the more you hear a language the better you learn it, how input and experience relate to the development and outcome of the language acquisition process is still very poorly understood.

If two or more languages are part of the linguistic and socialization environment of the child, then we can talk about bilingual first language acquisition (De Houwer 2009; Meisel 1994, 2001). Amazingly, young children are able to comfortably handle and develop two grammatical systems simultaneously and to different degrees if they are exposed to two languages in the environment. But children and adults can also acquire another, second, language after the core structural foundations of the first language are relatively set. The acquisition of a second language can start at different times in life: it can take place in infancy, after infancy, in later childhood, adolescence, and in adulthood.

First language acquisition, bilingual first language acquisition (the simultaneous acquisition of two languages), and second language acquisition are all established disciplinary fields with specific theoretical and methodological traditions and clear implications for clinical interventions and education.

What is, then, the acquisition of heritage languages, and why do we need a book about it? Heritage language acquisition is a type of early bilingual acquisition that takes place in a specific sociolinguistic environment. The acquisition of heritage languages deals with the study of the developmental stages and outcome of learning a heritage language from childhood and into adulthood, as well as the wax and wane of the heritage language in response to input factors. Broadly defined, heritage languages are culturally or ethnolinguistically minority languages that develop in a bilingual setting where another sociopolitically majority language is spoken. Heritage languages are commonly spoken by immigrants and their children, but they can also be spoken in their own territories when national or regional languages and indigenous languages share space with a majority language. Heritage speakers are child and adult members of a linguistic minority who grow up exposed to their home language – the heritage language – and the majority official language spoken and used in the broader speech community. From a psycholinguistic, individual perspective, the group of heritage speakers encompasses different types of early bilingual learners, exposed to the heritage language and the majority language in childhood before puberty, as we will see in Chapter 4.

As the product of a language contact situation, the study of heritage languages and heritage speakers – although not always called this way – has been around since the existence of linguistics as a science. Sociolinguists and historical linguists have long been interested in issues related to language change and emergence of new language varieties (Weinrich 1953), including the creation of creole languages from pidgin situations, and the demise of languages and their speech communities, as with endangered languages and situations of language death (Dorian 1989). Since the 2000s, the study of heritage speakers as bilingual language learners has taken on unprecedented prominence for both theoretical and practical reasons, attracting keen interest from fields such as theoretical linguistics, psycholinguistics and language acquisition, applied linguistics, and education, among others.

Why are heritage speakers suddenly so interesting or relevant for the language sciences? The modern era of globalization has brought about several far-reaching economic and geopolitical changes, and this special group of bilinguals speaks to the daily challenges faced by educators and clinicians in many parts of the world. Nearly all the high-income countries of the world are experiencing substantial growth in their immigrant-origin student populations. Concurrently, globalization is placing new demands on education systems the world over. As a consequence, school systems are facing the challenge of educating large and growing numbers of recently immigrated children of increasingly diverse origins to greater levels of competence and skill. Schooling systems worldwide are concerned about the full development of the second language (or the language of the host country) in immigrant children. At the same time, the field of heritage language acquisition makes its focus the development, stagnation, regression, and reacquisition of the family language. While school systems strongly emphasize the development of immigrants' competence in the majority language of the society, adolescent and young adult heritage speakers may become interested in further developing their skills in the heritage language for potential career advantages.

These days, for example, in many colleges and universities in North America, heritage speakers of many languages turn to second/foreign language classes originally developed for second language learners with no previous knowledge of the language to learn, relearn, or develop their heritage language. Realizing that these speakers are very different in many ways from traditional second language learners who initiate their acquisition of a second/foreign language in adulthood, teachers, language practitioners, and language program administrators have been pondering and debating how to best deal with this educational challenge, and in many institutions special language programs or curricular tracks have been developed for these students. If heritage speakers already know the language because they speak it at home, an obvious question is why they seek language instruction in a formal setting. Heritage speakers of Spanish and of Hindi in the United States (all university students in their twenties) that I have tested in my research over the past 6 years have provided reasons such as the following:[1]

> "I want to be just as comfortable writing, speaking, reading, and
>   listening in Spanish as I am in English."
> "I would like to improve my writing skills as well as reading. Also,
>   my speech needs work and my vocabulary is very limited."
> "I want to be grammatically correct."
> "I want to embrace my culture as much as possible and I feel that
>   I lost a vital part of speaking it while I was growing up."
> "Because I am weaker at my native language."
> "I don't want to start talking in English when speaking in Hindi."
> "I don't know how to read or write so I would like to improve that.
>   I also want to improve my speaking abilities so that I can be confi-
>   dent if I ever have to speak with a stranger in India."

[1] This research was funded by a National Science Foundation Grant ARRA 09175939 (2009–2013) to Silvina Montrul, Rakesh Bhatt, and Roxana Girju.

As these responses indicate, these speakers consider the heritage language a *native language* and part of their *cultural heritage*, but it is also a *weaker language* when compared with English because some speakers feel *they have lost parts of it as they were growing up*. A central issue in the study of heritage speakers and heritage language acquisition is what specifically gives credence to these self-reflections. What, specifically, has been lost or changed in comparison to adult speakers like their parents who were raised in a predominantly monolingual context where the heritage language is the majority language of society? These comments portray an undeniable awareness of weaknesses in their grammatical competence, and their collective voices call for expanding vocabulary, learning the grammar, and improving their speaking and fluency so that they can feel comfortable and confident speaking the heritage language without resorting to code-switching in English. Still, the most common answer is that they want to learn how to read and write or develop their vocabulary and grammatical skills further.

These personal accounts challenge at least two common myths about language and language learning. The first one is that the acquisition of a language since childhood uniformly and universally results in native-like command of the language in adulthood (Chomsky 1981; Crain and Thornton 1998). The second one is that once acquired by the end of the preschool period, the structural integrity of the native language is stable. Naturally, these assumptions take for granted the linguistic environment and the conditions of language use because they have been formulated on the basis of an "ideal" monolingual speaker who has not been raised in a language contact situation, or whose native language is not a minority language.

This book focuses on the grammatical development of the heritage language and the language learning trajectory of heritage speakers, and synthesizes the research of the last 20 years. It is intended for professionals, students, and researchers interested in understanding the factors that play a role in the acquisition of heritage languages. Readers with a background in linguistics, sociolinguistics, psycholinguistics, education, language policies, and language teaching who have little background in the field of language acquisition, will find this book most useful. The book should also be of interest to those already familiar with first and second language acquisition who want to further their knowledge of heritage languages.

The main argument I advance in this book is that heritage languages are native languages even though they may not always look that way. This is because the process of language acquisition and mastery is long and not all native languages acquired in a bilingual context develop in the same way into adolescence and beyond. Without proper environmental support, the heritage language remains unstable after the age of basic grammatical development, leading to incomplete acquisition or attrition of different aspects of the grammatical system. By the time many heritage speakers reach early adulthood, their heritage language displays many characteristics typical of adult second language acquisition in some modules of the grammar, but they maintain native-like mastery in other grammatical modules. The sociopolitical status of the heritage language as a minority language plays a fundamental role in the degree of language acquisition, maintenance, and loss of the heritage language throughout early childhood, middle childhood, and adolescence; that is, the entire span of the language learning period. Furthermore, for languages that have a written and literary tradition, academic support of the language and development of literacy skills during the school-age period can contribute significantly to language maintenance and the degree of linguistic competence acquired in the heritage language in early adulthood.

Just as the impetus that gave rise to the field of second language acquisition originated from pedagogical concerns (Thomas 2013), the field of heritage language acquisition is also driven by:

- a need to understand the nature of linguistic knowledge of the heritage language that heritage language learners bring to the classroom as young adults;
- how their linguistic knowledge has been acquired and forgotten or actually never acquired throughout their childhood;
- how it is represented, accessed, and processed when used in comprehension and production;
- how it is affected by literacy;
- how it differs from that of other speaker groups, such as the parents, native speakers who do not grow up or live in a language contact situation, children acquiring the language as a first and only language, and adult second language learners with whom they may share the classroom.

Some of these questions are eminently practical, whereas others are theoretically profound and at the core of several disciplines within the language sciences, especially bilingualism.

Heritage languages and their acquisition exist in a natural language contact environment and although sociolinguists have led the way in the study of bilingual societies and the language varieties that emerge from these situations, the focus in the last 20 years has shifted to the study of heritage languages as an individual phenomenon in the minds of speakers. Naturally, issues related to language development, linguistic knowledge, and language use interact with social variables. Among heritage speakers, we find simultaneous and sequential acquisition of a variety of pairs of languages that may be more or less typologically and genetically similar to each other, and this situation allows us to tease apart universal versus language-specific aspects of language and language development. The linguistic effects of the quantity, quality, and type of input from native speakers and from bilinguals with different degrees of proficiency in the two languages are other enduring questions that the study of heritage languages can help inform. Even more intractable but no less important is how the changing nature of input throughout the lifespan of heritage speakers contributes to the acquisition, maintenance, and loss of the heritage language at the individual level and across generations. The interaction of type and amount of input with age of onset of bilingualism in heritage speakers has opened new ways to investigate the nature of the linguistic systems that develop in heritage speakers.

Embedded in this context, heritage language education has found a place and a voice of its own within theoretical, experimental, and applied linguistics. As a field that emerged out of necessity, driven primarily by demographic changes, heritage language education has been strongly concerned with issues of cultural identity (i.e., who exactly are heritage speakers?) as well as pedagogical and practical questions, including *what* to teach and *how* to best instruct heritage language learners so that their personal, cultural, and linguistic needs can be properly met (Brinton, Kagan, and Bauckus 2008). In countries where heritage languages are national languages, such as in Ireland or in the Basque country, the realization that children may not develop their native language at age-appropriate levels under pressure from the majority language (English, Spanish) has led to substantial national efforts being invested to reintroduce the minority languages in the education system and to educate children bilingually or monolingually in these languages (Cenoz and Gorter 2008). But in countries where the heritage languages come and go with the waves of immigration, as in the United States, some schools in areas with a high concentration of speakers have developed special classes and programs for heritage languages, such as Spanish, Russian, Asian languages, and many others. Nonetheless, Valdés (1995, 2005) and Lynch (2003) have raised concerns about the atheoretical character of the field of heritage language education that emerged from this situation and its "blind appropriation and adaptation of foreign language methods" (Valdés *et al.* 2006, p. 235). The implication of such claim seems to be that if the heritage language education wants to move forward as a field of inquiry, it must develop a theory of heritage language acquisition.

In the last decade, the acquisition of heritage languages has moved from the margins to become a central focus of study within linguistics and applied linguistics. Another argument I advance in this book, therefore, is that the study of heritage languages and the acquisition of heritage languages can be profitably embraced by existing theoretical approaches to language and language acquisition within linguistics and applied linguistics. Because heritage language acquisition is another instance of multilingual language acquisition (see Figure 1.1), extending mainstream approaches and methods to this particular acquisition situation allows comparability of results of heritage languages with data from first language learners, second language learners, simultaneous

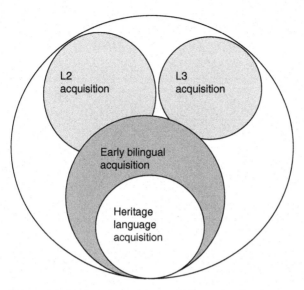

Figure 1.1. Heritage language acquisition as another instance of multilingual language acquisition.

bilinguals, and child second language learners. Through these comparisons we can identify the need to develop new methodological and data analyses methods to study aspects of heritage language acquisition that may not lend themselves to be easily investigated with the methods and tools we already have from sister disciplines.

Perhaps a particular attraction of the study of heritage speakers and heritage languages for theoretical linguistics is its focus on real, contemporary, bilingual native speakers. Generative linguistic theorizing (Chomsky 1981) in particular has been based on the study of "idealized" monolingual native speakers. When theories of language abstract away from the actual contexts of language learners and real speakers, they risk becoming weaker in real-world relevance, psychological validity and, ultimately, explanatory power (Jackendoff 2002). Given the complex nature of heritage language acquisition, where cognitive, social, cultural, and biological factors interact, another important appeal of heritage speakers is that their study invites a multidisciplinary approach within linguistics, especially bridging sociolinguistics, theoretical linguistics, and psycholinguistics, as shown in Figure 1.2. This kind of interdisciplinary collaboration also has real implications for education, clinical practices, and language policies.

A positive development in the last two decades has been the surge in descriptive studies (both large scale and single case studies) of heritage speakers'

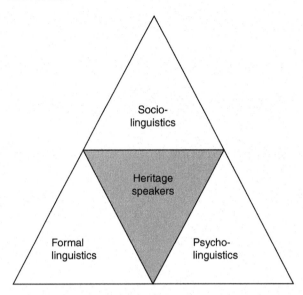

Figure 1.2. Multidisciplinary approach to the study of heritage speakers.

linguistic profiles of different heritage languages. In addition, we have increasingly seen more theoretically oriented research on heritage speakers of different ages, heritage language acquisition, and the psycholinguistic processes involved in this type of learning at the individual level. Existing theories of acquisition from related fields in linguistics have so far proved to be eminently appropriate to use with heritage languages and heritage speakers, as we will see in Chapters 5, 7, and 8.

Given the current interest in heritage speakers from all these theoretical perspectives, the objective of this book is to present a comprehensive overview and critical synthesis of the state of this field. Examining the vast body of theoretically oriented research that has accumulated over the last two decades allows us to assess how our knowledge has advanced in the last few years and predict what lies ahead, so that we can articulate clearer implications for advancing research, instructional practices, and language policies on heritage languages.

The book, therefore, discusses the development of linguistic, grammatical knowledge of heritage language speakers from childhood to adulthood, and the political, educational, social, cognitive, and affective conditions under which language learning does or does not occur in these minority-language-speaking populations. Placing heritage language acquisition as central to current and viable cognitive and linguistic theories of acquisition, the book showcases what research has uncovered so far about heritage speakers of different languages

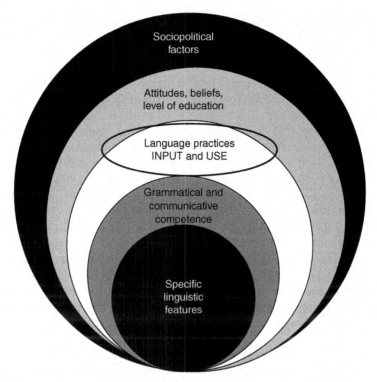

Figure 1.3. Factors affecting specific linguistic features in heritage language competence and use.

and their language learning process, offering crucial information for peda-gogical practices, curricular development, and language policies. Ultimately, this work attempts to be a landmark in the field of heritage language acquisi-tion, both as a reference source and as a catalyst for further research and dis-cussion in expanding the field.

Although the main focus of this book is on the advances in our understand-ing of the linguistic and psycholinguistic nature of heritage language acquisi-tion, the development and linguistic outcome of heritage language acquisition cannot be understood in isolation from its socio-affective context. Therefore, sociolinguistic and attitudinal factors are taken into account to some extent as well. There is no doubt that the study of heritage speakers encourages us to examine in more depth the indirect relationship between the individual psycho-linguistic level and language change at the sociohistorical level by way of the development of the language, conceptualized in Figure 1.3.

Figure 1.3 attempts to capture the fact that language is both a sociopolitical and a grammatical construct represented in the individual minds of speakers: in fact, language as a grammatical and psycholinguistic construct is embedded within language as a sociopolitical construct. If linguists and psycholinguists are interested in investigating specific linguistic features of heritage speakers, as the inner circle in Figure 1.3 shows, these cannot be properly understood without consideration of how the status of the language indirectly affects knowledge, acquisition, processing, and use of those features in communicative situations.

Furthermore, the sociopolitical status of the language (majority versus minority status) affects the attitudes and beliefs of its speakers toward the language, as well as the availability of the education in that language, and its degree of public use, for example. Language attitudes, in turn, affect language practices and patterns of language use: if a language is not used in education and outside of the home, it will not be heard and used as much by its speakers because they may not see its value. Input and use affect, in turn, grammatical and communicative competence, as manifested in particular linguistic features that are now part of the psycholinguistic representation of the speaker. In sum, as depicted in Figure 1.3, input seems to be the key ingredient that links psycholinguistic and sociolinguistic factors in heritage language acquisition. Understanding proximal and distal aspects of input in heritage speakers is crucial (Armon-Lotem *et al.* 2014). Proximal factors refer to basic input quantity, such as length of exposure and proportion of daily input in a given language. Distal factors are the broader environmental influences that contribute to a child's language development in qualitative ways, such as socioeconomic status, sociopolitical status of the language, language attitudes, and vitality of the language in the broader speech community.

To elucidate the interrelationship between macro-sociopolitical factors, micro-sociopsychological attitudes and practices as they bear on language acquisition, retention, and loss, the study of heritage languages and their acquisition necessitates a multidisciplinary approach where sociolinguistics, psycholinguistics, theoretical linguistics, and applied linguistics among other disciplines come together. In this book I show that while purely linguistic factors play a major role in determining the specific linguistic structures and constraints that arise under language contact at the psycholinguistic level, the effects of the social and ideological contexts are also relevant, although sometimes more indirectly and less immediately apparent. Questions that arise, but which are not answered in the book are, how can these be linked more directly? How can sociopolitical factors affect attitudes and language practices, which in turn affect the quantity and quality of input that forms the raw material for language acquisition? I hope that these questions can be taken up for further research.

The study of heritage languages and heritage speakers has significant implications for language policies and education, especially for second and third generation children and adolescents. Key dilemmas are whether, when, and how instruction in the heritage language should be provided; the timing of the introduction of the majority language as a second language; and modifications in the educational programs, instructional methods, materials for instruction, and teacher training to accommodate the linguistic needs of heritage speakers.

For these reasons, basic understanding of the language development of heritage speakers from early childhood to early adulthood is essential, and although the field of heritage language education has seen impressive growth in the last decade, to date there is no single book that provides a comprehensive and authoritative overview of the state-of-the-science of heritage language acquisition. This book aims to fill this gap by presenting the outcome of linguistic research conducted in the last decade and by addressing theoretical, empirical, and practical issues in heritage language acquisition.

The rest of the book is organized as follows. Because defining heritage speakers has not been an easy task, Chapter 2 introduces some current definitions of heritage languages and heritage speakers, the definitions and assumptions adopted in this book, and the problems that they may present. Because the main focus of this book is on grammatical development, Chapter 3 focuses on describing the language of heritage speakers and many of the structural properties displayed by heritage speakers in the context of the structural properties of the parental generation and of native speakers who did not grow up in a language contact situation. I argue that the characteristics of heritage languages described in Chapter 3 are largely due to how the heritage language was acquired, and for that reason Chapter 4 takes the reader through the language learning process in a language contact situation, discussing heritage language acquisition as bilingual acquisition in a specific sociolinguistic context. In describing the process and timeline of heritage language acquisition from birth to adulthood, I also consider several environmental factors and psycholinguistic processes that may contribute independently or collectively to language shift (gradual transition from speaking the heritage language to speaking and using the majority language predominantly) and the resulting divergent grammatical systems of heritage speakers in early adulthood. The main empirical evidence for many of the claims made in Chapter 4 is presented in Chapters 7 and 8, but before getting to these chapters the reader is introduced to some theories and methods that have been applied to the study of heritage speakers most recently. Chapter 5 provides theoretical approaches to heritage language acquisition and illustrates how mainstream theories of first and second language acquisition have been profitably extended to address the problem of heritage language acquisition. Because research design is (or should be) intimately linked to the theoretical assumptions that motivate the research questions, Chapter 6 emphasizes key methodological considerations when developing experimental research with heritage speakers and discusses many of the challenges that still remain when studying heritage languages and heritage speakers. Chapter 7 showcases recent research and research designs that addresses the nature of heritage language grammars in relation to linguistic theory, language change, and first language acquisition. Chapter 8 changes the focus to the differences and similarities between heritage language acquisition and second language acquisition, including a discussion of the few studies that have addressed research in the classroom. Finally, Chapter 9 takes stock of the theoretical, empirical, and practical advances in the field to date, considers implications for language policies and education, and points to areas of future research and development.

2   Heritage languages and heritage speakers

What is a heritage language and who qualifies as a heritage speaker? This chapter presents some common definitions and discusses the terminological problems brought about by using the term *heritage* to classify languages and speakers. Because most existing definitions of heritage languages and heritage speakers may not capture all the individuals and language situations represented in current research, I provide several concrete examples of situations that would fit the characteristics of heritage languages and heritage speakers assumed in this book. As caveat, I must mention that the examples provided are representative of the different types of heritage speakers studied to date but are hardly exhaustive.

2.1   What is a heritage language?

The *American Heritage College Dictionary* defines the word *heritage* as something acquired from birth, a property that can be inherited, or something passed down from a preceding generation. If the property acquired is language, then all human languages are heritage languages as long as they are acquired from birth and transmitted to the next generation. But the term *heritage* as applied to languages and speakers is a relative rather than absolute characterization because what makes a given language a "heritage" language is its local social context. As used in linguistics, education, and language policy, among other fields, the term *heritage language* is hardly neutral because it has sociopolitical connotations related to the distinction between majority and minority languages. Originally coined in Canada in the 1970s, the term *heritage language* began to be used in the United States in the 1990s to refer to minority languages (Cummins 2005, p. 585). Other commonly used terms in different parts of the world to refer to heritage languages are *international, community, immigrant, ethnic, indigenous, minority, ancestral, third*, and *non-official language* (Duff 2008a; Fishman 2006; Lo Bianco 2008; Wiley 2008). Common terms used in Europe to refer to immigrants and their children are *ethnic minorities*, or depending on reasons for immigration, *migrant workers, immigrant families*, and *refugees* (Extra and Verhoeven 1993). In Europe, the term *European*

Community language refers to the official national languages of the European Community member states (Coulmas 1991), and does not include indigenous and non-indigenous minority languages, whereas in Australia, *community languages* refers to immigrant languages and the indigenous languages of Australia (Clyne 1991). Thus, in Australia, *community languages* are heritage languages as defined in North America.

The distinction between a majority and a minority language is sociopolitical. Majority languages typically (but not always) have official status and recognition, are used in the media, and are the language of government administration and education. For example, English is the majority language in the United Kingdom, the United States, Canada, and Australia and so is Spanish in Spain and in Spanish-speaking Latin America, or French in France and in Quebec. Minority languages, on the other hand, are the languages of ethnolinguistic minority groups, and may or may not have co-official status. For different reasons, minority languages are often marginalized within nations or territories. The ethnolinguistic group in question may be a demographic minority, or may have a large population but be considered a minority by virtue of its lower social, cultural, and political status related to factors surrounding immigration or colonization. Examples of minority languages are (1) indigenous or aboriginal languages in the Americas (Inuttitut in Canada, Quechua in Peru, and Guaraní and Ticuna in Brazil) and in Australia (Dyirbal and Warlpiri), (2) national languages in many territories (French in Canada, Irish in Ireland, Welsh in Wales, Basque, Catalan, and Galician in Spain, and Sámi in Norway, Sweden, and Finland), and (3) immigrant languages all over the world (see Table 2.1). Fishman (2001, 2006) includes colonial languages (spoken during the formation of the American colonies and throughout the seventeenth and eighteenth centuries) like French, German, Welsh, Dutch, Finnish, and Swedish in the United States as heritage languages as well.

The majority/minority distinction is not inherent to any language but is determined by the local context. Sociohistorical and economic-political factors like colonization, territorial annexation, and migration determine the status of a language. Some languages can in fact have dual status as minority or majority depending on territory: Spanish is a majority language in Spain and Spanish-speaking Latin America, but a minority language in the United States. Spanish is also the most widely studied second/foreign language in US schools. Similarly, Hindi is an official majority language in India, but a minority language in the United Kingdom and in the United States. Global languages such as Spanish, English, Dutch, Portuguese, Hindi, Chinese, and so on are majority languages in their own territories but minority languages in diaspora contexts. Romani – the first Indian language to be spoken in Europe and the language of the gypsies – is predominantly known as a heritage language. Because gypsies

Table 2.1. *Examples of heritage languages*

Heritage languages	Examples
Immigrant languages	Spanish, Hindi, Russian, Korean, Mandarin, Arabic, and Tagalog in the United States and Canada, Turkish and Polish in the Netherlands and Germany, Finnish in Sweden, Dutch in Australia and South Africa, English in Israel and the Middle East, German in Brazil, Italian and Korean in Argentina, Amharic in Italy, and Polish and Hindi/Urdu in the UK
National minority languages[a]	Basque in Spain and France, Catalan in Catalonia, Irish in Ireland, Welsh in Wales, Walloon in France, Greek and Aromanian in Albania, and Frisian in the Netherlands and Germany
Aboriginal languages	Navajo in the United States, Inuttitut in Canada, Dyirbal in Australia, Quechua in Peru, Náhuatl in Mexico, and Sámi in Scandinavia

[a] These may have official status.

(Roma people) have always been a migrant group they do not have their own national territory (Kenrick 1993).

As currently used in the United States, a *heritage language* is a language other than English spoken by immigrants and their children (Valdés 2001). In Canada, the term heritage language refers to languages other than French and English (the official languages) and aboriginal languages (Duff 2008a). *Heritage language* may also refer to an ancestral language that may or may not be spoken in the home or in the community. Although a great bulk of the content of this book will refer to research on immigrant languages, the term *heritage languages* will be used to refer to minority languages co-existing with majority languages, including immigrant languages, national minority languages, and aboriginal languages, as summarized in Table 2.1.

2.2 Who is a heritage speaker?

Because heritage languages are defined by their local sociolinguistic status and situation and encompass several possibilities, defining precisely who can be classified as a heritage speaker has not been simple, and the elusive problem of identifying heritage speakers is familiar in the literature. In fact, most articles about heritage speakers spend a significant portion of their introductory sections discussing issues concerning the label *heritage speaker* and its connotations (Beaudrie and Fairclough 2012; Carreira 2004; Carreira and Kagan 2011; de Bot and Gorter 2005; Fishman 2001; He 2010; Hornberger and Wang 2008; King and Ennser-Kananen 2013; Polinsky and Kagan 2007; Van Deusen-Scholl

2003). All the terms available to date are appropriate for the specific context and communities they describe but are often hard to apply beyond that. If a heritage language can be an immigrant language, a colonial language, and official minority language in its territory, and an indigenous language, Carreira (2004) and Beaudrie and Fairclough (2012) are justified in their assertion that no single definition can embrace all these situations. Because as Carreira aptly puts it, we do not have a "size that fits all" when it comes to defining heritage speakers, it is instructive to give examples of how the term has been used so far.

As used in the United States, *heritage speaker* refers to individuals from language minority groups who grow up exposed to a minority language in the home and the majority societal language. In essence, this is a bilingual situation, and heritage speakers are bilingual individuals. The typical heritage speaker is a young adult, although age itself does not define a heritage speaker. A widespread definition in linguistic research and the teaching of heritage languages is Valdés' (2000, p. 1): "a student who is raised in a home where a non-English language is spoken, who *speaks or merely understands the heritage language, and who is to some degree bilingual in English and the heritage language* [emphasis mine]." Valdés's definition, like many other definitions available, is not without problems. For example, it is odd to describe a language as "non-English" and restrictive if we want to extend this definition to heritage speakers living in other countries or in other language contact situations, or to indigenous languages in countries where the majority language is not English. I often quote Valdés's definition because it underscores two important characteristics of heritage speakers, and these characteristics provide, in my view, sufficient operational criteria to characterize linguistic knowledge properly. First, a heritage speaker is somebody who grew up in a bilingual and bicultural environment where the home language and the majority language were spoken. Second, Valdés' definition takes into account bilingual competence.

Two notions related to bilingual competence are language dominance – the idea that one language of the bilingual will be used more often (in specific contexts) and will likely be processed more easily than the other – and proficiency, actual grammatical ability, and fluency in a language. Linguistic proficiency is one dimension of dominance, and although it often correlates with dominance, it cannot be entirely equated with it (Montrul in press). Some bilinguals may exhibit similar patterns of language dominance but may differ on the levels of proficiency in each language when compared to each other, as I will discuss in more detail in Chapters 3 and 4.

Heritage speakers are a precise example of this situation. Therefore, degree of proficiency in the heritage language is important in defining a heritage speaker, even when their degree of proficiency in the heritage language is relative and may vary considerably from heritage speaker to heritage speaker, within speakers of the same language, and across heritage languages. Although there are exceptions, heritage speakers tend to be dominant in the majority language and the heritage language is their weaker language. Even within this general pattern of majority language dominance, proficiency levels in the heritage language varies widely from individual to individual. That is, some speakers can be fully fluent in the language (including in spoken and formal written registers), while others may only possess very limited productive ability and more developed receptive ability (understanding of some words and phrases). The vast majority of heritage speakers of many languages, however, lies in-between these two extremes, displaying low to advanced overall proficiency in the heritage language, with important dissociations or different proficiencies by skill (speaking, listening, reading, and writing).

The current situation of mainland China provides another layer of complexity to define and characterize heritage speakers in terms of linguistic balance and relative proficiency in the majority language and in the heritage language (Ramsey 1987). In China, there are over a hundred languages spoken by at least fifty-six recognized ethnic groups (Cantonese, Mandarin, Han, Hmong languages, Tibetan languages, etc.). Putonghua – a variety of Mandarin – is the standard, official, Chinese language. The majority of Chinese speakers with no university education are heritage speakers of their local language and second language speakers of the official language Mandarin. Thus, many Chinese children and adults with low levels of education may have high competence in their heritage language and lower proficiency in the majority language. Many speakers of Mayan languages in Mexico and Guatemala are also still more dominant in the heritage language than in the majority language, fitting this same profile.

My own definition of heritage speakers as "early bilinguals of minority languages" (Montrul 2008, p. 161) takes into account a developmental perspective. That is, heritage speakers are early bilinguals because they were exposed to the heritage language and the majority language in childhood. However, as explained above, their command of the two languages changes throughout the life course and the language learning period, as I will discuss in detail in Chapter 4. Although by the time heritage speakers are young adults they are dominant in the majority language, this does not mean that subtractive bilingualism of this sort is a crucial component of defining a heritage speaker. In other words, the outcome of acquisition is not relevant for defining a heritage speaker (Benmamoun, Montrul, and Polinsky 2013a,b; Kupisch 2013; Meisel 2013). There are heritage speakers who may be balanced or relatively balanced in the two languages, or who have a very fluent command of the heritage language (Kupisch *et al.* 2013) because the family, social, and political environment where they grew up in Europe supported the development of the two languages. In Chapters 3 and 4, I will discuss in more detail the reasons why heritage speakers show the particular pattern of language dominance that they show, and how the different possible degrees of proficiency in the heritage

Table 2.2. *Characteristics of a heritage speaker*

Characteristics of heritage speakers
• A bilingual individual who grew up in a bilingual home and has linguistic proficiency in two languages.
• The first language, or one of the first languages, spoken at home is a sociolinguistically minority language (the heritage language).
• The bilingual individual is usually dominant in the societal majority language (although balanced-heritage speakers also exist).
• The heritage language is often the weaker language.
• The degree of proficiency in the heritage language ranges from minimal and receptive ability to fully fluent and native-like.
• Proficiency in the societal majority language is typically native or native-like (depending on level of education).

language are related to their language learning experience. This experience would include variables such as age of acquisition of the majority language, amount of exposure and use of the heritage language throughout the language learning period, patterns of heritage language use in the family, access to a broader speech community, access to schooling and literacy development, among many others. Table 2.2 summarizes the basic characteristics of heritage speakers just described.

A suitable definition of a heritage speaker is critical for conducting basic research on the linguistic knowledge of heritage speakers. At the same time, a proper definition also has significant implications for language policies, education, language program administration, teacher-training, and curriculum and materials development. Because the main impetus for the emerging field of heritage language education in the last two decades has been pressing needs related to the maintenance, revitalization, or (re)acquisition of heritage languages in an instructed setting, educators and heritage language practitioners still struggle to characterize the prototypical heritage language learner (Benmamoun, Montrul, and Polinsky 2013a,b). However, not all heritage speakers are learning or wish to learn their language in the classroom. Therefore, a distinction must also be made between *heritage speakers* (HSs) and the *heritage language learners* (HLLs).

Polinsky and Kagan (2007) aptly capture this situation when they refer to heritage languages "in the wild" versus heritage languages "in the classroom." The study of heritage languages in the wild is the study of heritage speakers (HSs) and their linguistic knowledge for the purposes of linguistic research, typically tested in laboratory settings or in their natural setting (as in the sociolinguistic studies of communities). The focus of pedagogical and educational research and practices is, on the other hand, the heritage language learner (HLL). These are the heritage speakers who seek to (re)learn their heritage language in the classroom and are taking formal classes.

Now, it is tempting to jump to the conclusion that *heritage language learners* are a subset of *heritage speakers*, but if we assume that having some proficiency in the heritage language is crucial for our linguistic definition of a heritage speaker, not all the students who sign up for heritage language classes are heritage language speakers. In fact, some HLLs do not have any proficiency in the heritage language but may come to the classroom because they want to learn the language from zero. These HLLs, who do not speak or understand the language, may have a cultural connection to it, but they are in fact no different from the second language learners. Hence, a broad definition of a HLL emphasizes possible links between cultural and linguistic heritage and "a heritage motivation" (Polinsky and Kagan, 2007; Van Deusen-Scholl 2003). This could include, for example, African-American students seeking to learn Swahili, even when Swahili has not been part of their immediate family heritage. It can also include students of Jewish origin learning Yiddish or Hebrew, when Yiddish and Hebrew were not spoken in their family, or of learners of Czech in Iowa who come from Czech heritage but never learned the language. The situation of many Muslims who do not speak Arabic at home but learn it in the mosque also comes to mind. There are also aboriginal communities in the United States that hardly have any speakers left, as in the case of Yurok, a language that predates Spanish and English in California. The last speakers who passed away a few years ago were completely fluent, and the speakers that remain today are much less so (*The New York Times*, April 12, 2014). Therefore, if cultural connection is crucial to defining a heritage language learner, then Valdés' definition does not seem to include this learner profile.

On the other hand, the definition of heritage language learner offered by Hornberger and Wang (2008) relies heavily on cultural identity and self-definition. First, Hornberger and Wang (2008, p. 13) define identity as consisting of "hierarchical, multidimensional, ever-changing images, descriptions, projections, and evaluations of self and self in the eyes of others." Identity defined in this way determines one's sense of belonging and co-membership in a group. Following Erickson and Shultz (1982), Hornberger and Wang distinguish between primary and secondary membership. Primary members have deep knowledge of the cultural norms and appropriate ways of interaction within the community, whereas secondary members have partial knowledge and may not be actually intimately connected to the group.

Extending these notions to HLLs, primary HLLs are those with cultural and linguistic connections to the group, hence also HSs, whereas secondary HLLs are those who only have a cultural connection with the group. People may feel connections to a culture for different reason, and as Hornberger and Wang (2008) properly acknowledge, different groups may also have different norms and assumptions of what is required to be a member of a group. For example, the ability to speak Spanish is neither required nor sufficient for Hispanic identity in the United States. In some instances, Potowski (2012) has found that Spanish speakers from the Dominican Republic consider that speaking Spanish is crucial for Dominican identity, but according to Toribio (2003) this is more so for black Dominicans, who want to dissociate themselves from English-speaking African-Americans in the United States. On the other hand, many Puerto Ricans, especially those who grew up in the United States, do not think that knowing Spanish is critical to be considered Puerto Rican (Zentella 1990). Similarly, in the Arabic-speaking world, Palestinians have a stronger connection to their Arabic language than Egyptians (Albirini 2013), and speakers of Irish in Ireland and Scottish Gaelic in Scotland do not feel the need to define themselves according to language because linguistic distinctions are not seen as essential to the functioning of their ethnic community (Watson 1989).

Table 2.3 summarizes the differences between the linguistic and the cultural definition of heritage language learners. The table aims to illustrate that not all heritage speakers are heritage language learners and that some heritage language learners are not actually heritage speakers as defined in this chapter.

Table 2.3 shows that according to the linguistic definition, a heritage speaker is a bilingual speaker who grew up exposed to the heritage language and culture in the home and the societal majority language beyond the home, speaks the majority language fluently, and possesses productive or receptive ability in the heritage language. Not all these speakers seek to relearn, maintain, or further develop their heritage language in the classroom at school, community/church/Saturday school, or university. Those who do attend classes are *heritage language learners*. If a person has a cultural connection to the heritage language but was not exposed to the heritage language in the home, does not speak the language at all, and only speaks the majority language (and may have knowledge of a second language), then that person cannot be called a heritage speaker (see cultural definition column in Table 2.3). Although it is tempting to classify these speakers as heritage language learners when they go to the heritage language classroom (Carreira 2004), for pedagogical and language learning purposes they are *second language (L2) learners*, because they do not bring previous linguistic knowledge of the heritage language. An L2 learner begins acquisition of a second language after he or she has acquired their first language. L2 acquisition in adults can take place in a naturalistic setting (a second language environment in the case of immigration), in the classroom, or in both, as in many current study abroad programs that combine naturalistic exposure with instruction. Unlike typical L2 learners, HLLs

Table 2.3. *Characteristics of heritage speakers and heritage language learners*

	Linguistic definition	Cultural definition
Linguistic profile	Bilingual speaker/hearer	Monolingual speaker of the majority language
Characteristics	Some receptive and/or productive command of the heritage language	No knowledge of the heritage language
Connection to the culture	Deep and close	Remote and personal interest
Is this person a heritage speaker?	YES	NO
Is this person learning the language in the classroom?	If YES ⇩	If YES ⇩
	Heritage language learner (HLL)	Second language (L2) learner

bring knowledge of the heritage language acquired naturalistically at home in childhood.

As we will see in more detail in Chapter 4, the term *heritage speaker* encompasses a variety of psycholinguistic profiles that give rise to different types of bilinguals. Understanding the inherent heterogeneity of heritage speaker populations and how exactly HLLs are different from L2 learners becomes relevant for defining heritage speakers and HLLs, and has important implications for curriculum development and language program design and administration (Kagan and Dillon 2003; Montrul 2009). An empirical study that aimed to capture the heterogeneity found in a language program that serves HLLs and other learners is Kondo-Brown's (2005) linguistic assessment of 185 typical incoming learners of Japanese at the university level (see also Kanno *et al.* 2008). The purpose of the study was to contribute to a clear definition of who is a heritage language speaker and how different types of HLLs differ or not from L2/foreign language learners in their proficiency. Another aim was to identify whether different groups of HLLs and foreign language (FL) learners differed in linguistic subskills. Kondo-Brown's study took place at the University of Hawaii at Manoa, which hosts the largest Japanese language program in the United States. The group of 185 participants was divided into four main groups according to degree of cultural connection with the language, largely determined by birth place and relationship with Japanese-speaking relatives, as shown in Table 2.4.

Kondo-Brown (2005) used two instruments: a Japanese proficiency test developed at the University of Hawaii at Manoa for placement purposes and a linguistic background questionnaire that included self-assessments. The proficiency test included three subtests: listening comprehension, grammar, and reading comprehension. A summary of the results appear in Table 2.5.

Table 2.4. *Four groups of students of Japanese with or without heritage language background (adapted from Kondo-Brown 2005)*

Group	N	Characteristics
JFL learner	42	Born in the United States No Japanese-speaking relatives No background in Japanese or Japanese heritage
JHL descent	66	Japanese descent (with Japanese family name) but no Japanese-speaking parent or grandparent Never lived in Japan
JHL grandparents	47	Born in the United States No Japanese-speaking parent, but at least one Japanese-born grandparent Never lived in Japan
JHL parent (heritage speakers)	30	Born in the United States or Japan At least one Japanese-speaking parent

Table 2.5. *Scores on the Japanese proficiency test by group (adapted from Kondo-Brown 2005)*

Groups	N	Japanese proficiency			
		Listening (%)	Grammar (%)	Reading (%)	Total (%)
JFL learner	42	52.4	27.5	24.9	32.2
JHL descent	66	27.6	23.9	24.9	29.6
JHL grandparent	47	38.6	21	20.1	26.3
JHL parent (HS)	30	86.8	76.7	55.4	74.5

Kondo-Brown found that the results of the self-assessments and the proficiency test were highly correlated, and largely mirrored the pattern displayed in Table 2.4. Clearly, the heritage speakers with Japanese-speaking parents – those who actually received exposure to Japanese since childhood and used the language to some extent in the family on a daily basis – had significantly higher linguistic proficiency in Japanese than the other three groups. In all tests and measures, they scored as advanced, whereas the other three groups scored similarly low.

This study shows convincingly that while having a distant cultural connection to the language and culture may provide a strong motivation to learn the language in the classroom, it does not convey linguistic knowledge in and of itself. HLLs with a distant cultural or family connection with the heritage language are not *speakers* of the heritage language. For linguistic purposes, they are L2 learners, just like the Japanese FL learners, because they do not have previous linguistic knowledge of the heritage language acquired in the home (see also Chang *et al.* 2011). However, they may have sociolinguistic and contextual knowledge that could be useful when learning the heritage language in the classroom. The pedagogical implications of this study are that if the goal of students is to gain language proficiency then heritage speakers who are HLLs may be better served when placed in a different type of class, specifically geared to heritage speakers, whereas identity-defined HLLs belong in a classroom linguistically oriented toward L2 or foreign language learners.

This book is concerned with characterizing heritage language speakers as described in Table 2.2 – some may be learners and some may not be – but crucially, they all have some command of the heritage language. HLLs with no previous knowledge of the language and a strong cultural connection are not bilingual individuals but incipient L2 learners and, as such, they are not the focus of this book. However, in Chapter 8, we will discuss studies that may have included some of these learners in their research designs.

Beyond definitions of heritage speakers that assume language development as an individual phenomenon, heritage speakers are members of a community who share a history, a culture, and a language. In Chapter 3 and subsequent chapters, we will see that the grammatical systems of heritage speakers of different languages are intriguingly similar in many respects. At the same time, there are some differences between heritage speakers of different languages. Understanding the particular sociolinguistic characteristics of each immigrant and nonimmigrant heritage language community is also relevant to appreciate the diversity and variability of heritage languages. We consider next some representative heritage language communities in different parts of the world.

2.3   Heritage language communities

2.3.1   Immigrant communities

When immigrants move in search of a better life and economic opportunities abroad, their families follow, and in addition to economic and sociopolitical factors cultural and linguistic factors play a role in these movements. If the languages of the original country and the host country are different, immigrants and their families are naturally drawn into a situation of bilingualism, which affects their languages differently depending on generation and age. Table 2.6 summarizes the linguistic profiles of different generations of immigrants.

Immigrant adults are native speakers of the languages spoken in their countries, and depending on their socioeconomic and educational status (SES), they have different degrees of schooling. There are also many immigrants who are native speakers of their regional variety/ies and may also be illiterate in their native language (e.g., many Kanjobal speakers from Guatemala who immigrate to the United States, or many immigrants from Somalia). Those who immigrate in adulthood (18-year-olds and older) are typically referred to as the first generation, and they are fluent native speakers of their language. Some of

Table 2.6. *Patterns of language dominance and proficiency of heritage speakers and the parental generation*

Generation	Possible language characteristics	
First generation (parents)	Dominant in the native language	Non-native proficiency in the majority language
Second generation (children)	Dominant in the majority language	Low to high proficiency in the heritage language
Third generation (grandchildren)	Dominant in the majority language	Ranges from intermediate-low proficiency in the heritage language to monolingual in the majority language

them may have some knowledge of the language spoken in the host country while others learn it gradually as a second language when they start their life in the new linguistic environment.

The heritage speakers are the children of adult immigrants: some move with their parents in childhood (immigrant children) while others are born in the new country, and are exposed to the heritage language and the majority language from birth (children of immigrants). The children of the first generation are the second generation and grow up in a bilingual context. The children of the second generation (and the grandchildren of the first generation) are the third generation, and they are also considered heritage speakers if they still have some knowledge of the heritage language, although many are monolingual speakers of the majority language already. By the fourth and subsequent generations, the heritage language does not usually survive and is rarely used in the family. This pattern of declining bilingualism within families is common in many parts of the world even when the heritage languages are supported by continuous immigration.

The general language dominance characteristics illustrated in Table 2.6 are common to all immigrant groups in the United States and in many other parts of the world, and once established in the host country, so are the patterns of intergenerational transmission and loss. However, there are differences between immigrant communities that also play a role in the degree of acquisition, maintenance, and loss of the language by heritage speakers. These are related to the size of the immigrant community, age of immigration of the children, SES of the parents in the country of origin and in the host country, efforts by the communities to seek educational opportunities for language maintenance, among other specific cultural practices germane to each immigrant community.

The United States has been the adopted country of immigrants from all over the world since it was founded, although the type of immigration and the reasons for immigration to the United States have varied along these years.

For example, the sixteenth and seventeenth centuries welcomed a large number of immigrants from Europe, predominantly from Germany, Holland, and Scandinavia, whereas the most recent century has primarily seen immigration from Latin America, Asia, and Eastern Europe. Carreira and Kagan's (2011) national survey of heritage languages in the United States indicates that the last 20 years have seen a significant increase in immigrants and heritage speakers of Spanish (over 34 million), Chinese (almost 2.5 million), Tagalog (almost 1.5 million), Vietnamese (1.4 million), Korean (over 1 million), and Russian (close to 1 million). Other important immigrant languages are Arabic and Hindi. With a population of over 50.5 million, according to the 2000 United States Community Survey, Spanish is the largest language minority. The percentage increase of speakers between April 2000 and April 2010 was 43%, and the estimated Hispanic population for 2050 is projected to reach 132.8 million, which will make it 30% of the entire population of the United States (www .census.gov/2010census/).

Spanish is the second most spoken language in the United States. As described by Valdés (2006), Spanish in California – and in the south of the United States – is both a precolonial language and an immigrant language, with a long history in these regions. Stable Spanish-speaking communities in what is now the United States have existed since the arrival of Ponce de León in the fifteenth century, before the arrival of the English settlers. In addition, immigrants from Mexico make up more than 60% of the total Hispanic population in the United States, and Spanish-speaking immigrants continue to arrive from other Spanish-speaking countries in Latin America, as well as from Spain. There are many Spanish-speaking immigrants of low SES who may speak non-standard, rural, stigmatized varieties of Spanish (see profiles in Carreira 2003, Parodi 2008, and Valdés 1995), but this does not apply to all Spanish speakers in the United States. In the past few decades, Spanish-speaking immigrants have been gradually making their way into other regions of the United States, beyond the Southwest, and according to the 2010 US Census Hispanics are the largest minority in twenty-five states. For example, between 2000 and 2010 the Hispanic population in South Carolina grew by 148%.[1]

The findings of Carreira and Kagan's (2011) survey revealed that 75.3% of the Spanish-speaking respondents had been born in the United States or arrived before the age of 11, 95.5% of them used Spanish at home, and more than 30% used Spanish beyond the home. However, only 45.5% had experience studying their heritage language in an instructed context, and the rest had no access to schooling in Spanish. However, the level of proficiency in Spanish of many Spanish heritage speakers can vary significantly depending on the

[1] Retrieved from www.census.gov/newsroom/releases/archives/facts_for_features_special_editions/cb11-ff18.html, July 29, 2013.

region they live in the United States and the size of the Hispanic community. The typical adult Spanish heritage speaker in the Chicago and Central Illinois area are children of Mexican, working-class parents, who were either born in the United States or immigrated in early childhood. Some attended bilingual education programs in elementary school, but most did not. Others were placed in English as a Second Language classes until their English was deemed proficient to continue with mainstream education in English. According to what these speakers report, they mostly speak Spanish with their parents and other adult family members throughout their life, but their interactions with friends and siblings are typically in English. Other sources of Spanish input can be church or religious activities. When they come to college, most Spanish heritage speakers tend to have intermediate to advanced proficiency in standard Spanish and functional literacy in the language. However, Spanish heritage speakers born and raised in border towns, such as San Diego (California) and El Paso (Texas) and in Cuban enclaves in Hialeah (Florida) where Spanish is widely used, are very fluent in Spanish, as opposed to heritage speakers of Colombian or Mexican heritage raised in New York City who may not be.

Another prominent minority in the United States and Canada are East Asian immigrants, heritage speakers of Chinese (Mandarin), Japanese, and Korean. While the three languages are very different, it is possible to outline some very broad characteristics of this group. Unlike the majority of Spanish-speaking immigrants, East Asian immigrants come primarily from middle SES and are better educated. Because East Asian families regard education very highly, even if their children have no previous knowledge of English they quickly learn English and tend to perform well in school. Even when the heritage language may be spoken at home exclusively, heritage speakers of East Asian languages also exhibit weaker command of their home language than of English (Kondo-Brown 2006). An additional hurdle for these heritage speakers is the acquisition of literacy skills, especially because Mandarin, Japanese, and Korean have different writing systems. Carreira and Kagan (2011) report very low literacy rates for heritage speakers of these languages when compared to Spanish heritage speakers. Furthermore, within Chinese, there is also great dialectal variation as well as register variation. To preserve their language and culture, East Asian families have been very active in the development of their own church or community-based Saturday schools, whose mission is to provide language, literacy, and cultural education to their children. These are also important community and family centers where heritage language children foster their ethnic identity.

The Russian-speaking diaspora is also well represented in North America, in Israel, and in Europe, and has been featured prominently in heritage language research and education. The comprehensive profiles provided by Polinsky (2000) and Friedman and Kagan (2008) indicate that the last two waves of Russian immigrants in the twentieth century are urban, middle class families with a strong desire to achieve educational and professional success. Among Russian speakers born in the United States it is quite common to find that they have very low oral proficiency in Russian, are unfamiliar with other formal spoken and written registers and do not know how to read or write Cyrillic (Polinsky 2000, 2006). At the same time, Carreira and Kagan found in their survey that many Russian heritage speakers arrived later in childhood and received schooling in Russian in their home country compared to heritage speakers of other languages who are born in the United States or move there very young. Still, the ratings for reading and writing skills of these immigrant children fall within low and intermediate proficiency according to Carreira and Kagan (2011). In a study of Russian immigrants in Toronto, Nagy *et al.* (2014) report better maintenance of the language in heritage speakers compared to the first generation.

Heritage speakers of South Asian languages are another important group in North America and in the United Kingdom. These are typically the children of immigrants from India and Pakistan who speak Hindi/Urdu, although it is also common to find speakers of other South Asian languages, including Bengali, Malayalam, Tamil, and Telugu (Gambhir and Gambhir 2013; Moag 1995). Since 1965, South Asian immigrants to the United States have been upper middle class professionals with postgraduate degrees, unlike their peers in the United Kingdom who are of lower SES. As with many other speakers of heritage languages, the children of South Asian immigrants assimilate very well and rapidly to the American educational system and tend to do very well academically. Their exposure to the South Asian language is restricted to the home and religious environments, although Gambhir and Gambhir (2013) note the existence of parent-organized heritage language classes in some areas. South Asian heritage speakers are typically illiterate in their heritage language, also because the script of the heritage language is very different from the English writing system. Adult heritage speakers in Hindi language classes are reported to be only familiar with colloquial varieties and have little knowledge of other registers and sociolinguistic conventions (Moag 1995).

Arabic heritage speakers present a very intricate linguistic profile (Albirini 2013; Ibrahim and Allam 2006; Shiri 2010) when compared with speakers of other languages. Arabic heritage speakers are Muslims or Christians of Arab descent and non-Arab Muslims (Pakistanis and Iranians who learn the language for religious purposes). Unlike the other languages discussed, Arabic is a diglossic language, where two grammatically and functionally distinct forms of the language coexist: High code or Modern Standard Arabic (MSA) and Low code Arabic or dialect. Arabic speakers are typically competent in multiple dialects and MSA. For educated Arabic speakers, Modern Standard Arabic (MSA) is the written variety learned in school, the variety spoken in the media and used in written and spoken formal Arabic. Business involving documents and paperwork is also conducted in MSA. Standard Arabic, by contrast, is the language of liberal arts and sciences and the language of the Quran. There is also spoken or colloquial Arabic, which is rarely written and is used in TV and radio and for conducting daily business. In addition to these three main varieties (Modern Standard, standard, and spoken Arabic), there are several regional varieties of spoken or colloquial Arabic, and each variety also has different registers. Arab heritage speakers speak or understand one or more dialects of Arabic and may even code-switch in different Arabic accents and dialects, especially if the parents come from different regions of the Arabic-speaking world. Like many South Asian heritage speakers, Arabic heritage speakers possess different degrees of proficiency in some spoken variety. But because they learned the spoken variety primarily at home, they have limited or no literacy skills, and little or no knowledge of written/standard Arabic. In many ways, heritage speakers are comparable to illiterate Arabic speakers from the Arab World. By contrast, heritage speakers who are non-Arab Muslims may learn the written standard Arabic and typically have no competence in spoken Arabic dialects. They may learn to read Arabic at the Mosque rather than the home. Although they are more literate than Arab heritage speakers, the register they may command is also restricted. In general, Arab Americans are educated and belong to the upper middle class, yet their children, like the children of all the other minority language groups described, do not develop full fluency in all aspects of Arabic.

To summarize thus far, Europe and North America are the home of many heritage languages. Although heritage speakers in general share many characteristics, there are also important differences among the communities related to SES, education, age of immigration, and language practices within the home and in the community. These differences impact the language ability of university-level heritage speakers in their language. According to the findings of Carreira and Kagan's (2011) national survey of the United States, Spanish, Russian, and Persian heritage speakers receive the highest exposure to the heritage language, Korean, Mandarin, and Cantonese receive moderate exposure, and Vietnamese and Tagalog speakers the least exposure. With respect to access to schooling, Russian, Korean, Mandarin, Cantonese, and Persian heritage speakers receive significant exposure, Spanish speakers receive moderate exposure, and Tagalog and Vietnamese heritage speakers almost none. Yet, when it comes to average ability in reading and writing, Spanish and Russian heritage speakers display intermediate ability, while Korean, Vietnamese, Persian, Tagalog, Mandarin, and Cantonese display quite low ability. It is possible to find native to advanced heritage speakers of Spanish and Russian, whereas the level of most other heritage speakers ranges from low to intermediate.

The linguistic situation and proficiency patterns of ethnic minorities and their children in Europe and in other parts of the world where the majority language is not English are very similar to what has been observed in North America (Extra and Verhoeven 1993). Driven by socioeconomic or political concerns, most contemporary immigration in Europe consists of immigrants from Mediterranean countries (both from and outside the European Union), immigrants from former European colonies, and political refugees. The vast majority of research on language policies and the education of immigrants in Europe has been concerned with the L2 acquisition of the majority language, while policies and research on immigrant language varieties in Europe have been relatively scarce. The tendency of this research has been to focus on the philological tradition of historical analysis with little attention on the actual language spoken by speakers of these minority languages. By the 1980s research on immigrant languages in Europe within a sociolinguistic perspective gained ground (Boyd 1985; Lainio 1987; Pfaff 1991) and only recently has psycholinguistically oriented research begun to emerge as well (Bayram 2013; Bianchi 2013; Brehmer and Czachór 2012; Kupisch 2012, 2013).

Turkish and Moroccan-Arabic are two major immigrant languages in Germany, the Netherlands, and other countries in Europe. Turkish and Moroccan immigrants from rural areas in Turkey and Morocco originally came to these countries legally as migrant workers during the economic revival of the sixties and seventies, when Dutch and German companies and the governments of these two countries recruited them as cheap labor. A few years later their families joined them. At first it was thought that the Turkish and Moroccan immigration was temporary and transient, and that these immigrants would eventually return to their home countries. But changing political and economic conditions in their home countries led these families to settle in Germany and the Netherlands permanently. Hence, first, second, and third generations of Moroccan and Turkish immigrants can be found in these two countries today. Available sociolinguistic studies draw broad comparisons of the heritage language abilities in these two communities and suggest that child Turkish heritage speakers show better command of Turkish than Moroccan heritage speakers of Moroccan-Arabic or Berber (Aarsen, de Ruiter, and Verhoeven 1993; Scheele, Leseman, and Mayo 2010), and this is related to specific cultural practices and degree of integration of the communities, as well as the multilingual characteristics of the Moroccan population in particular.

One difference between the status of many heritage languages in Europe and heritage languages in the United States that may affect overall level of proficiency attained in the heritage language in adulthood is access to schooling in the language. For example, it seems that it is possible for Finnish heritage speakers in Sweden to have schooling in their language, but this is not common in the United States (Lainio 1993). At present there are both first and second generation Finnish-Swedes in Sweden and today Finnish children can get education in Finnish in Sweden. However, before the 1970s education in Finnish was not available for these children. Today, use and maintenance of Finnish in the first generation is strong in this group, as in the pattern described in Table 2.6, but the second generation – the heritage speakers – suffer the same fate as Finnish immigrants to the United States and Canada, and gradually become dominant in the majority language, in this case Swedish.

Some countries in Europe (e.g., Sweden and Norway) offer mother tongue instruction to heritage language children in the public school system (Bylund and Diaz 2012). Although there are some bilingual programs for some languages in some states in the United States, and Spanish is one of them, bilingual education in general is not widely available to all the children who speak a heritage language in this country. Moreover, the majority of the programs that exist in elementary schools are transitional in nature, restricting academic instruction in Spanish for 1 or 2 years until the children develop sufficient proficiency in English in order to continue with the mainstream education in English. It is not the purpose of these programs, or the majority of these programs, to promote bilingualism and biliteracy in the majority and the minority language. Access to education in the heritage language, as we will see in more detail in Chapter 4, plays an important role in the development and maintenance of the heritage language.

The examples of immigrant languages discussed above are in contact with English or with standard European languages in Europe, and the definition of heritage language adopted in this book stresses that the heritage language is acquired in a minority language context. Fishman (2006) also emphasizes minority status as a crucial part of the definition of a heritage language, and seems to imply that it would be hard to consider English a heritage language because it enjoys high prestige and is most readily available in almost all parts of the world. It enjoys wider presence in popular culture and media than any other language. Interestingly, in many countries where English was a colonial language, such as India, Hong Kong, Nigeria, and even Argentina, it has remained a standard component of the national curriculum. The question that arises is whether English can be considered a heritage language like the languages discussed so far, and in fact it can. After all, Spanish, French, and Chinese are also main international languages that enjoy a certain degree of global prestige, and are acquired as heritage languages by millions of speakers in the diaspora. Viswanath (2013) conducted a study of English as a heritage language in Israel, a country that boasts a vibrant English-speaking community and where many children are exposed to English at home and learn Hebrew at school. Although Arabic is an official language in Israel whereas English is not, English has a stronger presence in public signs in Israel than Arabic does (Spolsky and Shohamy 1999). Viswanah found that the thirty-three heritage

speakers of English who participated in his study had relatively high proficiency in English but like most heritage speakers of many other languages (see
Chapter 3), they also showed non-native fluency and grammatical features not
produced by native speakers of English.

This discussion of English suggests that, as I stated earlier, the term *minority
language* must necessarily be applied locally, rather than globally, to the notion
of heritage language. Hence, any language can be a (local) minority language,
regardless of its world wide status, as long as it is not the dominant language
of the country under discussion. English is no exception.

2.3.2   Nonimmigrant minority communities

Aboriginal or indigenous languages and historical co-official languages in
many countries are not the result of recent global movements, but have had
a presence in their respective territories spanning several centuries: they are
minority languages due to colonization and territorial annexation. Nonetheless,
the speakers of these languages undergo a similar fate as immigrants and their
children when it comes to using their language, having access to it in education
or public life, and transmitting it to their children. In the case of indigenous
languages, there is migration from rural to urban areas in search of a better
life. Contact with the majority culture and language in urban areas determines
the level of bilingualism and minority language proficiency of these speakers
(Escobar 2004; Sánchez 2003; Schmidt 1985).

In Europe and Latin America, minority languages can refer to languages
that are traditionally used within a nation-state by a group of people who
speak a language that is not the official language of the nation-state. Historical
minority languages spoken in many territories in some cases can be official languages of a country or co-official languages within their territories.
Numerically, these groups can be a minority (e.g., Irish speakers in Ireland,
speakers of Euskera in the Basque Country), but they can also be numerically larger, such as Catalan speakers in Catalonia or the Quechua and Aymará
population in Peru and Bolivia. These languages are in contact with the majority and politically stronger language (in these cases English and Spanish) and
all speakers of the minority language are also speakers of the majority languages, which are part of the national school curricula. Historical minority
languages vary widely in the degree of government protection and availability
of education.

Two relatively successful examples of minority languages in Europe that
have benefited from language laws and have been incorporated in a solid education system are Basque and Catalan in Spain, although historically this has
not always been the case (Montrul 2013). The Basque language or Euskera is
spoken in the Basque Country, a region in the north of Spain close to the border

with France. Basque is a pre-Roman language of uncertain roots that has been present in Iberia since before the arrival of the Romans in 300 BC. Catalan is a Romance language derived from Latin spoken in the regions of Catalonia, Valencia, and the Balearic Islands in the Mediterranean. During the Franco dictatorship (1939–1975), languages like Basque, Catalan, Galician, and others were banned from public use under threat of fines and punishment. After the Franco dictatorship and with the new democratic constitution adopted in 1978, the Basque Country, Catalonia, and Galicia were recognized as historical territories and their languages became co-official with Spanish within their own territories. Today Catalan enjoys high prestige in Catalonia, a region with about 7 million people. The elementary education system promotes the language by offering curricula with full immersion and instruction in Catalan. High school and university education are in Spanish and Catalan. As a result, more than 70% of the population speaks Catalan and there are very few monolingual Spanish speakers in the region, most of them immigrants from other non-Catalan speaking regions.

The Basque country has about 2 million people, and about 800,000 speak the Basque language (Euskera) together with Spanish or French. The percentage of bilingual speakers in the Basque country is lower than in Catalonia; however, the majority of people who speak Basque more natively (200,000) are younger than 30 years of age. This is related to the historical political developments that occurred in 1978. Unlike Catalan, Basque did not have such a developed written tradition, and before the language could be instituted in schools, it had to be documented and normalized. At present, the Basque country features three models of elementary education with different levels of emphasis in Euskera, and the most popular one is total immersion in Euskera with a few hours of Spanish a week as a subject but not as the language of instruction. These days, the Basque language enjoys prestige and popularity in its own territory and the government policies of protection toward the language since the constitution of 1978 have contributed significantly to revitalizing the language and to promoting its acquisition and maintenance in the younger generations.

Because the status, vitality, and overall health of a heritage language depends on its local conditions, in some cases, government policies and the education system are not sufficient to help maintain the language. Consider Irish. Despite having especially recognized status under the Republic's Constitution as a national language and a first official language (Constitution of Ireland, Article 8, Watson 1989, p. 44), overall proficiency in the Irish language has been diminishing in Ireland over the last 20 years. The language is spoken natively in local communities where the language is protected (Gaeltachtaí regions), and there are least three recognized local dialects. In addition to dialectal variation, since 1958 the state has been promoting a standardized written form of the language in schools and official government business (An Caighdeán) based on modern regional varieties, which is not a native variety (Hindley 1990, p. xv). Yet, despite efforts to create elementary schools that teach content in Irish, the children are not developing full proficiency in the language because they are surrounded and outnumbered by English speakers (Harris 2008; Ó Giollagáin 2011). Recent studies on the situation of Welsh conducted in Wales (Lewis 2008; Mueller-Gathercole and Thomas 2009) also show that the school environment is not enough to protect the use and maintenance of minority languages when there is so much outside pressure from the majority language. There is also no doubt that in the case of Irish and Welsh, the prestige of the language plays a role in the degree of use and language preferences of speakers, since English is seen as a highly prestigious language as compared to Irish and Welsh.

Compared to the situation of the historical languages in Spain, the situation of indigenous languages in America and Australia are very different. Except for Guaraní in Paraguay, which enjoys significant prestige and is an official language of Paraguay, most other indigenous languages in America have little if any government protection and are not often supported by a comprehensive education system at the elementary school level. A main obstacle is the fact that many of these languages do not have writing systems and, consequently, no written and literary tradition. Although isolated efforts to provide education in these languages have been made in some instances, like the teaching of Quechua and Aymara in Puno (Hornberger 1988), creating pedagogical materials, training teachers to teach the languages, and sustaining these programs has always been a challenge. Of all heritage languages, indigenous languages may be the ones that are most at risk of loss and eventual death. Other examples of recently studied aboriginal heritage languages are Inuttitut in Northern Quebec (Sherkina-Lieber 2011; Sherkina-Lieber, Pérez-Leroux, and Jones 2011), and Dyirbal (Schmidt 1985) and Warlpiri (Bavin 1989) in Australia. With the exception of some elders, most residents can speak English. Sherkina-Lieber (2011) reports that speakers of the younger generations are not fluent in Inuttitut or do not speak it at all. Schmidt (1985) also found that older people (40–90 years old) still spoke what she calls traditional Dyirbal, younger members of the community (15–39 years old) speak "imperfect" Dyirbal, and children in the 0–15 year age group could not talk Guwal (the spoken familiar dialect or everyday Dyirbal) (Schmidt 1985, p. 22). On many measures, Dyirbal seems to be a dying language in Australia because like Inuttitut, the intergenerational transmission of the language is fading rapidly. Bavin (1989) considers that the situation of Warlpiri is not as dire as that of Dyirbal, even when many speakers of Warlpiri have also been shifting to English over the years. Warlpiri is not dying in Australia because it is held in high regard by its own speakers, and there have been some attempts to create school programs and materials to teach the Warlpiri languages to Warlpiri children at school. Therefore, the attitude of the speakers and efforts to educate their children in the language may help indigenous languages attenuate the process of intergenerational loss so common in these languages.

To summarize, heritage languages such as immigrant languages, aboriginal languages, and historical languages are spoken all over the world. Although they are all minority languages, the level of command of the heritage language in the speakers depends on the different characteristics of the languages, the contact language and culture, and the particular characteristics of the local communities. These are related to length of presence in the territory, number of speakers, vitality of the language, access to education, attitudes, and other specific cultural patterns within each community.

2.4   Other heritage speakers

We have seen that heritage speakers are born into a particular sociolinguistic and political situation. The heritage language can be an immigrant language, a historical language or an indigenous language, and heritage speakers learn their heritage language in the context of their own family. It is also important to stress that many heritage speakers may not be part of a broader ethnic community as discussed in Section 2.3, but their language learning experience as individuals makes them heritage speakers. That is, they are bilingual individuals as described in Table 2.2, who learned a heritage language since infancy, but it was a minority language because there was no speech community around to develop the language beyond what could be offered at home, or because there was a change of environment and linguistic input and use of the heritage language was severely reduced, confined to only certain contexts and registers, or interrupted altogether. Three cases that come to mind are children of bicultural families living in environments where their language(s) are not spoken as official languages, returnees, and some international adoptees.

2.4.1   Simultaneous and sequential bilingual children

Since 1980, important research has been conducted on child bilingualism and bilingual first language acquisition in Europe (De Houwer 2009; Deuchar and Quay 2000; Ezeizabarrena Segurola 2001; Lanza 2004; Meisel 1994, 2001, 2007; Müller and Hulk 2001), Canada (Genesee 1989; Genesee, Nicoladis, and Paradis 1995), the United States (Bolonyai 2007), Hong Kong (Yip and Mathews 2006), and Australia (Döpke 1992), among others. Most of these studies have focused on children growing up in bilingual families, where the parents are professionals or academics and speak different languages. An

American in the United States or a German in Germany can marry a person from another country and speak another language; other couples may consist of people from different countries who immigrated individually before getting married and met in the host country. Many children who grow up in bilingual families such as these may not necessarily be part of a larger heritage language community. According to the definition of heritage speakers adopted in this book, the fact that one or two home languages spoken by these bilingual children is a minority language in the wider community makes them heritage speakers. Up until recently, these bilingual children have not been called child heritage speakers in the literature, but the term is beginning to be applied to them as well (Kupisch 2013).

In some cases one of the parents can speak the majority language of the country (e.g., English in the United States) and the immigrant parent speaks another language (Spanish, Hindi, and Russian). If the immigrant parent speaks his/her language to the children, then the children become heritage speakers of that language. In other cases, the two parents may speak different languages (e.g., Arabic and Mandarin or Japanese and Korean), which are not the majority languages of the host country (Canada), and they may either speak their respective languages and the majority language at home, or they may choose to speak one of the heritage languages and the majority language at home. Like the children of immigrants, speakers of historical languages, or aboriginal children, the degree to which these bilingual children eventually develop high proficiency and full command of the heritage language (or the two heritage languages of the parents) and the majority language is also variable and will depend on the specific environment they find themselves in. The immediate family situation, in addition to the majority language context beyond the home, will determine the extent to which these bilingual children will develop the two languages or only one.

Serratrice (2001, 2002) studied a child – Carlo – brought up in this situation. Carlo is the son of an American father and an Italian mother living in Scotland. The parents are academics. For the first 5 months of his life, Carlo's father addressed him in English (the majority language in Scotland) and his mother in Italian. When Carlo was 5 months old, he started to attend an English-speaking day care half a day every day of the week. At home he spoke Italian with his mother and his older sibling. On weekends he was cared for by an Italian-speaking nanny. Even though Carlo is reported to be bilingual in Italian and English, Italian is a heritage language in this case because it is not the language of the wider speech community. Similar examples are the Hungarian-speaking child studied by Bolonyai (1998), Manuela, the Spanish-speaking child from the United Kingdom described in Deuchar and Quay (2000), and the German-speaking child growing up in Australia followed by Döpke (1992).

People often assume that children growing up exposed to two languages end up knowing their two languages very well but this is not always the case. When children realize that their home language is a minority language and it is not spoken beyond the home, they switch to the majority language spoken by their social group. De Houwer (2009, p. 3) describes the child studied by Von Raffler-Engel (1965), who grew up in Florence, Italy. His mother always addressed him in Italian and his father, who was American, in English. The parents spoke English to each other but because the child's broader environment was Italian-speaking, the child refused to speak English although he understood it, despite the parents' best efforts. As a result, the child's Italian was much stronger than his English.

The study of these bilingual children tends to focus on the preschool period, and traces the emergence and simultaneous and independent but parallel development of the two languages, as we discuss in more detail in Chapter 4. Only recently have there been attempts to link the early linguistic development of these bilingual children with the language abilities of young adult heritage speakers. In Chapter 7, we will discuss Silva-Corvalán's (2014) longitudinal study of two English-Spanish simultaneous bilingual children in the United States and we will compare the results of this study with the results of the adult heritage speakers studied by Silva-Corvalán (1994). Ideally, we would like to see more connections between the bilingual development of young children, school-age children, and young adults as they acquire the heritage language.

2.4.2   Returnees

There are also families who immigrate to another country and return to their home country after a few years. Their children may be born in the host country, learn and identify with the majority language, and attend school for a few years. During their stay in the host country, the family language is the children's heritage language and the majority societal language is their L2 acquired in the community. When these families return to their home countries, these children – now called returnees – may be dominant in the language of what used to be the host country and may have weaker command of the heritage language. Their return, however, marks a reversal of the sociopolitical and functional status of the languages: what used to be the heritage language now becomes the societal majority language, and the L2 learned in the host country, even when it is not the primary language of the parents, could be considered a heritage language of the child in the new environment. It would be considered a heritage language because in addition to having high proficiency in the language, the child still has a connection with the language and culture which were part of the child's upbringing and socialization.

An example of this situation is provided by Flores (2010, 2012), who conducted a study with twenty Portuguese returnees who had lived in a German-speaking country as second generation immigrants. Most of these individuals were born to first generation Portuguese immigrants living in Germany and Switzerland at the time. The others were born in Portugal but moved with their parents to the German-speaking countries before the age of three. All these bilinguals grew up exposed to German and Portuguese, in some cases simultaneously, in others sequentially (Portuguese L1, German L2) and attended school in German, the official language of Germany and Switzerland. The families returned to Portugal when the children were between the ages of 7 and 14 (average 10 years old). Now in Portugal, Portuguese is the official and majority language and German, being part of the children's upbringing and cultural and linguistic heritage, became their heritage language. A few years after returning to Portugal and changing linguistic environments, German suffered drastic reductions in input and use, inevitably becoming their weaker language. Flores documents the degree of attrition of German depending on the age of return of the now German heritage speakers.

Heritage language reversal and concomitant language loss upon returning to the home country has been widely documented for Japanese returnees who lived in an English-speaking environment for several years. These cases are often described as L2 attrition, but in fact it is attrition of a heritage language of the child. There are several case studies of Japanese returnees in the context of the L2 attrition of English (Reetz-Kurashige 1999; Tomiyama 1999, 2008; Yoshitomi 1999), and these would also be examples of English as a heritage language. In all these cases, the children were born in an English-speaking country and lived for more than 2 years abroad. They went to public elementary schools with full instruction in English. After 2 years of living in these English-speaking environments, English becomes the dominant language and Japanese the weaker language. Once these children return to their home countries, input and use of English decreases significantly, and within 2 years of arrival the children start to forget words and the rest of their grammatical abilities begin to erode. All these studies have followed these children post arrival in Japan, and document different degrees of English language forgetting at different levels of grammatical analysis and by skills.

Potowski (2013) focuses on the attitudes and beliefs of Mexican-American children who were Spanish heritage speakers in the United States, many of whom find themselves at a loss when they return to Mexico and try to insert themselves in the Mexican educational system with English as their heritage language. One of the issues these children face is that their Spanish, which was acquired as a heritage language in the United States, is not up to the standards of Mexicans, who ridicule them. While in the United States, their Spanish was marginalized and their English had a privileged status. However, now in Mexico, their English is a liability although English is still more valued in Mexico than Spanish is in the United States. Because the Mexican returnees perceive that English still has high status in Mexico, even when it is a liability to their Spanish development they want to make an effort to keep English as they insert themselves in the Mexican culture.

In conclusion, returnees are cases of heritage language reversal, which results from transnational movement of families from one country to the other. The children are brought up with two languages and cultures that have different status in the two countries. When the language becomes a minority language, it runs the risk of undergoing attrition or not advancing further in development. As emphasized throughout this chapter, any language can be a heritage language, and this depends on the environmental conditions and circumstances of the speaker.

2.4.3   International adoptees

Children who immigrate with their parents continue to have exposure to the family language to different degrees, depending on language practices in the family. Even if the children do not use the language frequently, some of them may end up being receptive bilinguals or *overhearers*, a term used by Au *et al.* (2002) to describe bilingual children who do not necessarily speak the heritage language but have some understanding of it (see also Sherkina-Lieber 2011). In general, these receptive bilingual heritage speakers have some productive ability in their family language even though they may exhibit very low proficiency in it. In contrast, internationally adopted children are often adopted by families who do not speak their language, although some families make efforts to keep the culture of the child present in some way. Therefore, input in the first language is interrupted abruptly right after adoption. For this reason, internationally adopted children are rarely bilingual, representing instead a unique case of sequential monolingualism, by which one language is actually replaced by another as they go from monolingualism in the first language to monolingualism in the second language. In general, 80% of internationally adopted children are infants, 10% are adopted between ages 4 and 5, and the remaining 10% at age 6 or older (Glennen 2005; Hyltenstam *et al.* 2009). Studies suggest that these children tend to lose their language easily and faster than heritage language speakers who are immigrant children, although some children adopted in middle childhood may retain the language to some extent (Montrul 2011). One may ask what would make international adoptees *heritage speakers* under the definition assumed in this book, which subsumes some degree of linguistic proficiency in the language.

In recent years, there has been some interest in the extent of potential language retention in heritage speakers who were adopted internationally. The most intriguing recent studies addressing these questions are perhaps Pallier *et al.* (2003) and Ventureyra (2005). They reported that twenty Korean adults (age at testing ranging from 20 to 32 years) adopted by French families between the ages of 3 and 10 had become native-like in French but had no recollection of Korean basic vocabulary or sounds. Both neuroimaging and behavioral tests revealed no traces of Korean even in speech perception in these speakers, who did not differ from native speaker French controls in any of the behavioral or brain imaging measures. However, Pierce *et al.* (2014) did find retention of perceptual correlates of tones in Mandarin. Using functional MRI they showed that internationally adopted children from China living in Quebec and exposed to French since adoption maintained neural representations of their birth language despite functionally losing the language and not having conscious recollection of it.

Another reason why some international adoptees can be considered heritage speakers is because some of them seek to relearn their native language in the classroom, like other heritage speakers and L2 learners, and there is some suggestive evidence that they do retain remnants of that first language. Hyltenstam *et al.* (2009) and Oh, Au, and Jun (2010) tested adopted Koreans who were learning Korean as an L2 in the classroom, and compared them to instructed L2 learners of Korean who had not been exposed to Korean before. Although the Korean adoptees had no productive ability in Korean before enrolling in these classes, both studies found that the Korean adoptees were significantly better at discriminating phonetic contrasts of Voice Onset Time (VOT) in Korean than the L2 learners with no previous knowledge of Korean. Hyltenstam *et al.* also found that the highest performing adoptees in Korean were those with the highest age of adoption (9 and 10 years). This advantage was only apparent in phonological discrimination but not in grammaticality judgments of morphosyntactic aspects of Korean, where the second language learners outperformed the Korean adoptees. The fact that reexposure effects were observed in the Hyltenstam *et al.* and in the Oh *et al.* studies suggests that remnants of the L1 must lie in the mind in some sort of representation, and that total L1 loss is unlikely in these cases. It is also possible that the apparent age of adoption effect on language retention may be due to the length of time elapsed between the interruption to L1 input and the reexposure, such that for those adoptees who experienced a shorter span between interruption and reexposure the degree of retention or recollection may be stronger.

To summarize, heritage speakers are not only bilingual young adult speakers. Many bilingual children also fall within the scope of the term *heritage children*, and what makes them heritage speakers is the status of the languages and the

Table 2.7. *Examples of heritage speakers*

Heritage speaker profile	Examples
Immigrant child or child of immigrant	Children and young adult bilingual speakers of immigrant families who speak Spanish, Hindi, Russian, and other languages in the United States and Canada
Young speaker of historical minority language	Children and young adult bilingual speakers of Basque, Catalan, Walloon, Irish, Welsh, etc.
Young speaker of an indigenous language	Children and young adult speakers of Navajo, Náhuatl, Dyirbal, Inuttitut, and Quechua
Bilingual children of professional families	Simultaneous bilingual children raised under the One parent one language strategy in Europe and Canada Sequential bilingual children of professional families
Returnees (heritage language reversal)	Immigrant children and young adults who return to their home countries after several years of immigration
International adoptees	Internationally adopted children who may retain some knowledge of their first language as young adults

conditions under which the languages are learned. Table 2.7 summarizes the three other cases discussed in this section: bilingual children living in different sociopolitical circumstances, returnees, and adoptees.

2.5   Summary

This chapter presented the definition of heritage languages and heritage speakers to be used in the rest of the book and discussed the controversies associated with these terms. Although I gave several examples of heritage languages and heritage speakers in different parts of the world, the examples are not exhaustive but just representative. In the rest of the book, I discuss the linguistic characteristics of these populations, the factors that play a role in the outcome of acquisition, the theories and methods used to date to study these populations, as well as some of the most recent findings and their implications.

3 The language of heritage speakers

In the previous chapter, we saw that the term *heritage speaker* encompasses a wide variety of individual profiles. Heritage speakers come from different language backgrounds and cultures, they possess different levels of education and socioeconomic status, and they are exposed to different varieties and registers of their home language. Interestingly, the vast majority of heritage speakers share a common characteristic: they are often dominant in the majority language and the levels of proficiency in the heritage language vary widely, from merely receptive ability to very fluent speech. Because the vast majority of heritage speakers grow up in a situation of subtractive bilingualism, their language abilities and the structural properties of their heritage language show differences when compared to the grammatical abilities of their parents and of age-matched peers raised in their home countries. Such broad range of variation in acquisition outcomes needs to be understood and explained.

In this chapter, I present a broad overview of the typical characteristics of the linguistic skills of heritage speakers, including structural features common to different heritage languages at the level of vocabulary, morphology, syntax, semantics, discourse pragmatics, and phonetics/phonology. My focus is on describing common linguistic characteristics of heritage language grammars, and I will discuss the potential reasons behind the particularly recurrent patterns in Chapters 4, 7, and 8, where comparison with other language learning situations will also be emphasized. In order for the reader to get a sense of what the language of these speakers looks like, I draw on a wide variety of recent and older studies from different heritage speaker populations as exemplified in Chapter 2 and from different parts of the world. Naturally, the studies referred to involve different participants and use different methodologies and are not always strictly comparable, but the goal of this chapter is to present general observations. More extensive discussion of the challenges involved when comparing different studies, as well as other methodological considerations, are the focus of Chapter 6.

I begin by providing background on bilingual competence, language proficiency, and language skills followed by a description of different linguistic levels of analysis that are systematically affected in heritage grammars.

3.1   Bilingual competence in heritage speakers

3.1.1   Dominance and proficiency

Bilingualism is knowledge (and use) of two languages, although not necessarily to the same degree. Linguistic knowledge is multidimensional at the linguistic (grammatical) and psycholinguistic (processing and use) levels, and most bilinguals typically develop unbalanced command of the two languages in one or more dimensions (Mackey 1962). Grosjean's studies (1997, 2008, 2010) captured this observation in the Complementarity Principle, which states that bilinguals use their languages in different situations and for different purposes and develop different degrees of fluency and proficiency in each language and language skill (listening, speaking, reading, and writing) as a result of this complementarity.

Two notions related to bilingual knowledge or competence are *language dominance* – the idea that one language of the bilingual will be used more often (in specific contexts) and will likely be processed more easily than the other – and *proficiency*, actual grammatical ability and fluency in a language. Linguistic proficiency and language dominance are intimately related, and the two are often treated as equivalent in many studies. However, I see linguistic proficiency as one dimension of dominance. Although proficiency often correlates with dominance, it cannot be entirely equated with it.

Except for those who may have relatively balanced competence in the two languages, the vast majority of heritage speakers exhibit similar patterns of language dominance but may differ in the levels of proficiency in each language when compared to each other, as shown in Figure 3.1. The majority language (ML) is stronger than or as strong as the heritage language (HL). One can certainly find some heritage speakers with very advanced or even native-like proficiency in the two languages as also depicted in Figure 3.1, and their existence is theoretically interesting and worth studying. In fact, the likelihood and incidence of heritage speakers who are fully fluent in the heritage language and balanced bilinguals in the general population of heritage speakers is an understudied topic at present, and I will discuss some examples in Chapter 7.

The concept of proficiency is widely used to describe and measure language development and language processing of the target language at the structural and discourse level. Basic and quantifiable features of linguistic ability are typically reflected in grammatical and textual knowledge, including phonology,

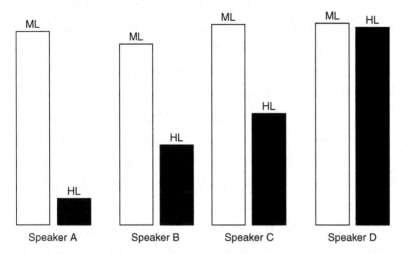

ML = English (United States, Canada, United Kingdom, Australia)
HL = Spanish/Japanese/Russian/Hindi/Irish/Dutch/Inuttitut/Dyirbal. . .

Figure 3.1. Same pattern of dominance but different levels of proficiency in the heritage language.

vocabulary, morphosyntax, semantics, and pragmatics or sociolinguistic competence (Hulstijn 2011, 2015). Fluency is characterized by the speed of lexical retrieval in receptive and productive skills, such as listening, reading, speaking, writing, and, in the case of bilinguals, translating as well. Proficiency is often measured in L1 acquisition and in only one language – the second language – in L2 acquisition.

While proficiency can be assessed in one language, dominance implies a relative relationship of control or influence between the two languages of bilinguals. As I argued in Montrul (in press), dominance includes a linguistic proficiency component, an external component (input), and a functional component (context and use). Furthermore, biographical variables such as age of acquisition, the place of birth and its language environment, and the place of previous and current residence and their language environment determine as well the type and amount of input in the languages. Hence, the dominant language is often the language to which the bilingual receives more exposure, and it is also the language the bilingual uses more frequently in specific contexts. Proficiency can be operationalized as the cognitive and linguistic component of dominance, measured in terms of actual language knowledge and linguistic behavior in one or the two languages. Figure 3.2 illustrates the distinction I draw between dominance and proficiency.

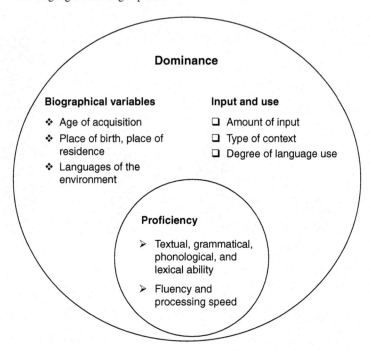

Figure 3.2. Relationship between dominance and proficiency (Montrul 2016).

3.1.2   Linguistic skills

As illustrated in Figure 3.1, heritage speakers can exhibit functional proficiency in both productive and receptive abilities, or in receptive abilities only.
That is, many heritage speakers with very low proficiency in the heritage language can barely speak the language but often retain the ability to comprehend it and translate it into the other language. In the literature, these heritage
speakers have been termed *receptive bilinguals* (Sherkina-Lieber 2011) and
overhearers (Oh *et al.* 2002). Additionally, some heritage speakers are literate
in their heritage language – they can read and write – while others are illiterate.
Therefore, heritage speakers display proficiency asymmetries in the productive
and receptive modes and in oral and written language.

Even when heritage speakers have functional ability in their heritage language, a hallmark of heritage speakers' proficiency is the wide range of
variability found (Figure 3.1). This variability is evident along three dimensions: productive/receptive skills (listening, speaking, reading, and writing),
communicative ability by discourse type (formal/academic and informal), and
grammatical domain (vocabulary, phonology, morphology, syntax, semantics,

and discourse). There are several variables that contribute to variability along these dimensions, such as the age at which the heritage speaker was exposed to the majority language, the degree to which the majority language was spoken at home together with the heritage language, whether the heritage language is spoken only by the parents or by other family members, including siblings (size and density of social networks), access to and amount of schooling in the heritage language, access to the heritage language in the public domain, the size of the speech community beyond the home, among many others. These factors will be discussed in more detail in Chapter 4.

By now, there is an important body of research documenting basic descriptive characteristics of heritage speakers of different languages in the United States, Canada, Europe, and a few other countries (Kondo-Brown 2005; Moag 1995; Pfaff 1994; Polinsky 2000; Potowski 2010; among many others), in addition to work on language death in a variety of immigrant, historical, and aboriginal languages (see chapters in Dorian 1989). Carreira and Kagan's (2011) comprehensive national survey of heritage language learners in the United States across different languages included information from 1,732 university students representing twenty-two languages (Arabic, Armenian, Cantonese, Hindi/ Urdu, Japanese, Korean, Mandarin, Persian, Russian, Spanish, Tagalog, Thai, and Vietnamese, among others). There were important generalities among the speakers surveyed, especially regarding heritage language use and proficiency. For example, when asked which language they used the most in different periods of their lives, the majority of respondents reported highest use of the heritage language in early childhood (before age 5) (70.2%) and lowest use after age 18 (1.3%), as shown in Table 3.1.

When asked about their self-assessments in English and the heritage language by linguistic skill, more than 65% of the informants rated their abilities in English at native levels, while only 7.5% rated all their linguistic abilities in the heritage language at native levels. The more developed skill in the heritage language is listening, followed by speaking. The least developed is writing, as shown in Table 3.2.

Montrul, Bhatt, and Girju's (2015) study of Hindi, Spanish, and Romanian heritage speakers in the United States, confirms this trend. Figures 3.3

Table 3.1. *Language used most at different periods in life (adapted from Carreira and Kagan 2011)*

Age	English (%)	Heritage language (%)	Both languages (%)
0–5 years old	11.2	70.2	18.7
6–12 years old	27.5	18.9	53.6
13–18 years old	44.0	4.0	51.9
18+ years old	44.4	1.3	54.3

Table 3.2. *Respondents' ratings of their abilities in English and the heritage language (adapted from Carreira and Kagan 2011)*

Self-estimated level

	None (%)	Low (%)	Intermediate (%)	Advanced (%)	Native (%)
Skills in the heritage language					
Listening	0.5	4.2	27.5	31.0	36.8
Speaking	1.0	16.8	37.8	24.3	20.1
Reading	4.0	28.8	39.6	15.4	12.2
Writing	4.8	40.3	36.2	11.3	7.5
Skills in English					
Listening	0.1	0.0	4.9	18.5	76.5
Speaking	0.1	0.2	7.8	19.5	72.3
Reading	0.1	0.5	8.2	20.8	70.3
Writing	0.1	1.1	12.7	21.3	64.9

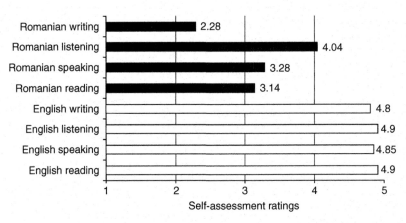

Figure 3.3. US-born Romanian heritage speakers' self-assessments of their English and Romanian abilities by skill (Montrul, Bhatt, and Girju 2015).

and 3.4 illustrate the Romanian and English self-assessments of forty-two Romanian heritage speakers, aged 21 years old (average). The averages given in Figure 3.3 are from twenty-three heritage speakers who were born in the United States and were exposed to Romanian and English since birth. Those given in Figure 3.4 come from 19 heritage speakers who were born and raised in Romania until about age 10, and attended some elementary schooling in Romania.

Figure 3.5 displays the self-ratings of 26 Hindi heritage speakers born and raised in the United States (mean age 20.6).

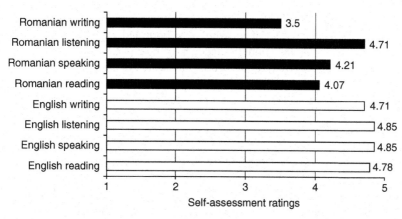

Figure 3.4. Romania-born Romanian heritage speakers' self-assessments of their English and Romanian abilities by skill (Montrul, Bhatt, and Girju 2015).

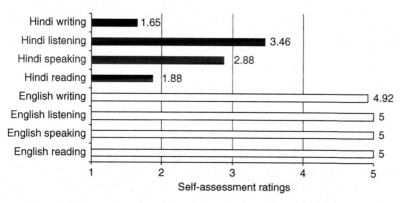

Figure 3.5. US-born Hindi heritage speakers' self-assessments of their English and Hindi abilities by skill (Montrul, Bhatt, and Girju 2015).

All the heritage speakers give themselves very high ratings in English, assessing their abilities in the receptive (listening and reading) and product-ive skills (speaking and writing) and by modality (written versus oral skills) equally high in the majority language. By contrast self-ratings in the heritage language (Romanian and Hindi) are significantly lower, and there are clear dissociations by skill. The three groups self-rated listening higher than all the other skills, followed by speaking. The lowest rated skill is writing. Hence, oral skills are stronger than written skills, and among the receptive skills lis-tening is stronger than reading. Notice that the Romanian heritage speakers who arrived in the United States later in childhood and attended some years of elementary school in Romania rated their abilities in Romanian higher than those Romanian heritage speakers who were born and raised in the United States. Notice also that the Hindi heritage speakers have the lowest self-rating scores, and these speakers did not receive much literacy instruction in Hindi. As a matter of fact, many of them were unable to read and write in the Hindi script. Unlike fluent speakers who received education in their native language, heritage speakers display dissociations in the linguistic knowledge by skills, and this is important in evaluating their linguistic knowledge.

Overall proficiency impacts the grammatical system. Just as heritage speakers display dissociations in proficiency by language skill, they also exhibit uneven mastery of different modules of the grammar. In the rest of the chapter, I focus on these areas to illustrate the characteristics of the grammatical systems of many heritage speakers in vocabulary, morphology, syntax, semantics, discourse pragmatics, and phonetics/phonology. As stated earlier, the examples come from a variety of languages, speakers, and contexts and are intended to show general trends found in heritage speaker grammars. In Chapter 4, I will discuss the language acquisition process and the fact that different aspects of grammar have different developmental schedules and present different degrees of difficulty in language learning in general.

3.2   The grammar of heritage speakers

3.2.1   Vocabulary

Knowledge of words, vocabulary size, formal and semantic changes, lexical productivity, and speed of retrieval of words during oral production are indications of the lexical proficiency of speakers. Knowledge of words also involves knowledge of productive morphological processes and the derivational morphology required to derive words from existing semantically related words (e.g., *real, unreal, construct, construction,* and *reconstruction*). The acquisition of vocabulary is context specific and depends largely on frequency of exposure and experience. Heritage speakers may know many words in their heritage language, but most often these are words related to specific semantic fields, such as common objects used in the home, body parts, basic nature terms, and childhood vocabulary. Compared to their parents or other speakers with proficient command of the language, their lexical repertoires tend to be reduced, especially if they did not go to school and did not learn academic vocabulary. In fact, many heritage speakers do not know words for many abstract concepts and may find it difficult to retrieve words they know but do not use very frequently. In general, and in comparison to other areas of the grammar, knowledge of the lexicon, which also includes lexical diversity in production, has not received much attention in heritage speakers, although lexical knowledge is related to proficiency and to general grammatical knowledge.

Schmidt's (1985) study of Dyirbal in Australia compared the lexical abilities of what she terms and classifies as "Young Dyirbal" speakers (ages 15–35) and "Dyirbal-speaking" children (ages 0–15). Young Dyirbal adult speakers were asked to give Dyirbal equivalents of English words in a 498-item list consisting of 322 nouns, 62 adjectives, and 114 verbs. Schmidt found that none of the 12 speakers was able to recall all of the 498 items (a 100% accuracy score), and scores ranged from 72% to 34% accuracy, average 45.6%. The speakers who were more fluent in English than in Dyirbal scored the lowest in the Dyirbal vocabulary recall task. Accuracy recall on verbs was 58.8%, which was higher than on nouns (41.38%) and adjectives (47.56%). Although the children had minimal ability to construct a Dyirbal sentence, they retained the ability to recall a few words. By comparison to the Young Dyirbal adults, the children received an average score of 10% on the same test, since they were able to recall at most fifty words. The children recalled words for body parts (*head, hand, foot,* and *eye*), animals (*kangaroo, dog,* and *crocodile*), and action verbs (*laugh, talk, drink, sit, lie down, sleep,* and *hit*). Schmidt also observed formal changes in the structure of words and nonsegmentation or lexical chunking of derivational morphology. For example, for some speakers the derivational affix *–gani* ("repeatedly") appeared to be incorporated into the root (*nyian* "sit") as a nonsegmentable unit. Instead of the word having the meaning of "sit repeatedly" as it does for the traditional Dyirbal speakers (the 60-year-old and above generation), it means simply "sit" for the young Dyirbal speakers.

A study that provides more vivid examples of changes in the internal structure of words is Gal's (1989) study of Hungarian heritage speakers in Oberwart, Austria, where German is the majority language. The speakers interviewed were peasant agriculturalists, especially the older generation (60+ years old) (Group A). They spoke Hungarian and learned German after age 15, as a second language. The participants in the other group (Group B) were the children of Hungarian peasants who grew up speaking Hungarian and German (i.e., bilingual heritage speakers). The participants in the younger group (Group C) were children of the bilingual heritage speakers and grandchildren of the first generation speakers (third generation heritage speakers). Although Hungarian was their native language, these speakers had been schooled entirely in German and had the lowest levels of proficiency in Hungarian, as described by Gal.

Following the sociolinguistic tradition, Gal conducted open-ended oral interviews to elicit speech samples, and calculated a lexical proficiency measure for each group based on a type/token ratio applied to verbs. The ratio for the first generation Hungarian speakers was 0.52, for the Hungarian heritage speakers of the second generation it was 0.47, and for the heritage speakers of the third generation (the younger speakers) it was 0.31. The focus of Gal's

Table 3.3. *Average frequency for five word formation devices in Hungarian heritage speakers in Austria (adapted from Gal 1989, p. 321)*

Word formation device	Group A	Group C	C as a % of A
1. Denominal and deadjectival causative *–ít*	1.4	0.5	35
2. Deverbal causative *–ít*	2.8	1.3	46
3. Deverbal causative *–tet/tat*	2.2	1.1	50
4. Preverb + verb	103	72	70
5. General verbalizer *–ol*	12.1	8.6	71
	N = 10	N = 16	

study was derivational processes in verbs; that is, how many other verbal forms with related meaning and words derived from verbs are formed by the productive addition of derivational suffixes. More specifically, Gal quantified five types of derivational processes: (1) denominal and deadjectival causative *–ít* (*rövid/rövidít* "short/shorten"), (2) deverbal causative *–ít*, (*fordul/fordít* "turn/ make turn"), (3) deverbal causative *–tet/tat* (*ír/irat* "write/have something to write"), (4) preverb + verb: *fel + áll* (up + stand) "stand up," and (5) general verbalizer *–ol*, as in *vásár/vásárol* "market/to shop." Gal compared the average frequency of these five derivational processes in the first generation speakers and in the third generation heritage speakers, those with the lowest ability in Hungarian, and the results are displayed in Table 3.3.

The third column shows the performance of the third generation heritage speakers as a percentage of Group A's frequency of words in required contexts. The results of the three causative patterns suggest that these causative affixes are practically not productive in the lexicons of the third generation heritage speakers (Group C), who omitted them very frequently in their speech. However, the use of preverb + verb and the general verbalizer *–ol* was higher for the heritage speakers (Group B) than for the first generation speakers (Group A) and these two patterns were very productive, resulting in what is typically described in the acquisition literature as over-regularization errors. Over-regularizations of this sort occurred more often when the speakers were filling in for lexical gaps, showing that despite having restricted vocabulary these heritage speakers have implicit, procedural knowledge of some productive word formation processes.

Schmidt's and Gal's studies were carried out within the sociolinguistic and anthropological traditions common in the early work on heritage language knowledge and use. More recent experimental studies of lexical knowledge in heritage speakers have taken a psycholinguistic and experimental approach, including Polinsky's (2004, 2006) study of American Russian, Hulsen's (2000) study of three generations of Dutch speakers in New Zealand, and Montrul and Foote's (2014) study of Spanish heritage speakers in the United States.

Table 3.4. *Russian heritage speakers' naming (in ms) and translation accuracy for the three word classes (adapted from Polinsky 2004)*

Word frequency	Naming (RT in ms)			Translation (% accuracy)		
	Verbs	Nouns	Adjectives	Verbs (%)	Nouns (%)	Adjectives (%)
High	460	580	698	82	73	55
Medium	612	766	780	80	64	27
Low	744	812	950	59	27	9
Average	605.3	719.3	809.3	73.6	56.6	30.3

Polinsky (2006) administered a basic vocabulary translation task from English into Russian – the Swadesh list – consisting of 100 words to 21 Russian heritage speakers who moved to the United States with their parents between the ages of 3 and 11 (the list included pronouns, nouns, verbs, and adjectives, but was not balanced by category in the sense that there were more nouns than other lexical classes, as in Gal's study). All the translations were elicited in spoken form in a direct interview with the investigator, and the number of correct translations was taken as a measure of proficiency in Russian. The heritage speakers were unsure about the proper citation of forms in Russian, and showed unstable knowledge with respect to word endings for gender in adjectives, plural versus singular nouns, or aspectual forms of verbs. Their lexical proficiency ranged from 74% to 90.5%. In another study of Russian heritage speakers in the United States, Polinsky (2004) examined the vocabulary proficiency of 5 adult Russian heritage speakers as measured by accuracy recalling nouns, verbs, and adjectives. The main task was a word recognition task done on a computer, which included 33 Russian nouns, 33 Russian verbs, and 33 Russian adjectives, each list divided into 11 high, 11 mid, and 11 low frequency words. In a second experiment, the participants were asked to give oral translations of the 99 words into English. The results showed that the first generation Russian immigrants were 100% accurate translating these words, while the second and third generation heritage speakers (data given in Table 3.4), manifested selective control of word classes: they had better command of verbs than of nouns and adjectives.

Verbs were named faster than nouns and adjectives and they were translated more accurately than nouns and adjectives. Polinsky noted that some of the verbs used in this task were verbs typically acquired very early in acquisition, some even earlier than many of the nouns tested, and Age of Acquisition (AoA) of words plays a role, independent from frequency, in lexical access and lexical memory (Ellis and Morrison 1998). But the most compelling explanation in Polinsky's view is that verbs are more "costly" to lose than nouns. Their structural properties as heads of clauses and their semantics (most often events) are more complex than those of most nouns because verbs take one or more arguments or other constituents and have different aspectual properties. Hence, because they pack more information, they are retained more than nouns perhaps because they are necessary for communicating events.

It is well established in studies of bilingual lexical representation and access that there are many word-related variables that contribute to how quickly and accurately words are identified and produced in a first or second language, including concreteness, imageability, frequency, length, morphological complexity, semantic relatedness, phonological relatedness and cognate status, and the age at which words are first learned (AoA). Hulsen (2000) investigated lexical access and retention of nouns in three generations of Dutch immigrants in New Zealand in their two languages, Dutch and English. The study also included a control group of Dutch speakers in the Netherlands. Hulsen used an oral picture naming task (with objects) and a picture-word matching task to test both accuracy and speed of lexical access in production and comprehension.

Results of both the Dutch and the English experiments showed main effects for generation, cognate status of words (cognate recognized easier and faster than noncognate), and frequency (high frequency words recognized faster than low frequency words). The first generation speakers were less accurate and slower in Dutch than the controls from The Netherlands, but only in production. The second generation speakers were significantly slower and less accurate in Dutch than in English in both measures, although they were much slower and more inaccurate in production than in comprehension. The third generation speakers showed the highest level of attrition. In fact, the picture naming task proved too difficult for these speakers, and the results had to be discarded. Performance on the picture matching task was better than on the picture naming task, suggesting that production is affected more than comprehension. At least for lexical retrieval and access, Hulsen found that, in fact, Dutch is the weaker language both in terms of use and speed of access in heritage speakers of Dutch.

Inspired by Polinsky's (2004) and Hulsen's (2000) findings, Montrul and Foote (2014) investigated the Age of Acquisition (AoA) of words using a lexical decision task and a visual translation judgment task. The heritage speakers tested in the United States were from a Mexican background, exposed to English before age 5. Their mean age at time of testing was 21.18. The stimuli included high and low frequency nouns, verbs, and adjectives. The main variable investigated was how early in life these words were acquired in the L1 of the heritage speakers (Spanish) and in their L2 (English). Each lexical class included words acquired early in L1 Spanish but late in L2 Spanish (Early L1–Late L2), late in L1 Spanish but early in L2 Spanish (Late L1–Early L2), and early in both L1 Spanish and L2 Spanish acquisition (Early L1–Early L2). For example, the word *pañal* "diaper" is acquired early in Spanish as L1 but late in Spanish as L2; the word *correo* "mail" is acquired early in Spanish as L2 but late in Spanish as L1, whereas the word *perro* "dog" is acquired early in Spanish as L1 and in Spanish as L2. Montrul and Foote (2014) found that AoA was a significant factor in speed of lexical access and translation recognition for both groups. The heritage speakers were faster and more accurate when accessing words learned early in Spanish (their L1) and early in English (their L2) (*pañal* "diaper," *perro* "dog") than when accessing words typically acquired later in life (*correo* "mail"). Montrul and Foote found that heritage speakers have good retention of words learned early in life, but they did not find an advantage for verbs as opposed to nouns and adjectives, like Polinsky (2004) did. Table 3.5 summarizes the general trends in the studies discussed.

One question that these studies raise is whether lexical proficiency is a significant predictor of overall linguistic competence in heritage speakers. As we will see in Section 3.2.2, lexical proficiency tends to correlate positively with morphosyntactic proficiency. The size of vocabulary and the types of words that heritage speakers know vary significantly from speaker to speaker because words are acquired in specific contexts. In general, heritage speakers retain (at least receptively) words that were acquired early in life, and semantic fields related to concrete nouns and everyday life. Loss of some derivational affixes and overgeneralization of others have been attested in some languages but, to my knowledge, there are no recent studies examining knowledge of derivational morphology and different semantic fields in heritage speakers. In general, the acquisition of the lexicon in all its dimensions is highly understudied in heritage language acquisition.

Table 3.5. *Summary of findings on the lexicon*

1. Smaller vocabularies than first generation speakers in both comprehension and production.
2. Vocabulary size and productivity is related to level of proficiency (i.e., lower proficiency and smaller vocabulary).
3. Knowledge and retention of early-acquired concrete words.
4. In some studies, nouns seem to be retained and accessed better and faster than verbs and adjectives (cf. Polinsky 2006).
5. The cognate status of words also facilitates knowledge and retention.
6. There are errors of misanalysis (chunking) of derivational morphology and there are errors of overgeneralization of regular processes of word formation to irregular forms.

3.2.2   Inflectional morphology

In comparison to the lexicon, there is significantly more recent research on the morphosyntactic abilities of heritage speakers, probably because inflectional morphology is the linguistic domain most noticeably affected in heritage language grammars, and structural changes in this module are very salient. Inflectional morphology is the locus of crosslinguistic variation. It carries grammatical information but does not change the basic lexical category of the root or base (e.g., *work–work-s*). In the nominal domain, many languages mark number (e.g., *one dog, two dogs*), gender (e.g., Spanish *la mesa* "the table-fem," *el libro* "the book-masc"), definiteness (e.g., *the book* versus *a book*), and case (e.g., *he* versus *him* or *who* versus *whom*); in the verbal domain languages often mark person and number agreement (e.g., *I play, he plays, they play*), tense (present *I jump* versus past *I jump-ed*), aspect (e.g., Spanish progressive and imperfective *jugaba* "I would/was playing" versus perfective *jugué* "I played"), and mood (e.g., Spanish *vengo* "I come" versus *venga* "I would come"). Languages are also typologically classified on the basis of their morphological makeup. In inflected, synthetic languages like Spanish, English, Russian, and Hindi, a word can consist of a root, and inflectional morphemes as suffixes (e.g. *car* singular, *car-s* plural). In isolating, analytic languages like Chinese, Vietnamese, and Yoruba each word is a morpheme and words are not inflected (e.g., Chinese *Tǎ* (he) *yǒu* (have) *sānzhāng* (three) *huà* (picture) "He has three pictures"). Agglutinative languages, like Turkish and Inuttitut, combine several morphemes into one word (e.g., Turkish *evdekiler* "the people in the house"). Inuttitut is classified as a polysynthetic language because a highly inflected word can actually be a full clause (e.g., *tusaatsiarunnanngittualuujunga* "I can't hear very well"). In addition to these broad morphological classifications, synthetic inflected languages exhibit at least two types of morphology: concatenative morphology (when one morpheme follows another in a linear fashion: *car, car-s*) as in English, Spanish, Russian, Japanese, and Dyirbal, and nonconcatenative morphology, when the morphological make-up of a word consists of a template and a consonantal root that maps onto the template, a very common pattern in Semitic languages like Hebrew and Arabic (e.g., the Arabic consonantal root *ktb* derives *katab-a* "he wrote," *kitaab* "book," and *kaatib* "writer").

Despite these typological differences in the morphological expression of the grammatical meaning of nouns and verbs, heritage speakers of diverse languages with overt morphological markings show strikingly similar patterns of omission of obligatory inflectional morphology and regularization of irregular forms, processes leading to overall simplification of inflectional morphology in their heritage languages. The next two subsections provide examples of these processes with nominal and verbal morphology.

3.2.2.1 Nominal morphology: gender, number, and case

Heritage speakers of languages with overt gender, number, and case marking do not often mark these categories consistently, compared to fluent speakers, including their own parents. Many languages classify nouns arbitrarily in the lexicon according to gender. Spanish has two genders (masculine *el carro* "the car," feminine *la silla* "the chair"), Russian and German have three (masculine, gender, and neuter). Many languages distinguish between singular (one) and plural (more than one) on nouns as well. Other languages mark definiteness with inflectional morphology on noun phrases, like Swedish and Dutch (e.g., Swedish *ingen ny bok* "no new book," *den nya boken* "the new book"). In these languages, all the elements of the noun phrase (determiners and in some languages adjectives) must agree with the noun. To make grammatical relations in a sentence, many languages mark case on noun phrases overtly: subjects are marked with nominative case, direct objects with accusative case, indirect objects with dative case, etc. The classic example is Latin, which had six cases (e.g., *porta* "door," nominative *porta*, genitive *portae*, dative *portae*, accusative *portam*, ablative *porta,* and vocative *porta*). Russian also has six cases, marked with regular and irregular morphological patterns. In some languages, gender, number, and case morphology interact in complex ways at the morphological level yielding thirty or more different forms depending on the language. Mature native speakers usually produce the appropriate morphological form in required contexts. When language learners do not produce morphological forms in all required contexts consistently or use different forms compared to adult native speakers, we speak about developmental "errors." In monolingual acquisition, morphological errors of this sort eventually go away with no need for instruction. In L2 acquisition, morphological errors tend to fossilize in many speakers at different percentages below native speaker norms.

Gender, number, and case in nouns are mastered at an early age by monolingual children, especially in languages that have relatively rich morphology such as Spanish (Montrul 2004a), Hungarian (Gábor and Lukács 2012), and Russian (Rodina and Westergaard 2012). Monolingual Russian- and Spanish-speaking children control gender marking by age 3 or 4 with almost 95–100% accuracy, with the exception of most irregular, less frequent, and marked forms.

In a study of 5 expatriate Swedes, who had lived in English, French, and Norwegian-speaking countries before returning to Sweden to attend university, Håkansson (1995) found that these heritage speakers of Swedish had problems with gender, number, and definiteness agreement. As assessed from spoken samples and written compositions in Swedish, they were all highly inaccurate on nominal agreement, producing an average of 53% errors. Another example comes from Greek, a language with three genders (feminine, masculine, and neuter), three different forms for masculine and feminine, and four different forms for neuter. Gender marking interacts in complex ways with plural marking. The default plural suffix for feminine is –s, for masculine it is zero, and for neuter is –s. Zobolou (2011) conducted a study of second and third generation Greek heritage speakers in Argentina. Although Spanish has gender and number, it does not have as many paradigms and irregularities as Greek. Zobolou found that instead of extending the ending –es or –s to every noun, as it would be done in Spanish, Greek heritage speakers in Argentina overgeneralized the default plural ending for each gender. For example, they pluralized *apantisi* (fem. sg. nom.) "answer" as *apantises instead of apantisis, eboros (masc. sg. nom.) "trader" as *ebores instead of ébori and pátoma (neuter sg. nom.) "floor" as pátomas instead of patómata. Zobolou (2011) notes that these patterns are similar to the errors produced by preschool children acquiring Greek in Greece before they completely master all these irregularities (Gavriilidou and Efthymiou 2003).

Agreement in noun phrases has also been studied in Arabic as a heritage language. Arabic is a language with a very complex system of gender and plural morphology: there are different endings for masculine and feminine plural nouns and adjectives. Furthermore, Arabic makes an important distinction between nouns for people (human) and nouns for things (nonhuman). Arabic also presents both concatenative morphology with suffixes attached to word roots, like English, Spanish, Turkish, and noncatenative morphology with consonantal roots and vowel changes within the word, like in other Semitic languages (Amharic, Hebrew, Tigrinya, Aramaic). An example of concatenative morphology is the feminine human suffix –aat – the most frequent ending – and the masculine human ending is –uun/–iin (mudarris "teacher," mudarrisun "teachers"), but there are numerous other alternative forms to these two forms. An example of nonconcatenative morphology is the broken plural, which is a very productive process involving a change of root rather than simply suffixation (similar but not identical to ablaut verbs in English, such as bring-brought). Examples of broken plurals are kitaab "book," – kutub "books" and film "film," – ?aflaam "films."

Albirini, Benmamoun, and Saadah (2011) found that young adult Palestinian and Egyptian Arabic heritage speakers make gender and number agreement errors in spontaneous production, although the error rate was different for the two groups: 8.76% the Palestinians and 20.8% the Egyptians. To follow up on these results, Benmamoun et al. (2014) investigated productive control of plural agreement patterns in heritage speakers of Egyptian Arabic, heritage speakers of Palestinian/Jordanian Arabic, and native speakers of the two dialects in spontaneous oral production and elicited oral production tasks. Benmamoun et al. found that the native speakers performed at 99–100% accuracy; but the heritage speakers produced up to 30% error rates with some words. While the

Arabic heritage speakers retained knowledge of broken plurals and Semitic roots in general, they tended to use the wrong pattern. El Aissati (1997) also investigated knowledge of plural formation in Moroccan-Arabic heritage speakers living in the Netherlands. The participants were asked to give the plural forms of a list of singular nouns, and unlike Moroccan monolinguals, the heritage speakers used the suffixation strategy for regular and irregular plurals when producing broken plurals.

Polinsky (2008a) found evidence of simplification of the gender agreement system as a function of proficiency in heritage speakers of Russian in the United States. Polinsky conducted an oral elicitation task consisting of feminine, masculine, and neuter animate and inanimate words that twelve heritage speakers had to use in a phrase. The speakers also completed a comprehension-based test, where animate and inanimate Russian nouns were presented with adjectives matching in gender or not. Participants were asked to detect the grammaticality of these noun-adjective combinations based on gender agreement with the adjective. The heritage speakers showed an 11% error rate with masculine nouns, 30% with feminine nouns, and 55% with neuter nouns. The higher proficiency Russian heritage speakers displayed a three-way gender system like the Russian speakers tested as baseline, but lower proficiency speakers had a two-way distinction, consisting of only masculine and feminine, and no neuter. Feminine nouns ending in a palatalized consonant were treated as masculine and neuter nouns were treated as feminine.

By now there are several studies on gender assignment and agreement conducted with Spanish heritage speakers in the United States, both with adults (Alarcón 2011; Montrul, Foote, and Perpiñán 2008a; Montrul *et al.* 2014; Montrul *et al.* 2013) and with children (Anderson 1999; Montrul and Potowski 2007). Spanish has only two genders, masculine and feminine, and masculine is considered the default (Harris 1991; McCarthy 2008). Although about 90% of Spanish nouns have regular ending for gender, there are irregular nouns that do not end in the canonical masculine –*o* and canonical feminine –*a* ending. They end in nontransparent endings like –*e* or a consonant. All these studies found that gender is problematic for heritage speakers with low to intermediate proficiency in Spanish. Higher proficiency heritage speakers can achieve native-like levels with gender assignment and agreement (Alarcón 2011; Kupisch *et al.* 2013; Montrul *et al.* 2013). When Spanish heritage speakers make gender errors, these are most frequent with feminine nouns and with nouns with noncanonical or nontransparent word endings. If masculine gender is considered the default in Spanish and feminine is the marked form, clearly Spanish heritage language grammars also show simplification of marked forms and retention of the default. In sum, with respect to gender agreement in nouns, the consistent finding across studies of different heritage speakers, languages, and majority/contact languages is that heritage speakers of lower proficiency in the heritage language apply gender to nouns inconsistently, unlike native speakers.

Case marking is another candidate for erosion and non-native mastery in heritage language grammars, and like gender agreement, erosion of case marking has been found in several heritage languages including Dyirbal (Schmidt 1985), Estonian in Sweden (Maandi 1989), Pennsylvania German (Huffines 1989), Greek in Argentina (Zobolou 2011), Hindi (Moag 1995; Montrul, Bhatt, and Bhatia 2012), Finnish (Larmouth 1974), Spanish (Montrul 2004b; Montrul and Bowles 2009), Russian (Polinsky 2006), and Korean (Song *et al.* 1997) in the United States, among many others. These languages vary significantly in the number of cases they mark overtly, yet the general pattern observed in the grammars of heritage speakers is that of reduction of case systems and simplification.

For example, full Russian has a six-way distinction in nouns: nominative, accusative, dative, instrumental, oblique, and genitive. According to Polinsky (2006, 2008b), the case system is severely reduced in heritage speakers: dative is replaced by accusative and accusative by nominative in many constructions with subjects, direct, and indirect objects. Thus, while native speakers of Russian use the six-case markings, heritage speakers tend to use only two: nominative and accusative. Huffines (1989) studied the loss of case marking in sectarian and nonsectarian Pennsylvania Germans of different ages, generations, and degrees of bilingualism. The Pennsylvania German spoken by the oldest native speakers in the nonsectarian community has three genders (masculine, feminine, and neuter), two numbers (singular and plural), and two cases (common and dative), like standard German. Genitive case is found in restricted cases. Huffines conducted sociolinguistic interviews with 33 sectarians and 19 nonsectarian adults (ages 25–60), consisting of free conversation, translation of English sentences into Pennsylvania German, and picture descriptions. The second and third generation speakers, all bilingual in English, produced significantly less dative forms than the elders. The second generation speakers tended to replace many dative forms by common case. The third generation speakers hardly used any datives in obligatory contexts, and used accusative and common case forms to express dative functions.

In terms of case systems, ergative languages contrast with nominative-accusative languages. Nominative-accusative languages (Spanish, English, Russian, Greek, and German, among others) generally mark subjects of transitive verbs and intransitive verbs with nominative case, and mark objects with accusative case. In Korean, subjects are case marked with the nominative particle *-ka* and direct objects with the accusative particle *-lul*, as shown in (1).

(1) Yeca-ka   namca-lul mil-ess-ta.
    girl- NOM boy-ACC push-PAST-DECL
    "The girl pushed the boy."

Ergative-absolutive languages (Hindi, Greenlandic, Dyirbal, and Euskera, among others) mark the subject of transitive verbs overtly with ergative case. Subjects of intransitive predicates and objects are marked with absolutive case, which is typically null (Butt 2006). In Hindi/Urdu, ergativity is conditioned by aspectual distinctions (perfective versus nonperfective). The ergative case in Hindi/Urdu is confined to the subjects of finite transitive verbs with perfective morphology, as in the example in (2), which shows the ergative clitic –ne on the subject *Ram*. The object can be nominative (i.e., no overt case and controlling verbal agreement). Example (3) is ungrammatical because the verb is intransitive, and the intransitive verbs do not license ergative –ne.

(2) Ram-ne   gaaRii   calaa-yii   hai.
    Ram.MSG-ERG car.FSG.NOM drive-PERF.FSG   be.PRES.3SG
    "Ram has driven a car."
(3) *Siitaa-ne   bahut   haNs-ii.
    Sita.MSG-ERG a lot   laugh-PERF.FSg
    "Sita laughed a lot."

Heritage speakers of nominative-accusative marking languages omit case marking with subjects and objects, as has been attested in Korean by Song *et al.* (1997).

Although nominative and accusative case markers are typically dropped in Korean spoken discourse, monolingual children and adults gain full control of the case system in comprehension and production, including the discourse-pragmatic conditions under which case markers can be dropped or retained. Song *et al.* found that while 5-to 8-year-old monolingual Korean children were 86% accurate at comprehending O-V-S sentences in Korean with nominative and accusative case markers, 5-to 8-year-old Korean heritage speakers performed at less than 34% accuracy. They tended to interpret O-V-S sentences as S-O-V sentences, ignoring the case markers.

Nominative case in Spanish is not marked overtly with morphology, but some objects are overtly marked with the accusative marker *a* (*Juan vio a María* "Juan saw Maria"), which is also the preposition appearing with dative case (*María dio un libro a Pedro* "Maria gave a book to Pedro"). Montrul (2004b) and Montrul and Bowles (2009) showed that adult Spanish heritage speakers omit the dative preposition "a" with the subjects of *gustar*-type verbs (**Juan le gusta la música* instead of *A Juan le gusta la música* "Juan likes music"), and they omit the same preposition when it appears with animate direct objects (**Juan vio María* instead of *Juan vio a María* "Juan saw

Maria"). However, when the preposition marks the prototypical dative case of indirect objects (*María dio un libro a Pedro* "Maria gave a book to Pedro"), Spanish heritage speakers hardly ever omit it in these cases.

Although Hindi is an ergative language, the case marking of direct and indirect objects is similar to Spanish. Montrul, Bhatt, and Bhatia (2012) studied Hindi heritage speakers in the United States and, as in Spanish, they also found that many heritage speakers differed from the first (parental) Hindi-speaking generation in that they frequently omitted the case marking particle *–ko* with specific direct objects and with dative subjects, but hardly ever omitted it when it marked dative case on indirect objects.

Heritage speakers of ergative languages like Hindi (Montrul, Bhatt, and Bhatia 2012), Euskera (Austin 2007; Ezeizabarrena Segurola 2011), Inuttitut (Murasugi 2012), and Dyirbal (Schmidt 1985) frequently omit or no longer use ergative case marking. In traditional Dyirbal, ergative case is formally marked by the suffix *–ngu* and a wide range of phonologically conditioned allomorphs (*–gu, –ju, –ru, –bu, –du, –ju*). Schmidt (1985) shows that young speakers of Dyirbal display allomorphic reduction to five forms (*–ngu, –du, –bu, –du, –ju*), two forms (*–ngu, –du*), and one form (*–gu*) depending on the proficiency of the speakers, and is absent (zero marking) in the youngest speakers, the children, who already show a nominative-accusative system. When these speakers lose the ergative inflection they use the strict word order of English, where transitive and intransitive subjects appear before the verb.

In Hindi/Urdu, ergative marking interacts with tense and agreement. The ergative case *–ne* is confined to the subjects of finite transitive verbs with perfective morphology. Montrul, Bhatt, and Bhatia (2012) investigated whether Hindi heritage speakers make case and agreement errors in oral production and in a bimodal grammaticality judgment task, which allowed for testing of sentences with different manipulations of the tense and agreement patterns that were not likely to be produced spontaneously. Participants were adult native speakers of Hindi raised in India, who arrived in the United States as adults and Hindi heritage speakers, who were enrolled in college or had completed college in the United States. They were all exposed to Hindi and English since birth (the self-ratings displayed in Figure 3.5 are of these speakers). Participants were shown pictures of the children's tale *Little Red Riding Hood* and were asked to narrate the story in the past. The Hindi heritage speakers showed instability in their case marking of ergative subjects with *–ne* and human animate and specific direct objects with *–ko*. Case marking was significantly more affected than agreement. Table 3.6 summarizes the rate of omission of ergative marking and of overgeneralizations.

The study also tested grammatical and ungrammatical uses of case marking in a bimodal acceptability judgment task (with auditory and visual stimulus presentation). Some sentences manipulated transitivity, and other targeted

Table 3.6. *Mean percentage accuracy, omission, and overgeneralization of ergative* –ne *marking (adapted from Montrul, Bhatt, and Bhatia 2012)*

	N	Number of predicates marked with –*ne*	–*ne* with transitive perfective (%)	–*ne* omission (%)	–*ne* overgeneralization to other predicates (%)
Hindi native speakers	21	214	95.98	< 1	3.59
Hindi heritage speakers	28	164	56.74	35.9	8.36

agreement and its interaction with ergative. Like the Hindi speakers from India, the Hindi heritage speakers in the United States distinguished between grammatical and ungrammatical transitive perfective predicates with ergative –*ne* and grammatical and ungrammatical sentences with intransitive perfective predicates with ergative –*ne*. Yet, the heritage speakers were more accepting of omission and overgeneralization errors with –*ne* marking based on transitivity than the native speakers from India, confirming the pattern attested in the oral production task.

To summarize thus far, regardless of the complexity of the case system and the typology of case in different languages (nominative-accusative or ergative-absolutive systems), case marking is significantly affected in heritage speakers who speak highly inflected languages. In general, some forms tend to be omitted, others are regularized, and the case system is simplified.

3.2.2.2 *Verbal morphology: agreement, tense, aspect, and mood*
The verbal domain exhibits similar morphological changes in heritage language speakers, especially with subject-verb agreement, complex tenses, aspect, and mood, although verbal morphology in general appears to be more stable and less vulnerable to omission and changes than nominal morphology.

Many languages mark person and number agreement on the verb, which agrees with the subject (e.g., *He know-s me*). There are also languages that have object agreement, like Hindi, where the verb also agrees in person, number, and gender with the object. Heritage speakers with low proficiency in the language display errors of subject-verb agreement (Huffines 1989; Polinsky 2006), but speakers with higher proficiency do not seem to have problems. For example, the four lowest proficiency Russian heritage speakers studied by Polinsky (2006) were only 30% accurate on verbal paradigms and agreement. The more proficient speakers in her sample were 66% accurate on agreement. Most common errors involved the use of third person singular in any tense, including in plural forms, and infinitives elsewhere. Sherkina-Lieber, Pérez-Leroux, and Jones (2011) studied comprehension of morphology violations in Inuttitut-English bilinguals with receptive knowledge of Inuttitut. Despite their inability to produce the language, receptive bilinguals with high levels of aural comprehension detected errors with subject-verb agreement mismatches with 70% accuracy or above, while those with lower receptive ability performed at chance (at about 50%). Montrul (2006a) showed that intermediate and advanced proficiency heritage speakers of Spanish in the United States were highly accurate on subject-verb agreement in an oral narrative task (above 96%). Similarly, Albirini *et al.* (2011) compared accuracy on nominal agreement and on verbal agreement in Palestinian and Egyptian Arabic heritage speakers in the United States and found that accuracy on subject-verb agreement was above 90%; the error rates were 6.4% for the Egyptian heritage speakers and 2.6% for the Palestinians. When agreement was not accurate, some speakers extended singular masculine agreement morphology to other verbal and nominal forms, particularly when the target forms were feminine plurals. There were also more errors produced when the subject and the verb were separated by a prepositional phrase. As for Hindi in the United States, Moag's (1995) observation that the vast majority of Hindi heritage speakers do not control subject-verb agreement was not confirmed by Montrul, Bhatt, and Bhatia (2012). The Hindi heritage speakers hardly made subject-verb agreement errors, and the few errors made involved object-verb agreement.

Tense is another verbal category that may be affected in heritage language grammars. Tense locates the event in the time axis and signals the difference between present-past and future. In general, there are few if any reports of errors with tense in heritage grammars (Fenyvesi 2000). The Inuttitut heritage speakers with receptive command of the language studied by Sherkina-Lieber *et al.* performed above 80% accuracy, identifying errors involving tense and agreement reversal of morphemes. Silva-Corvalán (1994, 2014), who studied oral samples from Spanish heritage speakers in the United States, did not record errors with tense and temporality either. The heritage speakers of Spanish used all the simple tense forms, and distinguished between past, present, and future. However, with respect to the future, they used the periphrastic form (*ir a* + infinitive "go to") instead of the simple future synthetic form (ending in *−r−* as in *ama-r-é* "I will love," *teme-r-é* "I will fear," *vivi-r-é* "I will live"). Unlike the first generation speakers, second and third generation speakers did not have productive use of the complex compound tenses (pluperfect indicative and subjunctive, future, and conditional perfect) and analytic forms in Spanish (future) (Silva-Corvalán 1994, p. 30). All in all, the general observation so far is that heritage speakers' accuracy with verbal morphology, including different verb tenses, seems to be related to proficiency: low proficiency speakers make errors, higher proficiency speakers do not. Errors with tense are rare with simple tenses, but many heritage speakers do not actually develop many complex forms.

Aspect is another verbal category concerned with the internal temporal constituency of a situation (state or event), such that these can be regarded as having an endpoint or not. Aspect can be expressed lexically by the inherent lexical semantics of the verb and its interaction with direct and indirect arguments and adjuncts (Dowty 1986; Verkuyl 1994). This is called Aktionsart, lexical aspect, or situation type (Smith 1991) and represents the way humans perceive and categorize situations. Aspect can also be expressed grammatically, through the use of inflectional morphology on the verb. This is termed viewpoint aspect (Smith 1991). Viewpoint aspect, which refers to the partial or full view of a particular situation type, is marked by an overt grammatical morpheme (e.g., preterite and imperfect in Spanish). Aspectual morphology is quite vulnerable in heritage language grammars, but the degree of vulnerability depends on the complexity of this category in the language and the grammatical means for marking it. Aspect can be calculated at the lexical, at the sentence, and discourse-pragmatic level. At the lexical level, verbs and predicates can be telic (with an endpoint) as in (4) or atelic (without an endpoint), as in (5).

(4) Mary baked a cake.   (accomplishment predicate, telic)
(5) Mary sang for hours.   (activity predicate, atelic)

At the grammatical level, one of the most common aspectual oppositions is the perfective-imperfective opposition. Perfective aspect is concerned with the beginning and end of a situation and is thus "bounded" (it can be inceptive, punctual, or completive).

(6) Mary read a book.

Imperfective aspect is "unbounded." It focuses on the internal structure of the situation instead, viewing it as ongoing, with no specific endpoint (imperfective aspect can be durative or habitual).

(7) Mary was reading a book.

Notice that grammatical aspect, like lexical aspect, makes reference to complete versus ongoing situations. However, while telicity is used to describe the aspectual nature of events at the lexical level, the notion of "boundedness" (Smith 1991), which is also related to endpoints, is relevant to grammatical aspect. Furthermore, viewpoint aspect is not categorical. Comrie (1976, p. 4) observes that "it is quite possible for the same speaker to refer to the same situation once with a perfective form, then with an imperfective, without in any way being self-contradictory." For instance, in (8) we can see that reading may be used with the progressive or the simple past to refer to the same event:

(8)   John read that book yesterday; while he was reading it, the postman came.

Finally, it is important to point out that verbal morphology (simple past versus progressive, in this case) may override the lexical aspectual value of verb phrases. While in Spanish telic predicates go well with the preterit and atelic with the imperfect (those are prototypical combinations), it is possible for the preterit verbal ending to appear with stative verbs and the imperfect with achievements. There are, however, some ways in which the grammaticality of preterit or imperfect may be conventionally determined. As an example, consider the sentences in (9) and (10).

(9)   Marisa pintaba (IMP) un retrato y todavía lo está pintando.   (unbounded)
      "Marisa was painting a portrait and is still painting it."

(10) Marisa pintó (PRET) un retrato y todavía lo está pintando.   (#bounded)
      "Marisa painted a portrait and is still painting it."

The imperfect in the first clause of (9) does not specify whether the situation is complete or not, and a clause indicating the continuation of the event is possible (not a contradiction). In contrast, the preterit in (10) frames the situation as bounded (completed). Hence, a clause indicating that the event is still in progress is a contradiction (thus the symbol #), although such interpretation is not necessarily impossible given appropriate context.

Some languages mark some aspectual distinctions through verbal morphology and others do not. In comparison to English, Russian has a very complex aspect system. In their citation forms (the form found in dictionaries), verbs are classified as basically perfective or imperfective with aspectual morphology instantiated as preverbal prefixes. For example, the verb *čital* "read" is imperfective in its citation form, and the verb *po-nravilos* "like" is perfective, containing the perfective prefix *po–*. In Spanish, some verbal paradigms contain explicit inflectional morphology that marks aspect, for example in participles and in the preterit/imperfect distinction that marks perfectivity and imperfectivity in the past tense of the indicative mood. In addition, some verbs can appear with reflexive pronouns to signify a change of state or the completion (telicity) of an event. For example, in Spanish, the preterit and imperfect distinction in the past tense marks grammatical aspect, as in (11) and (12).

(11) Pedro leyó   un libro.   (preterit, perfective)
      Pedro read-PRET. a book
      "Pedro read a book."

(12)   Pedro leía   un libro.   (imperfect, imperfective)
       Pedro read-IMPF a book
       "Pedro was reading a book."

A recent comprehensive study of aspect in Russian heritage speakers is Laleko (2008, 2010), who advances an account of grammatical aspect as a category representative of interface effects, and operating at the level of lexical semantics, syntax, and pragmatics. At the lexico-syntactic level, Russian aspectual distinctions are tied to lexical aspect, that is, telicity of the verbal predicate. The default aspectual value for verbs that are inherently specified as telic or atelic is based on the semantic properties of the verb. When the verbs are not overtly marked with aspectual morphology, the object of the predicate can also contribute to the aspectual value of the predicate. In the English example in (4), the object "a cake" contributes telicity to the predicate "bake." But in Russian telicity can also be overridden at the sentential level by habitual and progressive imperfectivizers on telic events or by delimiting perfectivizing prefixes such as *po–* and *za–*. In addition, other pragmatically conditioned aspectual triggers can also contribute to telicity. Thus, even in the absence of atelic interpretations of the verbal phrase at the lexical level or imperfective operators at the sentential level, Russian verbs may receive imperfective marking for pragmatic reasons.

Laleko (2010) showed that monolingual native speakers raised in Russia have knowledge of the interaction of these levels of analyses – lexical, sentential, and discourse-pragmatic – but the three levels of aspectual structure are affected selectively in heritage language acquisition. In particular, heritage speakers exhibit significant reduction of the pragmatically conditioned functions of the imperfective aspect, as well as imperfective forms with completed events, even in the presence of contextual discourse-pragmatic triggers of imperfectivity. At the same time, advanced heritage speakers did not exhibit errors with aspectual morphology in their speech. Thus, highly proficient heritage speakers are native-like in production even without the apparent complete mastery of the intricate contextual uses of the Russian imperfective.

Laleko's (2010) model of aspect in Russian makes further predictions with respect to the directionality of aspectual changes (restructuring) observed in heritage speakers as a function of proficiency. If advanced heritage speakers exhibit problems with the syntactic-pragmatic level of aspect, low proficiency heritage speakers will have problems with the discourse-pragmatic level and the intermediate sentential level, where grammatical aspectual triggers operate. Thus, lower proficiency heritage speakers may not be consistently sensitive to aspectual distinctions at the sentence level, paying more attention to the default lexical aspect of the predicate. Indeed, Polinsky's (2006, 2008b) lower proficiency Russian heritage speakers revealed multiple instances of perfective aspectual forms occurring in the presence of habitual adverbs when predicates are telic. According to Polinsky (2006), the perfective-imperfective morphological opposition is even lost in low proficiency Russian heritage speakers. Most verbs become lexicalized perfectives or lexicalized imperfectives, depending on lexical class. That is, the telic classes – achievements and accomplishments – are lexicalized in the perfective (with a perfective prefix), while the atelic classes – activities and states – are lexicalized in the imperfective (with an imperfective prefix). Examples of these tendencies in American Russian are shown in (13) and (14) (from Polinsky 2006, pp. 227–228, exx. 31 and 34).

(13) a. Ja nikogda ne pročital ta kniga.   *American Russian*
          I never NEG PERF-read [this book]
          "I never read this book."
     b. Ja nikogda ne čital   etu knigu.   *Full Russian*
          I never NEG read.IMPERF [this book]-ACC
          "I never read this book."

(14) a. Mne   nravilos'   v   Princeton   no   ja   ljublju   žit'   v
          Chicago   *American Russian*
          ME-DAT liked.IMPERF in Princeton but I like to live in
          Chicago.
          "I enjoyed Princeton but I would prefer to live in Chicago."
     b. Mne   po-nravilos'   v   Princeton   no   ja   ljublju   žit'v
          Chicago   *Full Russian*
          ME-DAT PERF-liked in Princeton-PREP but I like to live in
          Chicago.
          "I enjoyed Princeton but I would prefer to live in Chicago."

Thus, degree of erosion of aspect and the structural level affected seem to be related to the level of proficiency of the heritage speakers in their language.

Spanish has a much simpler aspectual system than Russian: as shown in (6) and (7), there is an aspectual contrast in the past tense, with two forms: preterit (perfective) and imperfect (imperfective). Using very different methodologies and theoretical approaches, both Silva-Corvalán (1994, 2014) and Montrul (2002, 2009) found that young adult Spanish heritage speakers in the United States confuse aspectual distinctions between perfective and imperfective forms. Spanish heritage speakers use preterit for imperfect forms and vice versa in oral production, and have been shown to have difficulties interpreting the meaning of preterit and imperfect morphology in experimental tasks involving truth value judgments (Montrul 2002, 2009). Silva-Corvalán (1994) and Montrul (2002) also found that Spanish heritage speakers had difficulty with stative verbs that shift aspectual value in the preterit (*sabía-supo* "knew-found out") in both oral production and in interpretation tasks.

Perhaps the verbal category that is most affected in heritage languages is mood in languages that express it morphologically. That is, not all languages express modality overtly in the grammar, but those which do present a challenge to heritage speakers when it comes to the expression of mood. For example, many Spanish heritage speakers do not reliably distinguish between the indicative and the subjunctive moods in comprehension and prefer to use the indicative mood in oral production in contexts where the subjunctive would be required or preferred by monolingual Spanish speakers (Montrul 2007, 2009; Silva-Corvalán 1994), and so is the conditional (Silva-Corvalán 1994). Although monolingual Spanish-speaking children start using subjunctive forms with a set of restrictive verbs that subcategorize for the subjunctive and in negative commands by age 3 (Montrul 2004a), semantically and pragmatically conditioned uses of the subjunctive and subjunctive in adverbial clauses is not mastered until about age 12 (Blake 1983).

First generation Spanish-speaking immigrants in the United States retain the subjunctive in all these contexts, but second and third generation heritage speakers tend to replace the indicative for subjunctive in contexts where the subjunctive is required, or they fail to use the subjunctive to signal different semantic and pragmatic meanings of a given expression based on context. For example, in her study of Mexican-Americans in the Los Angeles region, Silva-Corvalán (1994) found that low proficiency speakers did not produce subjunctive forms, using the indicative exclusively in both obligatory and in variable contexts, as in (15) and (16) (Silva-Corvalán 1994, p. 42).

(15)   *I hope que no me *toca* (PI) la misma problema.[1]   (= toque PS)
       "I hope I don't run into the same problem."
(16)   Quizás *vengo* mañana (= venga (PS)).
       "Maybe I come tomorrow."

In some cases, the use of the indicative or subjunctive depends on meaning and implicatures. The indicative implies a fact, whereas the subjunctive implies a hypothetical situation. In a study with intermediate and advanced proficiency Spanish heritage speakers, Montrul (2007) found a high rate of errors with the subjunctive in written tasks and little discrimination between the semantic implicatures of indicative and subjunctive morphology in variable contexts, such as with relative clauses (*Busco a una profesora que enseña*-indic./*enseñe*-subj. *francés*. "I am looking for a teacher who teaches/would teach French"). The indicative implies that the teacher exists, whereas the subjunctive implies that such teacher might not exist. Thus, the simplification of the subjunctive in adult heritage speakers appears to extend to comprehension as well.

---

[1] PI = present indicative, PS = present subjunctive. These abbreviations are from Silva-Corvalán (1994), and so are the examples.

Table 3.7. *Overall error rates with preterit and imperfect, subjunctive and indicative by Spanish heritage speakers in two oral elicitation tasks (adapted from Montrul 2009)*

Groups	N	Preterit (%)	Imperfect (%)	Indicative (%)	Subjunctive (%)
Advanced	29	3.8	8	4.1	26
Intermediate	21	1.9	2.5	14.5	27
Low	15	0.7	3.6	2.2	62.8
Overall	65	1.8	3.8	6.7	41.3

Comparing grammatical and morphological categories within the verbal domain, mood is significantly more affected than aspect. Montrul (2009) tested knowledge and use of tense/aspect and mood in Spanish heritage speakers of three proficiency levels: low, intermediate, and advanced, as well as a comparison group of monolingually raised native speakers. Although the heritage speakers used preterit/imperfect and indicative/subjunctive in two oral tasks, many of the errors evidenced in production also showed up in written recognition and in tasks of semantic discrimination. Montrul's results reflect the same developmental trends reported by Silva-Corvalán (1994). That is, many of the Spanish heritage speakers who exhibited unstable knowledge of mood displayed better command of grammatical aspect, as shown in Table 3.7.

The heritage speakers' knowledge of grammatical aspect appears more solid with prototypical grammatical aspect-predicate type combinations, such as achievements and accomplishments in the preterit or states in the imperfect. By contrast, those conditions where the lexical semantic features of the verb and the semantic features of the aspectual form clash, such as achievements in the imperfect and states in the preterit, proved more problematic for the low proficiency speakers as well. Therefore, the results of Montrul (2009) are consistent with the attrition effects observed with tense/aspect and with mood in childhood (Merino 1983; Silva-Corvalán 2003, 2014), even when all these studies used very different methodologies and tasks.

The simplification of subjunctive, future, and conditional forms has consequences for the expression of hypothetical discourse, an area of difficulty for heritage speakers with low proficiency in the language. For example, inflected infinitives, a type of subjunctive form at least in meaning, are another verbal form often missing in some heritage language grammars. Among the Romance languages, Portuguese is the only language that has infinitives inflected for person and number, as in (17):

(17)   nós saí+r+mos,   vocês/ eles/   elas   saí+r+em
        we to leave.AGR.1PL, you.PL./they.MASC./they.FEM to leave.
        AGR.3PL

Like subjunctive forms, inflected infinitives must appear in embedded clauses, as in (18). Inflected infinitives have different referential properties from noninflected infinitives.

(18) Eu   esperei   um pouco para nós   saírmos juntos.
      1SG.NOM wait.PERF.1SG a little for   1PL. NOM get out.INF.1PL
      together.
      "I waited a little for us to get out together."

According to Rothman (2007) and Pires and Rothman (2009a), inflected infinitives occur in both colloquial and formal varieties of European Portuguese, and heritage speakers of Portuguese in the United States use inflected infinitives in their speech and know their semantic properties. However, it seems that inflected infinitives do not occur in colloquial Brazilian Portuguese (BP), although they occur in written Brazilian Portuguese, the formal register. Pires and Rothman (2009a) argue that inflected infinitives in Brazilian Portuguese (BP) are part of academic discourse, and native speakers in Brazil develop knowledge of these forms through formal schooling. Pires and Rothman (2009a) present experimental data from 87 Brazilian children/teenagers of high socioeconomic status (ages range from 6 to 15), and their results show that, with very few individual exceptions, the children do not command the syntax and semantics of inflected infinitives until the ages of 10–12, after which they give evidence of adult-like knowledge with no significant individual variation. A written morphology recognition task and a written grammaticality judgment task administered to eleven Brazilian Portuguese heritage speakers in the United States, who were very fluent in their heritage language, confirmed that these speakers had not acquired the formal properties and semantics of inflected infinitives in Brazilian Portuguese.

If ... then conditional sentences are complex sentences, requiring specific combinations of tenses and moods depending on the degree of factuality or hypotheticality. In Spanish, as in many other languages, there are three types of conditional sentences that vary in their hypotheticality and (counter-)factuality. The first type is the simplest and takes simple present in the *if clause* (protasis) and simple future in the *then clause* (apodosis).

(19) Si llueve   mañana   no regaré   las plantas.
      if it rains-PRES tomorrow not I water-FUT the plants
      "If it rains tomorrow I will not water the plants."

The other two types are more complex, and represent irrealis and hypothetical meanings. In Spanish, they require subjunctive and conditional forms:

(20) Si tuviera   tiempo, terminaría de leer este libro hoy.
      if I had-SUBJ time, I finish-COND reading this book today
      "If I had time, I would finish reading this book today."

(21)   Si hubiera sabido   que venías   a las 4,
       te habría esperado.[2]
       if I had known-PLUPERF SUBJ that you come-IMP at 4,
       I you would have waited-COND PERF
       "If I had known you were arriving at 4 I would have waited
       for you."

Several studies (Fairclough 2005; Gutiérrez 1996; Lynch 1999; Silva-Corvalán 1994) have found that while first generation Spanish-speaking immigrants produce the three types of clauses with the most typical tenses as shown in (19–21), second and third generation heritage speakers show considerable variation in the use of verbal paradigms with Type 2 and Type 3 conditionals, the ones requiring conditional and subjunctive verbal forms. The general tendency is to replace subjunctive and conditional forms with the indicative, and the compound tenses with simple tenses. Silva-Corvalán (1994) observed that the first generation immigrants had a complex system of verb morphology that allowed them to convey different degrees of possibility, assertiveness, predictive certainty, etc. By contrast, second generation heritage speakers exhibited a more restrictive set of choices, using almost exclusively indicative morphology to convey a strong degree of assertiveness and predictive certainty, without differentiating morphologically between more or less possible situations in the hypothetical world created. The second–third generation children recently studied longitudinally (Silva-Corvalán 2014) hardly used the future and the conditional forms, but retained the past tense. Similar trends with the reduction of verbal forms in conditionals have been reported by Dorian (1981) for Gaelic and by Trudgill (1976–1977) for Arvanitika, an Albanian language in Greece.

In conclusion, this selective overview of verbal morphology in heritage speakers of different languages shows that the degree of erosion and simplification observed in different speakers and languages seems to be related to the degree of proficiency of the heritage speakers and the complexity of the verbal forms. In general, heritage speakers develop and retain solid knowledge of agreement and tense, but the categories that interface with semantics and pragmatics (aspect and mood) are more prone to simplification, and more so if they require complex syntax, like inflected infinitives, subjunctive, and conditional forms that must occur in complex sentences. Another observation is that nominal morphology tends to be more affected than verbal morphology. Table 3.8 summarizes the tendencies observed.

---

[2] However, the imperfect conditional is hardly used in most varieties and speakers replace it with the imperfect subjunctive in the two clauses.

Table 3.8. *General trends observed with the morphological competence of heritage speakers*

Nominal morphology	1. Inconsistent use of gender in nouns and gender agreement in noun phrases (Spanish, Russian, Swedish, Greek, and Arabic)
	2. Regularization of irregular plural forms (Greek and Arabic)
	3. Omission of overt case marking (marked accusative, inherent dative, and ergative)
	4. Simplification of case marking (from more to fewer forms)
	5. Allophonic reduction and regularization patterns
	6. The lower the proficiency in the heritage language, the more affected the nominal morphology
	7. Nominal morphology tends to be more affected than verbal morphology
Verbal morphology	1. Tense and agreement morphology tend to be better preserved than aspect and mood
	Tense<Agreement<Aspect<Mood
	2. Within Tense, the morphological future is more affected than present and past
	3. Within Aspect, imperfect morphology is more affected than perfective morphology
	4. In languages that have morphological mood, subjunctive and conditional are often replaced by indicative morphology
	5. The lower the proficiency in the heritage language, the more affected the verbal morphology

3.2.3 Syntax

Although under some theoretical accounts morphology is part of syntax, in this section I discuss features of sentences, like word order, and dependencies between elements in the sentence, such as pronoun interpretation. With respect to word order, the simplification of case and agreement morphology characteristic of many heritage language grammars has consequences for the basic clause structure and for pronominal reference. Yet, Håkansson's (1995) study of Swedish heritage speakers found that the speakers were quite native-like on the placement of verbs in Swedish, which follows the V2 Germanic rule. But in languages where word order and case interact, the erosion of case in heritage languages has consequences for word order. In languages with flexible word order, case markers allow the speaker and hearer to keep track of the participants (and their grammatical relationship) by explicitly marking the subject and different objects (e.g., in Latin *puella* ("the girl"), *portam* ("the door"), *videt* ("sees"), and *portam puella videt* mean the same thing, "The girl sees the door"). For example, Russian and Spanish heritage speakers mostly use S-V-O word order, while Korean speakers prefer S-O-V order (Song *et al.* 1997). Montrul (2010a,b) found that while Spanish heritage speakers accepted and comprehended S-V-O sentences accurately, they were much less accurate with sentences with preverbal, dislocated objects (O-V-S, *Las carpetas las dejó Juan en la oficina* "The folders Juan left in the office"). Similarly, Montrul, Bhatt, and Girju (2015) found that Spanish and Romanian heritage speakers had difficulty comprehending sentences with postverbal subjects (V-S) in a picture-based comprehension task and assigned lower grammaticality judgment ratings to these sentences compared to S-V-O sentences in a bimodal grammaticality judgment task. Albirini *et al.* (2011) report data from Egyptian heritage speakers, where the S-V-O order is predominant in the speech of these speakers, although the language allows for V-S-O as an alternative option. The prevalence of the S-V-O order could be due to transfer from English, but it could also be due to the complex syntax of the V-S-O order. Another intriguing recent explanation relates cognitive biases in learning to efficient communication and transmission. In a series of experiments with artificial languages that manipulate reliability of case marking and word order, Fedzechkina, Jaeger, and Newport (2012) and Fedzechkina, Newport, and Jaeger (2014) found that at the cognitive level and to ease communication, learners introduce changes during learning that are compatible with language universals: learners exposed to a fixed word order language drop case, those exposed to a variable system maintain case to track information. Thus, the case-word order trade off observed in heritage language grammars is compatible with these typological universals.

Another syntactic domain that is affected in heritage language grammars is long-distance dependencies, including pronominal reference within and beyond the sentence. The interpretation of anaphoric expressions such as reflexives (*himself/herself*) and pronouns (*him/her*) is known to be restricted by structural constraints, traditionally called the Binding Theory (Chomsky 1981). The syntactic conditions on the interpretation of reflexives is that they must refer to a noun phrase within the clause, such as *Charles* in (22). The pronoun *him* in (23), by contrast, can take the matrix subject *Peter* as antecedent or may refer to a discourse-salient antecedent, but it cannot refer to *Charles*.

(22)   Peter$_i$ said that [Charles$_j$ cut himself$_{i*/j}$ with the broken mirror].
(23)   Peter$_i$ said that [Charles$_j$ cut him$_{i/*j}$ with the broken mirror].

In English, reflexive pronouns (*himself/herself*) are typically subject oriented and take local antecedents (i.e., *Charles* in 17). Korean has three reflexives – *caki, casin,* and *caki-casin* – which differ in their distribution and interpretation. *Caki* is subject oriented and prefers long-distance antecedents (beyond the clause, like *Peter* in 22). *Caki-casin* requires a local antecedent (within the clause). *Casin* can take local or long-distance antecedents. Kim, Montrul, and Yoon (2009) found that long-distance preferences were affected in adult Korean heritage speakers in the United States. Heritage speakers preferred local, instead of long-distance, binding for *caki* and seemed to treat *casin* and *caki-casin* indistinguishably, as if they had a two-anaphor system. Their interpretations differed sharply from those of monolingually raised Korean speakers. A recent expansion of this study with eye-tracking (Kim *et al.* 2014) confirmed that Korean heritage speakers who were simultaneous bilinguals adopted local binding interpretations for long-distance binding anaphors. Similar problems of establishing reference with reflexive pronouns are reported by Polinsky and Kagan (2007) in Russian heritage speakers.

These data on long-distance binding preferences suggest that heritage speakers have difficulty with discourse dependencies between referents, especially if these dependencies are at a distance within and outside the sentence. As a result, other long-distance dependencies that require keeping track of noun phrases in a complex sentence, such as relativization, wh-questions, and passives are likely vulnerable domains in heritage language grammars as well.

With respect to passives, Polinsky (2009) compared English-dominant young adult heritage speakers of Russian to monolingual Russian controls of similar age in a sentence-picture matching task. Participants matched pictures to active/passive constructions, with verb-initial and verb-medial orders in Russian, as in (24) and (25). The results showed that the heritage speakers made errors comprehending sentences when the word order is different from S-V-O, regardless of voice, and also had difficulties with the passive voice in general.

(24) a. morjak   spas   pirat-a   (active S-V-O)
          sailor.NOM   saved   pirate-ACC
      b. spas   pirat-a morjak   (active V-O-S)
      c. spas   morjak pirat-a   (active V-S-O)
          "The sailor saved the pirate."
(25) a. pirat   spas-en   morjak-om   (passive S-V-O)
          pirate.NOM   saved-PASS sailor-INSTR
      b. spasen   morjak-om pirat   (passive V-O-S)
      c. spasen   pirat morjak-om   (passive V-S-O)
          "The pirate is saved by the sailor."

Putnam and Salmons (2013) also report on the loss of passive voice constructions in German heritage speakers from South Central Kansas. Eleven adult speakers (mean age 77.5) who grew up speaking German and English and had limited opportunities to use German on a daily basis were asked to translate English sentences into German and to comprehend written German sentences with passive voice by judging the grammaticality of the sentences in a grammaticality judgment task. Putnam and Salmons found that the German heritage speakers only produced impersonal passives in the translation task and, similar to what Polinsky reported for Russian heritage speakers, the heritage speakers of German had significant difficulty comprehending and giving grammaticality judgments on passive sentences. Thus, basic comprehension of word order in passives is a problem for low proficiency heritage speakers.

Relative clauses can also appear in complex sentences, modifying noun phrases that involve long-distance dependencies (through movement of constituents and a gap, or through a binding relationship between the head of the relative clause and the referent of the relative clause in some syntactic analyses). O'Grady, Lee, and Choo (2001) tested comprehension of subject and object relative clauses by Korean heritage speakers and Polinsky (2011) did so with Russian heritage speakers using a picture sentence-matching task. Both studies found that heritage speakers had more difficulty with the comprehension of object relative clauses (*The cat that the dog is chasing*) than with the comprehension of subject relative clauses (*The dog that is chasing the cat*). Sánchez-Walker (2013) tested written comprehension of subject and object relative clauses with inanimate objects and subjects in young adult Spanish heritage speakers in the United States. Subject relative clauses in English have V-O order within the relative clause, as in (26). Spanish has the English order, as in (27a), but also has object-verb inversion and displays O-V order, as in (27b).

(26)   The submarine that sank the boats.   (V-O)
(27)   a. El submarino que hundió los barcos.   (V-O)
        b. El submarino que los barcos hundió.   (O-V)

In object relative clauses, the complementizer *that* is optional in English, and the word order within the relative clause is S-V, as in (28). In Spanish, the complementizer *que* is not optional, and both S-V and V-S word orders are possible within the relative clause, as in (29a,b).

(28)   The submarine (that) the boats sank.   (S-V)
(29)   a. El submarine que los barcos hundieron.   (S-V)
        b. El submarino que hundieron los barcos.   (V-S)

Compared to the Russian and Korean heritage speakers studied by Polinsky and O'Grady *et al.*, Sánchez-Walker (2013) found that in general the Spanish heritage speakers in her study were quite accurate comprehending relative clauses, probably because they were of higher proficiency than the heritage speakers of Russian and Korean tested in other studies. At the same time, Sánchez-Walker found that the Spanish heritage speakers were very accurate with the sentences whose word order was like English yet inaccurate interpreting the sentences with the word order that is different from that of English (27b and 29b).

An interesting property of Arabic relevant to long-distance dependencies is the use of resumptive pronouns in restrictive relative clauses. Resumptive pronouns appear in the position of the gap left by movement of the head of object relative clauses. In subject relative clauses, however, there is a gap (like in English, Spanish, and Russian) (Aoun, Benmamoun, and Choueiri 2010). The difference between subject- and object-relative clauses are illustrated in (30) and (31): *ha* in (31) is the resumptive pronoun used to mark the site of the relativized lexical head in the relative clause.

(30)   saafer   maʕ š-šab   lli bjištiʁil bi-l-maktabi
        traveled.3s.M with the-young man who works in-the-library
        "He traveled with the young man who works in the library."

(31)   ʔakalt t-təffaaħa lli laʔeit- ha bi-t-tallaaži
        ate.1s the-apple that find.1s-it in the refrigerator.
        "I ate the apple that I found in the refrigerator."

The resumptive strategy is used in both Palestinian and Egyptian dialects in nonsubject positions, the two dialect groups tested by Albirini and Benmamoun (2014a). In both dialects, the resumptive pronoun agrees with its antecedent in gender and number. Twenty heritage speakers of Arabic and 20 native speakers of Arabic (half Palestinians and half Egyptians) completed three oral tasks (two narrative tasks and an oral interview). The two heritage speaker groups displayed higher accuracy on subject relative clauses (90% Palestinians and 78.95% Egyptians) than on object relative clauses (53.33% Palestinians and 48.15% Egyptians). Most of the speakers either dropped the resumptive pronoun or used one that does not agree with the antecedent in gender of number, as the examples in (32), (33), (34), and (35) illustrate (exx. 43–45 from Albirini and Benmamoun, p. 266).

(32)   l-žinni   xalla-h   ynaʔʔi tlət ʔašyaaʔ lli bəddu   yyah
        the-genie let.3s.M-him choose three things that want.3s.M it.M
        "The genie let him choose three things that he wants." (PHS)

(33)   ba-sawwi- l-projects lli huwwi yaʕTiini ʔiyya-h
        ASP-do the-projects that he   give-me it.m
        "I do the project that he gives me." (PHS)

In examples (32) and (33), the speakers use the resumptive pronoun -*h* "him/it.m" to refer to nonhuman plural antecedents, namely, *ʔašyaaʔ* "things" and *l-projects* "the projects." The use of a singular masculine pronoun in reference to the relativized singular feminine noun is a gender mismatch between the pronoun and its antecedent, which for Albirini and Benmamoun indicate problems with establishing long-distance dependencies.

(34)   l-žinn   ʔall-u   ʔaddi-hal-lak ʔay ħaaga lli ʔinta ʕaawiz9
        the-genie told-him give.1s-it-you any thing that you wanting
        "The genie told him that I give you any thing that you want." (EHS)

(35) miš mətzakkra šu hummi   l-təlaati lli saʔal
      NEG remembering.F what they the-three that asked.3s.M
      "I do not remember what are the three things that he asked
      [for]." (PHS)

In (34) and (35), however, the heritage speakers drop the resumptive pronoun altogether, thus leaving the position of the relativized noun phrase in
the relative clause empty. As noted above, a gap is not allowed in the position of the relativized noun phrase in object relative clauses. Therefore, dropping the resumptive pronouns in these contexts is ungrammatical. Albirini and
Benmamoun consider that such consistent omission of the resumptive pronoun
may be attributed to the influence of English, a language that uses the gap
strategy in both subject and object relative clauses. Finally, Montrul, Foote,
and Perpiñán (2008b) investigated knowledge of wh-movement, subject-verb
inversion and the use of complementizers in Spanish heritage speakers of intermediate proficiency in Spanish. In English, complementizers are not required
and actually ungrammatical if expressed – compare (36a,b). In contrast, the
complementizer is required in Spanish, as in (37a,b).

(36) a *Who do you think that came?
      b. Who do you think came?
(37) a. Quién crees que vino?
         who you-think that came?
      b. *Quién crees vino?
         who you-think came?

The heritage speakers rated grammatical and ungrammatical sentences with
subject and object questions in a written grammaticality judgment task. Montrul
et al. found significant differences between native and heritage speakers
because the ratings of the heritage speakers were more variable. Nonetheless,
the heritage speakers were quite accurate with subject-verb inversion and complementizers even though Spanish and English differ in this regard.

In sum, complex sentences like passives, relative clauses, and other referential dependencies present challenges for production and comprehension in
heritage speakers with lower proficiency in the heritage language as summarized in Table 3.9.

3.2.4   Interfaces

The interaction of syntax with semantics and pragmatics is considered an interface phenomenon, because it requires different levels of linguistic representation to interact with each other. One example of interface phenomena is lexical
semantics, which refers to how aspects of verb meaning that originate in the

lexicon are encoded in syntax. For example, unaccusativity is a semantic distinction that classifies intransitive verbs into unaccusative (with a nonagentive subject, as in *John fell*), or unergative (with an agentive subject, as in *John walked*). Under some analyses (Burzio 1986), unaccusative verbs involve displacement of the subject from the verbal phrase to the subject position, just like passives.

In generative linguistics, unergative verbs are syntactically characterized by having an external argument (the agentive subject occupies the structural subject position) and no internal argument, as in (38b), while unaccusative verbs have no external argument, and the patient is base-generated in object position, as an internal argument, like the object of transitive verbs, as in (39b). The patient then moves to subject position to receive nominative case and act as the grammatical subject of the verb, leaving a trace behind (39c). Thus, although they may have the same word order at the surface level, unaccusative and unergative verbs are structurally different.

(38) a. John walked.   *unergative*
      b. [John [$_{VP}$ walked]]
(39) a. John arrived.   *unaccusative*
      b. [e [$_{VP}$ arrived John]]
      c. [John$_i$ [$_{VP}$ arrived t_i]]

The distinction between these two classes of intransitive verbs appears to be universal, and may have language-specific syntactic and morphological consequences, depending on the language. For example, in English, certain unaccusative verbs can appear with existential subjects (*There appeared three men*) and in the resultative construction (*The bag fell open*), while unergative verbs cannot (*There worked three men, *Mary laughed hoarse*). In Italian, Dutch, and French, unaccusative verbs take the perfective auxiliary *essere, zijn, être* "to be" (*The man is gone*), while unergative and transitive verbs take the auxiliary *avere, hebbe, avoir* "to have" (*The children have laughed*). And in Japanese, the adverb *takusan* "a lot" has two distinct readings depending on the verb: with unaccusative verbs, the adverb quantifies the argument of the verb (*Many books fell*), whereas with unergative verbs the adverb quantifies the activity described by the verb and not the argument (*The children laughed a lot*, and not *Many children laughed*) (Kageyama 1996).

Montrul (2006) tested knowledge of unaccusativity in Spanish heritage speakers of low, intermediate, and advanced proficiency in Spanish. They completed a written grammaticality judgment task in English and one in Spanish, and an online probe recognition task in Spanish. The Spanish grammaticality judgment task included sentences with bare plurals (*Llegaron bomberos* "arrived firefighters") and absolute constructions (*Muerto el perro se acabó la rabia*, "Once the dog died, there was no more the rabies"), which discriminate between the two types of verbs. Unaccusative verbs are grammatical in these constructions, while unergative verbs are ungrammatical (*Caminaron mujeres, "women walked," *Cantado el coro se acabó la misa "Once the choir sang the mass ended"). The results showed that syntactic knowledge of unaccusativity was quite robust in the heritage speakers' two languages at all proficiency levels: they distinguished statistically between unaccusative and unergative verbs in the different constructions, largely patterning with the native speakers of English and Spanish tested as comparison groups in the two languages. However, a more recent study by Lee (2011) on the unaccusative/unergative distinction in Korean found that in a written acceptability judgment task Korean heritage speakers born and raised in the United States were unable to distinguish between the two verb types in constructions with quantifiers (the quantifier float construction), which is an unaccusativity diagnostic in Korean. Korean heritage speakers who were born in Korea but moved to the United States as children did better on the task but were still significantly different from the Korean native speakers who acted as a comparison group. It is possible that unaccusativity is acquired later in Korean children than in Spanish-speaking children, and many Korean heritage speakers do not develop this knowledge.

Semantic interpretations of articles in discourse are also affected in heritage grammars. Montrul and Ionin (2010, 2012) investigated the interpretation of definite articles with plural noun phrases in Spanish heritage speakers in the United States. In both Spanish and English, the syntactic and semantic distribution of definite and indefinite articles is largely similar, but the two languages differ in the expression and interpretation of plural noun phrases. Consider the English examples and their Spanish equivalents in (40–43). Spanish plural noun phrases with definite articles can express generic reference, as in (40), or specific reference, as in (41). English plurals with definite articles can only have specific reference, as in (42), while generic reference is expressed with bare plural noun phrases, as in (43).

(40)   Los elefantes tienen colmillos de marfil.   (generic reference)
       the elephants have   tusks of ivory
(41)   Los elefantes de este zoológico son
       marrones.   (specific reference)
       the elephants of this zoo are brown
(42)   Elephants have ivory tusks.   (generic reference)
(43)   The elephants in this zoo are brown.   (specific reference)

Misuse and omission of articles is very common in Spanish heritage speakers with intermediate to advanced proficiency in Spanish, especially in written compositions. Montrul and Ionin developed a written truth value judgment task and an acceptability judgment task to test the generic/specific interpretation of plural determiners in Spanish. They found that the Spanish heritage speakers incorrectly accepted bare plural subjects with generic reference in Spanish (*Cebras tienen rayas* "Zebras have stripes") and interpreted definite articles as having specific rather than generic reference, as in English. Kupisch (2012) conducted a study with adult Italian heritage speakers in Germany. Italian, like Spanish and German, is comparable to English in that it has generic bare plurals. Kupisch also found that the Italian heritage speakers who were dominant in German accepted incorrect bare plurals in Italian and tended to interpret the definite article in Italian as having a specific rather than a generic meaning. Kupisch and Barton (2013) report similar results in French (i.e., preference for specific rather than generic interpretation of articles) from French heritage speakers who are dominant in German.

Cuza and Frank (2011) investigated the syntax–semantics interface by focusing on the meaning associated with embedded interrogatives. Embedded interrogatives in Spanish differ from statements in that they have two complementizers. Consider the sentences in (44) and (45).

(44)   María le dijo a Juan <u>adonde</u> fueron los niños.   *statement*
       "Maria told Juan where the children went."
(45)   Maria le dijo a Juan <u>que</u> <u>a dónde</u> fueron los niños.   *question*
       Maria asked Juan where the children went.

In (44), the sentential complement [<u>adonde</u> *fueron los niños*] is interpreted as a reported assertion, whereas in (45) [<u>a dónde</u> *fueron los niños*] is a reported question introduced by the complementizer *que* "that." The main verb is the same in both sentences (*decir* "say") and the complementizer *que* introduces the question. Of course, the same sentence in (44) could be introduced with the verb *preguntar* "ask," in which case the complementizer *que* would be optional. In English, two complementizers are not possible, and the meaning of a complex sentence as assertion or indirect question is marked by the meaning of the main verb. Cuza and Frank tested thirty-two heritage speakers of Spanish in the United States, 74% on their knowledge of the meaning of these sentences. The heritage speakers ranged from low to advanced proficiency in Spanish. The main tasks were a written sentence completion task, an acceptability judgment task, and a preference task. The results showed that the heritage speakers used indirect questions with two complementizers very infrequently in the completion task (23%) as compared with the comparison group of fluent native speakers of Spanish (60%). In the acceptability judgment task, unlike the native speakers, the heritage speakers were not sensitive to the semantic difference between structures with two complementizers and structures with one complementizer. A few heritage speakers with advanced proficiency showed sensitivity to the semantic distinction between the two types of sentences in the preference task, but they were still less inclined to accept these options than the comparison group of native speakers. Therefore, the few available studies testing structures at the syntax–semantics interface suggests that semantic knowledge at the level of the lexicon (verb classes), reference and discourse (article semantics), and syntax (embedded interrogatives) is also affected in heritage speakers, as summarized in Table 3.9.

Finally, an interface phenomenon that has also been observed in a variety of heritage languages concerns the licensing of null and overt subjects, especially in null subject languages such as Spanish, Greek, Italian, Russian, Hindi, Arabic, and many others. In these languages, both null and overt pronouns are grammatical because the person and number information is recoverable from the agreement morphology, as shown in the Spanish sentence in (46).

> (46) Ella/ Ø llegó   de Madrid.
>   she   arrived-3RD SG from Madrid
>   "She arrived from Madrid."

However, the distribution of null and overt subjects is licensed by discourse-pragmatic factors, such as topic continuation, topic shift, or switch reference. Overt subjects are strictly required when new information is introduced and a contrast is established in discourse, as examples (46) and (47) show. The answer to question (47) requires a focused NP, and it must be expressed by an overt subject. In (48), the overt subject *él* is a topic if unstressed, but it can also be a contrastive focus if it is stressed. The pronoun in this case can co-refer with the subject of the previous clause because it emphasizes the subject.

> (47) ¿Quién vino?   El/Mario*Ø vino.   *focus*
>   "Who came?   He/Mario/*Ø came."
> (48) El periodista$_i$ dijo que él$_i$/ÉL$_i$ no había escrito ese reporte.   *topic*
>   the journalist said that he (himself) not had written that report
>   "The journalist said that he had not written that report."

The use of null and overt subjects is also relevant to establishing reference in discourse. For example, when there is no switch in reference between a series of sentences, null subjects are appropriate when there is topic continuity, whereas overt subjects are pragmatically infelicitous, as in (49). By contrast, overt subjects are appropriate when there is topic shift and a different referent is introduced, as in (50). Null subjects are infelicitous in these switch reference contexts (examples from Silva-Corvalán 1994, p. 148).

> (49) Pepe no vino hoy a trabajar. *Pepe/?él/Ø estará enfermo.   *same reference*
>   Pepe no came today to work Pepe/?él/Ø will be sick
>   "Pepe did not come to work today. He must be sick."

(50)   Hoy no fui a trabajar. Pepe/él/*Ø pensó que estaba enferma.   *switch reference*
        today I no went to work Pepe/él/*Ø thought that I was sick
        "Today I did not go to work. Pepe/he thought I was sick."

To recap, Spanish overt and null subjects in discourse are regulated by topic, focus, and topic-shift features (as proposed by Sorace 2000 for Spanish and Italian). In contrast, while the distribution of overt and null subjects in English may also be regulated by discourse-pragmatic factors, null subjects are rare in English (Torres Cacoullos and Travis 2015).

In prodrop or null subject languages like Spanish, higher uses of overt subjects in lower proficiency heritage speakers may be related to the simplification of agreement morphology and more frequent use of canonical (S-V-O) word order. Sometimes, the features of the null pronoun cannot be reliably and consistently retrieved from overt agreement on the verb (Albirini, Benmamoun, and Saadah 2011). However, the rate of null and overt subjects is also affected in heritage speakers who do not show problems with agreement and word order: lower rates of null subjects and overuse of overt subjects have been documented in several heritage languages: Hungarian (De Groot 2005), Hindi (Mahajan 2009), Tamil and Kabardian (Polinsky 1997), Spanish (Silva-Corvalán 1994, 2014; Montrul 2004b; Montrul and Sánchez-Walker 2015; Otheguy and Zentella 2012), Polish (Polinsky 1997), and Arabic (Albirini *et al.* 2011). What is reported in all these language is erosion of the pragmatic features that regulate the use of null subjects and higher rates of overt pronominals in discourse contexts, where a null pronominal would be more felicitous. This phenomenon has been observed in production and in interpretation tasks (Keating, VanPatten, and Jegerski 2011). Sorace (2000), who also finds a more restricted use of null pronominals in first generation Italian immigrants, attributes the difficulty to the attrition of phenomena that lie at the syntax–discourse interface rather than direct influence from English. Finally, the same difficulty with the pragmatic constraints on null and overt subjects in null subject languages has been reported in studies of bilingual children (Montrul and Sánchez-Walker 2014; Paradis and Navarro 2003; Serratrice *et al.* 2009; Silva-Corvalán 2014). Table 3.9 gives a summary of the patterns observed in syntax and other interfaces.

To summarize, different aspects of syntax, semantics, and pragmatics are affected as a function of different levels of proficiency in heritage language speakers. Basic word order is quite robust, but noncanonical word orders and complex structures involving long-distance dependencies, movement or displaced constituents, and embedding present different levels of difficulty to heritage speakers. There is also evidence of loss of meaning associated with articles or embedded interrogatives. Finally, the findings on the expression of null and overt subjects in heritage languages indicate difficulty with the pragmatic

Table 3.9. *Changes observed in heritage language grammars with core syntax and other interfaces*

Core syntax
1. Preference for canonical or strict word order (when case marking is eroded).
2. Difficulty with variable word order.
3. Difficulty establishing long-distance dependencies (binding interpretation of pronouns and anaphors, keeping track of referents in passive sentences and in relative clauses).
4. More difficulty with object than with subject relative clauses.
5. Omission and errors with resumptive pronouns in languages that use them.

Syntax–semantics–discourse interfaces
1. In some languages, lack of distinction between unaccusative and unergative verbs.
2. In languages with articles, difficulty with the semantic interpretations of articles in discourse.
3. In some languages, loss of meanings associated with complementizers.
4. In null subject languages, overuse of overt subject pronouns in topic continuity contexts.

---

distribution of overt pronouns and subjects in null subject languages. This finding, in particular, has been widely documented in first and second generation speakers of different languages (Montrul and Polinsky 2011), as well as in bilingual children in their minority language.

3.2.5   Phonetics/phonology and pronunciation

The observation that emerges from the studies of vocabulary, inflectional morphology, syntax, semantics, discourse, and pragmatics discussed above is that heritage speakers who are not very fluent in the heritage language display non-native patterns. Yet, pronunciation, as we will see, is the linguistic domain most spared from this impression. Recall from Section 1.2 that heritage speakers' stronger skill is usually listening, followed by speaking. In comparison to work on inflectional morphology and syntax, there are fewer studies on the phonetic and phonological abilities of heritage speakers. Heritage speakers are typically described as having the phonological skills of native speakers, especially when they are compared to adult L2 learners of similar morphosyntactic proficiency.

For example, Au *et al.* (2002) and Oh *et al.* (2003) studied the phonetic perception and production abilities of Korean and Spanish heritage speakers of very low proficiency in the languages (*overhearers*). Tests of pronunciation and voice onset time (VOT) measurements for Spanish voiceless stops (labial /p/, dental /t/, velar /k/) and for the denti-alveolar Korean stops (aspirated /tʰ/, plain /t/, and tense /t'/) revealed that the heritage speakers were significantly more native-like than comparison groups of L2 learners who had not been exposed to Korean or Spanish since childhood. At the same time, the heritage speakers also differed from the Spanish and Korean native speaker groups, suggesting that heritage speakers display some non-native phonological features as well. Hrycyna *et al.* (2011) and Kang and Nagy (2012) studied VOT changes in three generations of heritage speakers of Korean, Italian, Russian, and Ukrainian in Toronto, Canada. They found drift toward English in Russian and Ukrainian but not in the Italian heritage speakers. Kim (2012), who investigated the perception and production of stop consonants (/ptk/ and /bdg/) in Spanish heritage speakers in the United States, found that the heritage speakers did not differ from native speakers in perception but they did differ slightly in production. Rao (2013) investigated the spirantization rule in Spanish voiced stops (when [b, d, g] become [β, δ, γ] between vowels), and found that the more proficient heritage speakers in the sample were better at producing the spirantization rules than the less proficient ones.

Kupisch *et al.* (2013) investigated how foreign accent is affected if a first language is acquired as a minority (heritage) language as compared to a majority (dominant) language in a given national society. They compared the degree of foreign accent in the two languages of 38 adult speakers who grew up as simultaneous bilingual heritage speakers (German-French and German-Italian) to that of monolingual speakers and L2 learners. Naturalistic speech samples were judged by 84 native speakers of the respective languages. Kupisch *et al.* found that the majority language was spoken without traces of a foreign accent, and although the results for the heritage language were not native-like, they were significantly better than those of the L2 learners. For the heritage language, they further showed that a native accent is correlated with length of residence in the country of origin during childhood but not during adulthood. Finally, they showed that raters had comparatively more uncertainty judging the heritage language of these bilinguals (French) than judging their accents in the majority language (German). The consensus reached so far is that when it comes to overall accent as measured by VOTs or judged globally, heritage speakers have significantly more native pronunciation than L2 learners, and we will review some more studies in detail in Chapter 8. In some studies, heritage speakers are very close to native speakers and in others they are less so. There is individual variability in pronunciation.

If traces of non-native accents are found in heritage speakers, where are these localized more specifically? Or what specific aspects of their phonology and pronunciation are affected in heritage speakers of different levels of proficiency in the heritage language? Beyond global measures of pronunciation like VOT, other recent studies have looked at the acoustic and articulatory properties of specific sounds, as in production and categorical perception of vowels and consonants. Although heritage speakers may make all the phonological contrasts in each of their languages, another question is whether they make phonetic contrasts across their two languages between similar, yet acoustically distinct phones.

An example of this type of study is Godson (2004), who investigated the vowel system of young adult heritage speakers of Western Armenian in the United States. Godson found that the vowel quality of the heritage speakers showed some transfer from English in some Western Armenian vowels, but only for the Armenian vowels closest to English vowels; furthermore, the influence did not necessarily neutralize contrasts between other Armenian and English vowels. Saadah (2011), who investigated production of long and short vowels in Arabic, reports similar trends. Arabic has three vowels that contrast in length (/i, iː, u, uː, a, aː/). Formant measures of F1 and F2 showed that the Arabic heritage speakers produced vowels very close to the native speakers' values.

Chang *et al.* (2011) examined how closely heritage speakers of Mandarin pattern with native speakers with respect to production of language-internal phonemic contrasts. The study included 6 native speakers of Mandarin born and educated in mainland China or Taiwan who came to the United States after age 14, and fifteen heritage speakers of Mandarin. The heritage speakers were born to Mandarin-speaking parents but reported speaking English most of the time. Nine heritage speakers were classified as a high-exposure group and 6 as a low-exposure group (because some of the Mandarin learners originally recruited did not have actual exposure to Mandarin before age 18 they were classified as L2 learners, as described in Chapter 2 under cultural definition of heritage speakers). The participants completed three experiments: Experiment 1 tested production of the back vowels /o/, /u/, and /y/, Experiment 2 tested production of aspirated and unaspirated plosive consonants, and Experiment 3 tested production of retroflex /ʂ/ and alveolo-palatal /ɕ/ fricatives. The participants were asked to read aloud words containing the target sounds. Chao *et al.* found in the three experiments that the heritage speakers were very accurate at producing the within-language contrasts. Because the Mandarin heritage speakers were also tested in English, Chang *et al.* found that not only did they maintain the language-internal contrasts (as in minimal pairs contrasting /u/, /y/, and /o/), but they also distinguished crosslinguistic contrasts that do not produce a change of meaning, such as the difference between Mandarin /ʂ/ and English /ʃ/.

Lukyanchenko and Gor (2011) investigated the perceptual correlates of the hard-soft /t-t'/ and /p-p'/ stop contrasts in Russian heritage speakers in the United States. The 24 heritage speakers who participated in this experiment had Russian-speaking parents, were exposed to Russian from birth, and heard it on a daily basis at home. The Russian heritage speakers considered themselves dominant in English, yet the results of two discrimination experiments (AXB and AX tasks) showed that the Russian native speakers and the heritage speakers did not differ from each other, at least on this measure. At the individual level there was variability, however, because not all heritage speakers were uniformly similar to native speakers: some did experience difficulties in hearing contrasts that are less acoustically salient (such as /p-p'/ in the word-final position).

Finally, Kim (2012) focused on the perception and production of voiced /b, d, g/ and voiceless /p, t, k/ stops by seven Spanish heritage speakers born and raised in the United States. Since native speech perception reaches stability prior to native speech production, Kim wanted to find out whether Spanish heritage speakers would perform similarly to native English speakers and differently from five native Spanish speakers in their production and perception of English and Spanish stop consonants. Kim's results showed that the Spanish heritage speakers did not differ significantly from Spanish native speakers in perception, but they did differ somewhat in production. The heritage speakers produced Spanish /b, d, g/ with less prevoicing than the native speakers.

Overall, the studies on the phonological abilities of heritage speakers in both perception and production suggest that many heritage speakers display native-like abilities in this domain, and especially when compared to L2 learners, as we will see in more detail in Chapter 8. The few studies that have compared phonological and morphosyntactic abilities in very low proficiency heritage speakers (Au *et al.* 2002; Oh *et al.* 2003) have found that the same speakers show more native-like performance in phonology and pronunciation than in morphosyntax (cf. Kupisch *et al.*'s 2013 finding on superiority in morphosyntax compared to phonology). The apparent advantage for heritage speakers with aspects of phonology suggests that phonology and morphosyntax are acquired and preserved differently, and are probably regulated by different learning mechanisms, and sensitive to different developmental schedules for acquisition and loss. Still, the precise nature of heritage accents and the conditions that drive their native or non-native performance is a topic that deserves more in-depth study.

3.3   Natural linguistic processes at work

The main goal of presenting a general overview of the grammatical patterns at different levels of linguistic analysis observed in heritage speakers of different languages and heritage languages in contact with different majority languages is to appreciate the striking similarities found. The grammatical patterns observed in the sampling of heritage grammars illustrated in this chapter are the same grammatical patterns found again and again in languages of the world, and in developmental processes, such as language acquisition and the history of languages. Other processes are the result of languages in contact or bilingualism.

Morphological use in production by linguistically mature native speakers is highly accurate and stable – it is a domain of language where speakers do not vary. This stands in contrast to other linguistic domains such as frequency of use of complex sentences or vocabulary size, which are more normally distributed in the population of native speakers. If the target language as spoken by native speakers of the full variety is taken as the norm, the linguistic systems of heritage speakers display smaller vocabularies, reduced morphological paradigms in some areas (gender, number, case, and aspect), fewer tenses, and stricter word order. Heritage speakers know core aspects of vocabulary and grammar but what we see is a general tendency toward simplification, reduction, and reanalysis. The question is what drives these changes.

McWhorter (2007) defines grammatical complexity along three dimensions: overspecification (degree of grammaticalized semantic distinctions), structural elaboration (number of rules or foundational elements required to generate phonological, morphological, and syntactic forms), and irregularity (degree of morphological regularity and suppletion). These changes have also been observed in standard languages like English, Mandarin, Persian, colloquial Arabic, and Malay diachronically (McWhorter 2007). In different accounts of language change, contact between two or more languages at the psycholinguistic and sociolinguistic levels – as in bilingualism, second language acquisition, and creole formation – is one of the main factors driving change (DeGraff 1999; Lightfoot in press; McWhorter 2007; Meisel 2011; Silva-Corvalán 1994; Thomason 2001).[3] McWhorter (2007), for example, advances the hypothesis that language change in standard languages, and simplification in particular, can result from imperfect L2 acquisition by adults: "When Scandinavians invaded England, the result was not a hybrid between English and Old Norse as complex as both, but a language somewhat less complex than both, as the Vikings acquired a robust but abbreviated version of English grammar" (McWhorter 2007, p. 17). L2 learners have notorious difficulty mastering the phonology and morphosyntax of the L2, and do not usually achieve native-like competence in these domains.

---

[3] Language contact or multilingualism could not account for language change in Icelandic, a language that has remained relatively isolated from other languages (Hróarsdóttir, 2001, Lightfoot in press).

A widely documented and studied reason for the lack of success of second language learners is linked to age and maturational effects (Abrahamsson and Hyltenstam 2009; Birdsong 1999; Bley-Vroman 1990; Granena and Long 2013; Johnson and Newport 1989), a topic that we will cover in Chapters 4 and 8.

In Chapter 8, we will also discuss that many of the structural patterns found in heritage language speakers are similar to the errors made by adult L2 learners during the process of language development and in their ultimate (fossilized) attainment. Furthermore, many of the patterns found in heritage language grammars arise naturally from indirect (Otheguy and Zentella 2012; Silva-Corvalán 1994), and sometimes direct, transfer from the majority language (Albirini and Benmamoun 2014b; Montrul and Ionin 2010). For example, the erosion of gender and case marking in Russian, Spanish, and Korean heritage languages in contact with English as the majority language find a natural explanation because English does not grammaticalize or overtly mark these categories. Less difficulties with gender agreement, for example, have also been documented in Polish heritage speakers in Germany (Brehmer and Czachór 2012), and German is a language that also marks gender in nouns.

However, some studies have also suggested that contact between languages leads to some innovations, and changes in a heritage language do not always lead to simplification of the grammar. Complexification, the emergence of a significant linguistic constraint on the use of a linguistic structure, also occurs. For example, English developed *do*-support in questions and negation (McWhorter 2007). North Frisian, a minority language spoken in Germany, developed two definite articles (Ebert 1971), and varieties of Volga German spoken in Kansas have developed a new prepositional case (Keel 2015). Shin (2014) analyzed subject pronoun use with third person singular verbs produced in sociolinguistic interviews with first generation Latin American immigrants and second generation heritage speakers. Shin found that singular subject pronoun expression (*ella canta~canta* "she sings~sings") was constrained by tense/mood/aspect (TMA) in the heritage speakers, but not in the first generation immigrants. Shin's analysis shows that this complexification effect reflects a strategy of increase in attention to ambiguous verb morphology aimed at clear referent identification.

Change in the heritage language may also be independent of language contact. Many of the patterns of simplification, overgeneralization, and reanalysis found in heritage grammars are strikingly similar to the developmental errors attested in monolingual acquisition by young children, and these cannot be due to language transfer, as we will see in Chapter 7. An intriguing new line of research in cognitive science pioneered by Fedzechkina, Jaeger, and Newport (2012, 2013) suggests that many of these changes at the diachronic and synchronic level occur during language development, independent of another language. The nature of these recurrent patterns has sparked a lively debate: Are these universal tendencies due to constraints specific exclusively to language which are not shared by other aspects of human cognitive systems (Chomsky 1965), or are they due to general cognitive constraints on perception, memory, and learning (Hawkins 2004; Newport 1981; Slobin 1973)? Using an artificial language learning paradigm with native speakers of English, in a series of experiments Fedzechkina and colleagues provide behavioral evidence for the existence of linguistic universals. They found that crosslinguistically common correlations (e.g., word order flexibility and the presence of case marking) can be at least partially explained by domain-general learning biases stemming from a preference to balance the amount of information provided by the cues to sentence meaning during language processing and learning. They suggest that through language acquisition (or learning) these biases arise and shape language structure.

Coming back to heritage language acquisition, the changes observed in this particular learning situation also seem to be related to proficiency in the language, such that the speakers with the lowest proficiency in the heritage language display more structural changes at different levels of linguistic analysis than speakers with higher proficiency. This is different from what happens in situations of language change when new dialect varieties may be emerging because the structural changes observed in those situations are not necessarily related to proficiency in the language (Sharma 2005a,b). Although heritage speakers display gaps in their linguistic knowledge this does not mean they have acquired a "rogue" grammar or that their knowledge is somehow chaotic. In fact, heritage languages preserve basic structural aspects of the language, yet they get reorganized to accommodate or reassemble – in the sense of Lardiere (2009) – formal, semantic, and pragmatic features in different lexical and syntactic configurations.

3.4   Summary

This chapter presented a general overview of the language proficiency profiles of heritage speakers in terms of linguistic skills, to illustrate that the vast majority of heritage speakers show unbalanced bilingualism with a pattern of majority language dominance. Heritage speakers of different languages and social environments – whose heritage language is the weaker language – show strikingly similar patterns of erosion and simplification in vocabulary, morphology, syntax, and interfaces, whereas phonology and pronunciation remains quite strong. Many of the structural patterns exhibited by heritage speakers arise from normal and natural processes of language acquisition and language change in a bilingual situation. But a key question is how and why these patterns arise. The answer is provided in the next chapter, where we look closely at the process of language acquisition in monolingual and bilingual settings and at the factors that lead to the interrupted transmission of these grammars from the first to the second and third generations.

4   The bilingual development of heritage speakers

Chapter 3 presented a variety of grammatical changes in the heritage language of bilingual speakers from different parts of the world, as documented in a vast body of earlier and recent research. The extent of the changes observed in individual speakers is generally related to their degree of proficiency in the heritage language which, as we discussed, varies significantly and spans the entire spectrum from low/receptive to full productive ability. If heritage speakers are in some sense native speakers of their heritage language, or at least they start as such, why do they vary so much in the levels of proficiency eventually attained in the heritage language? The answer I provide in this book is that the wide variation in proficiency levels that develops in these speakers as reflected in several aspects of their linguistic knowledge is largely due to how the heritage language was acquired, and many individual and contextual factors played a role in their development.

In the first part of this chapter (Section 4.1), I cover very basic facts about bilingual language acquisition, assuming that not all readers are familiar with these. In Section 4.2, I discuss what it means to master a native language and the typical time it takes. Here, I support the distinction between emergence, acquisition, and mastery of different properties of language at native levels, and propose in Section 4.4 that many heritage speakers exhibit acquisition without mastery of several aspects of their heritage grammars. In Section 4.3, I turn to age of acquisition, an undeniably significant variable in heritage language development that explains the extent of language attrition in children and adults or incomplete or delayed linguistic development in children. (Readers who are familiar with language acquisition, language attrition, and age effects can skip the first three sections.) Finally, Section 4.4 considers the range of contextual factors that interact with the psycholinguistic and socio-affective development of heritage speakers from birth to adulthood. We will see that the social context takes a central role in understanding heritage language acquisition because it is far less homogeneous than in L1 and L2 acquisition.

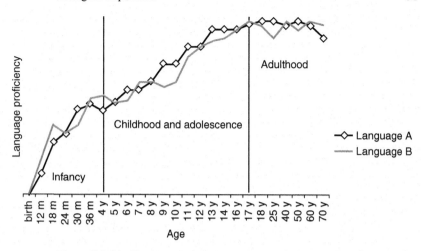

Figure 4.1. Idealized longitudinal development throughout the lifespan of two languages acquired since childhood in simultaneous bilinguals.

4.1 Bilingual acquisition

When you ask somebody to define a bilingual person the usual answer is that a bilingual is an individual who has learned two languages since birth and has balanced knowledge and use of those two languages in adulthood. Figure 4.1 is a hypothetical and idealized representation of what the language development of a simultaneous bilingual child would look like if we were to trace the growth of the two languages longitudinally throughout the life course, assuming that this individual was exposed to and used the two languages fairly often during his everyday life. (Note that the bilingual reaches what could be construed as full development in the two languages, but there is always fluctuation in the relative strength of the languages with respect to each other.)

Yet, the study of bilingualism from multidisciplinary perspectives has shown that these two conditions – exposure to the languages since early childhood and fluent use of the two languages in adulthood – are not always met because unbalanced bilingualism (when one language is stronger than the other) is actually the norm. There are many factors that come into play in the resulting degree of command of the two languages by an individual at a given time and in the relationship between the two languages throughout the process, both at the neuro-psycholinguistic and sociocultural-political levels. Heritage speakers are early bilinguals who meet the condition of having acquired two languages early; they often do not meet the second part of the definition because they are generally not balanced bilinguals. In fact, their proficiency in the heritage language can vary widely from individual to individual.

Table 4.1. *Dimensions along which the languages of a bilingual may vary*

Order of acquisition	Dominance	Function	Sociopolitical status
First language (L1)	Stronger language	Primary language	Majority language
Second language (L2)	Weaker language	Secondary language	Minority language
Simultaneous (A, B)	Balanced	No preference	Same status

When bilinguals know two languages, those two languages are in a special relationship with each other along several dimensions. Table 4.1 lists three dimensions that characterize the relationship between the languages of a bilingual person: order of acquisition, dominance, and sociopolitical status.

Focusing first on the columns in Table 4.1, *order of acquisition* refers to when the languages were acquired and in what order. A first language (L1) is acquired first, and a second language (L2) is acquired after the basic foundations of the first language are in place. Children exposed to two languages simultaneously since birth (Meisel 2001) have two native languages, referred to as language A (alpha) and language B (beta) (De Houwer 2009).

Dominance (second column) is a relative term that refers to the strength of the two languages of bilinguals with respect to each other. The stronger language is the language that the bilingual is more proficient in, as measured by level of accuracy in its structural components, and the one that is processed faster, measured by speed of response or production, as discussed in Chapter 3, Section 3.1.

Language dominance is very often related to function, the other variable listed in Table 4.1 (third column). A *primary language* is usually the language that is used the most on a daily basis or in more contexts, and the *secondary language* is the language that is used less often or in more restricted contexts. There are bilinguals who use both languages equally often or who consider that the two languages are not in a primary-secondary relationship. They can also consider that their two languages are equally strong, only used for different purposes and in different domains of life (Grosjean 1997, 2008, 2010), or as in a diglossic situation (Ferguson 1959). The level of fluency in the heritage language or language skills (listening, speaking, reading, and writing) will depend on the use of the language and will often be domain specific in terms of vocabulary and grammatical structures.

Finally, the sociopolitical status of the languages (fourth column) is a key variable in heritage language acquisition, which is perhaps less crucial in L1 and L2 acquisition. The distinction between *majority* and *minority* language indicates a power relationship. Majority languages are languages spoken by members of a majority group (who may or may not be members of a state), have official status and recognition, are used in the media, and are imparted in education. Minority languages are usually not official languages (although they can be), are spoken by ethnolinguistic minorities, are used in restricted contexts, and are typically not used in government, the media, and education.

Focusing on the rows in Table 4.1, the first two rows can describe the situation of L2 learners, such as Americans who learn Spanish as a foreign language at school. English is their native language: it is the language they use the most in their daily lives (dominant) and the majority language in the United States. By contrast, Spanish is the L2 (acquired around puberty at school), it is weaker in proficiency than English, and it is a minority language in the United States. The third row represents individuals who acquired the two languages since infancy. In parts of Canada and in some European countries it is possible to find simultaneous bilinguals with balanced command of the two languages, who use their two languages on a daily basis and to the same extent, feel equally proficient in the two languages, and the two languages are official and equally represented in the society (e.g., French and English in Montreal). Very few heritage speakers end up being balanced bilinguals of this sort (Kupisch *et al.* 2013).

For heritage speakers who are simultaneous bilinguals, one of their native languages (A or B) happens to be a sociopolitically minority language, and its minority status plays a role in the degree of linguistic competence or mastery attained in it, which often results in the minority language being weaker than the majority language. If the heritage speakers start as monolingual speakers of the heritage language (their L1) and then learn the majority language (the L2), there is eventual language shift when the L1 becomes the weaker language and the L2 the stronger language. So, while in L1 and L2 acquisition the dimensions of order of acquisition, dominance, function, and sociopolitical status are aligned, in heritage language acquisition they are not.

What makes studying heritage speakers challenging is the fact that the label *heritage speaker* subsumes a variety of psycholinguistic profiles defined by the complex relationship of order of acquisition of the languages (age of onset of bilingualism), patterns of dominance, and strength of the languages. We saw several examples in Chapter 2.

The age of acquisition of one or the two languages also defines different subfields within the study of bilingualism and a very important distinction is that between children and adults. *Early bilingualism* refers to the acquisition of two languages in childhood, before puberty. *Late bilingualism*, also known as adult L2 acquisition, typically occurs after puberty. The field of L2 acquisition is concerned with the development of the L2 and the learning of the L2 in the classroom (Thomas 2013). Within early or child bilingualism, researchers also distinguish between simultaneous bilingualism and sequential bilingualism, or child L2 acquisition. In sequential bilingualism, the languages are acquired

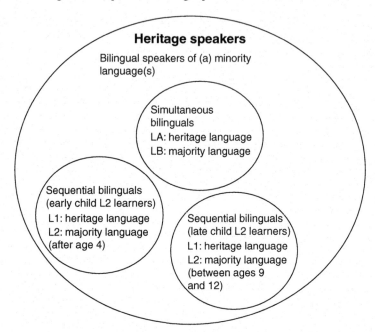

Figure 4.2. Most common profiles of bilingual heritage speakers based on age
of onset of bilingualism.

one after the other typically after age 3–4, that is, *after* the bases of the L1 are
acquired (Meisel 2011). All these different types of bilinguals can be heritage
speakers, as illustrated in Figure 4.2.

Simultaneous bilingualism is also called *bilingual first language acquisition* (De Houwer 2009; Genesee and Nicoladis 2009; Genesee, Nicoladis, and
Paradis 1995; Meisel 2001). Much research in this field has followed young
children between 1 and 3–4 years of age longitudinally to investigate how the
two languages develop simultaneously, starting with the emergence of first
words until the emergence of morphology and syntax (Barreña 1995, 1997;
Ezeizabarrena Segurola 1996; Müller and Hulk 2001; Paradis and Navarro
2003; Silva-Corvalán 2014; Yip and Mathews 2007; among many others). The
two languages of simultaneous bilingual children are typically compared to the
only language of children growing up in a monolingual context because much
of the research on the development of the two languages simultaneously since
the 1990s has been motivated by the Unitary System Hypothesis (Leopold
1939–1949; Volterra and Taeschner 1978). This hypothesis stated that, initially,
bilingual children are in a sense monolingual, and although they are receiving
input in two languages, they only posit one system. In addition to setting out
to verify whether bilingual children start off as "monolinguals," the developing

relationship between the two languages was also important. Do the languages develop autonomously and in a compartmentalized way or interdependently, interacting with each other throughout development (Genesee and Nicoladis 2009; Paradis 2001; Paradis and Genesee 1996)? Interdependent development would arise from the influence of one language on the development of the other, resulting in patterns or rates of development that differ from what would be expected in monolingual children.

The research conducted in Canada and in Europe has uncovered that bilingual L1 acquisition is very similar in significant respects to monolingual acquisition and different in others. Like monolingual children, bilingual children seem to reach the same linguistic milestones (e.g., babbling, one-word stage, two-word stage, emergence of inflectional morphology, and so on) at approximately similar ages in each of the languages, showing similar patterns of phonological, lexical, and morphosyntactic development. The two languages develop independently and children are "bilingual" – with two linguistic systems – from the initial state (Kovács and Mehler 2009; Petitto *et al.* 2001). Because they manage two systems, bilingual children also exhibit structural influence from one language to the other and code-switch naturally. They are also very sensitive to social context and know when and how to use the languages and with whom. Several studies of children growing under the one parent-one language approach, which assures that the child receives sufficient input in each language on a daily basis, show relatively balanced and age-appropriate development of the two languages at this early stage of development. Representative examples are Barreña (1995, 1997) for Basque-Spanish, and Paradis (2001) and Paradis and Genesee (1996) for French-English. In stark contrast to these findings, Hoff *et al.* (2014) found that very young bilingual children (22–30 months) from high SES families in the Miami area fall short of monolingual standards in the two languages in vocabulary size and morphosyntactic development, a difference that may have to do with language policies and the status of Spanish in the United States.

As stated earlier, many heritage speakers born in a bilingual territory start off as simultaneous bilinguals, but they end up as unbalanced bilinguals with weaker knowledge of the heritage language by adulthood. The study of bilingual first language acquisition tends to focus on the preliterate child, and unfortunately we know much less about what happens with the two languages of these bilingual children beyond age 4. One recent example of a study that followed two simultaneous Spanish-English bilingual children in the United States until age 6 is Silva-Corvalán (2014). Silva-Corvalán showed that the two children had autonomous and simultaneous development of Spanish and English until age 3, which matched the development of monolingual English-speaking children and monolingual Spanish-speaking children. After age 3, however, the bilingual balance of these children changed in response to changes in the input. We will return to other details of this study in Chapter 7.

Coming back to Figure 4.2, many heritage speakers are second language (L2) learners of the majority language. In the case of immigration, some move with their family to the host country between ages 4 and 9 (early child L2 learners) or after age 10 (late child L2 learners). There are also children who were born in the country/territory but were exposed to only the heritage language until the time they go to school. These children also acquire the heritage language as their L1, and the majority language is the L2. Typically in these cases, intense exposure to the L2 begins at school, where the majority and official language of their territory is the predominant medium of instruction. Of course, some heritage speakers have access to instruction in the heritage language, especially in some European countries (Norway and Sweden), including different types of immersion or bilingual education programs depending on where they live (e.g., Ireland, the Basque Country, Catalonia, Canada, United States, etc.).

A main difference between the field of L2 acquisition (also SLA) (by children and adults) and simultaneous bilingual acquisition is that the main object of study in SLA is the development of the L2, independently of what happens to the L1. The focus on only "one" language (the L2) does not take into account the L2 learner as a bilingual person with two languages. A principal theoretical concern of SLA has been to understand the nature of L2 acquisition, the route of development from the beginning to advanced stages of acquisition of different aspects of the language, and why L2 learners rarely reach the same level of attainment in the L1 of a native speaker. Other concerns are to what extent, why, and how does the L1 interfere with the linguistic development of the L2 from initial state, throughout development, and until the end state? Due to the focus on the target language only, L2 learners are also typically compared to monolingually raised native speakers of the target language.

The vast majority of studies in SLA and L2/foreign language teaching focus on adult learners, and this research suggests that acquiring a second language after puberty leads to nonuniform levels of attainment in the L2. Although it is possible for some people to attain very high levels of proficiency in the L2, this is an elusive goal for many others (Abrahamsson and Hyltenstam 2009; Long 2007). Second language acquisition is characterized by variable degrees of "success" (Bley-Vroman 1990; Selinker 1972), with "success" usually being meaningful convergence on the target grammar (i.e., sounding like a native speaker). Fossilization, or arrested development of particular aspects of the target language (phonology, morphology, syntax, collocations, etc.), is very common in this acquisition situation (Tarone and Han 2014). Figure 4.3 illustrates a common developmental pattern found in late, sequential bilinguals who began acquisition of a second language (L2) at around puberty. Note that the development of the native language (L1) followed its natural course.

Because L2 learners are not usually considered bilinguals in SLA, the (in)stability of the L1 of L2 learners and speakers has not been part of the research

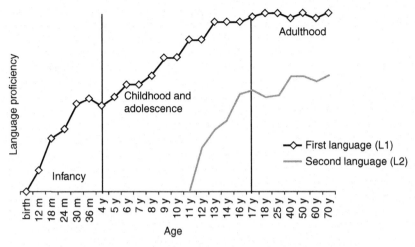

Figure 4.3. Idealized development of the first and second languages in late, sequential bilinguals (adult L2 learners).

agenda. In fact, the (in)stability of the L1 is the main theoretical concern of L1 attrition (Gürel 2002, 2004; Köpke 2007; Schmid 2011; Seliger 1991, 1996; Sorace 2000). Language attrition researchers have amply demonstrated that as L2 speakers learn the L2 and become proficient in it, some adult individuals immersed in a L2 environment for more than 10 years also tend to lose linguistic ability in their own native, family language. Adults undergoing L1 attrition exhibit reduced fluency (Schmid 2011, p. 1): they tend to talk hesitantly and slowly, with many pauses, repetition of words, self-corrections, and difficulties finding the words. They resort to code-switching to make up for lexical gaps and avoid complex constructions like embedded clauses or passives. They may have a foreign accent and make what many fluent native speakers would consider grammatical and lexical errors. Language attrition is defined by Schmid (2011, p. 3) as "the (total or partial) forgetting of a language by a healthy speaker." Many of the changes observed in the native language of a L2 speaker who may have been living in the L2 environment for many years are likely due to the influence of the L2 on the L1 (Bylund 2009a; Gürel 2002), but not all changes can be explained by L2 influence on the L1 (Schmid 2011). First generation adult immigrants may exhibit patterns of attrition, although it is important to clarify that L1 attrition is subject to high individual variation and is hard to anticipate: some native speakers show signs of attrition and others do not.

Figure 4.4 represents the hypothetical bilingual development of an adult undergoing L1 attrition. Research on L1 attrition tends to focus on one language only, the one suspected of undergoing attrition. The potentially attrited L1 is compared or measured against the nonattrited version of the L1 as spoken

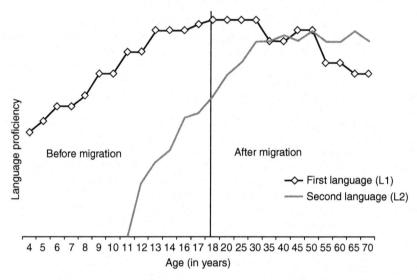

Figure 4.4. Idealized bilingual development of an adult undergoing first language attrition in the context of second language acquisition.

by fluent bilingual or monolingual speakers not living in an L2 environment (see Major 1992 for an example).

Most heritage speakers are simultaneous bilinguals or early sequential bilinguals, that is, child second language learners, as shown in Figure 4.2. Due to the impressive amount of scholarship on age effects (Section 4.3), there is also a generalized belief that children are better L2 learners than adults, and that starting acquisition of a L2 in childhood significantly enhances the chances of reaching native-like ability in the L2 later on (assuming, of course, sufficient and sustained exposure and use of the language). Support for this belief comes from studies of adults at time of testing, who were immigrant children. The participants in the famous Johnson and Newport (1989) study were Korean immigrants or children of Korean immigrants in the United States. Similarly, the Hungarian-L1 speakers studied by DeKeyser (2000), or the Spanish and Chinese speakers in Birdsong and Molis (2001), the Chinese immigrants in Spain studied by Granena and Long (2013), and the Spanish-speaking immigrants in Sweden studied by Abrahamsson and Hyltenstam (2008, 2009) are all immigrants or children of immigrants learning English, Spanish, or Swedish in the L2 environment where these languages are the national languages (Sweden, Spain, and the United States).

But there is a downside. Recent research has also demonstrated that as they learn the second language and become proficient in it, child L2 learners immersed in a situation where the L2 is the majority language tend to lose linguistic ability in their own L1, especially when they do not receive academic instruction in their L1 during the school-age period (Jia and Aaronson 2003; Jia and Paradis 2014; Merino 1983; Montrul 2008; Yeni-Komshian, Flege, and Liu 2000). When these children start school in the majority, official language (their L2), input and use of the L1 decreases as input and use of the L2 increases, progressively leading to language shift. Eventually, the L2 takes over in total frequency of use, as well as in the type of contexts of use. The patterns of language proficiency and dominance are such that the L2 continues developing whereas linguistic ability in the L1 diminishes or stabilizes before reaching its potentially full linguistic development (Jia and Paradis 2014).

Figure 4.5 shows a common pattern in heritage speakers who were simultaneous bilinguals in early childhood. The figure shows that their language development was "balanced" during early infancy, but the development of the languages diverges after age 5–6 when they begin to attend school in the majority language and significant exposure to the L2 increases. Some of these heritage speakers seek to relearn the L1 in the classroom when they reach college age, and in some cases they make progress in some areas as adults, as the figure attempts to capture.

Figure 4.5 also shows a typical scenario of a child who grew up monolingually in the heritage language during the preschool period (36 months), and began acquiring the L2 at school, at age 4. If this is an immigrant child, the child may have had an opportunity to attend school in the country of origin and in his native language. The language shift is clear in this graph, as the two lines cross over at about age 7. Many children from immigrant families in the United States usually experience subtractive bilingualism (Oller and Jarmulowicz 2009, p. 381), as shown in Figure 4.5. The majority language takes over and impinges on the development of the L1 – preventing these children from becoming balanced bilinguals as in Figure 4.1, even when in some cases they started as such (e.g., Silva-Corvalán 2014). These general tendencies, however, do not imply that achieving balanced bilingualism after age 4 is not possible in heritage speakers; it is just apparently not common in the United States.

Before considering the many factors that affect the development of the heritage language in heritage speakers (Section 4.4), we first turn in Section 4.2 to a discussion of what it means to acquire and master a language, followed by consideration of age effects in language acquisition in Section 4.3.

4.2   Acquisition and mastery of a language

4.2.1   Early language development

Every human language consists of sounds/gestures, morphemes, and words combined in language-particular ways into sentences to express a variety of meanings in diverse social contexts. To acquire a particular language means

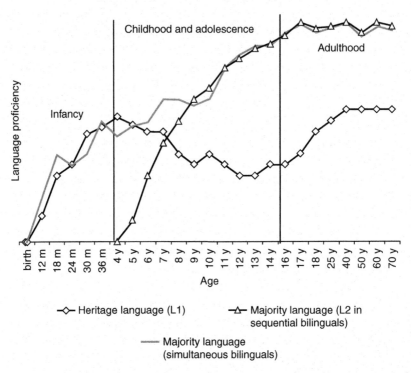

Figure 4.5. Idealized bilingual development of a simultaneous and a sequential bilingual undergoing minority language decline.

to acquire (or select from a universal inventory) its basic elements, that is, the set of sounds that when combined in a particular way define the phonology of the language and a set of words that feed the computational system that generates phrases and sentences that conform to the possible phonological, morphological, syntactic, semantic, and pragmatic "rules" of the language. Although the computational system and many linguistic principles may be universal and innate (Chomsky 1965), a language can only be acquired through exposure to it in the environment. On the usage-based approach (Tomasello 2003), rules of language emerge from the input and through language use.

A bilingual child needs to figure out the components and rules for each of the languages from input in two languages. Hoff (2006) provides considerable evidence that many social factors affect language development in children, ranging from the amount of time children spend in conversation with interlocutors to the contexts in which they talk and hear the language. How many opportunities children have to exercise their communicative skills, and how well their language model matches their abilities for analysis will have an effect on the rate of their particular language development (Shatz 2009). Social-linguistic environments need to provide multiple cues a child can use to discover how to act and interact both linguistically and nonlinguistically in her community. The developing child actively and selectively attends to the cues as she grows cognitively.

Although some approaches to language acquisition by children stress the rapidity and universality of the process (Crain and Thornton 1998; Crain and Lillo-Martin 1999; Guasti 2004), language acquisition develops in time: it begins at birth, if not in the womb, and it takes several years for a child to become an adult native speaker of the language. Many factors may come into play that can influence the process of acquisition as the child's cognitive maturity evolves throughout childhood and into adulthood. The acquisition of the different linguistic components of language (vocabulary, phonology, morphology, syntax, semantics, and pragmatics) interacts with physiological, neurobiological, cognitive, and social factors.

There are also well-attested linguistic milestones in both monolingual and bilingual acquisition that children reach at specific ages. Children who are a few days old can discriminate their own language from another, and bilingual children recognize the two languages (Sebastián-Gallés 2010). By 6 months of age, infants recognize the sounds of their native language(s). By about 7–10 months, infants begin to babble, producing reduplicated CV syllables, and by 10–12 months children produce their first words (excluding "mama"). They understand the meaning of several words several months before they begin to produce any words (Huttenlocher and Smiley 1987). These developments are independent of language modality, since similar milestones are observed in children acquiring oral or sign languages (by deaf children) (Bonvillian and Folven 1993). By about 18 months, there is rapid acquisition and use of new words, and a vocabulary spurt is observed in most children. Carey (1978) estimated that children acquire about nine new words a day from the age of 18 months to 6 years. At about the same time, children start to combine words into two-word phrases (*big toy, mommy go*) – the two-word stage – but do not produce inflectional morphology. Studies of monolingual and bilingual children show that at the two-word stage, children respect the word order of the languages they are exposed to. For example, if the language, or one of the languages, is S-V-O, the child will tend to produce words that stand for S-V (*mommy go*) or V-O (*eat cookie*), but not for O-V (*cookie eat*). Bloom (1990), Braine (1987), Brown (1973), and Pinker (1984), among many others, have noted that word order "errors" are very infrequent in L1 acquisition. These utterances are also characterized as "telegraphic" speech because they are composed of lexical categories only (nouns, verbs, adjectives, and prepositions) and lack function words and grammatical morphemes. English-speaking children, for example, frequently omit subjects at this stage (**eating soup*

"I am eating soup"), and this is not a grammatical option in the adult language, the main source of input to the child.

Children at first omit grammatical morphology, especially in a language such as English, and when inflectional morphemes appear, they start to emerge and develop in a fixed order. Children learning two languages follow the developmental sequence established in each of the languages (Meisel 1990, 1994). The omission of a morpheme in an obligatory context and the use of the wrong morpheme in a given context are referred to as developmental "errors" in child language. Developmental errors eventually go away, naturally. By 30 months, children's utterances become longer and more complex, and the children gradually produce the required morphemes in the contexts where they are required. This, of course, depends on the particular language being acquired, since not all features exist in all languages and not all features are acquired at the same speed from one language to another. For example, gender in nouns and definite determiners in Dutch are acquired quite late by Dutch-speaking children, after age 4 (Gillis and De Houwer 2001) or even by age 6 (Unsworth and Hulk 2010), whereas in Spanish gender agreement is mastered by age 3 (Montrul 2004a).

Comprehension-production dissociations are common during early syntactic and phonological development. Children begin to produce a variety of complex sentences during the preschool period. The earliest complex sentences in English-speaking children emerge around the second year (bare infinitives, *wanna* construction, complements of verbs *think, said, know*, and conjunctions *and* and *but*) (Diessel 2004). By age 3, children produce relative clauses, adverbial clauses, participial clauses, and modal verbs. Yet comprehension-based experiments have shown that children do not understand many complex sentences until well into the school years (Chomsky 1969; Clark 1971; Sheldon 1974; Tavakolian 1977). This may be due to the fact that the acquisition of complex sentences is related to the complexity of relating two clauses on the one hand, and to the frequency of the constructions in the input, on the other. For example, *if* and *when* clauses are more frequent in the input than *so* and *but* clauses, but *if* and *when* clauses are acquired later because they are more complex than *so* and *but* clauses. *If* and *when* clauses appear in the first clause instead of the second clause (*If/when you come tomorrow I will give you ice-cream*), and they are more difficult to plan, produce, and comprehend than *but* and *so* clauses appearing in the second clause (*I will give you ice-cream but/so you have to come tomorrow*). Finally, pragmatic and cognitive factors also play a role in the acquisition of complex sentences. For example, presentational relative clauses, which require the use of the indicative in Spanish (*Juan necesita un empleado que sabe*-indic *computación* "Juan needs an employee who knows computers"), are acquired earlier than presuppositional relative clauses, which require the use of the subjunctive (*Juan necesita un empleado*

Table 4.2. *Developmental milestones in early language development*

Age	Milestone	Linguistic characteristics
Birth to 5 months	Cooing	Early speech perception and phonetic discrimination
6–8 months	Babbling	Production of CV syllables Attuned to sounds of the native language
12–18 months	One-word stage	Production of first word(s) (form-meaning matching)
18–24 months	Two-word stage	Telegraphic speech Memorized chunks No productive use of inflectional morphology
24–36 months	Early multiword speech	Basic syntax Emergence of morphology
36+	Later multiword speech	Complex sentences

que sepa-subj *computación* "Juan needs an employee who would know computers"). The subjunctive in Spanish is used with complex syntax, and is not mastered until age 12–13 (Blake 1983). Table 4.2 summarizes key milestones. As we discuss in more detail in Chapter 7, many adult heritage speakers display morphological and syntactic errors typical of early language development in monolingual children.

4.2.2   Later language development

Language acquisition is primarily concerned with the preliterate child, who acquires the structural foundation of her native language – linguistic competence – largely orally and implicitly through interaction with the environment. Later language development refers to the school-age period, and this period has not been as intensely investigated in linguistics as the preschool period, perhaps because the Chomskyan view of language acquisition portrays becoming a native speaker as a fast and efficient process, with a continuous and effortless transition from the initial state to the final state (Crain and McKee 1985, p. 94). In stark contrast to this view, Berman (2001, 2004), considers that becoming a *proficient* native speaker takes a long time because, in addition to basic linguistic competence, she takes into account language use in a variety of contexts. Her studies show that the language of 9- and 10-year-old children differs markedly from that of adults, not only in content, but also in morphosyntax and lexicon. Many linguistic forms, even those that emerge at early preschool age, have a long developmental history to become acquired and mastered, i.e., entrenched (Albirini 2014a; Berman 2004, p. 10). Keijzer (2007) showed that in a number of tests of morphology and syntax in Dutch, 13- and 14-year-olds

Table 4.3. *Mean accuracy percentages on an oral real-word plural task in Jordanian Arabic (adapted from Albirini 2014a, p. 13)*

Age group	N	Mean accuracy (%)
3 years	10	24
4 years	10	36.25
5 years	10	50.25
6 years	10	68
7 years	10	80.75
8 years	10	91.50

were still very different from adult Dutch speakers as measured by a grammaticality judgment task and an elicited production test. Table 4.3, from Albirini (2014a), shows that it takes a while for Jordanian Arabic children to produce plural morphology in Arabic with more than 90% accuracy. Only at ages 5 and 6 years do the children appear to have internalized the complexity of plural morphology in Arabic. The children use all the forms but make mistakes until about age 8, when they behave like adult native speakers.

Crucial to understanding later language development is the distinction between *emergence, acquisition,* and *mastery.* For Berman (2004), a native speaker is somebody who has mastered and become proficient in several dimensions of knowledge and use of the native language through a constant interaction of competence and performance. Several general properties characterize changes from emergence to mastery in Berman's view. For example, children may have acquired the grammar of number and gender agreement, yet still be at an "item-based" phase of person marking (Tomasello 2001), what for Berman would be "partial" knowledge. Command of linguistic knowledge develops and is successfully reintegrated with increased ability in the domain of language use, which in the case of school-age children is reinforced by reading and writing. With increased age and cognitive and social maturation, the linguistic behavior of speaker-writers comes to have an increasing effect on their internal linguistic representations.

Let's consider some examples. Across languages that mark case overtly, children produce case marking relations between ages 2 and 3 (Perdue and Bowerman 1990). Hebrew-speaking children acquire the direct object marker *et* (accusative, definite) by age 2. Ravid (2004) shows that Hebrew-speaking children know and use the passive participle *–u* by age 3–4. Yet, the acquisition of passive morphology in Hebrew is not fully mastered until age 9. In a test administered to school-age children of different ages, Ravid showed that 6-year-olds gave consistently nonpassive responses when presented with obligatory contexts for passive formation. Speakers of Hebrew tend to avoid the passive in colloquial speech. Only 11- and 12-year-olds regularly provided passive constructions where required on the same test. This delay is not related to lack of morphosyntactic, syntactic, or pragmatic knowledge but to the fact that Hebrew affords speakers a range of readily accessible alternative means of expressing the discourse functions associated with passive voice, like the middle voice, impersonal passive, and topicalizations. Therefore, the morphology and syntax acquired during early language development is not mastered until later.

By the time children start elementary school, at age 5 or 6, they exhibit a vocabulary of 4,000–6,000 words (Carey 1978), inflect nouns and verbs with the correct morphology (90% accuracy according to Brown 1973), and articulate most of their words correctly. Bilingual children develop an amount of concepts equal to or greater than monolinguals, except that they are distributed between the two languages because the acquisition of vocabulary is context-dependent. Bilingual children who attend school in only one language – like many heritage speakers in the United States and in other countries – show faster and more development in the language of school (Merino 1983). Input is particularly important for vocabulary development (Menyuk and Brisk 2005). During the preschool period, children also gradually develop awareness of the language, and begin to discriminate between grammatical and incorrect forms. Because they cannot verbalize the rule, their grammaticality judgments are based on intuitions. Metalinguistic awareness develops at around age 4 (Doherty and Perner 1998) and is crucial for literacy development.

At school, children fix, restructure, and expand their basic linguistic competence, gaining more communicative competence as they learn to read and write (Barriga Villanueva 2004). They are also exposed to different types of discourse that require the expansion of more abstract vocabulary, and the use of more complex syntactic, semantic, and pragmatic structures. For example, children are encouraged to describe abstract objects or processes, to talk about cause and effect, to formulate hypotheses, and to support arguments. Depending on children's interests, they develop vocabulary for specific areas of knowledge, and their vocabulary size can range from 8,000 to 13,000 words by the end of first grade (Menyuk and Brisk 2005). During this period, children also learn semantic and formal relationships between words (synonyms, antonyms, homophones, etc.) and morphological relatedness (*rapid-rapidly, amaze-amazement-amazingly*). Children learn to use their language as a medium to express their thoughts and experiences in speaking and writing. Syntactically, children develop the ability to use low frequency structures such as the passive voice, common in scientific reports and writing, as well as generic statements (*Dogs have four legs*). Table 4.4 gives some of the features of later language development.

Table 4.4. *Structural and pragmatic development in 6- to 8-year-old children (adapted from Menyuk and Brisk 2005)*

Category	Change
Grammar syntax	Sentence length increases
	(e.g., *I see the boy who I played with yesterday*)
	Combining structures becomes more frequent (through
	complementation, conjunction, and subordination)
	(e.g., *She likes me to do homework before watching television*)
Morphology	Prefixing and suffixing increases
	(e.g., *unhappiness, disapprove, discussion*)
Lexicon	Use of abstract categories increases
	(e.g., *liberty, vast, imagination*)
	Synonyms and antonyms used more widely
	(e.g., *large, big, huge, small, little, minute*)
	Multisyllabic words appear more frequently
	(e.g., *disappointment, unhappiness*)
Phonology	Stress rules of language acquired
	(e.g., *history, historical, influence, influential*)
	Morphophonological rules
	(e.g., *a car, an apple*)
Pragmatics in conversation	Begin to take perspective of others
	Begin to make relevant responses
Storytelling	Begin to be listener-friendly
	Begin to follow story grammar
Explanation	Begin to move from personal reference to abstract knowledge

However, mere exposure to, and analysis of complex language at school is not sufficient for learning to occur. It is critical that older children have the opportunity to use the language in academic assignments requiring formal speaking and writing (Nippold 2004). Compared to the oral discourse of conversation, expository discourse stimulates the use of longer utterances containing greater clausal density through adverbial, relative, and nominal clauses (Nippold 1998). Analyzing poetry or writing about controversial topics also stimulates use of complex thought and language. By engaging in these activities, children are called upon to employ the sophisticated lexical and syntactic elements they have been learning.

At school, children acquire advanced levels of spoken and written language competence (Scott 2004). Learning to write requires learning to use more abstract language and to move from simple noun phrases (*my house*) to complex nominalizations (*the housing project that was inaugurated last year*). It also requires use of modal verbs, conditionals, and adverbial conjunctions (*meanwhile, consequently, and therefore*) in complex sentences. Children must also acquire knowledge of different registers and the ability to recognize when to use formal or informal language. Many languages, like Korean and Japanese, grammatically encode honorifics and other forms of address in verbs and nouns. Another critical aspect of written proficiency is spelling. Writing offers important advantages over speaking for linguistic development because it allows the learner more time to search the lexicon for the precise vocabulary and to organize the discourse more concisely, and to devote more thought to the formal aspects of language (Nippold 2004).

At school, children also learn about variation in the target language. The source of such variation may be dialectal, as in the standard language of school compared with the local dialect of the home; and/or contextual, as in register differences between everyday colloquial usage, standard intermediate-level usage of the media or of academic discourse, and the normative requirement of the official language establishment. Ready and flexible access to diverse linguistic registers, varied levels of usage, and different types of texts are prerequisites for "linguistic literacy" (Ravid and Tolschinsky 2002), and require both protractive cognitive maturation and extensive experience with different communicative settings. These demands are met, if at all, only in adolescence and beyond.

A very important question that few have asked is how literacy and the school context affect children's grammatical competence in general, including spoken language, especially when children's linguistic knowledge changes as a function of their experience with how the language is used in different circumstances. Jisa (2004) studied French-speaking children aged 9–11, 12–13, and 15–16 and adult university students on their knowledge and use of nonfinite clauses, such as *avant de partir au travail* "before leaving for work," which requires maintaining referents in subject position. The children and the university students were asked to discuss their ideas about violence in school in an oral presentation and in a written text. Jisa found that the university students produced more nonfinite subordination in the written text, regardless of order of production (written before oral or oral before written). For the younger children, however, the order of presentation produced a structural priming effect. Those children who were asked to produce the written text first showed more use of nonfinite subordination in both the written and oral texts they were asked to produce, unlike the 15- to 16-year-old children. This study shows that producing a written text before discussing the same topic in speech had an effect on the syntactic structures deployed by 9- to 13-year-old children in both their spoken and written versions of the task.

Jisa (2004) also examined the production of passive sentences in spoken and written expository discourse in French-speaking children, ages 9–10, 13–14, 15–16, and adults. The two structures targeted were the impersonal passive with *on* (generic, indefinite) and the verbal passive, as in (1) and (2):

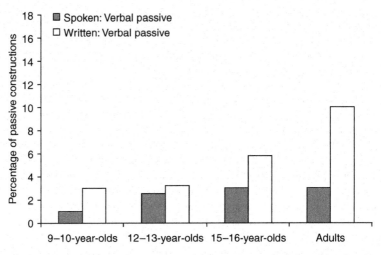

Figure 4.6. Percentage distribution of passive constructions in spoken and written expository texts in French monolinguals (adapted from Jisa 2004).

(1) On a résolu le problème
     "(Some) one resolved the problem."
(2) Le problem a été résolu (par moi)
     "The problem has been resolved (by me)."

The generic passive with *on* is more frequent in spoken than in written discourse, and all the participant groups produced more passive *on* than verbal passive in spoken discourse. At the same time, the use of the *on* passive decreased with age. This is because as children learn to write, the verbal passive is more frequent in written discourse and becomes another option to express a passive event. Figure 4.6, adapted from Jisa (2004), shows that 9- to 10-year-olds use some passive constructions in written discourse, but very few in spoken discourse. At about age 12, the children begin to use the passive in written and spoken discourse, and as they grow up, the verbal passive is used more in written than in spoken discourse.

The results of the younger children show that they write the way they speak, but they also show that learning to write influences speech. Experience with the use of the passive construction in writing makes the passive construction more accessible during speech. Jisa's study shows that generalizations based on just a single modality may fail to do justice to the developing linguistic knowledge of school-age children, particularly at more advanced stages of general cognitive development.

To summarize, the process of native language development is long. Mature and proficient knowledge and use of the native language require several years of cognitive and linguistic maturation and experience with literacy-related school-based activities. At the same time, many aspects of later language development continues across the lifespan, since the language used by adult speaker-writers of a standard dialect differs in significant ways from that of high school seniors (Reilly, Zamora, and McGivern 2005). Recent studies have documented proficiency differences in linguistically mature adult native speakers, as a function of SES and education (Dąbrowska 2012; Pakulak 2012; Pakulak and Neville 2010).

4.3   Language development and age

The discussion above shows that it takes several years of substantial exposure and use of the language in a variety of social contexts in order for a person to become a *proficient native speaker* – monolingual or bilingual. The basic linguistic competence developed during the preschool years gets expanded and solidified as the child grows cognitively and socially, and is exposed to written language at school. The two main ingredients for language acquisition are the

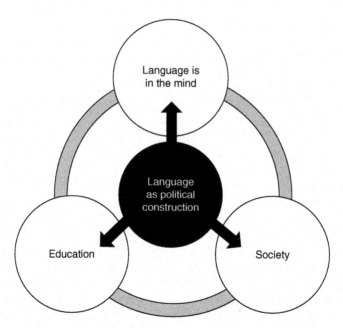

Figure 4.7. Nature, nurture, and age: factors affecting native language acquisition and entrenchment.

innate linguistic capacity for language – known as the *Language Acquisition Device* (LAD), *Universal Grammar* (Chomsky 1965), the *latent language structure* (Lenneberg 1967) – and input, or exposure to actual samples of the language. However, mere exposure to samples of language is not sufficient: both the comprehension and the production systems need to be engaged for the speaker to use and produce the language in meaningful contexts. Literate children and adults need exposure to written and oral language. Another key factor that interacts with the LAD and input is timing, conceptualized as the age of the learner, as in Figure 4.7.

Successful language acquisition is subject to a maturational schedule. More precisely, the LAD must be set in motion early, through exposure to the language. The idea that the elements and structure of language must be learned in childhood to be mastered at native levels has been around for many years, and is supported by scientific evidence from brain development (Lenneberg 1967; Mayberry 2010; Penfield 1953; Penfield and Roberts 1959). The biological foundation of language and its relevance to the critical period hypothesis for language was proposed by Penfield (1953). This hypothesis states that the capacity for implicit and unconscious native language learning is lost if it is not activated during the "critical" period in childhood. Although Lenneberg (1967) set the terminus of the critical period at age 13 (or puberty), other ages were proposed in later research, as well as multiple ages for different components of language (Bialystok and Hakuta 1999; Long 1990; Seliger 1978). Age effects are relevant both for L1 and L2 acquisition, as well as for L1 attrition.

4.3.1   Age effects in first and second language acquisition

Evidence for a critical period for language abilities in children can only be assessed indirectly. Original supporting claims came from a number of case studies of linguistic deprivation in children acquiring their first and only language: Victor (Itard 1801), Genie (Curtiss 1977), Isabelle (Brown 1958; Mason 1942), and Chelsea (Curtiss 1989). These children were discovered at different ages in childhood, and efforts to teach them language after they were found were not always met with success. Beyond the learning of a few words, there was little language development in Victor or Genie, for example. These cases suggest that not receiving linguistic exposure before the age of 6–7 years of age has dramatic and irreversible effects in the ability to develop the native language beyond that age (see comparisons and discussion in Gleitman and Newport 1995). At the same time, the fact that all these children were socially isolated, and in some cases also emotionally and physically abused like Genie, makes it hard to tell whether their inability to develop basic language (phonology, syntax, and morphology) is solely related to lack of exposure to language or to social and emotional deprivation as well.

The acquisition of signed languages by individuals who are born deaf is another more realistic situation that has allowed investigating the potential role of maturational effects in L1 and L2 language acquisition (Mayberry and Lock 2003). Deaf children acquire the elements and rules of sign language, and reach the same linguistic milestones (babbling, phonology, one word, two words, emergence of morphology and syntax, complex syntax, etc.) at approximately the same time as hearing children acquiring spoken languages like English, French, or German (Mayberry and Squires 2006). But an important difference between the acquisition of signed and spoken languages is that whereas hearing children begin exposure to their native language(s) from birth, many deaf children begin exposure to a sign language after birth and at different ages in childhood (Mayberry 2010). Because of this fact, the deaf population has allowed researchers to address whether variation in age of acquisition affects the development of sign language proficiency in adulthood.

Several studies have found that the later the onset of sign language acquisition, the lower the level of overall proficiency in the language (Mayberry and Fischer 1989), and of morphology in particular (Newport 1990). Mayberry (1993) found that L1 acquisition facilitates L2 acquisition in sequential bilinguals. Deaf learners who became deaf at different ages in childhood, had acquired a spoken language, and began acquisition of the sign language as L2 at different ages, achieved greater linguistic accuracy in the sign language than individuals for whom the sign language was the only language. Other studies have shown that when acquisition of sign language occurs in adolescence, very limited proficiency in the language is achieved, with serious comprehension deficits (Morford 2003). Mayberry (2010) supports the view that there is a critical period for L1 acquisition: only early acquisition in childhood leads to native-like development of the L1. At the same time, early language acquisition facilitates the acquisition of additional languages, even if many L2 learners do not always reach native-like ability in the L2. Mayberry's findings suggest that age of acquisition is more crucial and critical for L1 acquisition than for L2 acquisition (see also Herschensohn 2007 for a similar conclusion).

With respect to later language development, some theoretical approaches to literacy hold that oral language needs to be developed in order for children to learn and to read, because in many writing systems children need to relate sounds to graphemes. Furthermore, the size of vocabulary and language proficiency in general predict reading achievement in children (Dickinson *et al.* 2003). Mayberry and colleagues found that adult deaf individuals with low proficiency in American Sign Language had significant difficulties with reading comprehension in English, whereas those with higher proficiency achieved higher reading comprehension scores.

In conclusion, delayed acquisition in these otherwise cognitively normal deaf signers has deleterious consequences for their ability to process and acquire language from signed or written input. Their inability to achieve native levels of linguistic proficiency is not related to input but to input timing, or age of acquisition, as it impinges on the operation of the LAD.

4.3.2   Age effects in first language loss

Although the Critical Period Hypothesis has been implicated to explain degree of L1 and L2 acquisition as a function of age, the hypothesis is also relevant to explain patterns of L1 loss in an L2 environment (Bylund 2009a,b; Montrul 2008; Pallier 2007) and in cases of international adoption (Montrul 2011; Pallier *et al.* 2003). L1 attrition in a bilingual environment takes several forms in individuals who immigrated as adults. As explained earlier in Section 4.1, it can be manifested as a difficulty with lexical retrieval during production and associated disfluency, in addition to slowed processing during lexical access (Hulsen 2000; Schmid and Jarvis 2014). As a result, many individuals undergoing attrition may also resort to code-switching and lexical borrowings in order to make up for lexical gaps in their L1 during production (Paradis, Genesee, and Crago 2011). Furthermore, individuals undergoing attrition may be perceived as having a foreign accent in their native language (Hopp and Schmid 2013; Major 1992; Stölten 2013). Language attrition has also been shown at the syntax–pragmatics interface, including overproduction of overt subjects in pragmatically infelicitous contexts in speakers of null subject languages (Sorace 2000; Tsimpli 2007) and in the interpretations of pronouns and anaphors (Gürel 2004; Kim, Montrul, and Yoon 2010).

When attrition occurs in adulthood, the L1 grammar appears to undergo minor changes (Schmid 2014), which in some cases can be induced by the L2. Bylund (2009a) reported changes in the expression of motion events in the L1 Spanish of speakers living in Sweden, which seem to be influenced by the way the same events are syntactically expressed in Swedish, their L2. Bylund found that Swedish speakers verbalize endpoints while Spanish speakers do not necessarily do so. Thus, language attrition can also manifest itself as the avoidance of language-particular structures in favor of structures common in the L1 and the L2.

In general, individuals undergoing attrition in an immigrant setting retain the ability to understand and use the language at an advanced level. It appears that reduced input and even disuse of the language for several years in adults does not seem to affect the integrity of the native grammar substantially (Schmid 2007, 2014). In some reported cases, the effects of L1 attrition have been minimal: after more than 50 years of language disuse, Schmid (2002) found that German Jews living in the United States exhibited some transfer from English but very few actual morphosyntactic errors that could be attributed to L1 attrition. No adult undergoing attrition in a bilingual environment has been shown to regress to such an extent as to forget how to conjugate verbs, ask questions, or produce and discriminate native sounds (Keijzer 2007).

The situation is different, however, when intense exposure to the L2 starts in childhood, although it is not that acquisition of an L2 in itself necessarily causes loss of the L1 in childhood. After all, there are fully fluent bilinguals who are exposed to the L1 and L2 in childhood and do not exhibit L1 attrition (Kupisch *et al.* 2013). The studies documenting extensive effects of attrition at the lexical, phonological, and morphosyntactic levels are about children (Kaufman and Aronoff 1991; Turian and Altenberg 1991) or about adults who immigrated in childhood (Polinsky 2006; Vago 1991), suggesting important differences due to age of intense exposure to the L2 and reduced use of the L1. What causes severe L1 attrition is reduced input and lack of consistent and sustained exposure to and use of the L1 during a time when the native language is not fully fixed in the brain, most likely before and around the closure of the critical period (puberty) (see Figure 4.5). The L1 is used less because children growing up in an L2 environment spend most of their waking hours using the L2 at school and with peers, at the expense of the L1.

Studies of age effects in language development have been concerned with L1 acquisition (Gleitman and Newport 1995) and adult L2 acquisition (Herschensohn 2007; Johnson and Newport 1989). Recent research suggests that age of immigration and intense exposure to the L2 is also relevant for L1 loss in a bilingual environment. Bylund (2009b) and Montrul (2008) independently showed that the younger the individual when reduction to input and lack of use of the L1 take place, the more severe the extent of language loss at the grammatical level, such that the effects of L1 attrition in childhood are more dramatic than in adulthood.

Age of acquisition of the two languages or, in the particular case of heritage speakers, age of onset of intense bilingual exposure, is a key biographical variable that plays a role in bilingual acquisition in general, and in degree of fluency and proficiency in the heritage language, in particular (Jia and Aaronson 2003). Several studies have shown that child and adult heritage speakers who are sequential bilinguals and experienced a period of monolingualism or language dominance in their heritage language tend to have higher proficiency in the heritage language than children who are simultaneous bilinguals (Allen 2007; Allen, Crago, and Presco 2006; Montrul 2002, 2008; Montrul and Sánchez-Walker 2014). Montrul (2008) shows that within childhood and in a minority language context, simultaneous bilingual children are more vulnerable to attrition than sequential bilingual children, because sequential bilinguals were exposed to their L1 for a longer period of time than simultaneous bilinguals (Montrul 2002).

In addition to age and timing of L2 input, the quantity and quality of first language input play a significant role in the extent of L1 attrition: reduced input in childhood is not the same as completely interrupted input (Hyltenstam *et al.* 2009; Montrul 2008). Immigrant children continue to have exposure to the family language, even if they do not use the language very often and may end up being receptive bilinguals or overhearers (Au *et al.* 2002). In general, bilingual children who immigrate with their parents have some productive ability in their family language even though they may exhibit different degrees of incomplete acquisition and attrition (Montrul 2008; Polinsky 2006). By contrast, internationally adopted children are often adopted by families who do not speak the child's language, although some families make efforts to keep the culture of the child present in some way (Di Gregorio 2005). As a result, input in the L1 is interrupted abruptly right after adoption in international adoptees. For this reason, internationally adopted children represent a unique case of sequential L1 acquisition because one language is actually replaced by another, as they go from monolingualism in the L1 to monolingualism in the L2 (Ventureyra and Pallier 2007). The extent and speed of attrition and actual total loss of the L1 is even more severe in adoptees than in immigrant children (Montrul 2011). Figure 4.8 (Montrul 2008, p. 266) shows the hypothesized function between proficiency level in the L1 and age of onset of exposure to the L2 to illustrate degree of language loss in different bilingual populations.

The observed linear trend in the degree of language attrition illustrated in Figure 4.8 raises profound questions about the nature and stability of native linguistic competence until the end of the critical period and of bilingual dominance. In the previous section, we discussed that many aspects of language development extend beyond age 3 or 4, spanning the entire school-age period until adolescence. L1 attrition challenges the claim that language acquisition is largely complete by age 3 or 4 because it shows that the acquired linguistic competence is not very stable at this early age, and structures that are acquired that early can be lost or incompletely acquired (or not mastered) by children. L1 attrition also raises the question of when exactly a child becomes a native speaker of his or her language so that linguistic competence remains largely stable regardless of fluctuations in input and lack of use of the language for extended periods of time.

Possible answers vary. Approximately, the period before and after puberty is relevant for language entrenchment. Considering research on L1 and L2 acquisition on the interplay of the two languages in bilingual children, Montrul (2008, p. 267) proposed middle childhood, between ages 8 and 10, as a likely age of language fixation (see also Köpke and Schmid 2003). However, Bylund (2009b)

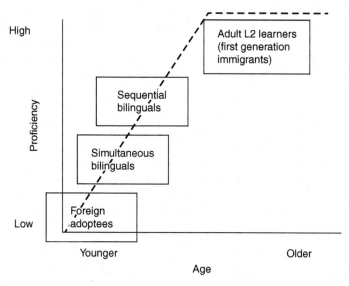

Figure 4.8. Positive correlation between age and proficiency for L1 loss (Montrul 2008, p. 266).

based his estimations on existing maturational effect trends for L2 acquisition, hypothesizing that age 12 – the onset of puberty – is the critical age for L1 attrition. This does not mean that if a child reaches age 8–9 or 12 when extensive exposure and use of the L2 begins he or she will retain the L1 intact the rest of his or her life irrespective of input. What it means is that, probabilistically, vulnerability to significant attrition due to reduced L1 exposure and use of the language is less likely at this age than at a younger age, and that substantial retention of the language is therefore more likely after this age. Literacy has also been shown to reduce the likelihood of L1 attrition in children (Zaretsky and Bar-Shalom 2010).

There may also be reasons related to brain plasticity and the myelination process of neurons during development as a cause underlying the critical period for language, as entertained by Ventureyra and Pallier (2007). It is widely documented that the human brain is not developed until about ages 10 or 12, and even later in adolescence. Brain development depends on the structural maturation of individual brain regions and their connecting pathways for the successful development of cognitive, motor, and sensory functions. When the brain is mature, there is a smooth flow of neural impulses that allows the brain to integrate multiple sparse areas. Plasticity is also related to cellular changes and molecular events (Zatorre, Fields, and Johansen-Berg 2012). The production of the myelin sheath, which insulates axon fibers and contributes to the density of white matter, is called myelination, and the process lasts until after adolescence. The myelin sheath is crucial for increasing the speed at which neural impulses propagate. The myelination process is plastic; during development, some axons grow, and other axons are eliminated in a pruning process also driven in part by experience. Underused axons are pruned away during childhood, and the remaining axons are increasingly myelinated. Although both myelination and pruning occur in the healthy adult brain, both processes are more active during development. The brain matures in a sequential manner by which some circuits develop and stabilize while others remain capable of plastic change. If the mechanisms of myelination and pruning are most active before puberty, and if experience with language contributes to fixing the language or languages in the brain, it follows that more input and use in the majority language in heritage speakers will accelerate the process of myelination and entrenchment of the L2, while disuse of the L1 will contribute to the pruning of the neurons that control L1 knowledge and behavior. Ideally, then, to develop full competence in the two languages so that both languages become entrenched at native levels and do not go away with fluctuations in input, bilingual children should be exposed to and use the two languages as much as possible during this crucial period of brain development.

There is a recent study that could speak to this possibility, even though it is not a study of language learning and forgetting but a study instead of reading development and brain plasticity. Yeatman *et al.* (2012) followed an initial cohort of 55 children between the ages of 7 and 12 longitudinally for 3 years to disambiguate the relationship between white-matter development and the maturation of reading skills. From the initial cohort, 39 children were measured at least three times with diffusion-weighted imaging; cognitive, language, and reading skills were assessed each year with norm-referenced standardized tests. Yeatman *et al.* found that there were individual differences between children in reading proficiency (good readers versus poor readers) that were related to differences in how the process of myelination and pruning developed in children longitudinally in the two groups. They suggested that successful reading development in poor readers can take place while the neural pathways are still developing if specific instruction is targeted at that time. Thus, timing of input during childhood is crucial.

In a functional Magnetic Resonance Imaging (fMRI) experiment, Mayberry *et al.* (2011) showed that a delayed acquisition of a first language in 22 congenitally deaf individuals results in changes in the functional organization of the adult brain. The participants varied in age of acquisition of American Sign Language (ASL): infancy (birth to 3 years); early childhood (4–7 years) and late childhood (8–14 years). Pénicaud *et al.* (2013) further investigated whether delayed acquisition of the L1 also modulates the structural development of the brain and carried out anatomical MRIs in the same group of deaf individuals who participated in the Mayberry *et al.* (2011) study. Pénicaud *et al.* used a neuroanatomical technique, Voxel-Based Morphometry (VBM), to explore changes in gray- and white-matter concentrations across the brain related to the age of L1 acquisition. The results show that delayed acquisition of a L1 is associated with changes in tissue concentration in the occipital cortex close to the area that has been found to show functional recruitment during language processing in these deaf individuals with a late age of acquisition. These findings suggest that a lack of early language experience affects not only the functional but also the anatomical organization of the brain. Furthermore, Ferjan Ramírez *et al.* (2013) used anatomically constrained magnetoencephalography to study behavioral and language processing data from two deaf individuals with onset of acquisition of ASL at age 14. They found that recently learned signed words mainly activated areas in the right hemisphere in these two individuals, in stark contrast from the typical left hemisphere activity pattern observed in young deaf adults who acquired ASL from birth, and from that of hearing young adults learning ASL as L2 for a similar length of time as the two individuals studied. These results provide more evidence that the timing of language experience over human development affects the organization of neural language processing.

To summarize, for a language to develop, stabilize, and not regress, a critical mass of input and use is required during an extended period of time, including the span of the language development period, which does not automatically end at age 4 and 5 but continues throughout the period of schooling and later language development. Whether a native language is susceptible to loss and to what extent between the ages of 12 and 18 is a matter that has not been investigated in any depth. The study of heritage languages leads us to reconsider the importance of this period which, as we will see, is what remains underdeveloped in heritage language speakers and learners.

4.4   Factors affecting the language development of heritage speakers

The discussion so far suggests that language development in a monolingual environment is a long process, if we take into account early emergence, acquisition, and mastery of simple and complex structures in production and comprehension, in addition to their subtle semantic and pragmatic implications. It takes at least 13 to 14 years, if not more, to achieve adult native levels of proficiency, and schooling plays a role in morphosyntactic development in adolescence (Keijzer 2007). A bilingual environment presents additional challenges since all these linguistic milestones must be achieved in two languages when the quantity of input in each language is not 100%, but it must be a proportion of 100% (i.e., 30–70% or 50–50%, etc.). When input is not optimal in quantity, many heritage speakers exhibit *acquisition without mastery* of several aspects of their heritage grammars. Input factors and use of the heritage language in the immediate family and school context and in the broader sociolinguistic context contribute to the acquisition and development of specific grammatical properties of the heritage language grammar.

How is quantity of input operationalized? In the previous section, we noted that, in general, young adult sequential bilingual heritage speakers show stronger language acquisition and maintenance in several areas than heritage speakers who are simultaneous bilinguals, and this was operationalized as an age of onset of bilingualism effect (early in simultaneous bilinguals and later in sequential bilinguals). Naturally, the time and cumulative amount of exposure as a simultaneous or sequential bilingual cannot be disentangled from the quantity of input and the type of input required to reach full linguistic proficiency in the two languages. In a study of French-English bilingual children in Montreal, where both English and French are valued and widely used in the community, Thordardottir (2013) found that 50% exposure to each language is sufficient to develop the language at monolingual levels in bilingual children. But the reality is that the amount of time or proportion of daily input a bilingual child is exposed to in the two languages can range from 0% to 100% in each language depending on circumstances.

In addition to mere quantity, the quality of the input and the contexts of language use also matter. The quality of input (and of output) refers to the richness of the language the child is exposed to in terms of diversity and complexity of structures and vocabulary (Jia and Paradis 2014). In other words, the type of vocabulary the bilingual is exposed to and actually uses, the specific syntactic structures used when speaking in a particular context or about a particular topic, and the type of discourse required depending on topic/context; that is, familiar and presentational versus descriptive, hypothetical, argumentative, etc. Examples of situations and activities that contribute to the quantity and quality of input in child heritage speakers are the percentage of time spent speaking the heritage language versus the L2; the number of different people with whom the heritage language is spoken; the percentage of time that the heritage language is used in leisure activities (i.e., playing games, reading books and magazines, watching TV and movies, or using the computer in the heritage language); and the frequency with which children attend activities conducted in the heritage language, such as playing with children who speak the heritage language, extracurricular activities, or weekend heritage language school.

If a language is not needed in some context or for some purpose, the vocabulary and linguistic properties associated with the context or purpose will not be developed, and if reading and writing skills are not needed in one of the languages, they will not be developed. Because many heritage speakers do not receive schooling in their heritage language, as a result they do not develop their language beyond basic, concrete vocabulary, and the syntactic structures required to talk about past and present events. Some heritage speakers may later lose many of the basics learned. Even if heritage speakers continue to use the language throughout their life, the language is used in restricted contexts and they may lack lexical and structural variety. Both the quantity and the quality of input are crucial for heritage language acquisition and eventual maintenance (Jia 2008).

Furthermore, the quality of input in a language contact situation can vary depending on the linguistic proficiency of the interlocutors. If the parents, for example, had lived in the immigration context for more than 10 years, they may experience attrition in some aspects of their grammar. One area that has been shown to be subject to change in first generation speakers, for example, is the use of null and overt subjects in null subject languages (Benmamoun *et al.* 2013a,b; Nagy *et al.* 2011; Sorace 2000; Tsimpli *et al.* 2004; among many others). Therefore, some heritage speakers may also be exposed to different input (with some changes affected by attrition) from their parents. Another possibility is that some heritage speakers may be exposed to heritage speakers from the same language but different dialect, and that the dialects may differ in a particular property. Otheguy and Zentella's (2012) study of pronoun expression in the Spanish of New York City is an example of this situation, because speakers of non-Caribbean dialects develop higher frequency of use of subject pronouns due to contact with speakers of Caribbean varieties and English. Although all heritage speakers report using the heritage language mostly with their parents or grandparents, in some families heritage speakers use the heritage language with siblings and friends, who are also heritage speakers themselves. Therefore, the social networks of the heritage speakers, the density of the networks (how many interlocutors), and the degree of proficiency of the speakers in the network, also contribute in important ways to the quality of input heritage speakers are exposed to.

There is no doubt that the immediate family plays a significant role in heritage language acquisition, but after the children start school the family is not sufficient for continued language development (Kerswill 1996). The broader sociocultural and political atmosphere contributes to language development as well. According to Armon-Lotem *et al.* (2014), political forces, identity, attitudes, and sociocultural and sociolinguistic preferences of the particular heritage language community also influence in significant ways the heritage language acquisition process. Even if the parents make an effort to use and transmit the heritage language to their children, the minority status and sociopolitical prestige status of the language in the broader society also plays a critical role in the degree of bilingual development, and can influence the degree of proficiency achieved in the heritage language. As children grow, the peer group and the broader society become the main sources of input and values about the heritage language. Associated government and educational language policies impact directly the eventual level of ultimate attainment of the minority language in heritage speakers. Because minority languages do not typically have official status, do not have the same public presence as majority languages, and are often not used as the medium of instruction in schools, there are few opportunities to use the language beyond the home.

Of course, this is not true of every heritage language, since some languages do enjoy more public exposure and schooling opportunities (e.g., Finnish in Sweden, or Spanish and East Asian languages in the United States). For example, heritage speakers of Irish and Welsh in the British Isles do have access to schooling and higher education in the heritage language. Still, in these cases it is very hard for Irish and Welsh speakers to develop high fluency in all domains when the presence of English is so prominent in numbers of speakers and in public life (Hindley 1990; Mueller-Gathercole and Thomas 2009). The languages of Spain are another example. During the Franco dictatorship in Spain, when historical languages like Euskera, Catalan, and the Galician language were banned from public use and their speakers punished if heard using the languages, many heritage speakers did not learn to read and write in their language. After the dictatorship and with the new Constitution of 1978, these languages regained co-official status and aggressive educational policies reinstated the active use and acquisition of these languages by the younger generation. It is possible today in Catalonia and in the Basque Country to go to schools where the main language of instruction is Euskera or Catalan and Spanish is just a subject. Aided by extensive active public use of the language in daily life, the heritage speakers who attend these schools develop very high proficiency in the heritage language. By contrast, political attitudes in the United States in favor of English-only policies have resulted in the banning of bilingual education in three states of the Southwest: California (in 1998), Arizona (in 2000), and Colorado (in 2001). The consequence of the new educational policy would be subtractive bilingualism, that is, English would eventually replace the child's home language, which would not continue to develop.

Other major factors related to sociopolitical status that also contribute to degree of heritage language development are internal to the individual and have to do with attitudes and identity. When a language is not important in a particular society, parents may also hold unfavorable attitudes toward their own language, leading them to neglect the language at home, impacting the heritage language development of their children. This is common with speakers of indigenous languages in parts of Mexico (Barriga Villanueva 2008). Very often, the parents do not have negative attitudes toward their language, consider that the heritage language is valuable, and insist on its exclusive use at home. Yet, the children may still refuse to speak the language or even feel ashamed about the language because they are aware of the minority status of the language in the broader society. For many immigrant children, reduced exposure and use of the heritage language begins as soon as they enter kindergarten (Shin 2002, 2005; Wong-Fillmore 1991, 2000), but the steepest decline is observed in early adolescence, ages 8–14 (Portes and Rumbaut 1996). During this time, rejection of the home language is accompanied by feelings of embarrassment, frustration over the widening cultural gap with parents, and cultural isolation (Tse 1998, 2001a,b). A move away from the heritage language and culture and toward the majority language and culture is common once children start schooling and their main peer group is other children.

The powerful influence of schooling and the social group for heritage language development is vividly documented by Caldas and Caron-Caldas' (2000) study of the bilingual development of their three children. The parents spoke French at home. The male child (12 years old) attended an English school in Louisiana, whereas his twin sisters (10 years old) attended a dual immersion French-English school. The family spent one year in the United States and summers in Quebec, where language input in the broader environment would change. Thus, though the children learned to speak French in a primarily French-speaking home environment, they were now reaching the point in the lifecycle (adolescence) where their propensity to speak French was determined primarily by their external social environments. Caldas and Caron-Caldas (2000, p. 375) state that the American school environment was detrimental to the French of the male child, who told his parents: "It's not cool to speak French in school." This comment was surprising because most of the boy's classmates were students of French descent. On a couple of other occasions, the boy expressed embarrassment when his mother and father spoke to him in French within earshot of his schoolmates. Because they want to fit in and their main point of reference is their majority language-speaking friends, during the school-age period heritage speakers refuse to use the heritage language at home.

In addition to their own feelings about their identity, some heritage speakers are often judged by elder speakers with higher proficiency in the language. Sherkina-Lieber *et al.* (2011) report that one difficult feature of Labrador Inuit communities has been the negative attitude of fluent speakers toward nonfluent speech in Inuttitut. Older fluent speakers have been described as producing negative reactions to nonfluent speakers' attempts to speak Inuttitut, so that nonfluent speakers' reported being discouraged from trying. Embarrassment at their language abilities and realization that their proficiency is not very high also affects heritage speakers' willingness to use the language at home during the period of later language development.

As learners' identification with the heritage language and culture evolves, so do their language choices and competencies, which in turn may change how they relate to parents, siblings, neighbors, teachers, and friends as part of the socialization process. He (2006) articulates how the ebbs and flow of heritage language competencies throughout the lifespan are intrinsically linked to ideologies and language choices that change as the heritage language learners grow up. The changes are conditioned by the bilingual learners' motivations to use the languages, social networks, and opportunities to use the languages. The quantity and quality of input in the heritage language, which feeds the Language Acquisition Device and determines the degree of acquisition and proficiency in the heritage language, is ultimately linked to all these sociopolitical, ideological, affective, and situational factors, as exemplified in Figure 4.9.

Once we establish the relationship between the biological, cognitive, political, social, and affective factors that contribute to language development we can see that there are several causes for lower proficiency in the heritage language than in the majority language in many heritage speakers that ultimately drive the structural changes at all linguistic levels discussed in Chapter 3. I list some potential causes below. In Chapter 7, we will discuss empirical studies supporting one or several of these possibilities.

4.4.1   Incomplete acquisition or acquisition without mastery

Normally developing monolingual children eventually develop native mastery of their first language. If the appropriate environmental conditions are available, bilingual children can also develop full linguistic competence in the two languages, although there may be areas of daily life where one language may be more dominant or preferred than the other (Grosjean 2008, 2010). When one language of the bilingual does not develop to the same extent as the other, it has little to do with cognitive inabilities or deficiencies germane to the bilingual individual. The main reasons, as discussed throughout this chapter, are likely due to age of onset of bilingualism, and reduction in input and use. Amount of exposure to and use of the minority language fluctuates during the life cycle of heritage speakers and many heritage speakers do not receive sufficient input and use of the language during crucial stages in childhood, such as, for example, during the school-age period, a time when significant cognitive and neurobiological development, critical language learning, and linguistic restructuring takes place.

Major language growth takes place in children of preschool age, when basic vocabulary, inflectional and derivational morphology, and simple and complex syntax are acquired. During this stage, monolingual children also show structural patterns typical of language learning in progress, like the use of root infinitives for conjugated verbs in English, or omission of case morphology

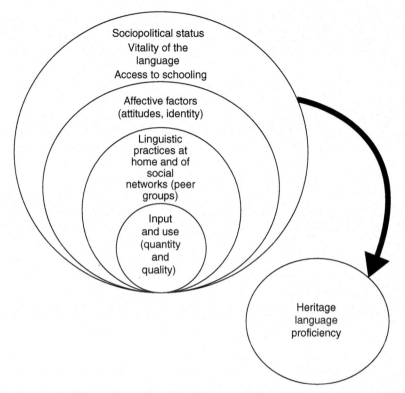

Figure 4.9. Interrelated factors that play a role in heritage language acquisition and proficiency.

in languages with a rich case system, confusion with gender assignment of nouns, etc. Children's language is compared to the adult language, which is the baseline and the target to be reached. In the language acquisition field, the nonadult structural patterns of children are called "errors," and these errors are eventually overcome without instruction. That is, by age 3 or 4, most children can conjugate their verbs and use them in several tenses, even moods. They can produce agreement and case, and they can displace elements in sentences to ask questions, express negation, or change the focus of the action (who is doing what). They control the basic grammar of their language. Although morphology may emerge in a piecemeal fashion at first, it eventually becomes productive and is used in obligatory contexts with 90% accuracy. That is, during the "acquisition stage" children may show productive use of a given form, but may not use it in all obligatory contexts. Once children master the form, it is always produced with 90–100% accuracy. As proposed by Berman (2004), a distinction must be made between acquisition and mastery.

We saw in Chapter 3 that heritage speakers of different languages appear to have acquired many aspects of their heritage language, like agreement, case, aspect, knowledge of passives, some conditionals, etc. but these do not seem to reach ceiling, the level of native speaker mastery, especially in speakers with lower proficiency in the language. It is very likely that due to insufficient exposure they did not receive the minimum threshold of input required to acquire and master different aspects of morphology and syntax, for example, especially those that are acquired after the age of primary linguistic development. (Establishing a minimum threshold of input for different structures is still an elusive goal.) This is what others and I have called *incomplete acquisition* (Montrul 2002, 2008; O'Grady *et al.* 2011; Polinsky 2006; Silva-Corvalán 2003) to describe the ultimate attainment of many adult heritage language speakers. The term has never been intended as a value judgment, although some may interpret it this way (see discussions in Otheguy and Zentella 2012 and Pascual y Cabo and Rothman 2012). Other less felicitous terms used by different researchers to describe the imperfect language abilities of heritage speakers include *reduced, partial, truncated, deficient, halted,* and *atrophied language acquisition.*

Jia and Paradis (2014) investigated the referring expressions used for first mentions of participants and entities in the oral narratives of 38 Mandarin heritage language (HL) and monolingual school-age children aged 6–10. The heritage speakers were living in Canada: they were all simultaneous bilinguals, half of whom were born in Canada and the other half immigrated soon after birth. Twenty-one of the children were attending an English-Mandarin bilingual school in Edmonton, Alberta, whereas the other 17 were recruited from English-only schools in the same city. The 15 monolingual Mandarin children who acted as comparison group were tested in Mainland China. Referring expressions for first mentions in Mandarin comprise lexical, morphological, and syntactic devices. Results showed that heritage language children used less adequate referring expressions (the general classifier *ge4*, the demonstrative pronouns *na4* "that," and nonspecific lexical items) for first mentions than the monolinguals. In other words, compared to the monolingual Mandarin children, the heritage language children overgeneralized classifiers and lacked vocabulary knowledge, a finding that Jia and Paradis (2014) attribute to incomplete acquisition of the classifier system and smaller vocabulary in Mandarin. At the same time, the heritage language children did not differ from the Mandarin monolinguals in their use of the possessive construction, the numerical determiner *yi*1 in the indefinite NP construction, and in the use of different postverbal and relative clauses. This result also suggests that incomplete acquisition of the heritage language may vary across different linguistic subdomains and not all grammatical areas show robust acquisition and maintenance (Montrul 2008); that is, domains requiring a great deal of input to acquire, such as vocabulary and the large repertoire of classifier morphemes, might be more vulnerable to incomplete acquisition than syntax, as we saw in Chapter 3. This study also showed that the children who were receiving schooling in Mandarin produced richer first mention expressions than those children who were not receiving Mandarin input at school. The statistical analyses revealed that older age of arrival, higher maternal education levels, and a rich and diverse Mandarin environment at home predicted stronger narrative outcomes, also pointing to an important role for input in heritage language acquisition.

In previous work (Montrul 2008), I have also referred to heritage language grammars as "incomplete grammars," the result of incomplete acquisition, but I now realize that referring to a grammar as incomplete can be theoretically problematic if one considers that languages are always changing in some way. It is also hard to tell when individual grammars can actually be acquired completely, as correctly pointed out by Otheguy and Zentella (2012) and Meisel (2013). Even more unfortunate is the fact that the term *incomplete grammar* can also unintentionally lead to a negative interpretation and portrayal of the ethnic minorities who speak these languages. Perhaps more appropriate is to suggest that incomplete acquisition can lead to a *divergent grammar* (see Benmamoun *et al.* 2013b), different from the target grammar or baseline, due to insufficient input and use to master the structural properties that children command by the end of the language learning period. An analogy would be the relationship between a pidgin and a creole language. Although related, one (the creole) is more elaborate than the other (the pidgin), and hence different from the other.

4.4.2   Heritage language attrition

It is possible that heritage speakers acquired structural properties of the heritage language by the closure of the period of early language development, but reduced input after that period (6–18 years of age) prevented them from mastering the properties at age-appropriate levels. Another possibility is that what was mastered by age 4–6 was subsequently lost as a result of L1 attrition, especially if the heritage speakers did not receive schooling in the language.

Language attrition is language loss of specific structural properties (vocabulary, sounds, and structures) at the individual level. For a grammatical property to be lost, it must first have been acquired, mastered, and retained as part of the speaker's knowledge for a sustained period. Subsequently, most likely as a result of fluctuations in input and language disuse, errors in localized areas of the language emerge. It is easy to establish or measure to some the extent language attrition in adults, since they may be assumed to have reached full linguistic development of their L1, although L1 attrition in adults is relatively superficial, and tends to affect lexical retrieval and fluency more than the integrity of the grammar itself (Montrul 2008; Schmid 2011).

Children can also undergo L1 attrition, and when they do, the effects on the linguistic system are much more dramatic than in adults: children can forget core aspects of grammar, like morphology and syntactic structures, in addition to vocabulary. As we will discuss in the next chapter, it is difficult to tease apart attrition from incomplete acquisition in heritage speakers in the absence of longitudinal data tracing the development of specific structural properties of the language. At the same time, it is also true that different grammatical properties have different maturational schedules. While some word order or prodrop are acquired very early, other aspects of complex syntax and semantics, which may also emerge early, take much longer to fully develop (subjunctive, binding properties, relative clauses, passives, conditionals, complex nominals, etc.). Thus, if a child does not receive sufficient input and exposure to develop these structures in spoken and written language, it is very possible that the subjunctive, binding principles, relative clauses, passives, conditionals, complex nominals, and the like, will not develop to an age-appropriate level. If heritage speakers exhibit high error rates with structures that were supposedly acquired during the period of early syntactic development, then attrition may be at play here. In Chapter 7, we will mention some studies that corroborate this possibility.

The lack of opportunity to attain an age-appropriate grasp of all points of the target grammar is what the term *incomplete acquisition* is supposed to capture. Assuming the distinction between acquisition and mastery, it is possible that heritage speakers acquired properties of their heritage language, like case, agreement, aspect, etc., but they did not reach the level of mastery of these structures. Given the discussion of later language development presented in Section 2.2, we could also describe the process as *(partial) acquisition without mastery* of specific areas of the heritage grammar. What becomes clear is that mastery and maintenance, attrition, and incomplete acquisition in heritage speakers are related to the quantity of input and use.

4.4.3   Different input

Another possibility that may contribute to what looks like attrition or incomplete acquisition may be related to changes in the quality of the input, not just in the quantity, although changes in both quantity and quality are not mutually exclusive. Changes may have to do with the fact that the main source of input to the heritage speakers – the first generation immigrants – is no longer native-like (Sorace 2004). After several year of intense contact with the majority language, some adult immigrants may exhibit minor attrition, or apparent changes in their grammars as well. First generation immigrants cannot be attrited upon arrival, so if attrition in the first generation is a factor in heritage language development, it can affect heritage speakers when they are older but not when they are young bilingual children. If the heritage speakers did not get enough input as children and did not fully develop some property of the heritage language, and several years later the parents display attrition of that property, then the property that was not mastered due to insufficient input earlier is later reinforced by the language produced by the parental generation. Many structural changes that happen under language attrition are related to majority language influence and structural dominance of the L2 over the L1. These effects can be present in the parental generation and exacerbated in the children, for whom the majority language is stronger than the heritage language. Thus, both quantity of input and different input can contribute simultaneously or independently and at different times during heritage language development.

Beyond the family, there is also the possibility that there is ongoing language change in the variety spoken by the heritage speakers and their speech community, changes that affect all the speakers to some extent and not just the younger generation. For example, Silva-Corvalán (1994) stated that many diachronic changes that are already in process in a given language get accelerated and magnified in a language contact situation. Therefore, it can happen that a given diachronic change or a change due to language contact is already becoming a distinctive feature of a new variety spoken by all the members of the community. If that is the case, then we would observe that all speakers exhibit the change, and the change is not related to degree of proficiency in the heritage language. The structural change has become a stabilized feature of the language (see Sharma 2005a,b).

Finally, schooling and different registers are another instance of different input that may lead to different grammars. In many languages, certain structures and grammatical features are only evident in standard, written registers. For example, the verbal passive is more common in the Romance languages in written discourse than in spoken discourse, and the order of pronominal elements (clitics) is different in colloquial and written/formal Brazilian Portuguese. East Asian languages have a grammatical system of honorifics and verbal agreement that must be used when interacting with different interlocutors in a formal situation. If heritage speakers are not exposed to the written, formal register of their language, and do not have the opportunity to interact with other interlocutors in more formal contexts, it follows that they will not get exposure to the vocabulary and structures related to those contexts. Simply put, the input necessary to develop these properties of the language is not available and the opportunities to use these properties of the language are not there either. Rothman (2007) and Pires and Rothman (2009a) present examples of this situation in Brazilian and European Portuguese (see Chapter 3).

To summarize, because heritage speakers are a highly heterogeneous population from the psycholinguistic and sociolinguistic point of view, age of onset of bilingualism and quantity and quality of input lead to mastery of some grammatical areas, and incomplete mastery and attrition of others. All these factors, or a combination of them, contribute to the particular language development of these individuals. In the next chapters, we will discuss in more detail theoretical approaches and research designs aimed at identifying and isolating these factors.

4.5   Implications

Heritage speakers are a type of native speaker because they were exposed to the heritage language early in life. Due to the variable conditions under which heritage speakers develop their family language, the study of heritage language acquisition helps us understand the role of different ingredients in the mastery of a native language. This is not always possible to do in monolingual acquisition because all these factors may play a role in tandem, whereas in heritage language acquisition they can be dissociated. Heritage speakers challenge traditional notions about the "stability" of linguistic competence acquired before a critical period, the organization of language in the mind, the limits of simultaneous bilingualism in early childhood, the positive and negative long-term effects of reduced input in early childhood; and the timing, quality, and amount of input required to maintain language skills. For example, heritage speakers force us to look deeper at the role of metalinguistic awareness and written language in language development in general. Only recently has research begun to uncover that there is more individual variability in native language attainment in monolingual acquisition as a function of education than previously thought (Dąbrowska 1997, 2012; Hulstijn 2015; Pakulak and Neville 2010). Heritage speakers also make us think about the distinction between knowing a language and mastering a language, which may be two different notions. And finally, because understanding heritage language acquisition does require comparison to monolingual acquisition where some of the variables of interest do not play a role, the study of heritage languages calls for more basic research on the acquisition of more languages, many of which are severely understudied and underdocumented. Therefore, comparing heritage language acquisition to monolingual acquisition crosslinguistically has the potential to inform and enrich the field of first language acquisition as well. Chapter 7 will cover studies that inform the relationship between monolingual acquisition and heritage language acquisition.

Heritage language acquisition also informs theoretical debates on L2 acquisition, and we will examine studies that compare adult L2 acquisition and heritage language acquisition in Chapter 8. Heritage speakers, like L2 learners, attain different levels of proficiency in the heritage language. While a handful of individuals attain full competence in a second language and in the heritage language, many others stall at intermediate or advanced stages of acquisition. Affective factors also play a role in the two situations, since both L2 learners and heritage speakers need special motivation to continue their language development. And because both L2 learners and heritage speakers command two linguistic systems, there is transfer from the dominant language onto the weaker language in the two groups.

The major difference between heritage speakers and L2 learners is the age of acquisition of the weaker language – the L2 in L2 learners and the L1 in heritage speakers. Age of acquisition is intimately related to the timing and nature of input in its sociocultural setting. Heritage speakers hear the heritage language from birth, whereas L2 learners do not typically receive exposure in the target language until early adolescence. Heritage speakers are exposed to the language at home and develop oral proficiency, whereas L2 learners most often start exposure in the classroom, where there is more emphasis on reading and writing skills. Furthermore, heritage speakers have underdeveloped metalinguistic skills in the heritage language, whereas L2 learners rely on metalinguistic skills to comprehend and use the L2. Thus, comparison between heritage speakers and L2 learners sheds light on the role of written input and metalinguistic awareness in L2 and secondary language development as well as on whether early auditory input brings advantages to heritage speakers in implicit aspects of language acquired in infancy.

Finally, the acquisition of heritage languages brings new information to the understanding of the mechanisms of language change in diachronic development when two languages are involved. Thomason and Kaufman (1988) note that when a population shifts to a new language and their rendition of the language ousts the original native one, as when the Scandinavians invaded England, transfer effects occur alongside incomplete acquisition. Even when the languages in contact have parallel or cognate structures, there can be reduction rather than language transfer. McWhorter's (2007) study traces signs of non-native acquisition in standard language grammars and his basic thesis is that present-day standard languages are "simpler" than they used to be and simpler than other related languages because they were "broken down" by large numbers of adult second language learners who did not acquire the language completely. He recounts that the Danes and Norwegians were largely illiterate and did not impose their language in writing or in government when they occupied England. Therefore, it is likely that the loss of inflections in Old English resulted from Old Norse speakers' non-native and incomplete acquisition of English. The suggestion is that incomplete acquisition and fossilization at the individual level become a language variety when there are large groups or intergenerational groups of

L2 learners who do not reach native-like ability in an L2. A powerful reason for the lack of success of L2 learners is linked to maturational effects, as discussed in Section 4.3.

To summarize, transfer, simplification, and arrested development in specific linguistic areas (fossilization) are not just common features of L2 acquisition. In fact, these mechanisms are also common and emerge naturally in an L1 that did not have a chance to develop fully in a bilingual environment, as in the acquisition of a heritage language. Heritage speakers are native speakers in some sense and, like L2 learners, can also be agents of diachronic language change in some circumstances. When certain structural changes are present in members of a speech community, they can be transmitted and reinforced, giving rise to what sociolinguists may call a language variety. Therefore, transfer, simplification, and fossilization, among others, are not only psycholinguistic phenomena that arise in individual grammars (idiolects) as a natural effect of language development and bilingualism, but they can also be important mechanisms of language change at the sociolinguistic and historical level.

An intriguing question that has not been explored yet is the relationship between the outcome of heritage language acquisition and creole genesis, where the input to the child is also underdetermined and nonconventional. Why is it that in heritage language acquisition insufficient input leads to truncated acquisition and a different grammar from the adult model, whereas in creole genesis, truncated input leads to a more complex and elaborated grammar than the one provided by the adult model? Assuming that children in the two situations share the same cognitive and linguistic mechanisms, the difference may lie in the development of two languages, like in heritage speakers, versus the development of only one, as in creole genesis. Heritage speakers who are dominant in the majority language show all the complexities that creole speakers manifest. But this is a question that remains to be investigated.

Chapters 7 and 8 will discuss studies that addressed the issues brought up in this chapter, but before doing so, Chapter 5 presents an overview of the theoretical approaches and linguistic traditions that have generated existing research on heritage language acquisition and loss, whereas Chapter 6 discusses key methodological issues in research with heritage speakers.

5   Theoretical approaches

In the previous chapters we covered basic descriptive phenomena about heritage speakers, the language of heritage speakers, and the learning and environmental conditions that give rise to the nature of the linguistic competence of heritage speakers. Because in recent years heritage speakers have increasingly been recognized as a unique source of insight into knowledge of language, the important question is what accounts for and explains the observed phenomena, and for that we turn to theories. Theories guide our search for these answers and also make predictions about what to expect under specific conditions. Lynch (2003) and Valdés (2006) have independently advocated for heritage language acquisition and education to have a theory of its own to advance empirical work. In this chapter, I present representative theoretical approaches to the acquisition of heritage languages that focus on language.

When the phenomenon to be explained is complex and multifaceted, it is unlikely that a single theory will be sufficient to explain it. Typically, there are different theories or families of theories to approach a given phenomenon and these theories tend to emphasize a particular aspect of said phenomenon. For example, language is both a grammatical system that develops in the minds of individual speakers and a social construct that allows individual speakers to communicate, to form groups on the basis of their communication and use of language, and at the same time to define their own linguistic identities through sociolinguistic and communicative practices. Existing theoretical approaches tend to emphasize either one of these aspects of language or the other, often presenting themselves as oppositional rather than as complementary approaches. The same applies to theories of language acquisition, theories of second language acquisition, and theories of bilingualism. It is unlikely that any one of these theories can account for all the facets of these language acquisition situations satisfactorily.

We have seen that the acquisition of a heritage language is a very complex phenomenon because of the many variables that play a role in their development. Heritage language acquisition would benefit from being grounded in contemporary mainstream theories of language, integrated within the purview of language learning more generally, and multilingualism in particular. Because heritage languages are native languages acquired early in life, the same theoretical approaches developed to explain the linguistic competence of native speakers and L1 acquisition can be extended naturally to explain and study different aspects of the heritage language acquisition situation. Heritage language acquisition is a special type of bilingual acquisition, thus it is natural to contrast it with other types of bilingualism. To date, the study of heritage languages has been approached from well-established theoretical traditions within linguistics and education such as sociolinguistics, anthropological linguistics, and generative linguistics, among others, and all these approaches are valid and relevant to advance the field.

This chapter presents the theoretical approaches to language, L1, and L2 acquisition that have been fruitfully extended to the acquisition of heritage languages so far. Section 5.1 covers the nativist and empiricist debate in L1 acquisition as well as some recent work on sociolinguistics. Section 5.2 focuses on mainstream cognitive and linguistic approaches to L2 acquisition and sociolinguistic approaches. Section 5.3 illustrates recent studies of heritage languages that have been guided by these theories. The variationist sociolinguistic, the generative, and the emergentist positions stress grammatical aspects of language acquisition, or the acquisition/emergence of grammatical knowledge, and the type of input needed to develop such knowledge. In contrast, sociocultural approaches emphasize instead what learners do with language and how they create and negotiate roles and identities through linguistic practices. As discussed in Chapter 4, the attitudes that heritage speakers and the majority society have toward the heritage language and their degree of identification with the heritage culture drive their use of the heritage language, and language exposure and use in context is what feeds the cognitive-linguistic system responsible for the psycholinguistic development of language. Because our focus is on the language of heritage speakers, we will limit our discussion to the approaches that deal directly with the language. For important insights of sociocultural theories applied to the acquisition of heritage languages, see He (2006).

5.1   Theories of native language acquisition

The study of language is concerned with understanding the human capacity for language, the formal properties of language, and the range of variability within and across natural languages, among other things. How is knowledge of language represented in the minds of speakers and how is it put to use in diverse social contexts? How are natural languages acquired or learned by young children, and how do they develop into mature linguistic systems? These essential questions are at the heart of formal linguistics, sociolinguistics, psycholinguistics, and L1 acquisition, and have guided significant research. The central focus of all these approaches has been the language of monolingual native speakers in order to tease apart the precise contribution of nature (Universal Grammar, genetic endowment for language, or Language Acquisition Device, etc.) and nurture (the linguistic environment and experience) in the ontogenesis of language. Many are familiar with Chomsky's delineation of the object of study in linguistics (1965, p. 3):

Linguistic theory is concerned primarily with an ideal speaker-listener, in a completely homogeneous speech-community, who knows its [the speech community's] language perfectly and is unaffected by such grammatically irrelevant conditions as memory limitations, distractions, shifts of attention and interest, and errors (random or characteristic) in applying his knowledge of the language in actual performance.

This notion of an idealized speaker is not unique to generative approaches to linguistics, but has also been characteristic within earlier work in sociolinguistics. Looking for the "best speakers" who will provide evidence of the most "unadulterated" form of the language has been a common practice in anthropological linguistics, in European dialectology, and in national folklore (Dorian 1981, p. 3). The rationale behind this particular focus is very much the same rationale behind any basic science: when attempting to discover the underlying principles of the faculty of language, we need to study "pure cases," without the interference of other confounding factors (Cook and Newson 2007). Variationist sociolinguistics (Labov 1966, 2006) emerged out of disagreement with this notion of the idealized speaker, and turned its focus instead to how people use language in different regions and social contexts. This approach also aims to discover, describe, and explain the underlying linguistic system that speakers possess.

Despite this intended emphasis on the monolingual norm, the same theoretical perspectives have been applied to the study of L2 acquisition and bilingualism with the aim of understanding the effects of knowing two or more languages for language learning in general. Even though the world is inhabited by more bilingual and multilingual speakers than monolingual speakers, a multilingual perspective in linguistics and language learning more generally has not been the norm. This situation is changing, however, and the study of heritage speakers represents an opportunity to redirect this important conversation (Benmamoun *et al.* 2013a,b). Roeper (1999) and Amaral and Roeper (2014) are recent attempts to unite L1 and L2 acquisition under a common representational theory of multiple grammars.

The study of language acquisition from a cognitive-linguistic perspective seeks to explain how a person constructs an abstract mental grammar through exposure to input. For example, how does the infant starting with apparently no grammar eventually develop native speaker competence and use of the language? How do bilingual children develop two linguistic systems at once? How does an adult who already knows a language learn a second language? At the heart of these tantalizing questions are the relative contribution of the genetic endowment (nature) and the environment (nurture) in the emergence and acquisition of language by children. The nature-nurture debate has figured prominently in theoretical accounts of this puzzle, although few will deny that some sort of special human capacity *together with* exposure to the target language in meaningful social interaction with ample opportunity to use the language bring about full native language attainment. Theories, however, tend to prioritize one factor over the other: whereas the theory of Universal Grammar (Chomsky 1981, 1986; Crain and Lillo-Martin 1999; Crain and Thornton 1998; Pinker 1984; Snyder 2007) emphasizes the role of genetic endowment in systematic language growth (nature), emergentist, and usage-based approaches (Bates 1976; Bybee and Hopper 2001; Mueller-Gathercole and Hoff 2009; Tomasello 2003) stress instead how language emerges, in a piecemeal fashion, from interaction with the environment (nurture).

5.1.1   Universal grammar

The theory of universal grammar (UG) is a theory of the human biological endowment for language representative of linguistic nativism. It assumes that linguistic behavior is unique to the human species: complex aspects of linguistic knowledge must be encoded in the genes. Innate knowledge of language involves knowledge of abstract rules (what is possible) as well as constraints (what is not possible). This knowledge is represented symbolically in the mind of human beings. Innate linguistic principles emerge early in life, are universal, and appear without decisive evidence from the environment.

UG is like a Language Acquisition Device, a mental construct that mediates between the primary linguistic data or input and actual linguistic behaviors (understanding and producing novel utterances by combining a finite set of elements). The theory assumes that young children implicitly make hypotheses about what is possible in their language as they receive input. UG contains the set of abstract rules and constraints that limit the data on which the child can make hypotheses and the types of hypotheses in human language. UG also defines the range of variation observed across languages (parameters, in Chomsky 1981) and characterizes the notion of possible human language. Accordingly, children are born with abstract grammatical knowledge (grammatical categories such as noun, verb, determiner, tense, agreement, etc., and the computational principles for combinations of these elements) that is triggered by exposure to input. The child selects the appropriate elements from UG (parameters, principles, functional categories, features, etc.) on the basis of the linguistic environment. While the environment is informative in some cases, as in the acquisition of words in context perhaps, it is not sufficiently detailed or transparent for children to derive the totality of the syntactic and semantic complexity of human language entirely from it, presenting a logical problem: how do children (and adults) come to know so much about language and its complexity when the input is not sufficiently informative? (Crain and Thornton 1998; Goodluck 2009; Guasti 2002; Roeper 2009; Valian 2009). For example, even when input is not robust, children develop implicit knowledge of the distribution of null elements (null pronouns, null objects, null case, null determiners, etc. depending on the language), and apply early on syntactic constraints on the interpretation of meaning (Lidz 2009). The nativist solution to the logical problem of how this might happen has been to attribute innate linguistic knowledge of the universal properties of language to the child.

The generative approach has focused on grammatical representations in children acquiring language and how these compare to the adult representations. Even though child and adult grammars do not look alike in many respects, the generative approach has tried to show that child and adult linguistic representations do not differ in fundamental ways, and very often children's nonadult behavior or "errors" are claimed to be due to performance or processing factors rather than to lack of abstract linguistic knowledge. This is the essence of the Continuity Hypothesis (Pinker 1989): there is continuity in development from child to adult grammar. Yet, children often entertain a different grammar throughout development (i.e., they make errors), but the nonadult grammar they entertain is always a grammar sanctioned by Universal Grammar. For example, English-speaking children produce sentences such as *What do you think **what's** in here? with a wh- copy instead of the intended question What do you think _is in here? (with a gap between think and is). Although the question with the wh-copy is not adult-like in English this is one way in which questions are asked in German (**Was** glaubst du, **was** gibt es hier drinnen?), so the child's grammar generates a question that is not target-like in English but is perfectly acceptable in German, another natural language. The developmental errors that children make are systematic, observe linguistic constraints, and fall within the range of variation attested in natural languages. Most importantly, they are overcome in due time.

Because the role of input has been generally downplayed in the generative framework, up until recently researchers have focused on investigating evidence of abstract linguistic knowledge when the input is scarce, ambiguous, or nonexistent (the poverty of the stimulus problem mentioned earlier with null elements), and cases where the input is abundant but the child grammar does not initially converge on the adult grammar, as with inflectional morphology. For example, young children acquiring English, Dutch, and French go through a stage when they do not produce tense and agreement morphology on verbs, as shown in (1). This is the root infinitive or optional infinitive stage. In languages like Spanish, by contrast, root infinitives are rare.

(1) a. Papa have it.   (English)
    b. thee drinken   (Dutch)
       tea   drink
    c. Dormir petit bébé   (French)
       sleep   little baby

This phenomenon shows that children do not simply repeat what they hear in the environment because caregivers do not omit tense morphology in this way or with the same frequency found in the child productions. On some syntactic accounts, the child grammar is incomplete in its structure and does not project a Tense node (Radford 1990; Rizzi 1994), or it does project Tense but it is not interpreted at logical form (Wexler 1994), or it is underspecified for Tense features (Hoekstra and Hyams 1998). Others attribute the omission of tense morphology to processing factors (Phillips 1995). These explanations have provided a representational account of this specific stage, but they do not explain how the child abandons these temporary representations and converges on the adult grammar later on.

Legate and Yang (2007) see the root infinitive phenomenon and its eventual demise in a different way, taking into account how Universal Grammar interacts with the input. The input leads the child to generate a series of hypotheses or grammars compatible with it, but the child eventually selects the grammar that is most consistent with the input. For the acquisition of Tense, the strength of the evidence for the postulation of this grammatical category is crucial, and it comes from the frequency of inflected verbs in the language and their position in the syntax. According to Legate and Yang, the rise of the target grammar is gradual rather than categorical and so is the demise of the nontarget grammar. When English-, Dutch-, or French-speaking children use root infinitives, they have adopted the grammar of Chinese, which does not instantiate Tense and allows bare forms. They adopt a Chinese-type grammar because it is a grammar sanctioned by Universal Grammar. Gradually, as they analyze their language-specific input and see evidence for Tense in verbal paradigms and verb placement, children postulate the grammar of English, or the grammar of French, or the grammar of Dutch. Because by comparison Spanish is a language that has more overt and reliable evidence, child learners of Spanish have abundant information from verbal paradigms and from syntax that Spanish is a [+Tense] language, and therefore do not adopt a Chinese-type grammar as often as English-speaking children do. An advantage of Legate and Yang's variationist learning model is that it explains crosslinguistic differences better than previous approaches. While keeping the role of abstract representations as sanctioned by Universal Grammar, another advantage of this model is that it takes into account the role of input in driving abstract syntactic knowledge.

In terms of syntax, adult grammars are hierarchically organized and children show evidence of having hierarchical representations from the earliest stages of syntactic development (Lidz, Waxman, and Freedman 2003). There are rules and constraints on interpretation that operate on the notion of c-command, or the idea that some syntactic constituents dominate others. For example, subject noun phrases are structurally higher than object noun phrases, and this fact has consequences for the interpretation of pronouns in backward anaphora, as shown in (2):

> (2) a. Hillary doesn't know if *she* will win the presidency in 2016.
>   b. *_She_ doesn't know if Hillary will win the presidency in 2016.
>   c. After *she* stept down as Secretary of State, Hillary didn't know if she would run for president in 2016.

The reason why the pronoun "she" can refer to Hillary in (2a) and (2c) is not due to linear order, but it has to do with where *Hillary* and the pronouns *she* appear in the hierarchical structure. In both (2a) and (2c), *Hillary* c-commands *she*, whereas *she* c-commands *Hillary* in (2b). Adults and children have implicit knowledge of these hierarchical relations. Children have been shown to respect c-command when interpreting sentences with backward anaphora, as shown in (2) (Crain 1991; Crain and McKee 1985; Kazanina and Phillips 2001).

The interpretation of anaphoric expressions such as reflexives (*himself/herself*) and pronouns (*him/her*) is known to be restricted by structural constraints. The Binding Theory (Chomsky 1980, 1981) posits distinct constraints for different types of noun phrases. Principle A defines syntactic conditions on the interpretation of reflexives, which are constrained to be referentially dependent on a c-commanding antecedent (*Charles*, in (3)) within a local domain. Principle B, on the other hand, prohibits a pronoun from taking a c-commanding antecedent within a local domain. Thus, in (4), the pronoun *him* can take the matrix subject *Peter* as antecedent or may refer to a discourse-salient antecedent, but it cannot refer to *Charles*, as it binds the pronoun within the Binding Domain.

> (3) Peter$_i$ said that [Charles$_j$ cut himself$_{i*/j}$ with the broken mirror].
> (4) Peter$_i$ said that [Charles$_j$ cut him$_{i/*j}$ with the broken mirror].

Children have been shown to respect c-command relations in the interpretation of reflexives (e.g., *Mamma bear combed herself/her*, Wexler and Chien 1985), showing early acquisition of Principle A of the Binding Theory.

In short, for the generative approach, linguistic knowledge is abstract and innate, available to children early on. Input is important, of course, because it triggers the operation of the linguistic constraints. However, input does not account for everything that children say or come to know. Even when children appear to make "errors" when compared to adults, their grammars fall within the range of variation of Universal Grammar, conforming to the structure of human languages.

5.1.2   Emergentism

Emergentism also focuses on grammatical knowledge but stands in contrast to the nativist approach. The essence of emergentism is that language is an epiphenomenon, emerging from the interaction of general purpose cognitive abilities with each other and with the linguistic environment. Innateness is also part of the emergentist position, but what is considered innate is cognition in general, and language is seen as a part of cognition rather than independent from it. The emergentist approach seeks to explain how the interaction between genes and the environment produces language (Ellis 2002; Elman *et al.* 1998; O'Grady 2005, 2008). The key question is what the emergent linguistic knowledge looks like, and the answers vary. For Ellis (2002), the emergent linguistic knowledge consists of local associations and memorized chunks; for Goldberg (1999) and Tomasello (2003), it is constructions; and for O'Grady (2005, 2008), it is memorized processing routines.

While for the theory of Universal Grammar input underdetermines knowledge of language, for emergentism input actually shapes it; provided by general learning principles and language processing mechanisms children extract inductive generalizations and statistical regularities from the input. Rather than being prewired, abstract grammar and linguistic complexity emerge from lexical learning. A central claim is that the child initially learns language by exposure to frequent patterns (defined at the phonological, morphological, semantic, and syntactic levels), drawing on analogy and statistical learning. Through statistical learning the child takes advantage of examples (data) of how language is used in order to capture its underlying probability distributions. By this procedure, the child automatically learns to recognize complex patterns from stress, prosody, syllable, and lexical patterns. The child then generalizes from the given examples, so as to be able to produce output in new cases.

The emergentist approach assumes functional and cognitive linguistics as a theory of language – like construction grammar (Goldberg 1995) – where constructions rather than abstract categories are considered basic units of grammar. There is no basic distinction between grammar and the lexicon, since both words and grammatical constructions as form-meaning/function mappings are considered symbolic units of language. Grammar is seen as a continuum ranging from isolated words to complex sentences that emerges from language use. There is no productivity and no rule-governed behavior at the beginning of language acquisition because representations of linguistic elements are assumed to correlate with frequency of occurrence (Bybee 1985). More frequent items and expressions are believed to be more entrenched in speakers' knowledge. Linguistic ordering of elements in syntax, for example, is shaped by processing (Hawkins 1999). Under this approach, the child is also attuned to social-intentional cues and social interaction, working hard to discern the communicative purpose of structural patterns in the language (Tomasello and Farrar 1986). Hence, abstract grammatical knowledge *emerges* from language use, the interaction of input, and innate aspects of cognition. Unlike the continuity approach advocated by nativists, this usage-based perspective holds that child and other representations are not continuous. In fact, they are different at first because children and adults do not share innate knowledge of language.

Lacking grammatical knowledge a priori, the child initially learns holophrases by rote, which can be either words or chunks (e.g., *Where is X?*, *It's a*, *wanna X*, *X gone*). These phrases are not analyzed at first. But once the child has learned a critical mass of such words and chunks (a substantial amount), the child is said to construct a grammar. The linguistic representations of young children are item-specific, as with the acquisition of verbal morphology: children use very specific linguistic expressions in very limited ways and do not generalize to other instances. At first, children store multimorphemic verb forms holistically (e.g., *swam* or *walked*), as chunks, and do not have abstract and productive knowledge of morphology or the category Tense. The frequency and consistency properties of stem + morphemes constructions and their distribution in sentences influence the emergence of productive schemas (Lieven and Tomasello 2008). Morphological schemas are acquired through a process of generalization across numerous stored items in an individual's lexicon and there is no mechanism for symbolic rules, contrary to what the generative model assumes (Pinker 1999).

For example, Freudenthal, Pine, and Gobet (2006) suggest that it is possible to explain the root infinitive phenomenon in Dutch and English (see discussion in Section 5.1) in terms of the interaction of utterance-final bias in learning and the distributional characteristics of child-directed speech in the two languages. Using a computational model to simulate the data on Dutch and English, they found that the variance in the two languages was explained by measures of mean length of utterance (MLU). They found that in Dutch- and English-type languages, root infinitives occur earlier in compound finite verbs than in nonfinite forms, and they also found that compound finites are more frequent in utterance-final position. Therefore, they were able to model the errors made by Dutch- and English-speaking children by examining the distribution of forms in the input.

Token and type frequencies are important determinants of learners' increasing accuracy with verbal morphology (Bybee 2008): they determine the acquisition and processing of individual words and the postulation of abstract schemas. Token frequency in the input and in the learners' output increases the lexical strength of the form-meaning/function mapping for that word, whereas type frequency determines the productivity of schemas, such as [[verb]ed] in English. Pinker (1999) proposed that regular verbs in English are generated by an abstract rule, whereas irregulars are stored in memory. For Bybee (2002), irregular verbs are inflectional islands that must be learned on the basis of token frequency. Regular verb forms are acquired on the basis of type frequency and this schema is overapplied to irregular verb forms, yielding typical child forms like *I falled down*, because of its superior lexical strength.

Paradis *et al.* (2010) investigated the predictions of the usage-based approach for the monolingual and bilingual acquisition of verbs in the past tense in French and English. They found that both monolingual and bilingual 4-year-olds were less accurate at producing irregular than regular past tense forms in the two languages. In general, the results supported the fundamental assumption of the usage-based approach predicated on type/token frequency. For all groups, past tense marking was a productive morphological process because children over-applied the regular form to irregular verbs. Paradis *et al.* (2010) also found that young bilingual children did not differ from monolingual children in their acquisition of regular verbs in the two languages (French and English), despite receiving less input in each language than monolingual children.

As for the acquisition of syntax, the emergentist approach holds that complex syntax emerges from words, expressions, and simple syntax, also in a piece-meal fashion. What generativists attribute to innate knowledge of hierarchical structure, emergentists attribute to ease of processing. Diessel (2004) investigated the emergence of complex and subordinate clauses in English, including relative clauses, and considered frequency of the construction in the input, complexity of the construction, and pragmatic function. He found that more frequent constructions are acquired before less frequent constructions, but that the processing complexity of the structure also interacts with the rate of acquisition.

In sum, unlike the generative approach, the emergentist and usage-based approach emphasizes the role of input in the emergence of grammatical knowledge and the gradient nature of language acquisition.

5.1.3 *Variationist sociolinguistics*

Some sociolinguistic approaches also examine the structure of language, but emphasize the role of social factors in understanding language development, language change, and language use. Variationist studies (Labov 1972) investigate the social and linguistic factors that account for variation and language change within a particular language, both intra- and interspeaker (Nagy *et al.* 2011; Otheguy, Zentella, and Livert 2007), such as the relationship between linguistic forms and gender, region, social class, ethnicity, and so on. It also assumes the existence of a standard or a norm and evaluates the language behavior and language use of various social groups with respect to that norm. In monolingual settings, language variation and change within a language is driven by certain social groups. In general, it tends to be working or lower class people and women (Eckert 1989; Labov 2001, 2006). In a bilingual environment or language contact situation, the change in the minority language is typically driven by the speakers who are more dominant in the majority than in the minority language (Silva-Corvalán 1994), although Shin and Otheguy (2013) recently found a role for affluent women in this situation as well. Variationist sociolinguistics has been primarily concerned with describing sociolinguistic variation and change in adult speakers, and studies of language development in children have been less common, although some have been conducted in recent years (Miller 2013; Miller and Schmitt 2012; Roberts 1997; Smith, Durham, and Fortune 2007). Like the emergentist position, variationist sociolinguists are more concerned with language use than with abstract knowledge of language, and the notion of input as a social phenomenon is also highly relevant in this framework, more so than in the generative approach.

Sociolinguistic variation involves the use of alternative linguistic forms in the same environment to express the same meaning, such as the pronunciation of the postvocalic /r/ in the North-Eastern region of the United States studied by Labov (1966, 2006). The use of different forms is conditioned by linguistic factors (phonological context, position, syntactic category, and pragmatic function) and extralinguistic factors (speech style, social class, etc.). These factors act together and interact. The little that is known about how children acquire variable rules of this sort suggests that phonological constraints are acquired before grammatical constraints and before extralinguistic social constraints (Labov 1989), while social constraints are learned relatively late (Miller 2007).

An example of developmental sociolinguistics that considers the process of language acquisition in the face of variable input of the sort identified by Labov are the studies by Miller (2013) and Miller and Schmitt (2012). These studies investigated the phonological realization of the plural morpheme –s (/s/) in two varieties of Spanish, Chilean and Mexican. Spanish syllable-final /s/ lenition is a widely studied stylistic variable in Spanish sociolinguistics (in Spanish this is referred to as *comerse las eses* "to eat up the /s/'s, or not to pronounce the /s/s'"). This phonological rule applies when the phoneme /s/ is in syllable-final position and is manifested as /h/ or /Ø/, as shown in (5). The rule is common in many varieties of Spanish, except from the Mexican highlands and the Andean region (Lipski 1994; Poplack 1980).

(5)   ¿Dónde están los libros?
        ¿Dónde e[h]tán lo[h] libro[Ø]?
        where are-3PL the-PL book-PL
        "Where are the books?"

Miller and Schmitt (2012) are the first to investigate the acquisition of plural marking on noun phrases – a morphologically categorical rule – when the pronunciation of the plural morpheme is variable. Due to the operation of the phonological lenition rule, plural –s sometimes surfaces as [s], sometimes as [h], and sometimes as [Ø]. Miller (2013) documented the use of syllable-final /s/-lenition in the naturalistic speech of 2- to 5-year-old Chilean Spanish-speaking children and their caregivers. The caregivers produced about 18% [s], 39% [h], and 43% [Ø] in spontaneous production interacting with their children, showing the same distribution of s-lenition in adult directed speech. Even more important, 4- and 5-year-old children patterned with their caregivers in their use of /s/-lenition. However, a sign that they were still developing knowledge of plural morphology is that the 2- to 3-year-old children showed more omission of [s] and incomplete mastery of plural morphology than the 4- and 5-year-old children.

The question guiding Miller and Schmitt's (2012) study was how the variable instantiation of plural /s/ in the input affects the acquisition of a categorical morphological rule of plural marking and the ability to associate that /s/ means "more than one" (form-meaning mapping). Instead of using speech samples commonly used in sociolinguistics, they investigated the comprehension and production of plural marking in Mexican and Chilean children with three psycholinguistic experiments. Since the lenition rule does not occur in Mexican Spanish, the assumption was that Mexican children are exposed to consistent input. The Chilean children, by contrast, are exposed to variable input. The experiments tested the production of the plural marker in 2- to 5-year-old children and the comprehension of plural and singular indefinite noun phrases (*una casa* "a house," *unas casas* "some houses"). According to the findings, by 4 years of age most Mexican children acquire plural morphology in Spanish (i.e., associate [-s] to "more than one") and produce plural morphology at adult levels. By contrast, Chilean children take 2 years longer to produce and acquire the meaning of plural in indefinite noun phrases, by age 6. The Chilean children produced bare nominals in plural conditions (*casa* for *casas*) while the Mexican children produced plural indefinites (*unas casas* "some houses"). Miller and Schmitt suggest that variable input leads to the postulation of different grammars initially. The Chilean children do not initially map [s] to plural while the Mexican children do. Similar to what Legate and Yang (2007) proposed, when the input is consistent and robust, children converge on the target grammar earlier than when it is not (see also O'Grady *et al.* 2011). Thus, Miller and Schmidt are pioneers in elucidating the role of sociolinguistic variation in L1 acquisition, and the role of variable input in the acquisition of categorical rules. After all, the ability to behave consistently despite variability in the input is also part of the competence of native speakers.

The positions illustrated in this section have been formulated primarily to explain language acquisition by children. Regardless of whether the child brings innate knowledge of grammar or abstract grammar emerges from the environment despite sociolinguistic variation, the amazing fact is that all typically developing monolingual children eventually become native speakers of their language. If they adopted different structural analyses of the input initially, or they were constrained by memory and processing limitations giving rise to what is referred to as "developmental errors," the unquestionable fact is that all (normally developing) children cease to make these errors at some point in development and converge on the grammar and patterns of use of the speakers in their speech community. All children become mature native speakers of their language despite sociolinguistic variation related to sex, region, education, SES, and the like. This is different from what happens in L2 acquisition, especially with adults, where full acquisition of the target grammar at native levels is not guaranteed (Bley-Vroman 1990; Meisel 2011). Although native-like attainment may be possible in some linguistic domains (Montrul and Slabakova 2003), it is not equally likely in all linguistic areas (Abrahamsson and Hyltenstam 2008, 2009; Granena and Long 2013).

There exists a large body of research on nativist perspectives (e.g., White 1989, 2003b), and on emergentism or usage-based perspectives (Ellis 1966, 2002; MacWhinney 2006) in second language acquisition.[1] In Section 5.2, we examine some of these approaches because they are also relevant to heritage language acquisition, as we discuss in Chapter 8.

5.2   Some theoretical perspectives on second language acquisition

5.2.1   *Linguistic and cognitive perspectives*

L2 learners must also construct a grammar of the target language on the basis of input, but a fundamental difference between children acquiring one or two L1s and adult L2 learners is that L2 learners already possess a mature linguistic system acquired early in life (the L1). Furthermore, adult L2 learners are already cognitively mature. Unlike children who eventually overcome developmental errors like mispronunciations, root infinitives, overgeneralization of regular morphology, misinterpretation of who is doing what in passives, etc., a characterizing feature of L2 learners is that their errors do not go away easily. L2 grammars, referred to as "interlanguages" (Selinker 1972), exhibit

---

[1] Sociocultural approaches applied to L2 acquisition are also prominent (Duff 2007; Lantolf and Appel 1994; Lantolf and Thorne 2006; Swain 2000, among many others), but because they do not focus on the language of learners – the scope of this book – we will not cover them.

fossilization or developmental arrest, such that localized errors with aspects of phonology, morphology, syntax, and collocations may persist after several years of intensive and extensive exposure to the language (Han 2014; Lardiere 2007; White 2003b). Very often, no amount of evidence from the input, explicit instruction, or correction, is sufficient to override non-native patterns in many L2 learners.

Much research on L2 acquisition since the 1960s has taken a cognitive and linguistic perspective, largely concerned with understanding L2 learners' linguistic competence and how it develops by exposure to explicit (instructed) and naturalistic input. L2 acquisition is characterized by significant transfer or crosslinguistic influence from the L1, especially at initial stages of development. L1 transfer can facilitate and accelerate acquisition in some cases but in other cases it can become an obstacle to progress. In addition to exhibiting transfer errors, L2 learners go through systematic sequences in their interlanguage progress, making errors like those produced by child learners (i.e., developmental errors). The challenge for theories of L2 acquisition is to explain the L2 learning process from initial state to ultimate attainment, the differential outcomes of L2 adult acquisition compared to L1 acquisition, and the similarities between the two learning situations. Theoretical approaches also need to account for how the social environment contributes to L2 learning.

By comparison to L1 acquisition, the nature-nurture debate has been less emphasized in L2 acquisition, maybe because other factors come into play in the L2 acquisition situation. For example, even if we accept that monolingual and bilingual children start the language acquisition process with no a priori grammar, as the emergentists contend, it is hard to say the same for L2 learners, who already constructed a grammar of their native language. Both the nativists and emergentists can successfully account for the fact that the native language plays a significant role in L2 learning. In Schwartz and Sprouse's (1996) Full Transfer/Full Access Hypothesis, a generative account, the entire L1 system (abstract rules and parameter settings) is the initial state of L2 acquisition. L2 learners analyze L2 input through the cognitive structure of the L1. Once the L1 grammar can no longer accommodate the L2 input, learners restructure their interlanguage system, incorporating elements from Universal Grammar (Full Access). When L2 learners make errors that are not necessarily due to transfer, they are also assumed to adopt linguistic analyses of the input sanctioned by Universal Grammar. Thus, according to this model, Universal Grammar remains accessible throughout the process. Native-like competence means the same kind of abstract linguistic competence as native speakers. In MacWhinney's Competition Model (1987, 1992), an example of an emergentist position, L2 learners transfer phonological, morphological, syntactic, and lexical cues from the L1 to the L2. Learners must discover which cues map directly onto L2 from L1, which ones will map only partially, and which ones will not apply. There is no assumption that the L2 grammar is like native grammar. The point of debate between the two approaches is whether L2 learners show evidence of being constrained by specific linguistic mechanisms in addition to their L1, or whether they work their way into the L2 grammar by staying close to the input, using their L1 grammar, and applying other general learning mechanisms.

Not all researchers working within the theory of Universal Grammar support the position that Universal Grammar is available in adult L2 acquisition (see Clahsen and Muysken 1986 and discussion in White 2003b). For example, it has been hypothesized that L1 and L2 acquisition utilize very different learning mechanisms, as spelled out in Bley-Vroman's (1989, 2009) Fundamental Difference Hypothesis (FDH). According to Bley-Vroman (1989, 2009) and Meisel (2011), child L1 acquisition is largely guided by Universal Grammar but adult L2 acquisition is not. To explain the apparent differences between L1 and L2 acquisition in terms of outcome (native attainment in L1 acquisition, non-native and variable attainment in L2 acquisition), the main claim of the FDH is that access to Universal Grammar is subject to a critical period. As applied to L2 acquisition the critical period has been taken to suggest that postpuberty L2 learners can no longer use the same linguistic mechanisms used by L1 learners. When learning a second language, L2 learners can only rely on their L1 knowledge (a particular instantiation of Universal Grammar, but not the full spectrum of linguistic options) and the principles and parameters active in their native language. Consequently, in addition to L1 knowledge, L2 learners must resort to domain-general problem-solving skills, like analogy or pattern matching, the patterns favored by the emergentist approach.

This particular "no access" or "deficit" position within generative linguistics shares the spirit of other cognitive and neurolinguistic perspectives on L2 acquisition, which do not view language and language learning by children as innate, but as part of general cognition, and take into account the distinction between procedural and declarative knowledge and implicit and explicit language learning (DeKeyser 2003; Paradis 2004, 2009). Implicit knowledge refers to what is learned beyond conscious awareness, and may be learned incidentally or not (depending on the author). Implicit knowledge is stored in procedural memory, and when this knowledge is accessed or recalled, it is executed automatically and quickly. By contrast, explicit knowledge is acquired with awareness of what is being learned, and with conscious effort. Because explicit knowledge is learned explicitly, individuals can verbalize this knowledge on demand. It is stored in declarative or episodic memory, where our world knowledge is stored.

Adult educated native speakers have both systems of learning available and use them as needed. According to Paradis (2004), when young children speak or comprehend language, they use implicit competence (or knowledge) only. This is also true of adults who are illiterate. Different from native speakers, incipient L2 learners use explicit knowledge of the L2 when producing or understanding the L2, and steadily and in tandem, develop implicit competence of it. In agreement with Bley-Vroman's (1989) position, DeKeyser (2000, 2003) also contends that adult L2 learners use a different cognitive system to learn an L2 because maturational constraints (due to the critical period) apply to implicit linguistic competence acquired early in childhood. The decline of procedural memory and loss of implicit cognitive mechanisms for language somewhere in childhood – what Bley-Vroman takes to be Universal Grammar and domain-specific mechanisms – forces late L2 learners to rely on explicit learning.

Although emergentism has been extensively applied to the problem of L2 acquisition (Ellis 2002; MacWhinney 1987; O'Grady *et al.* 2011a), with respect to the outcome of the acquisition process it is not clear how the "fundamental" differences between child L1 and adult L2 learners are captured by this approach if L1 and L2 learners utilize the same general learning mechanisms. One possibility is to say that the main differences between L1 and L2 acquisition are in the amount of exposure and use and in the influence from the L1. Another possibility is that children and adults vary in how they parse and process input, and the units they operate on, as stated in Johnson and Newport's (1989) Less is More Hypothesis. As we will see in Chapter 8, many heritage speakers show patterns similar to the patterns displayed by L2 learners. For this reason, these theoretical possibilities are very relevant when conducting and discussing research comparing heritage speakers and L2 learners.

Processability Theory (Pienemann 1998, 2005) is another theory that is closer to generative theory in terms of some of the basic universal and nativist assumptions but focuses on how language is processed and used. Conceived as a theory of L2 development guided by Lexical Functional Grammar (Bresnan 2001), Processability Theory relies on the architecture of the human language processor and states that at any stage of language development the learner can only comprehend and produce the linguistic forms that his/her language processor can handle. The acquisition of structures that require a lower level of procedural skills are a prerequisite for acquiring structures that require a higher level of processability. Pienemann (1998) proposed that there is an implicationally ordered processability hierarchy that constrains the language acquisition process, starting at stage 1 and ending at 6:

1. no procedure (e.g., producing a simple word such as "yes")
2. category procedure (e.g., adding a past tense morpheme to a verb as in "talked")
3. noun phrase procedure (e.g., matching plurality as in "two kids")
4. verb phrase procedure (e.g., moving an adverb out of the verb phrase to the front of a sentence as in "I went yesterday/yesterday I went")
5. sentence procedure (e.g., subject-verb agreement as in "Peter sees a dog")
6. subordinate clause procedure (e.g., use of the subjunctive in subordinate clauses triggered by information in a main clause as in "The doctor insisted that the patient be quiet")

Because it is essentially a model of production, Processabilty Theory incorporates Levelt's (1989) psycholinguistic incremental model of speech production to describe the automatic and unconscious mental operations that are applied to linguistic knowledge.

Pienemann's position is that the notion of Universal Grammar and language processing are not dichotomous, but should operate together, and the fundamental principles of language processing apply to L1 and L2 acquisition of grammar. However, L1 and L2 learners start from different initial hypotheses and the structural effects of these hypotheses bias how L1 and L2 learners process the target language and develop their linguistic systems. The theory seeks to explain the developmental process and stages of language learning and why there is a universal sequence of development in the acquisition of different aspects of grammatical knowledge. More recently, it has also come to address the logical problem, or why learners come to know more about language than what can be inducted from the input. Finally, Processability Theory looks at the grammars of L2 learners independent of how they differ from native speaker norms, so this is a theory that truly examines L2 acquisition in its own right.

The universal nature of Processability Theory, the relationship between morphology and syntax, and the plausibility of the stages of development proposed in different languages have been empirically tested across various typologically diverse languages (English, German, Italian, Arabic, Chinese, Japanese, Swedish, Spanish), especially in L2 acquisition situations (Baten 2011; Bonilla 2015; Di Biase and Kawaguchi 2002; Mansouri 2005; Pienemann and Håkansson 1999; Zhang 2005).

5.2.2   *Sociolinguistic perspective*

Variationist sociolinguistics has also been applied to understand systematic variability in L2 acquisition and how it deviates from the norm. This work was pioneered by Beebe (1980) and Tarone (1979, 1983), who addressed the fact that the speech of L2 learners varied systematically depending on speech style, along the lines proposed by Labov (1970). Beebe examined the pronunciation of 9 Thai learners of English in an oral interview and in a list reading task. The focus of the study was on the pronunciation of /r/ and /l/ and the main finding was that the more or less target-like pronunciation of different allophones of these phones depended on the task and phonological environments. Bayley and Tarone (2011) summarize the most recent research showing that L2 learners produce more target-like speech in more formal, written tasks when they pay attention to form and they engage in monitoring and editing. By contrast, they produce less target-like speech in more informal tasks that focus on meaning.

In addition to studying systematic variation in L2 performance, sociolinguistics addressed the observation that when it comes to ultimate attainment, L2 learners seem to set their own target for interlanguage development based on language norms in the social groups they identify with and want to participate in. Tarone and Liu (1995), for example, documented the impact of different interlocutors and social settings on the rate and route of one learner's acquisition of questions in English. In their longitudinal case study, Tarone and Liu showed how the L2 learner's patterns of language changed depending on his social context and his peers, starting in the informal context and spreading over time in interactions with his peers, and finally with his teacher. These social settings impacted the learner's acquisition of questions in English because some forms were first produced in some contexts and with some interlocutors rather than others. In this way, variationist sociolinguistics adds another important complementary dimension to the study of L2 grammars, and how they vary from native norms, not afforded by the generative and the emergentist positions.

To summarize, the main perspectives described – Universal Grammar/ Processability Theory, Cognitive approaches/Emergentism and Sociolinguistics – emphasize different components of the language learning process: innate linguistic knowledge, general learning processes, input and processing, respectively, all taking place in a sociocultural environment that determines social and attitudinal aspects of language learning and acculturation. Table 5.1 summarizes some of the main features of the theories discussed.

All the factors listed in Table 5.1 are critical components in heritage language acquisition. These approaches often present themselves as competitors in confronting challenges of linguistic analysis and acquisition, when in fact they complement each other even though they start from very different sets of assumptions about grammar, linguistic knowledge, learning, and language use in a social group. The three approaches, or perhaps a combination of the three,

Table 5.1. *Main features of nativism, emergentism, and variationist sociolinguistics as theories of L1 and L2 acquisition*

Nativist (Universal Grammar) Processability Theory	Emergentism/usage-based/ cognitive approaches	Variationist sociolinguistics
• Language is innate and independent of cognition • Emphasis on abstract knowledge and linguistic representations • Input triggers innate knowledge but does not determine the complexity of the language system acquired • Processability Theory emphasizes the developmental problem in terms of processing competence • Acquisition is implicit and is constrained by Universal Grammar and the language processor • Seeks to explain developmental and transfer errors • L2 acquisition is another instance of language acquisition (for some, not fundamentally different from L1 acquisition) • Knowledge of the L1, processing routines, and innate knowledge guide L2 acquisition	• Cognition is innate • Language is part of cognition and an epiphenomenon • Emphasis on language use in the context of social interaction • Grammar emerges from language use and cognitive processes (analogy, statistical learning) • Input frequencies and memorized chunks drive acquisition • Children learn the language implicitly and later develop explicit knowledge • L2 acquisition takes place through explicit learning • There is transfer of phonological, morphological, and syntactic cues from the L1 to the L2	• Emphasis on how language is used and what speakers say • Language learning is driven by language function and social context • Focus on relationship between systematic variability and social and regional variables (sex, SES, region, age) • Focus on L2 speech and patterns of language use with different interlocutors • L2 learners determine their own norms based on social context • Systematic variation by context (formal, informal) and task type (controlled, spontaneous social group, etc.)

are perfectly suitable to study heritage language acquisition, as I explain in the next section.

5.3   Theoretical approaches to heritage language acquisition

A tacit assumption in this book is that a theory of the acquisition of heritage languages should not look different from a theory of a monolingual or second language speaker of a language. The same goes for a theory of grammar: the syntactic or functionalist model that one uses for the monolingual speaker should be identical to one used for the multilingual speaker. This is not to say that there are no differences between heritage speakers and other speakers. For example, in Chapter 4, I mentioned several factors that contribute to shape heritage language grammars: differences in attainment, attrition over the lifespan, transfer from the dominant language, and incipient changes in parental/community input that get amplified in the heritage variety, among others. These differences do not entail that the theory of grammar and its acquisition for heritage speakers should be fundamentally different or have additional assumptions than a theory of grammar for a monolingual speaker. The same components that are crucial in monolingual acquisition, such as an innate linguistic/cognitive component, input, and socialization, are decisive in heritage language acquisition as well, except that input and the extent of socialization in the heritage language may be different. That is, heritage speakers, like L1 and L2 learners bring to the acquisition task access to innate properties of language and cognition, like L1 learners they start acquisition of the language very young, and like L2 learners they also bring knowledge of another language. Table 5.2 lists the facts that have been observed in heritage language acquisition and that need to be explained. In addition to these facts, a remaining

Table 5.2. *Observable facts to be explained about the acquisition of heritage languages*

1. Exposure to input and use of the language are necessary for heritage language acquisition
2. Most of heritage language acquisition happens incidentally and is acquired implicitly
3. Heritage language learners come to know more than what they have been exposed to in the input
4. Heritage language learners develop better command of the aspects of language that they use more frequently (informal, familiar language, oral skills and pronunciation, auditory skills)
5. There are predictable stages of heritage language development depending on age of onset of bilingualism and quantity and quality of input
6. The outcome of heritage language acquisition is variable: the vast majority of heritage speakers do not reach full linguistic competence in all aspects of the heritage language
7. Developmental and synchronic variability apply unevenly to linguistic properties and linguistic modules
8. There are limits to the effects of frequency of forms in the input in heritage language development
9. There are limits to the effects of the dominant language on heritage language acquisition
10. Explicit knowledge of the heritage language is less developed than their implicit knowledge
11. Affective and attitudinal factors play a role in heritage language acquisition (and relearning in a formal setting)

question is how attrition and incomplete mastery of the heritage grammar over the lifespan should be captured.

Collectively, the theoretical approaches presented capture most of these facts, but no theory can account for all of them single-handedly. To illustrate this point, the next section presents studies of heritage language speakers that have adopted the approaches to L1 and L2 acquisition described so far. We start with sociolinguistics because, historically, this was the first approach to heritage language grammars; generative, emergentist, and processability theory approaches are more recent developments.

5.3.1   Sociolinguistics

The study of heritage speakers as defined in this book has a long tradition in sociolinguistics, especially in variationist sociolinguistics, sociology of language, and ethnolinguistics.[2] Many studies have focused on describing the language of heritage speakers as examples of different emerging regional and community varieties of the language in the diaspora (e.g., the Spanish of Los Angeles, the Spanish of New York, Finnish in Sweden, Russian in America) and frequently address theoretical issues in language contact and change as a sociohistorical phenomenon (Dorian 1989).

To date, the most complete sociolinguistic treatment of Spanish heritage speakers is, without a doubt, Silva-Corvalán's (1994) study of the Spanish of Los Angeles mentioned in Chapter 3. Silva-Corvalán documented the oral production of a cohort of Mexican-Americans living in Los Angeles between 1983 and 1988 in order to understand language change in progress as a result of Spanish being in contact with English. The investigation focused on language maintenance and on changes generally characteristic of language shift or loss. The sample included adolescents and adults of three generations of immigrants. First generation speakers (group I) were born in Mexico and had immigrated to the United States after age 11. These speakers had native command of Spanish and their command of English ranged from near-native to poor. Speakers in group II were either born in the US or had arrived in the US before the age of 11. Group III speakers were also born in the US, but at least one parent had to be classified as a speaker of group II. All the US-born bilinguals had been exposed to the two languages from birth, had native command of English, and their ability in Spanish ranged from near-native to poor. All speakers were interviewed

---

[2] Sociology of language was pioneered by Fishman (1972) and studies society in relation to language. It focuses on attitudes, linguistic spaces, and who uses what language with whom, for what purposes, and when. Society, rather than language, is the focus of study. Ethnolinguistics studies the relationship between language and culture, and the way different ethnic groups perceive the world.

and conversations were later transcribed for analysis. In addition, all speakers completed fill-in-the-gap questionnaires designed to elicit additional information about their grammars.

Silva-Corvalán (1994) studied potential simplification of the tense-aspect and mood (TAM) verb system across the three generations, documenting seven implicationally ordered stages of simplification and loss. The first stage affected the use of future perfect and the conditional (as a tense) and the last stage represented the loss of the present subjunctive. The simplification (but not loss) of the preterit and imperfect forms of the past tense occurred in stage 3, with simplification of the preterit (with a closed class of stative verbs) occurring before simplification of the imperfect indicative. Silva-Corvalán (1994, p. 44) documented from speech samples that speakers often confused preterit and imperfect forms, using one for the other:

> (6) Yo fui el único hombre que *tenían*.   (for *tuvieron*)
>   "I was the only son they had."
> (7) En la casa mi mamá era la única que *habló* español y las demás *hablaron* en inglés.   (instead of *hablaba* and *hablaban*)
>   "At home my mom was the only one who spoke Spanish and the other ones only spoke English."

Silva-Corvalán discovered that the shrinking of the preterit at stage 3 affected only a small number of stative verbs: *estar/ser* "be," *tener* "have," and *saber* "have." Speakers from group I most frequently produced stative verbs in imperfective contexts, but in perfective contexts these speakers used the preterit with these verbs. However, speakers of groups II and III appeared to neutralize the morphological perfective-imperfective distinction, and the speakers with the lowest proficiency sometimes used the imperfect form in *both* perfective and imperfective contexts with stative verbs. Similar instability with the use of the imperfect was found by Zentella (1997) in the speech of five 8- and 9-year-old heritage speakers of the New York City area. Zentella also concluded that the children's use of tense and aspect marker distinctions was very different from that of monolingual Spanish speakers, considered the norm.

With respect to other tenses, Silva-Corvalán documented absence of the synthetic future, the conditional, and the pluperfect indicative, starting with the speakers of generation II. Simplification was also observed in the use of indicative for the subjunctive, especially in third generation speakers, as shown in (8).

> (8) Lo voy a guardar antes que *llega*. (instead of *llegue*)
>   "I am going to keep it before he arrives."

Other changes were the extension of the copula *estar* to cases where *ser* should be used, as with predicative adjectives (*la recámara está pequeñito* "the room is small," *yo estoy inteligente* "I am intelligent"); omission of the complementizer *que* in complement clauses (*Yo creo no la quiere ver* "I think that he doesn't want to see her"); loss of semantic-pragmatic constraints on SVX word order (*una señora entró y me preguntó si conocía* "A woman came in and asked me if I knew"). Finally, Silva-Corvalán also observed that overt pronominal subjects were used in cases where null subjects are more pragmatically appropriate (e.g., *Yo pienso que yo me olvido el español* "I think that I forget my Spanish"), as discussed in Chapter 3.

For Silva-Corvalán, the loss or simplification of tenses in the adults studied is not due to transfer from English – the majority and dominant language – but rather a result of reduced exposure and use of Spanish and other cognitive and interactional factors. She interpreted some patterns of simplification and loss of tense morphology evident in her data to apparently be the mirror image of development in creolization and in L1 and L2 acquisition (1994, p. 50). Silva-Corvalán considered that these and other morphophonological changes in the heritage speakers' verb forms were driven by an accelerated process of internal linguistic change already happening in other monolingual varieties of Spanish.

Another recent study of three heritage languages in Toronto, Canada, following variationist sociolinguistics is Nagy *et al.* (2011). They investigated the effects of language contact and, more precisely, the effect of English influence (a non-null subject language) on subject pronoun realization in Cantonese, Russian, and Italian, all null subject languages, and found that the influence from English was minor. Otheguy, Zentella, and Livert (2007), another variationist sociolinguistic study, found that Spanish speakers who had arrived in New York City after the age of 16 and had been living in the city for less than 6 years had a significantly lower rate of overt subject pronouns than those who were born and raised in New York City (or who had arrived before age 3). Otheguy, Zentella, and Livert (2007) claimed that contact with English resulted in a lower rate of null subjects in the Spanish speakers from New York. Polinsky (1995) also found evidence for a possible effect of contact with English on overt subject pronoun realization in six heritage languages. Although Polinsky did not use variationist methods, and examined only a few speakers per language, she found that the weaker the proficiency in the heritage language, the more overt subject pronouns the heritage speakers used. Thus, following this previous work, Nagy *et al.*'s investigation was concerned with degree of dominant language transfer and attrition in the three immigrant populations.

Cantonese, Russian, and Italian have well-established communities in the greater Toronto area. For each language, Nagy *et al.* obtained a corpus of spoken language with recordings of 40 native speakers, distributed across three generations. First generation speakers lived in the homeland until the age of

18, and had been in Toronto for more than 20 years. Second generation speakers had at least one parent who was a first generation speaker. Third generation speakers were those with at least one second generation parent. Each generation was represented by four age groups: 12–18, 19–38, 39–59, and 60+, although the data presented in this study focused on a subset of 16 Cantonese, 11 Italian, and 12 Russian heritage language speakers (second and third generation were collapsed). For comparison with English, Nagy *et al.* included 8 speakers of comparable ages from the Toronto English Archive (Tagliamonte and Denis 2010).

Speech was elicited through a sociolinguistic interview, then transcribed and coded for analysis. Nagy *et al.* examined the factors constraining variable null subjects in each language, and found no significant difference with respect to the rate of null subjects between the speech of Italian- and Russian-Canadians who were born in Italy and Russia and those born in Canada. Crucially, none of the languages in either generation were close to the 2% rate of null subjects in English. Nagy *et al.* concluded that contact with English is not causing a change in null subject heritage languages spoken in Toronto with respect to null subject variation because the first generation speakers and the heritage speakers produced comparable rates of null subjects. There was no indication of transfer from English in any of the heritage languages examined. The results of this study on heritage speakers in Canada seem to diverge from the results of null subject languages of heritage speakers in the United States.

In sum, these sociolinguistic studies have focused on potential divergence in the grammars of heritage speakers with respect to the norm or the standard of monolingual varieties. Heritage speakers show variability in the degree of ultimate attainment of specific properties of the heritage grammars, but their variability does not always match the variability of the standard monolingual norm. In some cases part of the variability in heritage speakers can be explained by dominant language influence but in other cases it cannot. As for the changes observed, debate exists as to whether they follow diachronic developments already in place in the language, or they are the result of direct contact and transfer from the majority language. Although these studies do not address the acquisition of the heritage language by bilingual heritage speakers of the second generation directly, they all mention that language contact and language use may be implicated in the linguistic change observed among immigrant generations and with respect to the monolingual varieties. From the facts listed in Table 5.2, this approach mostly addresses the following facts: (1) Exposure to input and use of the language are necessary for heritage language acquisition; (5) There are predictable stages of heritage language development depending on age of onset of bilingualism and quantity and quality of input; (6) The outcome of heritage language acquisition is variable; (7) Developmental and synchronic variability apply unevenly to linguistic properties and linguistic modules; (9) There are limits to the effects of the dominant language on heritage language acquisition; (11) Affective and attitudinal factors play a role in heritage acquisition.

5.3.2   Formal linguistics

Starting in the mid-1990s there has been increasing interest in heritage speakers from a formal linguistic and psycholinguistic perspective, where language change is seen as an individual phenomenon in the mind of the speaker. Polinsky (1997, 2000, 2006) conducted in-depth studies of the Russian spoken by second generation heritage speakers in the United States. By presenting examples of common patterns produced by these speakers in oral production, Polinsky attempted to capture the nature of the grammatical system that develops under reduced input conditions. The Russian spoken by these heritage speakers is also treated by Polinsky as a particular language variety, just as in sociolinguistics, although her focus is less on investigating external variables like age, social class, or gender, and more on explaining its morphosyntactic characteristics and the linguistic competence of its speakers. Polinsky shows that despite the fact that American Russian is a reduced version of what she terms full Russian (the variety spoken by first generation immigrants or *emigrés*), it is subject to the same grammatical constraints as other natural languages, even if those constraints operate in a gradient fashion, and are not always evident from the input. Thus, a grammar acquired partially or incompletely is still systematic and regular, rather than a collection of isolated pieces randomly put together or learned by rote.

   Polinsky (2006) used the techniques from field linguistics (vocabulary translation and oral interview) to elicit knowledge of basic vocabulary and different aspects of morphosyntax from 21 speakers of American Russian in their 20s and 30s who had immigrated with their parents to the United States between the ages of 3 and 11. The morphosyntactic areas examined were nominal morphology (case, gender, and number agreement in nouns), verbal morphology (agreement, lexical aspect, and conditionals), word order, and referential expressions (overt/null subjects, reflexives, and resumptive pronouns). Polinsky found a correlation between lexical proficiency and morphosyntactic ability. The speakers with the lowest scores in the vocabulary elicitation task were the ones who showed patterns of simplification and structural changes in all the morphosyntactic domains tested. Speakers with higher proficiency showed less deviations from the Full Russian variety. As presented in Chapter 3, the changes observed involved simplification of the case, gender and aspect system, loss of verb agreement, elimination of the conditional, loss, or simplification of reflexivization rules, development of resumptive pronouns, loss of null subjects, and increased pronominal redundancy in discourse. All these changes, according to Polinsky, are due to reduced input leading to incomplete acquisition or attrition at the individual level, as described in Chapter 4.

Larsson and Johannessen (2014) is another recent example of formal linguistic approaches to heritage languages that emphasize the emergence of structures that are not represented in the input. Their study focused on the varieties of the Scandinavian languages Norwegian and Swedish as spoken in the American Midwest. Heritage Scandinavian (both Swedish and Norwegian) produce word orders in embedded clauses that are different from the word order possibilities of European Norwegian and Swedish. Like in the sociolinguistic tradition, the data comes from oral recordings of heritage speakers of Scandinavian. From these recordings, frequency counts of subordinate declaratives, embedded questions, and relative clauses were obtained. The data showed a substantial amount of verb–adverb order in all such clauses in Heritage Scandinavian despite the fact that the verb–adverb order is ungrammatical in embedded questions and relative clauses in European Scandinavian. European Scandinavian does allow verb–adverb order in *that* clauses, but Larsson and Johannessen found this word order considerably more frequently in Heritage Scandinavian than in European Scandinavian. Larsson and Johannessen argue against the possibility that the new verb–adverb word order present in Heritage Scandinavian is a loan from English, and consider instead that the apparent change is due to incomplete acquisition of Norwegian and Swedish in the second generation heritage speakers. Evidence for their hypothesis comes from nontarget verb–adverb word order also found in developmental stages of the acquisition of verb movement in the Scandinavian languages. European Norwegian and Swedish L1 learners appear to also produce verb–adverb word orders for quite some time, well beyond age 6. We will revisit this study in Chapter 7.

Other studies within this general theoretical framework have adopted experimental methodologies from L1 acquisition, L2 acquisition, and psycholinguistics. The methodologies used involve oral narrative tasks, oral and written elicited production tasks, grammaticality judgment tasks, and truth value judgment tasks, in addition to other online techniques measuring speed of processing in real time, as we will see in Chapter 6. Groups of heritage speakers who differ on the variable of interest are compared with a control group of native speakers born and raised in the countries where the heritage speakers trace their roots, either residing in the country of origin or very recent arrivals in the host country. Like many sociolinguistic studies, these psycholinguistically oriented studies have also found significant differences in the performance of heritage speakers as compared to native speakers (Montrul 2008).

An example of the extension of nativist approaches to heritage language acquisition using experimental designs of L1 and L2 acquisition is Kim, Montrul, and Yoon's (2009) study with adult Korean heritage speakers living in the United States. Kim, Montrul, and Yoon focused on the interpretation of anaphors (reflexive pronouns), a topic that has received significant attention in generative syntactic theory and generative approaches to L1 and L2 acquisition, as it relates to universal principles and parameters of human languages. As shown earlier in Section 5.1, reflexive pronouns like *herself/ himself* obey c-command relations and must be locally bound in English; that is, they must refer to the immediate subject within the local clause (see examples 3 and 4 under Section 5.1.1). This knowledge is acquired implicitly. Korean has three types of reflexives, namely, *caki, casin,* and *caki-casin* which differ in their distributional and interpretive properties. According to Kang (1998), *caki* is subject oriented and prefers long-distance antecedents. On the other hand, *caki-casin*, which is less frequently used than *caki*, requires a local antecedent. The third reflexive *casin* is used less frequently than *caki* and allows both local and long-distance antecedents (see also discussion in Chapter 3). Studies on L1 transfer in L2 acquisition of binding showed L2 learners whose L1 has only local binding (such as English) have difficulty interpreting reflexives that can be bound long-distance in languages like Japanese and Chinese (Hirakawa 1990; Thomas 1995; White, Hirakawa, and Kawasaki 1996; Yuan 1998).

According to studies on the L1 acquisition of reflexive binding, Korean children initially show a preference for the local binding of *caki* between the ages of 3 and 6 (Cho 1989; Lee 1990; Lee and Wexler 1987). The preference for local binding begins to diminish around the age of 6 or 7 (Cho 1989; Lee 1990). Cho (1992) studied the long-distance anaphor *caki* with children between the ages of 6 and 12 and found that 6- to 8-year-old children preferred local binding, while this preference was weaker in 10- to 12-year-old children. These results suggest that although knowledge of binding theory in Korean emerges around age 3, it takes several more years for the adult system to be fully established, say around the age of 12 (see discussion on mastery in Chapter 4). The age of L1 acquisition of local and long-distance binding is important in understanding the linguistic performance of the heritage speakers in the Kim, Montrul, and Yoon (2009) study, since they began to be exposed extensively to English and significantly less to Korean at around the time that knowledge of the reflexive system is mastered in Korean monolingual children. With input reduction at this crucial time of development, the acquisition of Korean reflexive binding in this population is likely to be incomplete. On the other hand, assuming that the adult Korean binding system is acquired at age 12, for the late bilinguals who came to be immersed in the English-speaking community after their L1 had been robustly acquired (their mean age of exposure to English was 13.6), the properties of Korean reflexive binding will have been mastered before the onset of intense exposure to English.

Kim, Montrul, and Yoon also asked whether the influence of English, a language with local anaphors, would be apparent in the binding interpretations of long-distance reflexives by Korean heritage speakers, such that Korean-English bilinguals whose Korean was weaker than their English would show a marked preference for local, as opposed to long-distance binding in Korean as well. Because English has only one type of reflexive (*himself*), while Korean has three (*caki, casin,* and *caki-casin*), the interpretive distinctions among the three Korean reflexives were further hypothesized to be lost or neutralized in the bilinguals, regardless of reflexive type. Participants were 50 Korean heritage speakers living in the United States (mean age 21.4). Twenty-one were late bilinguals (age of arrival 11–15 years; length of residence 4–9 years) and the other 29 were early bilinguals exposed to both languages simultaneously since birth. In addition, 68 monolingual speakers of Korean were tested as the control group in Seoul, Korea. The main task was a truth value judgment task with pictures and the target items consisted of bi-clausal sentences illustrating each type of reflexive (*caki, casin,* and *caki-casin*).

The main findings were that long-distance binding preferences are affected in heritage speakers. With the reflexive *caki*, which allows both local and long-distance binding, the heritage speakers preferred the local interpretation, while the late bilinguals and the Korean control group accepted both interpretations. The results of the other two anaphors, *casin* and *caki-casin*, did not differ significantly among the groups. However, while the monolinguals and the late bilinguals retained a three-way anaphor system, the results of the early bilinguals (the heritage speakers) showed that they treated *casin* and *caki-casin* alike. They seem to have a reduced two-anaphor system. The heritage speakers acquired and retained universal knowledge of binding relations but there were also non-native effects in anaphor interpretation that could be related to dominant language transfer and other universal tendencies of reanalysis and simplification, as discussed in Chapter 3.

In sum, the formal linguistic approaches focus on linguistic knowledge and representations elicited from production and comprehension data. They have addressed the facts about variability in different linguistic domains as a function of reduced input, with particular emphasis on universal tendencies found in many heritage languages. These approaches have also emphasized the relationship between heritage language grammars and stages of development in child language, the implicitness of the heritage language acquisition process, and the role of dominant language transfer.

5.3.3   Emergentism

There are very few extensions of the emergentist position to heritage language acquisition, although many of the characteristics of heritage grammars that arise through insufficient exposure to input also seem to find a natural explanation within this theoretical perspective. O'Grady *et al.*'s (2011a) study is an example of a study that assumes the validity of the emergentist perspective applied to the study of heritage language acquisition (see also O'Grady 2013 and commentaries therein). Under the general view that language acquisition consists of pairing sounds and meaning at all levels of linguistic analysis and does not rely on innate knowledge, like Pienemann (1998), O'Grady also considers that the language processor is primarily responsible for strengthening form-meaning mappings made available by other cognitive systems. Now, the question that arises is how processing contributes to what is acquired, to what is retained, to what is lost, or to what is never acquired in heritage language acquisition. O'Grady *et al.* explore the acquisition of two types of phenomena: case marking and scope interpretations in Korean. Case marking, as we have seen extensively in Chapter 3, is often not mastered and sometimes lost in heritage language acquisition despite the fact that it is acquired early, and it is frequent in the input; i.e., in languages that mark case overtly, every sentence that has NP instantiates case to some extent. Scope is at the interface between syntax and semantics, and sentences exemplifying scope are very infrequent in the input. Intriguingly, scope appears to be successfully acquired in both L1 and heritage language acquisition.

Korean uses case marking to distinguish subjects and objects, as shown in (9), where *–ka* is nominative and *–lul* is accusative.

(9) Yeca-*ka*   namca-*lul* anacwue
     woman-NOM man-ACC   hug
     "The woman is hugging the man."

However, in spoken Korean, case marking is frequently dropped (Chung 2013): Cho (1982) found that in child-directed speech Korean mothers produced nominative case 56.8% of the time and accusative case less than 10%, which makes the input highly variable for children. At the same time, semantic and pragmatic notions play a role in the frequency of case-marked noun phrases (Chung 2013; Lee 2006). For example, accusative case is more frequently used when the object is focused, has a human referent, and is definite (as with differential object marking in other languages). Thus, the form-meaning mapping is not straightforward. As a result, acquiring case marking in Korean will require a significant amount of input, which is what heritage speakers typically lack. The study by Song *et al.* (1997) mentioned in Chapter 3 showed that child Korean heritage speakers have significant problems using accusative and nominative case during comprehension of relative clauses in Korean. For O'Grady *et al.* (2011a), reduced frequency in the input and opaque form-meaning mappings would explain the lack of mastery and the attrition of case morphology in Korean heritage speakers. Simply put, the processor does not receive sufficient exposure to strengthen the form-meaning mappings.

Scope is a semantic property that refers to the interaction between logical operators (negation and quantifier expressions) in sentences such as (10) in Korean and (11) in the English equivalent.

> (10)   Jane-i   motun yenphil-ul an   ss-ess-ta
>   Jane-NOM all   pencil-ACC NEG use-PAST-DCL
> (11)   Jane didn't use all the pencils.

These sentences have two interpretations in English: the partition set interpretation suggests that Jane used some pencils but not others. The other interpretation is called the full set reading, and suggests that none of the pencils were used. The full set reading is the preferred interpretation in Korean. These sentences are very infrequent in the input and present a typical poverty of the stimulus problem. Within the generative perspective, Han, Lidz, and Musolino (2007) have suggested that the partitioned set interpretation is available when the negation is structurally higher than the quantified object (*all the pencils*), and children come equipped with this abstract knowledge (see discussion in Section 5.1). Rather than relying on innate structural knowledge, O'Grady *et al.* (2011) consider that the preferred interpretation for these sentences in English and in Korean can be naturally accounted for by processing routines. O'Grady *et al.* (2011) conducted four experiments using truth value judgment tasks with pictures and stories to examine preferred interpretations of these sentences: one with Korean children in Korea (ages 5–6;9), one with Korean heritage speakers in the United States (ages 6–11;9), one with Korean adults in Korea, and one with young adult Korean heritage speakers in the United States (ages 18–26). The results showed that the child and adult heritage speakers of Korean strongly favored the full set interpretation of *not all* sentences in Korean, like the child and adult Korean native speakers tested in Korea. These results are summarized in Table 5.3.

Unlike what has been found for the acquisition of case marking, there is little evidence of incomplete acquisition or attrition of scope interpretations in Korean as a heritage language. At the same time, the heritage speakers did accept more partitioned set interpretations than the Korean native speakers, suggesting that there was also some transfer from English, but this was not their preferred choice. O'Grady *et al.* conclude that the full set reading is favored in Korean over the partitioned set reading because the full set reading

Table 5.3. *Interpretative scope preferences for Koreans in Korea and Korean heritage speakers in the United States (adapted from O'Grady et al. 2011)*

Experimental groups	N	Full set context (preferred in Korean) (%)	Partitioned set context (preferred in English) (%)
Korean children in Korea	20	98	25
Korean heritage speakers in the United States	16	98	42
Korean adults in Korea	51	98	9
Young adult Korean heritage speakers in the United States	10	100	33

places fewer demands on the processor. There is no need for the assumption of innate knowledge of abstract movement operations.

O'Grady *et al.* argue that heritage language acquisition can be easily captured by the emergentist perspective and is no different from language acquisition in a monolingual setting: it requires the same sort of input conditions and it draws on exactly the same resources. The processor is sensitive to frequency and consistency of form-meaning mappings, favoring those mappings that minimize the burden on working memory (the Amelioration Hypothesis, O'Grady 2013).

5.3.4   Processability Theory

Although Processability Theory has been around for a while, its extension to heritage language acquisition is very recent. In fact, this approach is quite promising for heritage language acquisition because it focuses on speaking, processing, the relationship between words, morphology, and syntax, and stages of development independently of native speaker norms. It is also amenable to use with longitudinal studies, which, as we will discuss in Chapter 7, need to be undertaken more extensively if we are to understand the course of heritage language development.

To my knowledge, Bayram (2013) is the first study that uses Processability Theory to understand the acquisition of Turkish as a heritage language in Germany. This study investigated the state of development (from words to complex syntax) and linguistic knowledge of 24 young third generation heritage speakers (mean age 12.8). The study investigated knowledge of case, flexible word order, passives, relative clauses, and other long-distance dependencies (see Chapter 3), using oral production tasks. Unfortunately, this was not a longitudinal study and tested heritage speakers assumed to be at different stages of heritage language development. Language production was elicited through four communicative tasks that required use of passive sentences and relative clauses, complex sentences at the highest level of expected development (stages 5 and 6 in Section 5.2). (Six child native speakers of Turkish in Turkey were also administered the tasks to make sure they elicited the complex structures that Bayram was hoping to elicit from the heritage speakers.) Recall from Section 2.1 that Processabilty Theory proposes implicationally ordered stages of language production such that words are the first stage, followed by morphology, followed by basic syntax, and later by complex syntax. A learner who produces complex syntax is assumed to be able to produce structures at the previous stages, but a learner who can barely produce morphology cannot be expected to produce and process structures that occur at stage 4 or 5. Rather than using a criterion based on the percentage of accurate use of these forms, at 60% or 90% accuracy, Bayram (2013) used an "emergence" criterion to identify five developmental stages in the acquisition of these structures in Turkish as given in Table 5.4, level 5 being the most advanced. The emergence criterion identifies the first use of a form, not necessarily its accuracy because according to Pienemann accuracy does not always correlate with order of acquisition.

Out of the group of 24 Turkish heritage speakers, two of them only reached stage 2 (canonical word order), 17 of them reached stage 3 (nominal, genitive possessive, verbal complement, sentence-initial adjuncts), three of them reached stage 4 (passives), and only two of them reached the highest developmental stage, stage 5 (relative clauses). As predicted by the theory, the heritage speaker who reached developmental stage 5 produced all other structures at lower stages, while heritage speakers at stage 3 were not able to demonstrate productive and systematic use of structures at stages 4 and 5.

Bayram concludes that the results demonstrate that the language acquisition of Turkish by heritage speakers in Germany is developmentally constrained by the availability of processing mechanisms, given credence to Processability Theory with novel data from heritage speakers. The participants displayed a clear hierarchy in their development, with competence in the processing of basic grammatical structures that are canonically mapped, but with gaps in the processing of complex structures, such as passives and subject relative clauses, that are noncanonically mapped and involve long-distance dependencies. This study in particular contributes important insights both to theoretical accounts of acquisition of Turkish and to the wider study of heritage language acquisition.

The extension of Processability Theory to heritage language acquisition is quite new, but it is a natural extension because this theory could potentially speak to several of the facts of heritage language acquisition listed in Table 5.2, especially those dealing with development. Processability Theory may be able to account for the fact that different structures have different developmental schedules, and heritage speakers who are at different stages of development display variability in levels of acquisition. Because the developmental

Table 5.4. *Processing procedures in Processability Theory corresponding to Turkish structures (adapted from Bayram 2013)*

Stage	Processing procedure	Level of information exchange	Syntax	Verbal morphology	Nominal morphology
1	Word, lemma	Words	Single words, Formulaic expressions	–	–
2	Category procedure	Lexical morphemes	Canonical word order (S-O-V) prodrop Topic = subject	Passive (participles) Tense person	Case plural
3	Phrasal procedure	Phrasal information	Adjunct + Canonical mapping (S-O-V) Topic = adj	Verb complemen-tation	Genitive possessive
4	Sentence procedure	Interphrasal information	Noncanonical mapping (O-S-V) Topic = object	Passive	–
5	Subordinate clause procedure	Interclausal information	–	Relative clauses Long-distance dependencies	–

hierarchy is constrained by processing, frequency of structures cannot alter the route of development so easily, according to this theory, but this is something that remains to be empirically verified. Finally, dominant language transfer could potentially be accommodated in this framework when the heritage language learner processes features of the heritage language that are also relevant in the dominant language. However, because this theory assumes that L1 and L2 acquisition start from different knowledge sources and that is why they diverge eventually, presumably heritage language acquisition will start like L1 acquisition (in sequential bilingualism cases) and how it eventually diverges from L1 development needs to be explained. Although Processability Theory does not state it explicitly, it seems that the other language (whether it was acquired before, simultaneously, or after the other) plays a role in language processing. A final point is that given its focus on emergence and development, this approach would benefit from studies that actually use longitudinal data.

In conclusion, as in L1 and L2 acquisition, the vast majority of recent studies on heritage language acquisition have been conducted within the linguistic and cognitive perspective, as we will see in more detail in Chapters 7 and 8.

5.4   Summary

This chapter presented several mainstream contemporary perspectives to L1 and L2 acquisition that seek to explain the nature of linguistic knowledge, how it emerges, how it develops, how it reflects the role of the input, and other universal properties of language. Due to the complexity of the heritage language acquisition process and outcome, all these theories, rather than only one, are needed to explain the phenomena at hand. Existing theories of L1 and L2 acquisition within linguistics, sociolinguistics, and psycholinguistics can be profitably extended to the acquisition of heritage languages. There is no need to create a special theory for heritage language acquisition.

6   Methodological considerations

In the previous chapter, we presented some common theoretical approaches to monolingual and bilingual L1 acquisition and adult L2 acquisition that have also been applied to understand the nature of linguistic knowledge and use in heritage language speakers. Chapters 7 and 8 will cover recent empirical findings on the internal and external factors that may contribute to grammatical changes in heritage language speakers, as discussed in Chapters 3 and 4. But before we do so, it is important to consider the issues that heritage speakers raise for research, as well as the most common research designs and methods that have been applied to this population to date. I discuss first how research methods are related to the research question and theoretical perspective assumed, followed by key considerations that arise when studying heritage speakers' linguistic knowledge and behavior.

The number of heritage languages and dialects, the different types and number of heritage language communities all over the world, and the inherent individual variation in heritage speakers' proficiency within a language are serious challenges for comparative research. A common dilemma is deciding the ideal baseline group against which we evaluate the linguistic behavior of heritage speakers. Another consideration is identifying who the heritage speakers in the study are, and describing as thoroughly as possible their biographical characteristics and level of proficiency in the heritage language becomes essential. Decisions must also be made regarding the most appropriate approach (bilingual or unilingual) to address the research questions, as well as the design of the tasks and instruments to elicit data. Finally, because individual variability is a hallmark of heritage speaker groups, finding a valid way to analyze, present, and interpret the data is key for advancing research in this field.

6.1   Research methods

In Chapter 5 we covered main theoretical approaches with very specific assumptions about the nature of language and the role of the environment and other social factors in language development. These assumptions guide the research questions, the research designs, and the methods used. Although research methods are not an end in themselves, methods affect results, which in turn drive conclusions about linguistic knowledge and behavior.

Emergentists are interested in the emergence of language from language use, the use of routines and chunks, and the frequency of constructions in the input. Their preferred methodology is elicitation of naturally produced speech. Variationist sociolinguistics also prioritizes spontaneous language use by means of oral interviews. On occasion, they can use oral translation tasks or elicited production tasks to elicit the use of particular linguistic features that may not occur frequently or naturally in a conversation. Different types of sociolinguistic and attitudinal questionnaires are used to gather information about the external variables of interest, such as sex, age, region, education, etc.

Generative linguists assume that language is independent of cognition and it is largely innate. Input triggers the inborn capacity to acquire and use language but at the same time it does not fully determine it. Given these assumptions, their main focus is to demonstrate that children and adults have complex knowledge of properties of language not obvious or directly acquired from the input. They also seek to demonstrate that child and adult native speakers have knowledge of abstract rules and constraints on form and meanings assumed to be part of Universal Grammar. Many studies of young children also rely on speech samples from spontaneous production, and this method is appropriate to investigate grammatical phenomena that occur in almost every sentence (e.g., subject-verb agreement, gender, case, etc.). At the same time, generativists believe that language use is a very narrow window into linguistic competence because many constraints on grammar and interpretation cannot be easily tracked in the input or observed from production.

From the 1980s, the study of language acquisition within the generative framework began to combine the computational-representational approach developed by linguists and the methods of experimental psychology to draw conclusions about the underlying grammar (McDaniel, McKee, and Smith Cairns 1996). Today, experimental linguists working on L1, L2, and bilingual acquisition use judgments of the target language typical of formal linguistics as well as production and comprehension methods developed by experimental psychologists. Online and brain-based techniques derived from psycholinguistics and neurolinguistics typically used to investigate processing, implicit knowledge, and the representation of language are increasingly being adopted as well (e.g., Kwon *et al.* 2013).

Another hallmark of the generative linguistic approach applied to language acquisition is its focus on universals. As a result, this framework has guided a vast body of research on languages other than English and crosslinguistic research designs comparing different languages are more common in this approach than in others. Having data and analyses already available from less commonly studied languages is very beneficial for research on heritage languages of the same understudied languages.

In general, the methods used by the generative, emergentist, and variationist sociolinguistic approaches can be broadly characterized as quantitative because numbers and frequencies are calculated from linguistic behavior, measured quantitatively and analyzed statistically. The instruments used are applied to groups of people, and once the data are analyzed, the findings can be generalized to the population where the sample was drawn from. Much of the earliest work on child language acquisition from a psycholinguistic (cognitive-linguistic) perspective consisted of longitudinal case studies of one or at most three or four children (Brown 1973; Stern and Stern 1907). Stern and Stern (1907) is a diary study, with sporadic written notes of spontaneous production data. Advances in technology allowed Brown (1973) to collect spontaneous production data by audio recording the children systematically often. The case study approach has been very common in language attrition studies of adults and children as well (Kaufman and Aronoff 1991; Olshtain and Barzilay 1991; Vago 1991), especially with international adoptees (Isurin 2000; Montrul 2011; Nicoladis and Grabois 2002). Because language attrition is rare, there is significant individual variation, and it is hard to find many subjects who share several of the crucial variables that need to be controlled in an experimental study.

Case studies present a number of advantages according to Duff (2008b): the possibility to study atypical cases, conduct in-depth analysis based on different sources of data, gather extensive background information, and the possibility to carry out longitudinal observations. But case studies also have limitations. Data drawn from case studies may be seen as problematic for theories of typical behavior. They also present constraints on quantitative analysis and limitations about generalizability because it is not always possible to run inferential statistics. However, case studies of spontaneous production data are useful if the data are collected systematically and with careful attention to details that affect the quality of the resulting corpus. If a large corpus is available, such as the CHILDES database created by Brian MacWhinney (macw@cmu.edu) or corpora collected from individual children, quantitative measures can be obtained from the data. So, although many case studies are qualitative and descriptive (Parodi 2008; Wiley 2008), many others are quantitative, like the longitudinal studies conducted by Anderson (1999) and Silva-Corvalán (2014).

Experimental studies are also appropriate when the topic, population, and situation warrant it. Experimental research on heritage language speakers and learners has been gaining ground in the last decade, and in the rest of this chapter I will discuss broadly different research methods that have been applied or can be applied to the study of heritage language learners. Important considerations in studying heritage speakers are the use of control groups or baseline measures, types of proficiency tests, and other experiential and sociolinguistic variables that can also affect the design of any experiment.

In sum, different theoretical approaches to the study of language have specific assumptions about the nature of language and what needs to be explained. The research question guides the selection of methods and research designs. In general, both experimental and case studies are appropriate and have been used to investigate the bilingual development of heritage speakers and changes in their linguistic development over time. More recently, the use of experimental studies has become increasingly common to investigate the linguistic knowledge and language processing of heritage speakers cross-sectionally, as we will discuss in the rest of this chapter, and to compare the linguistic knowledge of heritage speakers with that of other learner populations. Experimental methods raise a number of challenges that we consider next.

6.2   What is the baseline?

A main issue in studies of heritage speakers is the standard for comparison against which we measure their linguistic knowledge or development. The ideal research design to trace how the languages of heritage speakers change or not over time would be a longitudinal study following the same individuals and documenting changes in their linguistic behavior from time 1 to time 2 or time *n*. This would also be a within-subject(s) design, where the same individual(s) is/are compared to each other. This approach has been common in case studies of monolingual (Brown 1973) and bilingual children (Anderson 1999; Silva-Corvalán 2014) or child and adult L2 learners followed longitudinally for several months or years (Lardiere 2007; Li 2012). Unfortunately, for a variety of practical reasons longitudinal studies are not usually feasible, and hence not very common. Consequently, many researchers adopt instead group studies that measure participants only one time and use several groups for comparison.

6.2.1   Longitudinal studies

An example of a longitudinal study with Spanish heritage speakers in the United States is Anderson (1999). Anderson looked at the decline of gender morphology in two normally developing Spanish-speaking siblings – Beatriz and Victoria. The siblings came to the United States at the ages of 3;6 (Beatriz) and 1;6 (Victoria) with their parents. Data collection consisted of naturalistic observations and started almost 3 years after arrival, when the children were 4;7 and 6;7, and ended 2 years later, when the children were 6;5 and 8;5. The two parents were from Puerto Rico, and Spanish was spoken at home. At the beginning of the study, the siblings spoke Spanish and English with each other,

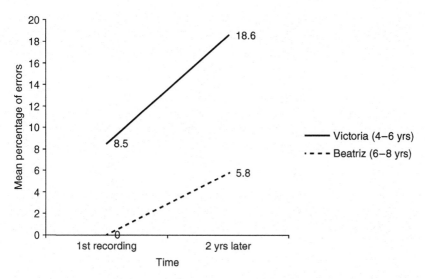

Figure 6.1. Mean percentage of errors with gender agreement in Spanish noun phrases in two Spanish-English bilingual children followed longitudinally (adapted from Anderson 1999).

but toward the end of the data collection period, the children shifted to using only English with each other and Spanish with their parents. When data collection started, the older sibling had some literacy skills in Spanish, and during the course of the study the two children developed literacy skills in English in daycare and preschool. The siblings were videotaped in play sessions with their parents every 1–2 months over a period of 22 months. The recordings were later transcribed, coded, and analyzed. Anderson (1999) focused on the development of gender agreement in noun phrases, which monolingual children control with close to 100% accuracy by the age of 3 years (Hernández Pina 1984; Pérez Pereira 1991), and found that the two siblings made errors with gender. The percentage of errors with gender increased markedly over time for the two children, as shown in Figure 6.1.

At the time of the first recording, Beatriz, the older sibling, produced gender agreement 100% correctly (0% error), like a typical monolingual child of her age (see Montrul 2004a). Two years later, she was producing 5.8% errors, which is very high for a native speaker. Victoria, the younger sibling, produced 8% errors during the first recording, which suggests that she had not yet mastered gender agreement at age-appropriate levels. By the end of the data collection period, Victoria's gender error rate increased steadily to 17.4%, 18.2%, and 25% in the last three sessions. That is, her error rate almost tripled. There is measurable change over time in the heritage language with respect to gender agreement, and each child is the baseline or control for herself.

To my knowledge, there are no longitudinal case studies of adult heritage speakers to examine whether they change over time as much as children. For that reason, I will give an example from L2 development that illustrates no change over time: Lardiere's (2007) study of fossilization in Patty, an adult L2 speaker whose L1 is Chinese. Patty was recorded after she had lived in the United States for 10 years and then again almost 9 years later. Lardiere (2007) examined Patty's use of past tense and agreement morphology, as well as other syntactic evidence of grammatical morphology in wh-questions and the nominal domain. Lardiere shows that there were no changes in Patty's grammar between the three recording sessions conducted 9 years apart. As shown in Figure 6.2, the results showed a clear dissociation between morphological and syntactic aspects of verbal inflection: Patty only supplied 4.41% of third person agreement morphology and 34.66% of past tense morphology in obligatory contexts (i.e., 95.6% and 65.34% errors), while production of overt subjects and nominative case was above 98% accurate.

These two examples show that longitudinal case studies are highly valuable and informative, and very suitable to extend to the acquisition of heritage languages if we are interested in understanding how their language changes in time and in response to fluctuations in input. Case studies analyzed in this way detect developments or changes in the characteristics of the target population at the individual level, and because they extend beyond a single moment in

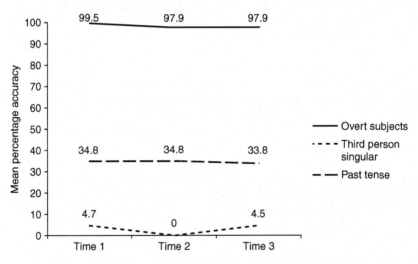

Figure 6.2. Mean percentage accuracy on overt subjects, third person singular, and past tense in English over time in an adult second language speaker (adapted from Lardiere 2007).

time, they can establish sequences of events. The most important feature of this design is that heritage speakers (or L2 learners) are their own baseline.

6.2.2   *Cross-sectional studies*

Snapshot studies or cross-sectional studies obtain observational measures only once and compare different population groups at a single point in time (for example, by collecting data at the same time from a group of 6-, 9,- and 12-year-old children). In order to make inferences about potential differences or changes in the linguistic behavior of the sample of interest, such as a group of heritage speakers, these studies must include one or more groups for baseline and comparison. Changes or differences are assessed (indirectly, of course) by comparing subjects between groups. To study language development in children or in adult L2 learners, for example, in addition to the baseline group usually consisting of a group of adult monolingual native speakers of the target language, these studies can include other experimental groups that differ on variables critical to understanding linguistic development, such as age at time of testing if it is a study of monolingual acquisition by children, or of different proficiency levels, if it is a study of L2 acquisition by adults. One advantage of a cross-sectional design is that it allows the comparison of many different variables at the same time. Studies that use the system of classifying speakers as first, second, or third generation speakers, such as Silva-Corvalán (1994), are considered cross-sectional studies.

It is possible to combine a longitudinal and a cross-sectional design. Merino (1983) carried out two related studies of language loss in Spanish-speaking children of Mexican origin, attending school exclusively in English, with no Spanish instruction. The first study was a cross-sectional design: it tested 41 bilingual children ranging from kindergarten to fourth grade (5–10 years old), and measured degree of language loss in comprehension and production in a variety of morphosyntactic features of Spanish (gender and number, tense, word order, relative clauses, conditional, and subjunctive) and their acquisition in English (equivalent or similar structures). Results showed steady chronological development – L2 acquisition – between the kindergarten children and the children in the higher grade in English (both in comprehension and production), but a significant decline – L1 attrition – in Spanish comprehension in the third and fourth grade children. These findings are summarized in Table 6.1.

Table 6.1 also shows that performance in the older children dropped dramatically in Spanish production (from 84% in first grade to 65% in fourth grade), while comprehension remained relatively stable (86% in first grade and 80% in fourth grade). With respect to the Spanish structures most affected in production, the children had significant difficulty with the subjunctive and

Table 6.1. *Mean accuracy scores on overall measures of production and comprehension in English and Spanish by Mexican-American children in a cross-sectional study (adapted from Merino 1983)*

Grade	N	Production		Comprehension	
		Spanish (%)	English (%)	Spanish (%)	English (%)
K	9	56	52	73	76
1	4	84	86	86	89
2	9	71	75	84	85
3	10	77	81	75	86
4	9	65	86	80	88

the conditional verb forms, the most complex forms. With the subjunctive in particular, the fourth graders performed at the level of the kindergarteners, and with the past tense, the fourth graders performed below the level of first graders.

For the longitudinal study, 32 children of the original sample were tested again 2 years later. The children were administered the same Spanish and English production and comprehension tests and their accuracy scores were compared to their scores obtained 2 years earlier. The results showed that performance in English continued to improve for all the Spanish-speaking children, while performance in Spanish deteriorated dramatically: 50% of the children showed loss of some sort; another 25% did not show any progress. The locus of the differences between the first and second test administrations was found in the past tense, the subjunctive, and relative clauses, as shown in Figure 6.3. Even when the Spanish-speaking children did not have full mastery of all these structures two years earlier, Merino suggested that the pattern of language was consistent with L1 attrition.

Hence, in the cross-sectional study the children were compared to other children who differed on age, and in the longitudinal study, the children were their own baseline, and were compared with each other over time. The two designs provide valuable information about linguistic change in time.

If the study does not measure the same participants at different times and instead includes a control group to establish that a change of some sort has taken place, a critical issue is who is the ideal baseline for heritage language research, or is there more than one? The vast majority of studies have compared the linguistic behavior of heritage speakers with either an "ideal monolingual" norm established from the theoretical and descriptive linguistics literature, or by also collecting linguistic behavior from monolingually raised native speakers assumed to speak the full variety of the target language. In some cases

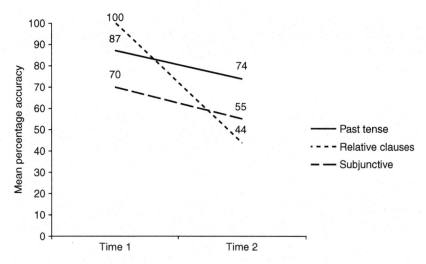

Figure 6.3. English L2 acquisition and Spanish L1 decline in Mexican-American children (n = 32): longitudinal study (adapted from Merino 1983).

the monolingually raised native speakers are tested in the country of origin (Montrul, Bhatt, and Girju 2015); in other cases they are immigrants who are recent arrivals (less than 5 years) in the host country (Montrul *et al.* 2013), yet in other cases the baseline consists of long-term immigrants, or the first generation immigrants who may or may not have undergone language attrition themselves but who are assumed to be the main source of input to the heritage speakers (Hulsen 2000; Polinsky 2006; Silva-Corvalán 1994). Crucially, the choice of baseline group should also be guided by the research question of the study, and justified accordingly. The language of these monolingually raised native speakers is compared to the language of heritage speakers. If significant quantitative and qualitative differences are found between these groups, then changes due to incomplete acquisition or attrition are assumed from the heritage speakers.

Language variety is a critical variable to take into account when choosing the best baseline group for the population of heritage speakers. Since many heritage speakers speak different regional varieties, or come from different socioeconomic backgrounds (SES), it is also important to control for language regional variety, level of education, and SES. Not much can be concluded about incomplete acquisition of phonology and morphosyntax if, for example, native speakers of European Portuguese are compared to heritage speakers of Brazilian Portuguese, when European and Brazilian Portuguese show important structural differences in their phonology and morphosyntax. Similarly, a control group of native speakers from Spain would be inappropriate to establish whether heritage speakers of Mexican background exhibit a different linguistic system, unless the grammatical feature of interest is not subject to dialectal variation. Controlling for regional variety becomes even more critical when testing heritage speakers of Arabic due to the ample diversity found in Arabic dialects. SES should also be controlled for because it contributes to vocabulary and morphosyntactic development (Hoff 2006). Comparing native speakers of Hindi with middle to high SES living in the United States to Hindi heritage speakers in England, who tend to be of low SES, would not be a methodologically sound comparison, unless the grammatical feature of interest is not subject to variation due to SES. At least for Spanish in the United States, Sánchez (1983) found that heritage speakers with low SES backgrounds used more Spanish daily than those with higher SES backgrounds, who were apparently more assimilated into the mainstream American culture.

In addition to the adult monolingual or L1 dominant-bilingual speaker, another necessary methodological comparison is that between adult heritage speakers and monolingual children of the heritage language. In the absence of longitudinal data from the same speaker(s), one way to assess incomplete acquisition of the L1 is to establish when in childhood a given grammatical phenomenon typically reaches adult norms. If adult heritage speakers are shown not to control the grammatical phenomenon to the same degree as monolingual or very fluent bilingual children – especially if onset of bilingualism occurred *before* the grammatical phenomenon is assumed to be fully acquired – then acquisition without mastery can be indirectly inferred in the adult heritage speaker. We will see examples of studies of this type in Chapter 7. One can rely on the already existing literature on L1 acquisition if the phenomenon and the language of interest have been studied. One problem of carrying out research with many heritage languages that are not main standard languages is that there may be very little to nonexisting research on the acquisition of these languages. Another problem is that the grammatical rules or the rules of language use may not be properly described in the available literature. Thus, collecting data from L1-acquiring children in the country of origin and of fully fluent adults becomes necessary before investigating the heritage language.

To summarize, there are different possibilities for the choice of a baseline group against which to compare the linguistic behavior of heritage speakers: heritage speakers themselves, monolingually raised native speakers of the same language variety in the country of origin, first generation immigrants with several years of residence in the host country or recent arrivals, and monolingual children in the country of origin. The choice of the baseline group, especially when it is monolingual, needs to be justified by the research question of the particular study.

Admittedly, using a baseline or comparison group of monolingually raised native speakers promotes the monolingual bias (Bhatt 2002; Ortega 2013) that is so prevalent in bilingualism and L2 acquisition research. Pascual y Cabo and Rothman (2012) view this tendency with concern for heritage language acquisition as well because the monolingual–bilingual comparison may contribute to unintended negative implications and value judgments about heritage speakers' grammars. This can be especially problematic when the monolingual speaker is perceived as superior to the bilingual speaker, both by researchers and the general public who may read the extant research (Bhatt 2002). I acknowledge that these ideological tendencies exist, but surmise that the monolingual–bilingual comparison cannot be avoided entirely, especially when it is necessary to answer specific and important research questions. If we did not compare monolinguals and bilinguals, we would not be able to answer whether simultaneous bilingual children start their acquisition process with one linguistic system like monolinguals or two. We would not be able to understand how one language influences the other during development, or to tease apart developmental versus transfer errors in second language and bilingual acquisition. We would not be able to understand diachronic language change in a language that develops independently versus change in the same language in contact with another language. We would not be able to understand what changes in L1 attrition in a bilingual environment when we cannot do a longitudinal study comparing the same individuals with each other. And as it turns out, the monolingual bias, as I discuss next, is quite pervasive in the field of bilingualism itself, where the most common research design to understand bilinguals has been *unilingual*, with a focus on *one language*, rather than bilingual by taking into account the interaction between the two languages.

6.3   Unilingual versus bilingual approach

If a bilingual has two languages, ideally we would study and compare the bilingual's command of the two languages either longitudinally or cross-sectionally. However, as Grosjean (1997, 2008) has pointed out, the vast majority of studies in bilingualism take a unilingual approach by which only one of the languages of the bilinguals is assessed, and this is especially true of studies of L2 acquisition and heritage speakers as well: most of the studies mentioned in Chapter 3 have evaluated the heritage language of heritage speakers in comparison to a baseline. Most of these studies assume (but do not test or confirm) that the majority language is the stronger language in heritage speakers. Testing knowledge of only one language of bilinguals provides a partial and fragmented picture, Grosjean claims, because the bilingual knowledge in its totality, which would include evaluating linguistic and communicative competence in the two languages as a whole, is not taken into account. Grosjean's holistic approach to bilingualism advocates the examination of the two languages of bilinguals at the same time. In situations of language contact, as in the case of heritage speakers, bilinguals usually acquire and use their languages with different people, for different purposes, and in different domains of life. Different aspects of life require different languages and this is reflected in what Grosjean termed the Complementarity Principle (Grosjean 2008, p. 23), illustrated in Figure 6.4.

The Complementarity Principle (Grosjean 1997) determines the fluency of bilinguals in their two or more languages. The level of fluency attained in a language (more precisely, in a language skill) will depend on the need for that language and will be domain specific. If reading and writing skills are not needed in a language, they will not be developed. If a language is spoken with a limited number of people in a reduced number of domains, it may be less fluent and more restricted than a language used extensively. If a language is never used for a particular purpose, it will not develop the linguistic properties needed for that purpose (specialized vocabulary, stylistic variety, some linguistic rules, etc.). Based on this reality, Grosjean suggested that the procedure used to evaluate the bilingual's competencies needs to be redefined. Bilinguals should be studied in terms of their total language repertoire, and the domains of use and the functions of their various languages should be taken into account. What this holistic view of bilingualism means empirically is that we should study bilinguals, and in our case heritage speakers, in their two languages, either cross-sectionally or longitudinally. This holistic or bilingual approach

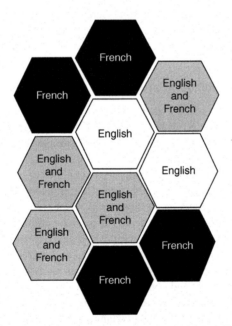

Figure 6.4. The Complementarity Principle (Grosjean 2008, p. 23)

would allow us to actually document more directly the impact of L2 learning on L1 loss, the mutual interaction and restructuring of the two languages throughout development, and the role of crosslinguistic influence as a function of dominance, among other important questions. Merino's study discussed in Section 6.2 is an example of this more holistic approach because the children were studied in the two languages. Three other recent examples of bilingual designs are Yeni-Komshian, Flege, and Liu (2000); Bylund, Abrahamsson, and Hyltenstam (2012) and Montrul and Ionin (2010).

Yeni-Komshian, Flege, and Liu (2000) investigated changes in pronunciation in 240 Korean heritage speakers in the United States who have learned English as L2 at different ages, and had immigrated to the United States between the ages of 1 and 23. The goals of the study were to examine age effects on L2 pronunciation, to determine if native L1 pronunciation is retained when an L2 is acquired, to compare the relative balance between L1 and L2 pronunciation proficiency, and to examine background factors that may contribute to different patterns of L1/L2 proficiencies. The heritage speakers were tested in Korean and in English, and were asked to produce sentences in each language, which were later rated and evaluated for foreign accent. The study also included two control groups, one of Korean speakers in Korea and one of American English speakers in the United States. The results showed a significant negative correlation between L1 and L2 pronunciation scores among those heritage speakers who had started L2 acquisition before puberty (i.e., before age 12), but not for those who started beyond this point. There was a tradeoff because as the Korean heritage speakers became more proficient in English over time, their Korean pronunciation became less native-like.

Bylund, Abrahamsson, and Hyltenstam (2012) used a similar design with 30 Spanish heritage speakers in Sweden to see whether some of the L1–L2 tradeoffs documented by Yeni-Komshian, Flege, and Liu (2000) in pronunciation would also obtain in morphosyntax. Their L2 acquisition began before the age of 12 (mean 6; range 1–11; SD 3.2) and their mean length of residence in Sweden was 23.7 years (range 10–41; SD 7.5). They completed grammaticality judgment tasks and cloze tests in Spanish and in Swedish. Fifteen monolingually raised native speakers of Spanish and 15 of Swedish were recruited as controls. Unlike Yeni-Komshian, Flege, and Liu (2000), there was no negative correlation between L2 proficiency and L1 proficiency in this study: the heritage speakers who were native-like in Swedish (the L2) were also native-like in Spanish (the L1). Language aptitude, as measured by an independent aptitude test, was also considered as a possible explanation of the main trends found.

Finally, Montrul and Ionin (2010) investigated the two languages of adult Spanish heritage speakers in the United States (Spanish and English) to assess both the dominance relationship between the languages, and potential transfer from the dominant language (English) onto the weaker language (Spanish). Written proficiency tests in each language verified that English was the stronger language of the Spanish heritage speakers. The study focused on knowledge of the meaning of definite articles with generic reference, which differ in the two languages. In English, definite articles have a specific meaning (*The elephants are big*), whereas in Spanish definite articles (*Los elefantes son grandes*) are used to denote generic (elephants in general) and definite expressions (these specific elephants). The 23 heritage speakers were tested on written comprehension tasks in English and in Spanish. A control group of monolingually raised Spanish speakers and another one of English speakers were recruited as well. Montrul and Ionin found that the heritage speakers' interpretation of English articles was native-like, assigning specific reference, and did not differ from the American English control group. However, the heritage speakers were less accurate in Spanish and differed from the Spanish control group: they assigned more specific than generic interpretations to definite articles in Spanish, unlike the Spanish native speakers. When the two languages of the heritage speakers were compared, there was transfer from English (the stronger language) onto Spanish (the weaker language). Many Spanish heritage speakers interpreted definite articles in Spanish with specific rather than generic reference, as they do in English.

The strength of these three studies is that they actually tested the dominance relationship between the two languages, and how one language influences the other in the same individuals, which is an ideal bilingual design to address the questions they set out to address. At the same time, these studies also included monolingually raised speakers as baseline, because these groups are still needed to validate the researcher-made tests and to understand and interpret basic differences between monolinguals and bilinguals in the two languages.

One can question, however, whether the control group of monolinguals is necessary at all when investigating bilinguals. Kupisch *et al.* (2013), who tested heritage speakers of German and French with French and German as majority languages on a variety of linguistic domains, did not include a group of native speakers of French, the language tested in the two bilingual groups, because the main goal of this study was to evaluate how the majority or minority status of the target language was related to the linguistic proficiency of the bilinguals in different structural aspects of their French. Yet, Kupisch *et al.* (2013, p. 24) felt compelled to justify the lack of a monolingual baseline group, suggesting that the notion of the native speaker cannot be avoided in bilingual research: "Even though we have not included a control group of monolingual native speakers in all experiments, we have made sure by consultation and pretesting with native speakers that our experiments and analyses were based on what monolingual native speakers accept as native-like behavior." Although Kupisch *et al.* included only bilingual participants, the study adopted a unilingual rather than a bilingual approach because overall proficiency in German, the other language of the bilinguals, was only taken into account as a grouping variable in the design. Knowledge of German was not tested with the same measures used to evaluate their competence in French.

In sum, despite the ideological and practical issues that relying on preestablished monolingual norms or using groups of monolingually raised native speakers present for the study of heritage speakers, the use of these baselines cannot be avoided. Groups of monolingually raised speakers or monolingual norms are required when one of the goals of research on heritage languages is to understand how this specific acquisition situation differs from other ones with less variability in the environment, or to establish that the measures used by researchers are valid and reliable when used with populations with relatively stable knowledge of language.

6.4   Defining and describing the population of heritage speakers

A significant challenge of studying heritage speakers is the wide variability in linguistic experience and contexts of acquisition. Therefore, it becomes crucial to describe their background characteristics in detail in order to interpret the results obtained. When reporting research, thorough description of the participants is required, especially to understand what type of bilinguals they are (see Figure 4.1 in Chapter 4) and their degree of proficiency in the heritage language. Background information is usually collected with detailed questionnaires. Estimates of language proficiency can also be obtained from language background questionnaires (see examples in Chapter 3), but it is highly recommended that proficiency be measured with available tests.

6.4.1   Background variables

Once participants are selected for a study, they need to be described in detail in order to gain insight into the extralinguistic variables that play a role in their linguistic knowledge at the time of testing. Basic information about gender, age at time of testing, age of acquisition of the languages, place of birth, educational level, current occupation, and level of education, among other topics, is a must. In addition, one may want to know the participants' age at immigration, languages of schooling, number and kind of relationships to other interlocutors in the heritage language (social networks), estimates of language ability and use in each language and exposure at different times in life or ages in childhood (e.g., preschool, elementary school, middle school, secondary school or high school, university), knowledge of other languages and their level of proficiency in each, languages of the parents, education and occupation of the parents, etc. A background questionnaire can also be used to elicit information about attitudes toward the heritage language, the vitality of the language, the perceived utility of the language, and ideas about whether and how to transmit the language to future generations.

Questions of this sort can be answered directly (e.g., *How old are you? When did you start learning your heritage language? How old were you when you started using English?*), or through binary choices (e.g., *Is your heritage language like your first language? yes, no*), gradable scales (e.g., *How often do you respond in your heritage language when your parents speak it to you? never, seldom, sometimes, often, always*), can-do scales (e.g., *I can read books in Spanish/ in English: 1, 2, 3, 4, 5*), or open-ended questions (e.g., *Why are you studying your heritage language in the classroom?*). Ethnic orientation questionnaires (Brooks and Nagy 2012) are used to elicit information about language use and identity. These questionnaires yield both quantifiable numerical data that can be reported as part of the required descriptive information in the study or can also be used to obtain measures of background variables to correlate with other dependent variables in the main statistical analysis. Qualitative data obtained through open-ended questions are not quantifiable but can be used to illustrate information from the perspective of the heritage speakers that cannot be conveyed with numbers (see statements by heritage speakers in Chapter 1).

Lengthy and detailed questionnaires of this sort are very common in sociolinguistic studies and are hardly used in language acquisition research or research with monolingual speakers. But because the sociolinguistic situation of heritage speakers is what defines them, sociolinguistic questionnaires are a must in studies of heritage speakers. In many situations, these questionnaires can be administered together with sociolinguistic interviews, which are likely to break the ice before and help put the heritage speakers at ease. They are also assumed to elicit the most unmonitored and implicit use of the language (Schmid and Jarvis 2014).

6.4.2 *Measuring proficiency*

Proficiency has to do with phonological, lexical, semantic, syntactic, and pragmatic ability in the language. Fluency is also a component of proficiency. Proficiency can actually be measured with a variety of linguistic tests. Although dominance is often estimated from questionnaires and background variables, and can be correlated with proficiency (Figure 3.2, Chapter 3), measuring proficiency in the two languages of heritage speakers is a way to measure language dominance.

Recall from Chapter 3 that heritage speakers can have differential proficiency in the heritage language in different language skills. They typically have more advanced oral and aural skills than reading and writing skills because they were exposed to the language at home. The levels of academic literacy in the heritage language also varies considerably depending on the availability of the language in the speech community, access to schooling, the writing system of the heritage language, the family socioeconomic class, and other environmental variables.

Language proficiency measures are widely used in L1 and L2 acquisition research to assess grammatical development, fluency, complexity, accuracy, and communicative competence in a given language. Some proficiency measures are standardized tests, but others are developed by researchers from samples of linguistic behavior. In principle, most of the oral and comprehension measures used with preliterate monolingual children can be used with heritage speakers, while not all the measures used with literate L2 learners may be appropriate, especially those requiring advanced reading comprehension and writing skills. For studies comparing L2 learners and heritage speakers, it is crucial to also take into account the degree of metalinguistic awareness involved in each task, since this is another variable that relates to the particular language learning experience of these two types of learners. Existing measures widely used in L1 and L2 acquisition need to be adapted for the heritage speaker population depending on the age and literacy level of the participants. We see some examples next.

6.4.2.1 Speech samples   With preliterate children and illiterate or low literacy adults, oral production samples are the best vehicles for obtaining proficiency measures in different languages. A common methodology used in L1, L2, and heritage language acquisition has been narration of the Frog Stories (Mayer 1969). Participants are asked to narrate the events portrayed in a wordless book about the adventures of a boy and his frog, by following the pictures. Speech samples are audio recorded, transcribed, and analyzed. From the speech collected, one can obtain the speech rate, which can be quickly measured as the word-per-minute output in spontaneous production. A lower speech rate results from difficulty with lexical access, hesitations, and disfluency, very common in heritage speakers with low productive ability in the language. A speaker can be asked to describe one set of pictures in their heritage language and another set in the majority language; doing so provides a standard of comparison for assessing individual variation in speech rate in the two languages.

Polinsky (2008a) used speech rate as a proficiency measure in her study of gender agreement in Russian heritage speakers. Recall from Chapter 3 that the heritage speakers in this study fell into two distinct groups: those who maintained the full three-gender system of noun classification (feminine, masculine, neuter) with various adjustments, and those who radically reanalyzed the baseline system as a two-gender system (masculine and feminine). Reanalysis of the baseline three-gender system as a two-gender system was strongly correlated with a lower speech rate, thus supporting the use of speech rate as a reliable diagnostic for identifying heritage speakers and tracking the variation in the population. Another study utilizing speech rate to compare the proficiency of heritage speakers and first generation immigrants is Brooks and Nagy (2012). Instead of using words per minute they used vowels per second as a proxy for syllables, and found that speech rate measured in this way was a good predictor of language choice and of generation: first generation immigrants had faster speech rates than second and third generation immigrants, the heritage speakers.

One can also perform morphosyntactic and lexical analyses of speech samples. For example, Mean Length of Utterance or MLU is a measure of linguistic productivity in young children. It is calculated by collecting 100 utterances spoken by a child and dividing the number of morphemes or words by the number of utterances (Bishop and Adams 1990; Rice 2010). A higher MLU is taken to indicate a higher level of language proficiency. A challenge that MLUs presents is that the measures are difficult to compare from language to language. This drawback is particularly evident when calculating MLUs in two typologically different languages, as Döpke (1998) and Yip and Mathews (2006) discuss for bilingual children. For example, an agglutinative language like Turkish, where a sentence can be expressed in a word with multiple morphemes, will yield a higher MLU at a comparable level of development than Chinese and isolating languages where one word typically has one morpheme. Even comparison between inflectional languages like English and French is difficult because morphological complexity varies from language to language. French is morphologically richer than English: a French article *le/la* contains information about definiteness and gender, whereas the definite article in English, *the*, only contains information about definiteness. MLUs are not usually used with older children and adults because their language is more complex than that of infants, and MLUs beyond a certain age are no longer informative or able to discriminate linguistic proficiency. However, MLUs are the most used measure with young children.

From speech samples produced by adults and older children, one can also calculate number of words, number of clauses, lexical diversity, syntactic complexity and variety, and grammatical accuracy, among others (Hulstijn 2011; Unsworth 2005). Daller *et al.* (2011) developed a way to objectively measure language proficiency and dominance from speech samples in adults, focusing on fluency. Their study included native speakers of Turkish learning German in a school setting and Turkish immigrant children who arrived in Germany before age 2 and returned to Turkey at around age 15. The returnees had been in Turkey for less than a year. Daller *et al.* administered a picture description task in the two languages of the bilinguals. The elicited speech samples were analyzed with regards to words per second and the Turkish speakers produced significantly more words in Turkish than the returnees (Turkish heritage speakers). Daller *et al.* concluded that the ratio of text length in each language (after computing typological differences between Turkish and German) was a good indicator of language proficiency because they validated their findings with other measures. For example, the speech samples were also analyzed through the computer program *Praat*, which revealed that the returnees were slower at retelling stories in Turkish than the Turkish speakers in Turkey. At least for the Turkish returnees, their proficiency scores in German and in Turkish correlated with other biographical variables, such as age of acquisition of German. In sum, from speech samples, Daller *et al.* were able to measure dominance in structurally different languages through measures of proficiency and fluency in each language.

Another oral proficiency measure that has been applied to heritage speakers of different languages, but whose validity is still controversial, is the oral proficiency interview (OPI), a standardized measure that follows the guidelines of the *American Council on the Teaching of Foreign Languages* guidelines (ACTFL). The OPI is widely used in L2 acquisition to assess functional ability in a language and has been used with some heritage speakers to establish its potential validity for this population. Valdés (1989) showed that when applied to Spanish heritage speakers in the United States, the OPI interview reveals the wide range of variability at all levels of language skills exhibited by heritage speakers. However, when applied to heritage speakers of Spanish, the OPI does not adequately capture the proficiency levels intended. In a study of Spanish and Russian heritage speakers in the United States Martin (2013) confirmed Valdés' assessment. For example, speakers rated in the ACTFL intermediate range must be able to engage in simple conversation, ask simple questions, and complete a simple, everyday transaction. Even at intermediate level on the ACTFL scale, heritage speakers may sound native-like in fluency and pronunciation but lack sustained functional ability to perform linguistic functions across a range of autobiographical and familiar situations using simple sentences and basic grammatical relationships. The text produced lacks connectors and organization and there is poor control of structures used to express time in the language.

Similar discrepancies between apparent fluency and language use emerged at advanced and superior levels. These speakers were unable to perform the task of producing well-organized extended discourse dealing with abstract concepts or situations. Instead, they would stay in the autobiographical discourse providing only examples from personal experience. Although they were more grammatically accurate than intermediate speakers, they lacked precise vocabulary and showed lexical interference from English. Because the OPI was designed to test functional proficiency in a second language, further research and testing is needed before any firm conclusions can be reached about its validity and implementation with heritage speakers.

All in all, valid proficiency measures can be obtained from speech samples from heritage speakers. Once obtained, these can be subjected to different types of analyses of grammatical accuracy, fluency, lexical diversity, and functional proficiency, in order to estimate heritage speakers' level of proficiency at the outset of a study.

6.4.2.2 Measures of vocabulary Polinsky (1997, 2000, 2006) and O'Grady *et al.* (2009) observed a strong correlation between a speaker's knowledge of lexical items, measured in terms of a basic word list, and the speaker's control of grammatical phenomena. Polinsky (2006) found that those Russian heritage speakers from her sample who knew more basic words from a list of 100 items exhibited better control of agreement, case markers, and subordination in spontaneous speech. Correlations between grammatical and lexical knowledge are further supported by results from several heritage languages, including Arabic (Albirini and Benmamoun 2014a) and Armenian (Godson 2004). This relationship between grammatical and lexical knowledge is not exclusive to heritage language competence; it has also been proposed for early child language (Fenson *et al.* 1994, 2000; Thal *et al.* 1997). If structural attrition and lexical proficiency are correlated, lexical proficiency scores, which are relatively easy to obtain, can serve as a basis for measuring proficiency in heritage speakers. The assumption behind using vocabulary tests as proficiency measures is that knowing more words results from more exposure and is a sign of proficiency skills.

A measure of lexical proficiency commonly used with children and adults is the standardized vocabulary tests such as the *Peabody Picture Vocabulary Test–Revised* (PPVT–IV; Dunn and Dunn 2007), which assess receptive vocabulary. This test is available in many other languages, including Spanish – the *Test de Vocabulario en Imágenes Peabody* (TVIP; Dunn *et al.* 1986). Each item has four simple illustrations arranged in a multiple choice format. The interviewer pronounces the word, and the child/adult points to the matching illustration. Items increase in difficulty and can be used with participants ranging from 3 to 70 years old. However, these tests are not available in many languages, and related languages that share many cognate words (e.g., Dutch and Frisian) may present a problem of reliability when using this test. A way around this limitation is for researchers to create another measure. Researcher-based tasks such as picture naming tasks have also been used as measures of proficiency in psycholinguistic studies (Kohnert, Bates, and Hernández 1999). Children and adults are shown pictures and are asked to name the pictures as fast as possible. The dependent variables speed and accuracy are taken as a reflection of lexical retrieval and access.

Lexical decision tasks and picture naming tasks have often been used in studies as a measure of proficiency in adult early bilinguals and L2 learners. Meara and Jones (1988) and Meara and Buxton (1987) found correlations for

L2 learners of English between accuracy on a lexical decision task and the Cambridge Proficiency Exam. Fairclough (2011) investigated whether the lexical decision task was a good tool for language placement for both L2 learners of Spanish and Spanish heritage speakers and she found high positive correlations between accuracy on a cloze test and accuracy on a lexical decision task in both groups. The results of Montrul and Foote (2014) were very similar to those reported by Fairclough (2011), confirming correlations between written proficiency as measured by parts of the DELE test (to be described in the next section) and accuracy on a lexical decision task close to $r = .70$ for the two groups.

Measures of lexical access during oral production have also been used to obtain measures of language dominance in heritage speakers. O'Grady *et al.* (2009) developed a "body-part naming task" as part of their Hawai'i Assessment of Language Access (HALA) project. This task, like the others in the HALA inventory, capitalizes on the fact that the speed with which bilingual speakers access lexical items and structure-building operations in their two languages offers a sensitive measure of relative language strength, or language dominance as defined by the authors. The HALA test also included a nature-image naming task, with words like *sun, moon, cloud, rain*, and a phrase building task, with noun phrases like *small cat, green leaf, pig's ear* and *shoe and fish*. The test included body parts because they have vocabulary counterparts in all languages, and the same applies to nature words. These words are relatively easy to elicit through pictures. In general, very low proficiency heritage speakers know body parts and basic nature terms, as these are the most resistant to language loss. In a pilot study conducted with Korean-English bilinguals, O'Grady *et al.* (2009) were able to establish a strong correlation between language dominance and naming times even in highly fluent bilingual speakers, in support of the central assumption underlying the HALA tests.

Montrul *et al.* (2013, 2014) used a similar measure of language proficiency in two studies investigating gender assignment and agreement in Spanish heritage speakers and L2 learners of Spanish in auditory and oral production tasks. The oral proficiency measure was a picture naming task (PNT), which the two experimental groups performed in English and in Spanish separately to establish their degree of language dominance, following O'Grady *et al.* (2009). Participants saw images on a computer screen and were prompted to say the name of the object as quickly as possible. In the Spanish naming task, participants were prompted by the instruction *diga*, and in the English version, by *say*. Both accuracy and reaction times were measured. Statistical analyses compared the three groups on speed and accuracy in the Spanish PNT. The heritage speakers and the L2 learners were also compared on their speed and accuracy of naming in English. The heritage speakers and the L2 learners did not differ from one another on either the Spanish PNT or the English PNT in terms of both speed and accuracy. The L2 learners and the heritage speakers were faster and more accurate naming words in English than naming the same words in Spanish, suggesting that they were dominant in English. These measures correlated positively with the results of the main tasks used to investigate knowledge of gender in the two groups.

Measures of lexical diversity and of knowledge of words in context, in addition to accuracy and speed of lexical retrieval, provide additional information about the lexical proficiency of heritage speakers. Lexical diversity is the range and variety of vocabulary deployed in a text by either a speaker or a writer. Treffers-Daller (2011) discusses a method to extract a measure of lexical diversity from speech samples in different languages (see also Treffers-Daller and Korybski 2016) using mathematical formulas. Mayer's (1969) frog stories were used to elicit oral narratives in the two languages of the two bilingual groups. Lexical diversity was measured by calculating a ratio of types and tokens in each language. These measures were used to compare two bilingual groups who differed in their age and context of learning French. Schmid and Jarvis (2014) used similar measures to investigate lexical attrition in first generation immigrants.

In sum, from speech samples and picture naming tasks that focus on vocabulary, reliable proficiency measures can be obtained for heritage speakers.

6.4.2.3 Other proficiency tests   Proficiency tests that rely on written language are most appropriate with literate monolingual and bilingual children and adults, and are typically used in L2 acquisition. It is common to group individuals in different levels of morphosyntactic proficiency by using vocabulary tasks, translation tasks, sentence completion tasks, cloze tests, and C-tests. Commonly used standardized tests like the TOEFL (*Test of English as a Foreign Language*) in English or the DELE (*Diploma de Español como Lengua Extranjera*) in Spanish contain subtests of this sort. When standardized measures are not available, researchers have resorted to developing cloze tests or C-tests as a fast, efficient, and reliable tool (Tremblay 2011). Cloze tests consist of a text with words deleted every n^{th} word (fixed-ratio deletion method) or deleted as a function of their nature or role in the text (rational deletion method). Participants are asked to provide the deleted word and answers can be multiple choice, exact word method, or acceptable word method. A C-test includes a number of short texts with at least twenty fill-in-the-blanks. From the second sentence onwards, every second half of every second word is deleted. Cloze tests and C-tests have been found to correlate highly with other standardized proficiency measures such as TOEFL (Bachman 1985; Brown 1983). With literate heritage speakers, compositions or written discourse can also be used to extract a measure of vocabulary knowledge and morphosyntactic complexity as it is done with speech samples (Henshaw 2013; Pérez Núñez (under review); Polio 2001).

The DELE (Diploma of Spanish as a Foreign Language) is the official accreditation degree of fluency in the Spanish language, issued and recognized by the Ministry of Education, Culture and Sports of Spain. This test has proven quite suitable to determine proficiency levels for L2 learners, and to predict linguistic performance in this population (Bruhn de Garavito 2002; White *et al.* 2004). It has also been extended to heritage speakers, and especially when the studies compare L2 learners and heritage speakers (Montrul 2005; Montrul *et al.* 2008; Montrul and Foote 2014; Montrul and Ionin 2012; Montrul *et al.* 2013; Montrul *et al.* 2014, among others).

But due to the fact that L2 learners and heritage speakers have very different language learning experiences, Carreira and Potowski (2011) have questioned the suitability of the DELE test to predict the linguistic performance of Spanish heritage speakers, especially those of apparent lower proficiency. The types of "explicit" metalinguistic awareness or knowledge required to complete language tests typical of second language classrooms or grammar courses (i.e., fill-in-the-blanks with the correct grammatical form, choose the correct form of the verb or the right word given a context, etc.) is developed and practiced at school, when children work on their literacy skills (reading and writing) and study language in language arts classes or in foreign language classrooms.

If we want to know how L2 learners differ from heritage speakers we need a tool to compare them, and we have to apply the same to both groups. Extending the tools that we have to another population is one way to start. Assessing and modifying the tools if they do not measure what we expect them to measure would be the next step, but first we need to establish whether the tools are valid and suitable or not. Several subsequent studies have used parts of the DELE test or a similar type of test to divide heritage speakers into proficiency groups (Cuza and Frank 2011; de Prada Pérez and Pascual y Cabo 2011) or to compare heritage speakers and L2 learners of Spanish to establish that the two groups of bilinguals were comparable at the outset of the studies (Alarcón 2011). In all these studies the written proficiency measure predicted the participants' accuracy in the linguistic area of focus. Finally, when standardized proficiency tests are not available, as may be the case for many heritage languages, researchers have constructed their own cloze tests as proficiency measures and have validated them with native speakers. This has been done for Hindi and Romanian, for example, by Montrul, Bhatt and Girju (2015).

In short, some available standardized proficiency tests can be used with heritage speakers, depending on the degree of literacy required to perform the task. Speech samples are very useful to extract measures of fluency (speech rate), lexical diversity and proficiency, and morphosyntactic complexity, which can all be used to establish proficiency in the heritage language. Especially for languages for which other standardized measures do not practically exist,

Table 6.2. *Examples of different proficiency tests and measures*

Type of tasks	Examples and what they measure	Other notes

Speech samples	Word/syllable per minute (fluency)
	Voice Onset Time (VOT)
	  (pronunciation)
	Lexical diversity (types and tokens)
	Grammatical complexity
	  (morphosyntax)
		
		Mean Length of Utterance
		  (MLU)
		Appropriate for children
		  younger than 4

Standardized oral tests	Oral Proficiency Interview (OPI)	Available in multiple languages Developed for L2 acquisition

Vocabulary tasks	Standardized receptive vocabulary tests
	  (Peabody Picture Vocabulary Task
	  or PPVT)
	Lexical decision tasks
	  (accuracy and reaction times)
	Picture naming task (accuracy and
	  reaction times)
	Body-part naming and phrase building
	  task (accuracy and reaction times)
	Multiple choice vocabulary tasks
	  (offline written recognition)
		Available in multiple languages
		
		Researcher-made
		
		Researcher-made
		
		HALA test developed by
		  William O'Grady in Hawaii
		Standardized tests for L2
		  learners

Written proficiency tasks	Cloze test/ C-test	Part of standardized test or researcher-made

researchers can create their own tasks based on what is known from previous research, such as picture naming tasks, lexical decision tasks, and cloze tests, and validate them and normalize them with monolingually raised native speakers before applying them to heritage speakers. Table 6.2 summarizes the measures discussed. This list is not exhaustive, of course.

6.5   Experimental data and types of tasks

With the advent of new technologies and growing interest in describing and explaining the linguistic knowledge of "real" instead of "ideal" speakers, linguistics and language acquisition have become increasingly more experimental in recent years, relying on methods from psychology, neuroscience, sociology and education, among other disciplines, to investigate linguistic performance and to reach conclusions about linguistic competence and processing in heritage languages. A number of recent books and review articles in prominent journals describe in detail many of the different tasks that can be used to elicit linguistic performance and knowledge from monolingual and bilingual children and adults, both healthy and language-impaired populations (Blom and Unsworth 2010; Crain and Thornton 1998; Ionin 2013; Ionin and Zyzik in press; Mackey and Gass 2012; McDonough and Trofimovich 2008; Sekerina, Fernández and Clahsen 2008; VanPatten and Jegerski 2010, among many others). Many of the methods described in these volumes are eminently suitable and adaptable to use with the heritage speaker population. The last decade has in fact witnessed an explosion of experimental research using many of these techniques applied to heritage languages.

Experimental tasks can be broadly derived into two categories: offline and online. Offline tasks include behavioral tasks such as comprehension and judgment tasks that measure the final response. Examples of offline tasks are written comprehension tasks, written production tasks, and judgment tasks usually performed under no time pressure with paper and pencil or with computer programs that record the answer. Online tasks, by contrast, aim to capture the dynamics of language processing and typically measure the time it takes to make a response. Oral production data are also considered online data because production unfolds over time. They additionally yield simultaneous information about the unfolding of the decision-making process and the processing of linguistic stimuli as it happens. Online tasks that measure reaction times, eye gazes, and brain activity require specialized equipment and technology. Online and offline tasks used with preliterate children, which typically minimize the role of metalinguistic awareness, are very appropriate to use with child heritage speakers and adult heritage speakers with low literacy skills in the heritage language. We focus on some next.

6.5.1 Oral production and auditory comprehension tasks

When studying heritage speakers of languages that have not been studied before, or to obtain general information about the linguistic ability of heritage speakers, one can always start by eliciting speech from oral narratives or video narration. In fact, Schmid and Jarvis (2014) found that free speech seems to be the most reliable method to capture implicit knowledge in individuals undergoing attrition. The Frog Stories (Mayer 1969) and similar stories have been widely used in many languages, with child learners, L2 learners, and with child and adult heritage speakers (Berman and Slobin 1994; Polinsky 2008b; Sánchez 2003). From these speech samples, one can identify general trends in the data and can observe whether there are patterns that merit being pursued with further experimentation. One limitation of these data is that the use of vocabulary and structures is constrained by the task, the topic, and the discourse. While many features of language are frequent in these data, such as agreement, word order, case marking, etc., infrequent structures, specific vocabulary, or other specific structures of interest may not show up. It is of course possible to conclude that speakers have knowledge of structures they produce, but nothing can be concluded from the absence of a structure in a speech sample. Therefore, elicited production and comprehension tasks, which are set up so that participants produce/comprehend the structures of interest as required by the discourse context and situation, are another option to be used by themselves or in conjunction with a narrative task.

A production task assesses the ability to use particular words, affixes, and structural patterns in one's own speech, whereas a comprehension test assesses the ability to understand particular words, affixes, and structural patterns in the speech of others. The assumption behind these tests is that production and comprehension of a given form reflect abstract linguistic representation of that form. If a person produces and understands a given form, it is because that form is part of the person's grammatical knowledge. However, the relationship between comprehension and production as mediated by underlying linguistic knowledge is not straightforward (see special issue of *Lingua* 120(8) on the relationship between production and comprehension). In child language, at least the first 2 years of life, comprehension seems to precede production, but after age 3 there are studies showing that children can produce grammatical forms but they do not really understand the grammatical meaning associated with that form (Johnson, de Villiers, and Seymour 2005; Miller and Schmitt 2014).

Montrul and Sánchez-Walker (2013) used an elicited production task to investigate productive knowledge of case marking in child and adult Spanish heritage speakers. Participants were presented with a PowerPoint presentation with twenty-eight pictures (one per slide) showing people and children's characters performing an action with animate or inanimate objects. The participants were required to form a sentence describing the picture using the words provided. The design consisted of 7 verbs appearing with animate objects (e.g., *atacar* "attack," *ayudar* "help"), 7 verbs that take inanimate objects (e.g., *beber* "drink," *comprar* "buy"), and 7 verbs taking animate or inanimate objects (e.g., *ver* "see," *tocar* "touch"). There were 28 target images (14 depicting animate objects and 14 depicting inanimate objects). Each image represented a character doing something, for example, Mafalda reading a book or Buzz Lightyear carrying Woody. The expected response for the slide with the inanimate object was *a Mafalda leyó el libro* "Mafalda read the book." The expected response for the slide with the animate object was *a Buzz llevó a Woody*, "Buzz carried Woody." The production of the heritage speakers was recorded and then transcribed for analysis of presence/ omission of "a" marking with animate, specific direct objects with different verbs. Accuracy rates on production of "a" marking were calculated for all participants.

When the grammaticality or acceptability of sentences depends on a specific context, sentences are asked to be judged in context, and the Picture Matching Task (PMT) has been widely used in L1 acquisition research (Gerken and Shady 1996; Schmitt and Miller 2010) to test these cases with passives, subject and object relative clauses, binding relations, and complementation. The PMT presents a single sentence in the context of two or more pictures, and the learner's job is to match the sentence to the correct picture. The successful matching of the sentence to the correct picture depends on the syntactic structure assigned to the sentence. O'Grady, Lee, and Choo (2001) investigated the comprehension of subject and object relative clauses by Korean heritage speakers using a picture matching comprehension task, and so did Polinsky (2011). In these studies, heritage speakers of Korean and Russian saw two pictures and had to choose the picture that matched the sentence they heard. Correct and incorrect choices were counted to obtain accuracy scores. In a recent study, Sánchez-Walker (2013) used a task similar to the ones used by O'Grady *et al.* and Polinsky to examine comprehension of subject and object relative clauses in Spanish, except that the task was presented via the psycholinguistics program E-Prime on a computer screen. In addition to recording accuracy, using E-Prime allowed Sánchez-Walker to collect information about processing, as measured by reaction times. All experimental items were embedded in a sentence starting with *Ésta/Éste es* "this is." Both NPs shown in the experimental sentences could be relativized as subject or object. Participants heard one of the sentences and had to choose the correct picture.

All relative clauses were created as reversible plausible contexts in which either NP could perform the action expressed by the verb, as in (1) and (2). Participants heard a sentence and were presented with two pictures, A and B. They were asked to choose the picture that described the sentence they heard, as shown in Figure 6.5. To make the correct choice, participants needed to pay attention to word order and verbal agreement in each sentence.

Accuracy was recorded for all sentences. Reaction times were also recorded to see if object relative clauses would take longer to process than subject relative clauses.

Another study of aural comprehension and picture matching with very low proficiency heritage speakers of Russian is Sekerina and Trueswell (2011). The experiments in this study involved the visual world paradigm investigated with eye-tracking technology. The study asked how monolingual Russian speakers and heritage speakers of Russian process contrastiveness online in split constituents in Russian.

The participants were presented with 5 colored cardboard objects/shapes (stars, birds, frogs) arranged in a 3 × 3 board, as shown in Figure 6.6 and

A   B

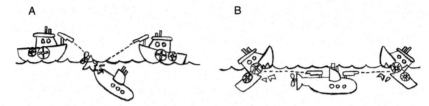

Figure 6.5. Example of pictures and sentences used in a Picture Matching Task (Sánchez-Walker 2013).

Subject Relative Clauses

(1) a. Éste es el submarino que hundió los barcos.   (V-O)
        This is the submarine$_{sg}$ that sank$_{sg}$ the boats
     b. Éste es el submarino que los barcos hundió.   (O-V)
        *This is the submarine$_{sg}$ that the boats sank$_{sg}$

Object Relative Clauses

(2) a. Éste es el submarino que los barcos hundieron.   (S-V)
        This is the submarine that the boats$_{pl}$ sank$_{pl}$
     b. Éste es el submarino que hundieron los barcos.   (V-S)
        *This is the submarine that sank$_{pl}$ the boats$_{pl}$

6.7. The heritage speakers heard sentences that instructed them to move particular objects and move them to an open position on the board. The instructions included contrasts of color or object (red star, red bird, blue bird), but the phrases also varied in word order and stress, as shown in (3).

In order to perform the instructions, the participants needed to notice and process case morphology. The rich case morphology of Russian allows speakers to track the grammatical role of the noun phrase. In all sentences in (3) *krasnuju zvezdočku* "redACC-FEM starACC-FEM" is the direct object regardless of its position in the sentence because it is marked with the accusative case, which is the default case for direct objects in Russian. Example (3a) represents the canonical word order of Russian, with the direct object *red star* following the verb while (3b) expresses the same proposition, and contrastiveness in expressed through word order permutations or scrambling. Example (3c) is a grammatically marked option of split scrambling, encoding contrastiveness with split constituents by separating the adjective from the head noun and moving it to sentence-initial position. Despite the surface word order variation, the three examples mean the same in terms of their truth value.

Sekerina and Trueswell investigated whether highly proficient heritage Russian speakers (Experiment 2) would have difficulty processing contrastive constituents in Russian compared to Russian monolinguals (Experiment 1). They used the visual world paradigm (VWP) that is sensitive to dynamics of real-time activation of referent, and offers a number of advantages for heritage speakers: it is a naturalistic task relying on oral comprehension, one of the strongest skills in heritage speakers, and does not require metalinguistic reflection. Eye movements reliably tap into the earliest phases of online processing, and have revealed robust correlations with linguistic behavior (eye movements are launched to the referent as soon as it is mentioned in speech). Sekerina and Trueswell also explored a relationship between factors such as years of exposure to Russian and self-rated proficiency that could possibly affect variability in processing efficiency in these bilinguals.

To summarize thus far, these examples illustrate some of the methodological possibilities available to use with heritage speakers, but there are many other suitable tests. Depending on the age and level of literacy of the heritage speakers, these and other production and comprehension tasks can also be done in the written modality. Other tasks include measures of elicited oral/written production (which cover a wide range, from fill-in-the-blank tests to elicited imitation tasks) as well as psycholinguistic tools (such as self-paced reading and eye-tracking) with auditory, visual, or bimodal presentation of linguistic materials.

In general, production and comprehension tasks yield valuable information about the linguistic knowledge of a language learner or speaker: if a learner/speaker produces and understands a particular linguistic expression (such as a word, a phrase, or a sentence), it is reasonable to conclude that this expression is part of the learner's/speaker's linguistic knowledge. At the same time, production and comprehension data have limitations. If a learner does not produce a particular word, phrase or sentence, or has made a production error, this does not necessarily reflect a lack of linguistic knowledge: factors such as frequency of the form and their availability for fast retrieval from memory may be responsible. Conversely, the production of certain frequent formulaic expressions may reflect rote memorization rather than linguistic knowledge. Comprehension-production dissociations are also common: sometimes learners comprehend structures that they do not produce, or produce linguistic forms that they do not fully understand. Sometimes, the structures of interest do not simply occur. For these reasons, researchers may use other data collection tools to study learners' linguistic knowledge, such as grammaticality judgment and interpretation tasks.

6.5.2   Judgment, preference and interpretation tasks

Grammaticality or acceptability judgment tasks (GJTs or AJTs) present lists of words, phrases or sentences in isolation and require participants to make a judgment based on their intuitions about the grammaticality or acceptability of the word, phrase or sentence. The acceptability judgment task is appropriate when sentences in isolation are clearly correct or incorrect, violating

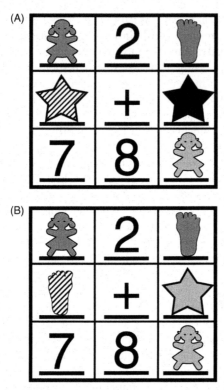

Figure 6.6. The two types of scenes compared in Experiment 1 (Monolinguals) and 2 (Bilingual HL Russian). (A) The 1-Contrast scene: Target red star (position 6), Color Competitor red bird (position 7), Target's contrast object yellow star (position 1), two distracters, blue frog and green frog (positions 2 and 8). (B) The 2-Contrast scene is the same except that the blue frog (position 2) has been replaced by a blue bird that serves as the contrast object for the Color Competitor (position 7) (Figure 1 from Sekerina and Trueswell 2011).

(3) a. Položite KRAS-nuju zvezdočk-u v Poziciju 4.
        Put   red-ACC.FEM star-ACC.FEM in Position 4
     b. KRASnuju   zvezdočku položite v Poziciju 4.
        REDACC-FEM starACC-FEM put in Position 4
     c. KRASnuju   položite zvezdočku v Poziciju 4.
        REDACC-FEM put   starACC-FEM in Position 4
        "Put the RED star in Position 4."

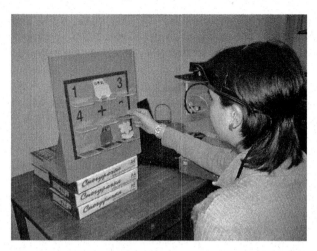

Figure 6.7. Eye-tracking system used in Sekerina and Trueswell (2011).

some grammatical rule of the language. According to Cowart (1997), however, *grammaticality* is an abstract concept: a sentence is either grammatical or not grammatical in a given grammar, but this cannot be tested directly. Experimental tasks can test whether the participant accepts a given sentence, and the speakers' judgments can consequently be used to make inferences about grammaticality.

The use of acceptability judgments as a window into grammaticality and linguistic competence has a long tradition in generative linguistics. Due to its focus on abstract linguistic knowledge rather than use, and on finding evidence that native speakers have implicit knowledge of rules and constraints of their own language that are not obvious in the input, generative linguistics is known for its extensive reliance on acceptability judgments. Native speakers' judgments of (un)acceptability are taken as primary evidence for the nature of speakers' linguistic competence: A sentence which is judged as acceptable by a native speaker is part of that speaker's mental grammar, while a sentence which is judged as unacceptable is in violation of a linguistic rule of the speaker's mental grammar. Generative syntactic theory has traditionally relied on introspective acceptability judgments rather than controlled experiments, on the assumption that the judgments of an individual native speaker are representative of those of other native speakers. This assumption has been challenged recently, and use of carefully designed AJTs with groups of adult native speakers is becoming increasingly common (Sprouse and Almeida 2012).

Variationist sociolinguistic methodologies do not accept grammaticality judgments and intuitional data as main sources of linguistic knowledge because they are not considered reliable (Silva-Corvalán 2001). The claim is that grammaticality judgments do not always reflect what speakers know and use; sometimes speakers respond according to what they think they should say or what should be said, letting prescriptive and other attitudinal factors affect their responses. This is important when the tests include sentences that may be grammatical in some dialects and not in others. Sociolinguists prefer instead spontaneous speech in general, elicited from oral interviews and naturally occurring conversations.

Acceptability judgments have been widely used in experimental methods applied on older children and L2 learners, where individual variation and other linguistic variables can be controlled. One may question the reliability of judgments elicited from L1 learners and heritage speakers with low literacy and metalinguistic awareness, yet acceptability judgment tasks have been used successfully with heritage speakers of different languages and of different levels of literacy and of proficiency in the heritage languages (Au *et al.* 2002; Cuza and Frank 2013; Montrul 2010; Montrul, Bhatt, and Bhatia 2012; Sherkina-Lieber 2011, among others). That is, in these studies, the judgments elicited from the heritage speakers did not show response biases or indeterminacy characteristic of somebody who has difficulty performing the task. If heritage speakers are relatively illiterate, aural acceptability judgment tasks with auditory stimulus presentation are appropriate, as used with young children. An example of a study with heritage speakers with receptive command of Inuttitut is Sherkina-Lieber (2011), mentioned in Chapter 3. If heritage speakers can read and write in the language, written acceptability judgment tasks are appropriate. Montrul and Bowles (2009) and Montrul (2010) used written acceptability judgment tasks with heritage speakers of Spanish ranging from low to advanced proficiency in Spanish, who could read and write in the language. And if the heritage speakers range in level of literacy, then bimodal presentation where sentences are given in written and auditory form simultaneously are ideal. Montrul, Bhatt, and Bhatia's (2012) study with Hindi heritage speakers used a bimodal acceptability judgment task. Therefore, level of literacy is crucial when deciding on the modality of the task (auditory/visual) with heritage speakers.

Another defining characteristic of many heritage speakers is that they have underdeveloped metalinguistic skills in their heritage language (Bowles 2011; Correa 2011). Therefore, the other key issue to consider when using acceptability judgment tasks with heritage speakers is the degree of metalinguistic awareness and reflection required of the task. The way the stimuli are presented or how the responses are elicited and measured contribute to making the task more implicit (relying more on intuition) or more explicit (relying on learned and verbalized grammatical rules). That is, acceptability judgment tasks vary widely in their form. Ellis (2005) lists tasks according to the degree of implicit or explicit knowledge required to complete them. Written untimed tasks give participants ample opportunity to read the sentences several times and think about them before making a final judgment. Instructed heritage speakers and HL learners have opportunities to recall grammatical rules learned and practiced in class, for example, to answer the test. On the other hand, aural acceptability judgment tasks do not leave time for conscious reflection, and require a more implicit response. If the auditory or written acceptability judgment task is timed, and the participant has 2–4 seconds to answer before the stimulus sentence disappears, this method leaves less time for reflection and the judgments can be more implicit than the judgments obtained with tasks that do not impose a time limit on each answer.

Untimed tasks are more appropriate for some populations of heritage speakers than others, depending on their level of education and technical skills. For example, computerized tasks may be appropriate for heritage speakers who are studying at a university but less so for heritage speakers of aboriginal communities like Quechua, Inuttitut, or Dyirbal, for whom online tasks would not be suitable. Cultural differences of this sort are important to take into account when collecting data with different groups of heritage speakers and in different parts of the world.

In addition to modality and timing, the instructions and stimulus presentation also contribute to making the task more or less metalinguistic. For example, sentences can be presented in isolation, or they can be presented in minimal pairs, contrasting the key grammatical feature of interest. When sentences are presented in isolation (with no preceding context) participants are asked to judge each sentence individually, one by one, and they are also told not to compare sentences or go back and change answers. Some AJTs additionally ask participants to indicate their degree of certainty. The sentences in a traditional AJT are designed to be either grammatically well-formed, or in violation of a rule of morphology (as in (4a), in which the agreement on the verb is missing) or syntax (as in (4b), which contains illicit adverb placement).

(4)   a.*Mary come to visit everyday
        b.*Mary watches often television.

Sherkina-Lieber (2011) presented the sentences to Inuttitut heritage speakers in auditory modality and as minimal pairs, as in (5).

(5)   a. Grammatical: N-sg V-3sg
        Sugusik   sini-juk
        child-ABS sleep-PART.3SG
        "The/a child is sleeping."
        b. Ungrammatical: *N-SG V-3PL
        *Sugusik sini-juit5
        child-ABS sleep-PART.3PL

Presenting the sentences one by one may prompt a more implicit response than when sentences are presented in pairs, because in the latter the participant's attention is explicitly drawn to the main grammatical difference between the sentences, such as number mismatch in subject-verb agreement in (5b), and the participant has to engage in a conscious process of comparison. Similarly, the instructions of an AJT can simply ask the participants to decide based on their intuition whether the sentences provided are acceptable or unacceptable, or it can ask the participants to do the same and in the case of unacceptable sentences require the participants to circle the error or even correct it. The latter instruction engages metalinguistic reflection more than just asking participants to express a judgment.

Sometimes, the acceptability of a sentence depends on its context. In this case, acceptability judgment task, are not appropriate. A methodology designed to test constraints on meaning in child language acquisition is the Truth Value Judgment Task (TVJT) (Crain and Thornton 1998; Gordon 1996), and this methodology has been extended to adult L2 acquisition (Ionin and Montrul 2010; White *et al.* 1997) and to heritage language acquisition (Kim, Montrul, and Yoon 2009; Montrul and Ionin 2012). In this task, participants are asked to judge the truth of the target sentence in the context of a preceding story, picture, or video. TVJTs used with young children are invariably oral in format, and typically involve a story either acted out with toys or told via a series of pictures. In the case of adult, literate L2 learners, and literate heritage speakers, the story can be provided in written form, possibly (but not necessarily) accompanied by a picture. Because TVJTs focus on the meaning of the sentence, they are most appropriate for investigating phenomena at the syntax–semantics interface (e.g., interpretation of pronouns and reflexives, tense and aspect, definite and indefinite noun phrases, overt and null subject pronouns). In a correctly designed TVJT, the interpretation of a sentence as true or false in a given context depends on the syntactic structure assigned to the sentence.

For example, Kim, Montrul, and Yoon (2009) tested the interpretation of the anaphors *caki*, *casin*, and *caki-casin* in Korean heritage speakers in the United States. The main instrument was a TVJT with pictures and written sentences. Examples of the sentences and pictures used are shown in (6).

(6)   Cheli-nun [Minswu-ka *caki*-ul   kuli-ess-ta-ko] malhay-ss-ta
      Cheli-TOP   Minswu-NOM self-ACC   draw-PAST-DECL-COMP said
      "Cheli said that Minswu drew himself."

In half of the sentences the picture used forced a locally bound interpretation for the reflexive, while for the other half, the picture forced a long-distance interpretation. All sentences were grammatical. The participants were asked to judge whether each sentence was a true description of the picture. As mentioned in Chapter 3, the heritage speakers seemed to have a two-way contrast

a. Long distance binding   b. Local binding

in their anaphor system because they treated *caki* differently from *casin* and *caki-casin*, but not between *casin* and *caki-casin*, like the monolingual controls and the late bilinguals.

Kim, Kim, Montrul and Yoon (2014) revisited the question of whether heritage speakers of Korean discriminate among reflexives by binding distance preference in online processing as well and used a visual world paradigm with eye-tracking technology. Participants listened to aural stimuli while looking at a visual display on a monitor. The visual display contained four images. For example, an image of Shrek, an image of Peter Pan, an image of a sheet of paper, and an image of a piece of cheese were displayed. An offline antecedent identification task measured final interpretations assigned to the reflexives. The two tasks used the same experimental materials, which consisted of Korean sentences with the three anaphors, as shown in (7).

(7)   a. 피터팬은 [슈렉이 넓은 종이에 자기(caki)를 멋있게 그렸
         다고] 말했습니다.
      b. 피터팬은 [슈렉이 넓은 종이에 자신(casin)을 멋있게 그렸
         다고] 말했습니다.
      c. 피터팬은 [슈렉이 넓은 종이에 자기자신(caki-casin)을 멋
         있게 그렸다고] 말했습니다.
      Peter Pan [Shrek on a wide paper self nicely drew] said
      (-TOP)   (-NOM)   (-ACC)
      "Peter Pan said Shrek drew himself nicely on a big piece of paper."

After the stimulus sentence, the participants heard a sentence such as "Shrek drew a picture" and had to indicate whether the sentence was true or false. Proportions of fixations to the two subject pictures (matrix subject pictures versus embedded subject pictures) were compared, from the onset of the reflexives.

An important variation of the traditional AJT is a task in which participants are asked to choose between two (or more) related sentences or forms in the target language, that is, a preference task. Preference tasks can be used to test grammaticality (i.e., one form is grammatically correct while the other is not) as well as interpretation (i.e., one form expresses the target interpretation better than another). If interpretation is targeted, then the choice of form is generally preceded by some context. The nature of the response can vary as well; the contrast may be between words, phrases, or sentences. Finally, in any preference task, the researchers must decide whether the participants can choose only one option, both, or neither.

Montrul and Ionin (2012) designed a picture-sentence matching task (PSMT) to test the interpretation of definite and possessive determiners in alienable and inalienable possession contexts in Spanish heritage speakers. Each test item consisted of two pictures, A and B, presented side by side with only one sentence underneath. Participants were instructed to read the sentence and decide whether it described picture A, picture B, or both pictures, by circling one of the three options, as in (8).

A   **B**

(8) a. Pedro levantó la mano   A   B   Both
        "Peter raised   the hand."
     b. Pedro levantó su mano   A   B   Both
        "Peter raised   his hand."

In English, the target response for a sentence like (8a) with a definite determiner would be *B*, the alienable possession interpretation; the target response for a sentence like (8b) with the possessive determiner would be *A*, the inalienable possession interpretation. In Spanish, by contrast, both definite and possessive determiners are grammatical with an inalienable possession interpretation. Hence, *A* or *both* was the expected response for sentence (8a) with the definite determiner, whereas *B* or *both* was the expected response for sentence (8b) with the possessive.

Since the PSMT tests acceptance of both determiner types, but does not test the *grammatical preference* for one over the other, Montrul and Ionin (2012) created another task, the sentence-picture acceptability task (SPAT). The test used the target sentences and pictures from the PSMT, except that each item in this task presented a single picture with two sentences underneath, one with a definite determiner (e.g., *Pedro levantó la mano* "Peter raised the hand") and the other with a possessive determiner (e.g., *Pedro levantó su mano* "Peter raised his hand"). Participants had to judge the acceptability of each sentence as a description of the picture on a five-point scale, where 1 = unacceptable and 5 = acceptable. Sample pictures and sentences in the SPAT appear in (9) and (10).

(9) a. Pedro levantó la mano   1   2   3   4   5
     b. Pedro levantó su mano   1   2   3   4   5
                                     unacceptable   acceptable

(10) a. Pedro levantó la mano   1   2   3   4   5
     b. Pedro levantó su mano   1   2   3   4   5
                                    unacceptable   acceptable

Native speakers were expected to rate sentences with definite articles slightly higher than sentences with possessives in the context of an inalienable possession picture, but probably lower than sentences with possessives in the context of an alienable possession picture.

Valenzuela *et al.* (2012) used a written preference task with heritage speakers of Spanish to investigate code-switching. The heritage speakers were asked to choose phrases and sentences that sounded most natural to them. Because the acceptability of code-switching depends on context and the interlocutors, the items on the preference task included a brief dialogue between bilingual speakers followed by a choice of determiner phrases that mixed a Spanish determiner and a noun in English (e.g., *la party* or *el party*), as in (11).

(11)   Juan: I had lots of fun anoche, pues, I ran into Sergio.
       Elisa: Seriously? ¿Dónde lo viste? *[Where did you see him?]*
       a. En la party
       b. En el party

The question investigated by Valenzuela *et al.* was whether bilingual speakers would opt for the determiner that agrees with the inherent gender of the noun in Spanish or whether they would prefer the default masculine form. Thus, in the case of "party," the speaker might prefer the feminine determiner to reflect inherent gender (*la fiesta* – fem.) or alternatively choose the masculine determiner as a default. Since code-mixed discourse is difficult to characterize in terms of grammaticality, a preference task was ideal for investigating the nature of bilingual grammars in this study.

Table 6.3. *Examples of some experimental tasks*

Test of	Task type	Notes
Oral/written production	Spontaneous, naturalistic story retelling elicited	Complete sentence, word, fill-in-the-blanks
Comprehension (written/ auditory/bimodal)	Written, auditory, or bimodal picture-sentence matching	Offline (pencil and paper, pointing) Online (Visual World Paradigm with eye-tracking)
Grammaticality (written/ auditory/bimodal)	Written, auditory, or bimodal Acceptability Judgment Tasks	Sentences presented in isolation or in context Can be timed/speeded or untimed (offline)
	Written, auditory, or bimodal Preference Task	Sentences presented in pairs for comparison (more metalinguistic)
Meaning	Written, auditory, or bimodal Truth Value Judgment Task	Offline Online (Visual World Paradigm with eye-tracking)
	Written, auditory, or bimodal picture-sentence matching	Offline Online (Visual World Paradigm with eye-tracking)

In summary, acceptability judgment tasks, truth value judgment tasks, and preference tasks can be used and have been used with heritage speakers of different languages, cultures, and degrees of ability in the heritage language. The modality, stimulus presentation, and type of response can be adapted to the level of literacy of the speakers and the degree of explicit knowledge required to make their judgments. Table 6.3 summarizes their characteristics.

6.6   Group versus individual results in experimental studies

Experimental studies test groups of people rather than individuals, and allow us to generalize the behavior(s) observed in a group to groups with similar characteristics. In many ways, applying experimental methods to heritage speakers and trying to generalize from one observation to other groups of heritage speakers is in itself a contradiction, if not an impossible task, when one of the key characteristics of heritage speakers is their heterogeneity and individual variability within and across heritage languages.

After collecting their data and analyzing their results, many experimental studies of heritage speakers report group results. Group results aggregate the individual results of all participants by computing a mean score, and appropriate statistical analyses are performed. For example, the studies by Sherkina-Lieber *et al.* (2011) and Sekerina and Trueswell (2011) report highly significant differences between heritage speakers and the baseline groups in knowledge of the grammatical order of inflectional morphemes in Inuttitut and processing contrastiveness in Russian with split constituents. In the two studies, the results are aggregated for all participants and presented as group results. The problem with group results is that they hide individual variability. It is hard to tell from means and standard deviations alone whether all the heritage speakers in the group behave differently from the baseline speakers or only some in each group. Although some variability is required of the data to be entered into statistical analyses, too much variability can be problematic for the statistical analysis itself and the potential interpretation of the results. One way to address this problem is to present both group and individual results, and this has been done in different ways.

Montrul, Bhatt, and Bhatia's (2012) study of case marking in Hindi presented the results as a group, as shown in Table 6.4. The native speakers were above 95% accurate on production of ergative *–ne* marking with perfective transitive predicates, while the heritage speakers as a group only supplied the overt marker 56.74% of the time, a difference that was statistically significant. The heritage speakers omitted *–ne* in obligatory contexts more than 35% of the time.

The wide variability within the group of heritage speakers was also discussed by looking at how many heritage speakers clustered in different accuracy rates: 5 heritage speakers (18%) were 100% accurate on *–ne* marking with transitive, perfective predicates while 6 heritage speakers (21%) were 0% accurate, showing no ergative marking. The remaining 18 heritage speakers (64%) produced 10–90% omission errors. In the same study the Hindi speakers were administered a bimodal acceptability judgment task testing overt marking and omission of ergative, accusative, and dative case in Hindi.

Mean acceptability ratings on all ungrammatical sentences with omission of obligatory case marking were compared statistically for the heritage speakers and the baseline group. The analysis revealed that the heritage speakers as a group accepted significantly more case omissions with ergative *–ne*, accusative *–ko*, and dative *–ko* with dative experiencers than with dative *–ko* indirect objects. Montrul *et al.* subsequently conducted an individual subjects' analysis to see how many heritage speakers consistently accepted ungrammatical sentences with missing case markers, as shown in Figure 6.8.

The individual analysis confirmed the group analysis and showed that out of a total of 28 heritage speakers, 9 (32%) accepted omission of *-ne* marking with transitive, perfective predicates, 13 (46%) accepted omission of *-ko* with animate and specific direct objects, and 8 (27%) accepted omission of *–ko* with dative subjects. Only 2 heritage speakers (7%) accepted omission

Table 6.4. *Mean percentage accuracy, omission, and overgeneralization of ergative* –ne *marking (adapted from Montrul, Bhatt, and Bhatia 2012)*

	N	# predicates marked with –ne	–ne supplience with transitive perfective	–ne omission	–ne overgeneralization to other predicates
Hindi native speakers	21	214	95.98	< 1	3.59
Hindi heritage speakers	28	164	56.74	35.9	8.36

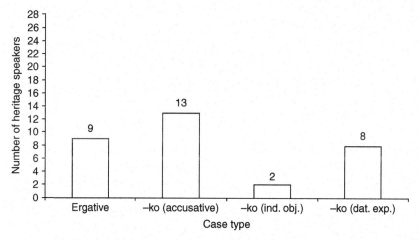

Figure 6.8. Number of heritage speakers who showed a tendency to accept ungrammatical sentences with omission of case markers (Montrul, Bhatt, and Bhatia 2012).

of –*ko* with indirect objects. The 2 heritage speakers who accepted omission of –*ko* with indirect objects also accepted omission of accusative –*ko* and omission of –*ko* with dative subjects. Except for one heritage speaker, all those heritage speakers who accepted omission of –*ko* with dative subjects also accepted omission of –*ko* with human animate specific direct objects. The other 6 only accepted omission of accusative –*ko* with animate specific direct objects. Of those 9 who accepted omission of –*ne* with transitive predicates, 7 also accepted omission of accusative –*ko* and of dative–*ko* with dative experiencers, while the other 2 accepted omissions of accusative –*ko* only. This pattern suggests that for those heritage speakers who display evidence of case erosion in their grammatical competence, ergative –*ne* and accusative –*ko* are quite vulnerable. And among the three realizations of –*ko*, accusative –*ko* is

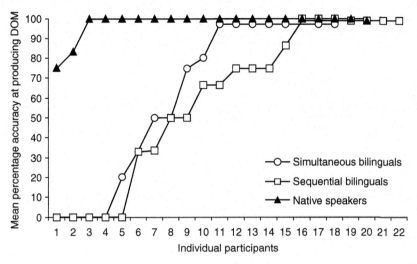

Figure 6.9. Story retelling task. Individual variation in accuracy at producing DOM with animate direct objects by the monolingual and bilingual children (Montrul and Sánchez-Walker 2013).

more vulnerable to attrition and incomplete acquisition than –*ko* with dative subjects. The –*ko* that marks indirect objects is the most resilient.

Similar individual variability with differential object marking was found by Montrul and Sánchez-Walker (2013), where the adult heritage speakers of Spanish showed an average 20% rate of omission of differential object marking (DOM) with animate specific direct objects, whereas children showed about 40% omission. When individual results were examined, they also ranged between 0% omission and 100% omission. Figure 6.9 displays the results.

The data were further analyzed based on responses to a lengthy language background questionnaire that included several questions estimating amount of input and use. Montrul and Sánchez-Walker found that heritage speakers who were exposed to more Spanish and used more Spanish were less likely to omit DOM than those who used less Spanish.

de Swart (2013) proposes instead that the field of heritage language acquisition deals with variability in a different way. Rather than treating variability as a post hoc problem, a follow-up analysis after group results are discussed, the research designs and statistical methods should perhaps assume individual variability first and then generalize from multiple instances. Adopting the multiple case studies methodology typically used with language-impaired individuals who are hard to treat as a group is one possibility. Another possibility is to find ways to integrate the experimental methods approach typical of psycholinguistics with the multifactor sociolinguistic approach, so that both group variables and individual biographical variables can be entered into the research design and explained appropriately. More recent advances in statistical methods that are increasingly using mixed linear models are moving in this direction. Because heritage speakers vary so much, caution should be taken when extending the results to other heritage speakers.

6.7   Summary

This chapter covered important issues to be taken into account when conducting research with heritage languages. Studying heritage speakers requires a deep understanding of their psycholinguistic and sociolinguistic characteristics. Because heritage speakers are a special type of bilingual population that vary from language to language and region to region, it is crucial to describe the population and use background questionnaires and proficiency measures to understand the level of linguistic knowledge of the speakers at the outset of the study. The research design of the study needs to be justified by the research questions, the theory, and theoretical assumptions assumed. Subsequently, the tasks designed to elicit data should be appropriate for the age and the level of proficiency of the heritage speakers, being specifically cautious with respect to the degree of metalinguistic awareness and explicit knowledge required of the task. The main challenges that remain to study this population are the general paucity of research on less commonly studied languages, many of which are heritage languages, and the lack of baseline measures. We still face challenges when it comes to adapting and creating culturally appropriate tests for understudied languages. Finally, we need to develop new data analyses methods to capture and understand individual variability.

7   How native are heritage speakers?

Chapter 3 presented general characteristics of the grammars of heritage speakers and in Chapter 4 we discussed the process of acquisition and several language-internal, language-external, and individual factors that may underlie the structural changes typical of heritage language grammars. With the theoretical and methodological background presented in Chapters 5 and 6, we are now in a position to examine the results of the most recent theoretically driven experimental research on the nature of heritage speakers' linguistic knowledge and how researchers have attempted to tease apart the factors that may explain the nature of these grammars. In a sense, heritage speakers are native speakers, because they start the acquisition of the heritage language early as native speakers but later undergo language shift. While some aspects of their language show age-appropriate and native-like attainment, others are not fully acquired in childhood (incomplete acquisition or acquisition without mastery) or manifest regression (attrition). Hence, the question we address in this chapter is how heritage speakers differ from monolingual or bilingual native speakers with full command of the target language. This question, naturally, calls for an approach that examines the development of the heritage language only – what I have called a unilingual approach in Chapter 6 – and direct comparison of the linguistic systems of heritage speakers with those of monolingually raised speakers, both adults and children. This comparison allows the assessment, although indirectly, of the nature of early input in a dual language context and its effect on the resulting grammars. Because heritage speakers are not monolingual, we also consider the comparison of heritage speakers to bilingual children as another way to understand their development from childhood to adulthood.

7.1   Native-like ability in some heritage speakers

Throughout this book, I have stressed the fact that heritage speakers are generally dominant in the majority language, but the range of proficiency in the heritage language varies from individual to individual ranging from mere receptive to fully productive ability, depending on a variety of life experiences and environmental circumstances. However, it is possible to find heritage speakers with very advanced proficiency in the heritage language or who do not differ from fully fluent speakers some grammatical areas.

7.1.1   High proficiency heritage speakers

An important question that few have attempted to answer so far is the following: How native can heritage speakers be in the heritage language in more than one grammatical area? Kupisch *et al.* (2013) and Kupisch, Akpinar, and Stöhr (2013) investigated the linguistic competence of 11 simultaneous bilingual heritage speakers of French who grew up predominantly in Germany with one German-speaking and one French-speaking parent. Some of these participants had attended a French school (the Lycée Français de Hambourg), where all instruction was in French, although they tended to speak German outside the classroom. Most traveled to France on a regular basis, but only 3 had been living in Francophone countries for several years. At the time of testing, they were between 20 and 42 years old. All but one preferred speaking German to speaking French, and they were more proficient in German according to a written cloze test. Instead of comparing them to monolingual French speakers or to child heritage speakers of French living in Germany, the heritage speakers of French were compared to 11 age-matched bilinguals who also acquired German and French simultaneously, but grew up predominantly in France. In other words, the comparison group was heritage speakers of German in France. The study investigated whether the majority or minority status of the language – in this case French in Germany (minority language) and in France (majority language) when the other language is German – contributes to its degree of acquisition of different grammatical areas of French.

The study targeted several properties on which German and French differ, including adjective placement, article use in noun phrases, gender assignment and agreement, choice of prepositions, and voice onset time (VOT). The bilinguals completed a structured oral interview and a bimodal grammaticality judgment task with 152 items covering all the grammatical areas mentioned above. Except for adjective placement, the results showed that the heritage speakers of French living in Germany did not differ significantly from the comparison group of German speakers who grew up in France, performing at above 90% accuracy in the sentences targeting the morphosyntactic and syntax-semantics properties under investigation. The heritage speakers of French in Germany only produced 1.7% errors with prepositions. In both the oral interview and in a grammaticality judgment task, they were 95% correct in marking gender agreement (Kupisch, Akpinar, and Stöhr 2013). In the acceptability judgment task, where speakers had to correct ungrammatical bare nouns (with no articles), the heritage speakers succeeded in providing the article 96% of the time. Statistically, there were no differences between the two French-German bilingual groups. Although this study did not include a group of monolingually raised native speakers of French, obtaining scores above 90% in most of these measures is indicative of very high proficiency in the language.

Despite the absence of overall statistically significant differences between the French heritage speakers and the speakers of French as majority language, some minor differences in performance between individuals in the two groups were noticed on closer inspection of the data. First, when the heritage speakers of French in Germany made errors, they were less accurate in gender assignment (*la nez* versus *le nez* "the nose"), which is a lexical property, than in gender agreement (*le petit nez* versus *la petite nez* "the small nose"), a syntactic property, while the bilinguals who grew up in France with French as the majority language showed no such difference. Second, the heritage speakers also made a few errors with the placement of adjectives when placement was dependent on certain lexical properties of the adjectives, while the bilinguals who grew up in France were equally accurate with all types of adjectives. This, again, indicates a problem of lexical entries and lexical access but not a problem with syntax. Third, the heritage speakers' VOT values for /t/ and /k/ differed significantly from those of monolinguals reported in the literature, while those of the heritage speakers with French as the majority language showed no significant difference from monolingual French VOT values. Finally, when the heritage speakers' accent was judged by 23 monolingual French speakers, most of the heritage speakers with French as the minority language were deemed foreign. In summary the few differences found between the German-dominant and the French-dominant bilinguals were related to lexical knowledge, not to morphology, syntax, or semantics. The most major differences found were related to accent.

The native-like abilities of the heritage speakers of French studied by Kupisch and colleagues are most likely related to their high proficiency and frequent use of the language. Unlike the vast majority of heritage speakers in North America, these heritage speakers of French in Germany received substantial schooling in French as well as multiple opportunities to spend a significant amount of time in French-speaking countries. This example serves to stress that under propitious conditions – specifically with consistent input, active use of the language in the society, and instruction at school – heritage speakers can become fully fluent, and in some cases, indistinguishable from native speakers in many aspects of their grammar. If we were to test more heritage speakers in Europe it is likely that they would fall at the higher end of the proficiency scale compared to the vast majority of heritage speakers in North America and in other parts of the world. In North America, and in the United States in particular, the incidence of young adult heritage speakers who are simultaneous bilinguals scoring above the 90% accuracy range in several areas of grammar, or who are native-like in several domains of their language, is a question that remains to be addressed.

7.1.2   *Native-like ability by linguistic domain*

Of enduring interest to linguists is the fact that when the grammars of heritage speakers display native-like ability, it does not occur across the board: that is, some areas of linguistic knowledge are very resilient and likely to develop at native levels whereas others are not. In other words, heritage speakers' grammars have areas of strength and areas of weaknesses. O'Grady *et al.* (2011), discussed in Chapter 5, pointed out that grammatical properties whose acquisition is highly dependent on input frequencies, like inflectional morphology, are very vulnerable to incomplete acquisition and loss in the heritage language, especially in speakers of lower proficiency in the heritage language. Yet other linguistic phenomena are less frequent in the input, like scope interpretations (*not all X did Y*), but are successfully acquired, independently of the proficiency of the speakers.

An example of the first type of phenomenon is gender agreement in nouns. Gender agreement is highly vulnerable in heritage speakers, as we discussed in Chapter 3. At the same time, command of gender marking and agreement does not affect all heritage speakers to the same extent. A significant percentage of participants with advanced proficiency in Spanish – but not all – in the studies by Alarcón (2011), Montrul, Foote, and Perpiñán (2008a), and Montrul *et al.* (2013, 2014) performed at the level of native speakers with full command of Spanish. Similarly, Bianchi's (2013) study of Italian heritage speakers in Germany found all the heritage speakers to be above 90% accurate on gender in German in the tasks used. Command of gender requires assigning or classifying nouns in the lexicon (gender assignment) and computing the rule of agreement in syntax (gender agreement). It is very possible that the Italian heritage speakers studied by Bianchi are quite accurate on gender in German as compared to the Spanish heritage speakers in the United States tested in all the other studies, because independently of how much they used the language on a daily basis, both Italian and German have gender agreement at the abstract syntactic level, and acquiring or maintaining the syntactic realization of agreement is not problematic for the Italian heritage speakers.

But a reason why many heritage speakers in some of these studies show errors of gender assignment at the lexical level is because not all languages with gender agreement classify the nouns in the lexicon as masculine or feminine in the same way. The studies that have teased apart lexical and syntactic aspects of gender acquisition have come to the conclusion that when heritage speakers make gender agreement errors, they have more problems with lexical assignment than with the syntactic rule of agreement (Albirini,

Benmamoun, and Chakrani 2013; Montrul *et al.* 2013). The very few errors documented by Kupisch *et al.* (2013) in the heritage speakers of French were very likely due to lexical assignment. Such errors are not surprising because gender assignment occurs in the lexicon, and many heritage speakers have lexical gaps and/or lexical retrieval difficulties in the heritage language (Montrul *et al.* 2014). All in all, although inflectional morphology is a very vulnerable area in heritage grammars, it is possible to find heritage speakers who show native-like ability in this area, especially among those heritage speakers who have very high proficiency in the heritage language. Two other very recent studies that found high proficiency heritage speakers to be like monolingually raised native speakers is Leal Méndez, Rothman, and Slabakova's (2014) and Leal Méndez, Slabakova, and Rothman's (2015) studies of a phenomenon in the syntax–semantics–discourse interface in Spanish – clitic left and right dislocations – two structures that are frequent in conversational Spanish.

With respect to another phenomenon underrepresented in the input that seems to be successfully acquired by heritage speakers, Kupisch *et al.* (in press) found quantitative and qualitative similarities between heritage speakers and monolingually raised speakers. Kupisch *et al.* investigated knowledge of definiteness effects in 15 German native speakers, 17 Turkish native speakers, and 21 Turkish heritage speakers living in Germany, mean age 28 years old. Eleven heritage speakers were exposed to Turkish and German before age 3 (simultaneous bilinguals), whereas the other 10 were first exposed to Turkish and began acquisition of German as a second language after age 4 (sequential bilinguals). The Turkish heritage speakers came from households where the two parents spoke Turkish, were schooled in German, and considered German their dominant language. About 80% of the heritage speakers self-assessed themselves as "native" in German and the remaining 20% as "native" in Turkish.

The study focused on knowledge of the definiteness effect with existential constructions in both Turkish and German. In English, existential constructions with *there* can only be followed by an indefinite noun phrase in both affirmative and negative sentences, as in (1a,c). Definite noun phrases with a definite article are ungrammatical (1b,d).

(1)   a. There is a man at the door.   (indefinite, grammatical)
       b. *There's the man at the door.   (definite, ungrammatical)
       c. There isn't a dog in my garden.   (indefinite, grammatical)
       d. *There isn't the dog in my garden. (definite, ungrammatical)

German has definite and indefinite articles and shows definiteness effects in affirmative and negative existential constructions just like English, as shown in (2).

(2)   a. Es ist ein Hund/es gibt einen Hund in meinem Garten.
         it is   a   dog/it gives a   dog   in my   garden
         "There is a dog in my garden."
      b. Es ist kein/es gibt keinen Hund in meinem Garten.
         it is no/ it gives no   dog in my   garden
         "There is no dog in my garden."
      c. *Es ist der Hund/*es gibt den Hund in meinem Garten.
         it is the dog/   it gives the dog in my   garden
         "There is the dog in my garden."
      d. *Es ist nicht der Hund/*es gibt nicht den Hund in meinem Garten.
         it is not   the dog/ it gives not the dog in my   garden
         "There is not the dog in my garden."

Turkish does not have definite articles and the indefinite article is the numeral *bir* "one." Definiteness can be expressed through prosody, word order, and case, or the use of a strong quantifier. Turkish shows definiteness effects with affirmative existentials, as in (3), but not in negative existentials, as in (4).

(3)   a. Bahçe-de birkaç çocuk var.
         garden-LOC some child exist
         "There are some children in the garden."
      b. *Bahçe-de her çocuk var.
         garden-LOC every child exist
         "There is every child in the garden."
      c. *Her çocuk bahçe-de var.
         every child garden-LOC exist
         "There is every child in the garden."
(4)   a. Bahçe-de çok ağaç yok.
         garden-LOC many tree not-exist
         "There aren't many trees in the garden. "
      b. Bahçe-de Ali yok.
         garden-LOC Ali not-exist
         "There isn't Ali in the garden."
      c. Ali bahçe-de yok.
         Ali garden-LOC not-exist
         "There isn't Ali in the garden."

Kupisch *et al.* (in press) adopted a bilingual approach because they tested implicit knowledge of the definiteness effect (DE) in the two languages of the heritage speakers (Turkish and German) by means of bimodal acceptability judgment tasks (sentences presented in auditory and in written form). The performance of the heritage speakers in each language was compared to the performance of the German and Turkish monolingually raised native speakers, respectively.

Group results comparing the heritage speakers divided into simultaneous and sequential bilinguals, the German speakers and the Turkish speakers, showed effects of grammaticality and sentence types within each group. Crucially, all the Turkish heritage speakers treated German and Turkish existentials differently: in German, the German native speakers and the Turkish heritage speakers accepted existential sentences with weak affirmatives and weak negatives with almost 100% accuracy, and there was complete rejection of existential sentences with strong affirmative and negative sentences. In Turkish, all groups accepted existentials with weak affirmatives and weak negatives with almost 100% accuracy, and also accepted existentials with strong negatives with between 70% and 90% accuracy. All groups distinguished between grammatical and ungrammatical sentences categorically in each language, with no evidence that the structure of German was imposed on Turkish or vice versa in the heritage speakers. Statistically, there were no significant differences between the Turkish heritage speakers and the Turkish speakers from Turkey in the Turkish AJT, or between the Turkish heritage speakers and the German native speakers in the German AJT. That is, the Turkish heritage speakers were "native-like," quantitatively and qualitatively, in the two languages. In sum, with respect to the definiteness effect, these heritage speakers of Turkish residing in Germany seem to have the linguistic competence of monolinguals in each of their languages, even though one of their languages (Turkish) does not have articles and was self-perceived as weaker by most of the heritage speakers. Furthermore, these results suggest that the definiteness effect with existential constructions can be acquired in both languages, independently of the age of exposure to the majority language. For Kupisch *et al.* these results contradict the assumption that heritage speakers who are simultaneous bilinguals are at a disadvantage compared to heritage speakers who are sequential bilinguals. On the basis of these results, Kupisch *et al.* also argue that reduced input during early life does not always lead to incomplete or divergent acquisition.

The results of Kupisch *et al.* contribute to the observation that some areas of grammatical knowledge are vulnerable to fluctuations in input while others are resilient and immune to changes, perhaps because they are universal and not dependent on amount of input for their development as much as other grammatical areas, as discussed by O'Grady *et al.* (2011). Kupisch *et al.* show that the acquisition of definiteness effects – a particular syntactic property of definiteness – is not susceptible to fluctuations in input or proficiency and may represent a universal property of language, although we do not know of any studies of other more general syntactic and semantic properties of definiteness in heritage speakers. This is further supported with evidence from L2 acquisition. White (2008) and White *et al.* (2012) found that L2 learners of English who speak Turkish and Chinese develop full knowledge of the definiteness effect in English, which is never taught in the classroom. Hence, rather than putting into question the well-attested observation that fluctuations in input often lead to incomplete acquisition in many heritage speakers – and in simultaneous bilinguals more than in sequential bilinguals – Kupisch *et al.*'s study shows that universal properties of language, like definiteness effects, are well-preserved in heritage language grammars and robustly acquired in other acquisition situations.

To summarize, there is recent research coming from Europe showing that *some* heritage speakers do achieve native-like ability in selected areas of the heritage language, and future research should endeavor to continue this line of investigation to uncover which other aspects of the grammar are preserved, testing like Kupisch has done, heritage speakers across different grammatical domains. We also do not know what the general incidence of native-like ability in a population of heritage speakers is likely to be, and which specific conditions lead to high levels of achievement. However, as we see next, many properties of language are particularly affected in heritage speakers when input and active use of the language are insufficient, leading to structural changes or non-native ability in the language. The changes exhibited by heritage speakers with lower proficiency in the heritage language have begged for an understanding and an explanation, since they have important theoretical and practical consequences for the nature of language and its (re)acquisition.

7.2   Non-native ability in most heritage speakers

The wealth of studies conducted in the past few years suggest that most heritage speakers who exhibit non-native mastery of several aspects of their grammar are able to communicate at basic levels and tend to have low to intermediate proficiency in the heritage language (Carreira and Kagan 2011). This suggests that the quantity and the quality of the input and active language use, as we stressed in Chapters 3 and 4, affect the full development of several aspects of their linguistic knowledge.

Quantity of input refers to the actual amount of language available in the environment; namely, daily hours of exposure and use of the language, and its cumulative frequency (every day, every other day, interrupted for a while, uninterrupted, etc.). As we discussed in Chapter 4, native-like language development can only take place through sufficient exposure to input during a critical period in childhood (Mueller-Gathercole and Hoff 2009). Of course, what exactly is "sufficient" exposure has been hard to determine. Monolingual children are exposed to their language more than ten hours a day, every day, for several years. Bilingual children's daily input to either language is much less, and if the language is a minority language and not instructed at school, the daily input can be less than five hours a day for school-age children. Furthermore, any changes in the linguistic environment of bilingual children affect the daily proportion of input in each language. Hence, children's length of exposure to their heritage language varies and fluctuates significantly in terms of amount and frequency of daily input. Several studies have demonstrated that heritage speakers who are simultaneous bilinguals are more vulnerable to language loss than heritage speakers who are sequential bilinguals because they are dominant in the minority language until they go to school. Simultaneous bilinguals have the longest exposure to the majority language and receive less cumulative input in the minority language (see Montrul 2008 for discussion). Consequently, aspects of language that require significant input to be acquired are likely to show differential degrees of acquisition or mastery, like morphology.

In addition to mere exposure to the language, actual use of the language is also critical for language acquisition and maintenance, including the number of interlocutors who speak in the heritage language (Gollan, Starr, and Ferreira in press). Very often, and driven by attitudinal and affective reasons, once they start school, children increase their interactions with majority language-speaking peers and want to fit in. If their parents were the main source of input in early childhood, now their peer group takes center stage. It is common for heritage language children to stop actively using (producing) the heritage language, even when their parents continue to speak the language to them. The general tendency is for the children to respond to parents in the majority language or to code-switch. There are well-documented sociolinguistic reasons related to these patterns (Labov 2007; Oh and Fuligni 2010; Tseng and Fuligni 2000). Furthermore, language prestige also plays a role. Children are much more likely to resist using a heritage language of low status, such as Spanish in Los Angeles, as opposed to French and Hebrew in Los Angeles. Both immigrant parents and children with higher SES background are more likely to speak the majority language and use it with each other. Oh and Fuligni (2010) further report that those adolescent heritage speakers in the United States who immigrated in childhood (sequential bilinguals) and immigrated at about age 9 reported speaking the heritage language with siblings and friends in addition to their parents, whereas those who immigrated at about age 4 used the heritage language less at home. Those adolescents who spoke more English also showed the lowest level of proficiency in the heritage language, and among the heritage language groups tested, Latino adolescents in the United States retained the heritage language at higher rates than Asian American peers. Thus, language use, in addition to just mere exposure, also contributes significantly to heritage language proficiency.

I have argued extensively (Montrul 2008, 2010, 2011, 2012) that insufficient input and use can lead to attrition and incomplete acquisition of the heritage language in second generation immigrants and beyond, and that it is difficult to tease apart the two possibilities *a posteriori*, in the absence of longitudinal data tracing the entire language development period. Attrition implies that the speaker knew linguistic property *x* at time 1 and later, at time 2, the speaker has unstable knowledge of linguistic property *x*, or can no longer recall linguistic property *x*. That is, there is regression rather than stability or progression (see Figure 4.4 in Chapter 4). Attrition is easier to demonstrate in adults assumed to have reached linguistic maturity in their grammar than in children, who may still be developing different structures of their language when input and use become reduced.

Several snapshot studies of first generation adult immigrants who have been living in the host country for more than 5 years have identified structural changes attributed to attrition at the level of syntax (Gürel and Yılmaz 2013; Perpiñán 2013; Yılmaz 2013), syntax-semantics (Bylund 2009), and discourse-pragmatics (Tsimpli *et al.* 2004). To my knowledge, except for Hutz's (2007) study of L1 lexical attrition in a German immigrant through the letters she wrote to her family for 57 years, there are no longitudinal studies of language attrition in adults, documenting a change in the same individuals from time 1 to time 2, as has been done for fossilization in L2 acquisition (see study by Lardiere 2007 mentioned in Chapter 6). Until now, attrition has been assessed through cross-sectional studies that include a comparison group of native speakers who are either more recent arrivals to the host country or native speakers in the country of origin (Hulsen 2000; Gürel and Yılmaz 2013; Iverson 2012; Perpiñán 2013). Although all these studies report different effects of attrition in the L1 acquired monolingually on the adults examined, most of the changes observed can be attributed to influence from the L2 onto the L1 after migration, and do not necessarily result in ungrammatical or erroneous performance. According to Schmid (2011), frequency of language use is not a strong predictor of language attrition in adults. In general, although L1 attrition occurs in some circumstances and in some speakers, it is neither highly likely nor widespread, as we show in Section 7.5.

But the situation is quite different with children. Children's language development and regression are highly susceptible to amount of input and frequency of use. Both Bylund (2009) and Montrul (2008) have independently argued that there are age effects for language attrition: the younger the child when there is reduction in input, the more severe the degree of attrition in adulthood. In general, then, the period before and after puberty is relevant for language entrenchment, as discussed in Chapter 4. This does not mean that if a child reaches age 8–9 when extensive exposure and use of the L2 begins the child will retain command of the L1 intact the rest of his or her life irrespective of input. What it means is that vulnerability to language regression due to reduced L1 exposure and use is *much less likely* at this age than at a younger age, and that substantial retention of the language is therefore *more likely* after that age. Admittedly, other social factors play a role as well, and more empirical research is needed to investigate these hypothetical ages for vulnerability to attrition more directly.

When a bilingual child receives significantly less input in the heritage language, and does not actively use the heritage language during the school-age period if not earlier, their developing competence in the heritage language is affected. We saw in Chapter 4 that many aspects of grammar require several years of exposure in specific contexts for the structure to be acquired at age-appropriate levels. Depending on the age when language shift occurred, the child may have acquired but not fully mastered a given structure (e.g., inflectional and derivational morphology, passives, relative clauses, subjunctive, conditionals, etc.) before then, thus leading to incomplete acquisition of the structure at a later age. At the same time, incomplete acquisition and attrition are not mutually exclusive: depending on the age and the developmental schedule of different grammatical properties, a child may show attrition in some areas that are acquired and mastered in the preschool age (gender agreement, case, aspect, and null subjects) and incomplete acquisition of structures that take several years to develop or are mastered during the period of later language development (verbal passives, subjunctive, and conditionals). It is also possible for a child to show incomplete acquisition of a structure (not acquired at age-appropriate levels) at time 1 and attrition of the same structure (higher error rates and regression) at time 2. The pattern of attrition of gender agreement in nouns displayed by Victoria, the younger sibling in the Anderson (1999) study mentioned in Chapter 5, illustrates this particular scenario.

It is also important to clarify that acquisition of an L2 in itself does not necessarily cause loss of the L1 in childhood. After all, there are fully fluent bilinguals who were exposed to the L1 and L2 in childhood and do not exhibit L1 attrition (see study by Kupsich *et al.* discussed earlier in section 7.1.2). What causes L1 attrition is disuse and lack of consistent and sustained exposure to the L1 during a time when the native language is not fully fixed in the brain, most likely before and around the closure of the critical period. The L1 is used less because heritage language children growing up in a L2 environment spend most of their waking hours using the L2 at school and with peers at the expense of their L1. Many studies documenting extensive effects of attrition at the lexical, phonological, and morphosyntactic levels are about children (Anderson 1999; Kaufman and Aronoff 1991; Merino 1983; Turian and Altenberg 1991) or about adults who immigrated in childhood (Polinsky 2006; Vago 1991). The most severe cases of attrition, when language loss happens very fast and is almost total, occurs with international adoptions (Isurin 2000; Pallier *et al.* 2003; Nicoladis and Grabois 2002). Input in the family language is reduced but still available in heritage speakers who immigrate with their parents. In the case of adoptees, input in the native language is interrupted altogether. Therefore, to reiterate once again, the inescapable conclusion is that the amount of input and use of the language affects the developing language of the child until about puberty significantly more than it affects the linguistically mature adult. We now turn to two examples of studies that document attrition and age effects.

7.2.1   L1 language attrition in childhood

Flores (2012) investigated the effects of age and quantity of input in a case of heritage language reversal. The target group were Portuguese-German bilinguals of Portuguese heritage who grew up in a country where German is the majority language (Germany and Switzerland). The German heritage speakers returned to Portugal some time in childhood, and at the time of testing, Portuguese was now the majority language and German was the minority, or heritage language in Portugal. All the returnees had attended school exclusively in German when they lived in Germany and Switzerland, and had been in Portugal between 5 and 10 years when they were tested. They all reported stronger fluency in Portuguese than in German. Age of return was the main predictor variable manipulated in the study, and the returnees were thus divided into two groups: the child and the postpuberty returnees. In the first group, there were 9 speakers with a mean age of 16.8 at the time of testing and a mean of 8.4 years at the time of return (range 7–10). The second group consisted of 9 speakers who returned to Portugal between the ages of 12 and 14 (mean 12.6) and were between 18 and 22 (mean 20.9) at the time of testing.

The goal of the study was to document potential attrition of German (the L2) and Flores focused on two properties: object expression (clitic pronoun versus null object) and word order (V2). It is possible to drop objects in Portuguese, especially when the object is a topic and must be identified by the discourse. In German, it is also possible to drop an object when it is a topic, but topic drop in German is far more restricted than in Portuguese and must obey syntactic and pragmatic conditions. With respect to verb placement, German is a V2 language and the verb in matrix sentences must be in second position. Portuguese is not a V2 language, and has S-V-O order. Object expression and verb placement in German were elicited through an oral task. If the returnees dropped objects in German in contexts where topic drop is not allowed, and if they did not respect the V2 rule for verb placement, these would be signs of attrition (as reflected by the influence of Portuguese on German).

The study was not longitudinal and there is no data on these returnees before their return. For baseline groups, Flores recruited a group of adult Portuguese immigrants with knowledge of German who had recently returned to Portugal, and child Portuguese heritage speakers in Germany, who would be the proxy for

Table 7.1. *Mean percentages of object and verb placement constructions in German (adapted from Flores 2012)*

Groups	Object expression			Illicit verb placement	
	Clitic (%)	*Null object (%)	Topic drop (%)	*XPSV (%)	*Vnfinal (%)
Child returnees	41.5	47.3	11.2	47.3	45.4
Postpuberty returnees	50.6	34.4	15	3.5	2.5
Adult control (Portugal)	88	1.9	10.1	0	0
Child control (Germany)	90.2	0	9.8	0	0

the returnees if they had been tested while in Germany as children. Table 7.1 summarizes the main findings. (*XPSV are ungrammatical sentences with the V in the third position, following XP and S; *Vnfinal are ungrammatical sentences where the verb is not in final position in embedded clauses.)

The results show that the two returnee groups produced significantly more illicit null objects in German (*null object) than the adult and child control groups, who still had contact with German. The returnees seem to have imposed the Portuguese pragmatic and syntactic conditions on object drop to objects in German. More revealing, however, are the findings of verb placement, where the difference in production of illicit orders between the returnees who returned in childhood versus those who returned after puberty is striking: the child returnees showed 47.3% and 45.4% errors with *XPSV and *Vnfinal, the postpuberty returnees 3.5% and 2.5%. These findings show that for core aspects of syntax, like V2, reduced input in childhood significantly affects the integrity of the grammar in heritage speakers of German, at least when the heritage language is also a second language.[1] Attrition in this case leads to producing ungrammatical constructions in the target language. When contact with the language is reduced or interrupted after puberty, the effects of attrition are relatively minor. Through the use of different age groups in this cross-sectional study, Flores (2012) confirmed age effects on L1 attrition, supporting maturational explanations for language loss (Bylund 2009; Montrul 2008).

Another clear case of language attrition in childhood is Montrul's (2011) study of Alicia, a 34-year-old woman from Guatemala adopted at age 9 by a

[1] This finding contrasts with Håkansson's (1995) study of Swedish returnees. The Swedish returnees were tested in Swedish, their L1, and despite showing very high error rates for nominal agreement, the V2 rule was intact. So, the vulnerability of V2 may depend on whether the attrited language is the L1 or the L2.

family from rural Illinois in the United States. Because she was adopted at age 9, she retained a great deal of her first language compared to children adopted at a much younger age (Nicoladis and Grabois 2002). Alicia reported not using any Spanish between ages 9 and 14 but reconnected with her native language in high school, at age 15, and took some Spanish courses in college. When tested at age 34, Alicia self-identified as a person of Hispanic origin with strong connections to other Spanish speakers in the community. Alicia was motivated to use Spanish: she could actually speak some Spanish and produce extended discourse. Her pronunciation sounded native, with occasional interference from English. Since Alicia was adopted at age 9 rather than as an infant, and lived 9 years of her life as a monolingual native speaker of Spanish, it is likely that her age at time of adoption may have contributed significantly to the level of language retention she exhibited. Yet, compared to the output of a 9-year-old monolingual child or an adult native speaker of Spanish, Alicia's Spanish was nonfluent and labored when it came to lexical retrieval and grammatical accuracy. She compensated for word-finding difficulties with code-switching and borrowings from English, as in (5) and (6) (underlined words represent grammatical errors, disfluencies, and code-switching):

(5)   *Sí, un poquito, mi abuelito nos <u>cuidan mí</u> a mi hermana y yo, nosotros <u>estamos adoptado juntas</u>*
      "Yes, a little bit, my grandaddy took care of me and my sister. We were adopted together."

(6)   *Tenemos tres, uno que nació el año que nos <u>daron,</u> que nos <u>adoptaron</u> mi familia, él <u>está</u> adoptado <u>con</u> otra familia ahí en Wisconsin, <u>so</u> nunca no no conocimos, pero <u>um</u> pienso que tenemos otros que nunca, que tal vez <u>mo- morieron</u> porque mi madre está enferma <u>en la cabeza</u> y por eso nuestro abuelito <u>nos cuidan</u> y él está enfermo con <u>diabetes*</u> y <u>alcohol* alco alcohólico</u> también, <u>so</u> por eso él <u>puse que alguien nos necesita nos adoptar</u>*
      "We had three, one who was born the year we were given out for adoption. He was adopted by another family in Wisconsin, so we never met, but I think that we have others who probably died because my mother was mentally ill and that is why our grandaddy was taking care of us and he was also sick with diabetes and alcoholism and that is why he found somebody to adopt us."

Alicia completed a written proficiency test in Spanish and a written acceptability judgment task (she could read and write in Spanish). She also completed a cloze test in English and a version of the English grammaticality judgment task used by Johnson and Newport (1989) and DeKeyser (2000) in written form. Alicia scored with 93% and 98.9% accuracy in the English proficiency test and acceptability judgment task, within native speakers' range, and 56% and 58% in the proficiency and acceptability judgment task in Spanish, well below the range of Spanish native speakers (91–100%).

In addition to these overall measures, Alicia returned for two more testing sessions and several other oral and written tasks in Spanish targeting verbal and nominal morphosyntax, including tense, aspect and mood, gender agreement in nouns, and differential object marking. Alicia's linguistic performance in these tasks was compared with the performance of a group of Spanish native speakers. In the tasks testing gender agreement, the native speakers obtained 99–100% accuracy scores whereas Alicia's scores ranged from 60% to 85% accuracy, showing a high attrition rate of gender. She showed poor control of differential object marking (about 60% accuracy), and very poor accuracy on verbs in the subjunctive (21%) and in the imperfect (27%). Accuracy on the preterit was 71%. She could not discriminate between the semantic implications of preterit and imperfect forms in a meaning judgment task, unlike the native speakers.

On the assumption that 9-year-old children have already mastered gender agreement (Montrul and Potowski 2007), differential object marking (Montrul and Sánchez-Walker 2013), and verbal morphology (Montrul 2004), and with the comparison of Alicia's results with those of native speakers on all the measures tested, Alicia's grammar of Spanish is not at the level of a 9-year-old in all these grammatical areas due to changes resulting from regression or L1 attrition. These changes were most likely caused by lack of input and active use of Spanish during a critical age of language development – 9 to 14 years old – and uneven use and exposure to Spanish after that. Hence, this study also shows that age is a crucial factor in language loss.

7.2.2   Incomplete acquisition in childhood

The ideal method to document incomplete acquisition is through longitudinal studies that capture changes in the same individuals, as discussed in Chapter 6. Even more ideal would be to follow heritage speakers from birth into adulthood and in the two languages to trace the acquisition of the two languages and their interaction in response to fluctuations in input. Silva-Corvalán's (2014) study of two simultaneous bilingual siblings, Nico the older and Bren the younger, growing up in Los Angeles is the closest to this ideal study to date. The mother was an English speaker, but the children were exposed to Spanish from interactions with the father, a second generation Spanish heritage speaker, and the paternal grandmother, a first generation immigrant from Chile with very high command of Spanish and of English. The siblings were observed from 1;11 until about 6 years of age (5;11). Using a bilingual approach, Silva-Corvalán documented the development of the two languages of the children and their interaction (crosslinguistic influence) in response to quantity of input, the potential vulnerability of particular grammatical areas in Spanish, the relationship between the children's grammatical systems and the input data from child-directed speech, and the effect of the frequency and complexity of the linguistic input on the attainment of proficiency in some aspects of the children's emerging lexicons and grammars.

The data came from diary notes and audio recordings of naturalistic productions in English and in Spanish elicited in interactions with the two Spanish-speaking caregivers in the family. The morphosyntactic and pragmatic distribution of subjects, S-V word order, the copulas *be* and *ser* and *estar*, and the verbal systems (tense-aspect and mood) were coded for analysis and investigated in the two languages The children's development in each language was compared to the monolingual development of English and Spanish by children of the same age.

On a daily basis, the children received approximately more input in English (about 70%) than in Spanish (about 30%), but the quantity of input changed after age 3, increasing for English and decreasing for Spanish, especially for the younger sibling. The estimated amount of input in each language for each child is illustrated in Figure 7.1.

Growing up in Los Angeles, English was the dominant language in the two children, and they had a similar level of proficiency when compared to each other or to monolinguals. By contrast, the rate of their developing proficiency in Spanish was unequal and had consequences for the development of some of the structures studied at different ages. Silva-Corvalán found that from the onset of production and up until age 3, the children showed independent and age-appropriate development of both English and Spanish morphosyntactic structures and this did not differ from the development of the same structures in the monolingual acquisition of English and of Spanish. After age 3, Spanish became the weaker language in the two children and began to display incomplete development and structural influence from English. As observed in many studies, the older sibling developed higher proficiency in the heritage language than the younger sibling (see also Anderson's 1999 study mentioned in Chapter 6). Overall, Silva-Corvalán showed that the younger sibling's Spanish was more distant from typical monolingual norms than the older sibling's Spanish and more vulnerable to direct and indirect influence from English. For example, the younger sibling resorted to English more frequently, had a smaller vocabulary in Spanish, and made more grammatical and pragmatic errors in Spanish than his brother.

Silva-Corvalán's analysis focused on the same grammatical areas investigated in her study with the three generations of Mexican immigrants in Los Angeles (Silva-Corvalán 2014). She found that the verbal system seems to be most affected by amount of input in the two siblings, whereas copular

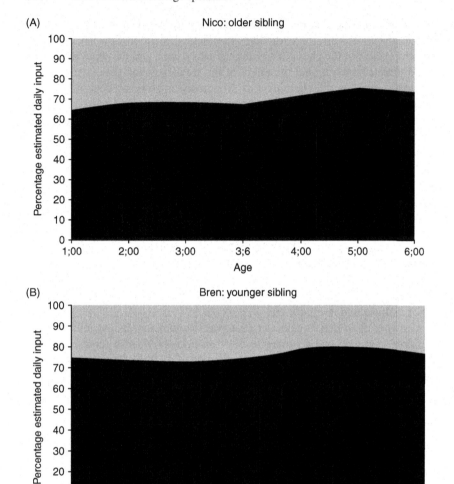

(A)   Nico: older sibling

(B)   Bren: younger sibling

Spanish   ■ English

Figure 7.1. Estimated percentage of daily input in Spanish and English in the language development of two simultaneous bilingual siblings (adapted from Silva-Corvalán 2014).

constructions followed the development in monolingual English and monolingual Spanish. The 32 different tenses and moods in Spanish showed signs of incomplete acquisition, especially in the younger sibling.

The longitudinal data from these two siblings provide an opportunity to revisit the question of whether the reduced verbal system identified in young adult heritage speakers of the second and third generation was the result of attrition or incomplete acquisition. In fact, they seem to provide a clear answer. Silva-Corvalán (2014) further compared the results of the two bilingual siblings with those of three Spanish-dominant children of the same ages and two adult bilinguals born and brought up in Los Angeles. One of the children had acquired Spanish and English from birth in Los Angeles; another child was a nearly Spanish monolingual with very low proficiency in English; the third child was a Spanish monolingual recorded in Chile.

Silva-Corvalán (2014) found that the two bilingual siblings developed age-appropriate command of tense in English, including tense morphology, modals, and auxiliaries. Both siblings followed a similar path of development in their stronger language and achieved essential verb system milestones at about the same age as English monolinguals. However, the development of the TAM system of Spanish was not age appropriate. During the period from 2;0 to 2;11 the siblings made the typical tense and person agreement errors characteristic of monolingual child Spanish language development (Fernández Martínez 1994; Mueller-Gathercole, Sebastián, and Soto 2002). Yet, the younger sibling showed weaker control of person agreement than the older sibling. Silva-Corvalán found that the tenses that are relatively more complex, and also less frequent in the adult input were acquired later or not acquired at all by age 6;0. The younger sibling developed a more reduced tense system than his older brother. Although at age 3;6 the younger sibling used the present subjunctive, by age 6 he no longer used it and he never developed the other complex tenses in Spanish. When these two bilingual Spanish-speaking children started kindergarten in the United States, they had not yet acquired the complete TAM system in Spanish, like monolingual peers.

Comparing the two young siblings to the adults studied in 1994, Silva-Corvalán (2014) concluded that the TAM system developed by the siblings and another bilingual child by age 6;0 is comparable to that of second and third generation Spanish-English bilingual adults who have not received formal education in Spanish. The argument that the processes of simplification and loss attested in adult bilingual Spanish are most likely the consequence of an interrupted process of acquisition of this language between the ages of 3;0 and 5;0, when more intensive exposure to English reduces exposure to and use of Spanish, finds substantial support in this study. Reduction in exposure and use leads to losing or at least weakening of the online command of the less frequent tenses. These two siblings are future adult heritage speakers, who by the age of 6;0 had unequal control of their heritage language, a feature that finds a parallel in the range of proficiencies identified across heritage speakers. Silva-Corvalán's study shows that while some grammatical areas exhibit target-like and robust development (copulas), other areas do not develop to the same extent and result from incomplete acquisition rather than attrition or loss of linguistic knowledge acquired earlier. More longitudinal studies like Silva-Corvalán's (2014) are needed, tracing the life-course development of the two languages of the heritage speakers, ideally until early adulthood.

Because it is not always possible or feasible to conduct a longitudinal study, another way to test indirectly whether a given phenomenon in heritage speakers may be due to incomplete acquisition or attrition is to link the data obtained from adult heritage speakers to that of child L1 learners and child heritage speakers. The next two sections present some examples of this approach to tease apart attrition from incomplete acquisition in the linguistic development of heritage speakers.

7.3   Heritage speakers and child L1 learners

If adult heritage speakers make errors that are similar to developmental errors produced by monolingual children during the course of acquisition, it is possible to conclude that the patterns in heritage speakers resemble an earlier stage of language development. In other words, comparing monolingual child L1 learners and adult heritage speakers allows us to assess the hypothesis that heritage speakers are, in a sense, "fossilized" child L1 learners (Polinsky 2011). Fossilization is a term commonly used in L2 acquisition to refer to the arrested development of grammatical features (Han 2014; Lardiere 2007; Long 2003; Selinker 1972), which characterizes interlanguage grammars (Selinker 1972), the linguistic systems of L2 learners. The reader may recall the concept of fossilization in an interlanguage grammar from Chapter 2, when we discussed Lardiere's (2007) longitudinal study of Patty showing no change over time. A few studies have found parallels between stages of L1 acquisition and the grammars of heritage speakers, especially in some aspects of morphology and word order.

One study is Benmamoun *et al.* (2014), who examined Palestinian and Egyptian Arabic heritage speakers' knowledge of plural formation in their colloquial varieties, which use both concatenative and nonconcatenative modes of derivation. In the concatenative derivation, a plural suffix like *–iin* attaches to the singular stem (*muhandis* "engineer-sg" → *muhandis-iin* "engineer-pl"); in the nonconcatenative mode, the relation between the singular (*gamal* "camel") and the plural (*gimaal* "camels") is less transparent and involves vocalic and prosodic alternations. The main similarity between the singular and the plural form is the consonantal root (*g-m-l*). The suffixal plural form is called the *sound* plural, and the plural with change in templates is called the *broken* plural. *Sound* plurals are the default form of plural derivation but they occur less frequently in the language than *broken* plurals (McCarthy and Prince 1990). In the first experiment, oral narratives were elicited from 20 young adult heritage speakers and 20 native speakers of Egyptian and Palestinian Arabic. In the second experiment, another group of 24 heritage speakers and 24 native speakers of the same dialects completed an oral picture description task. Monolingually raised native speakers of Egyptian and Palestinian Arabic were tested as baseline. In the two experiments, the heritage speakers produced "errors" that were not attested in the native speakers.

Interestingly, the error patterns produced by the heritage speakers with sound plurals are very similar to the developmental errors produced by child native learners of Arabic, as reported by Omar (1973), Ravid and Farah (1999), and Albirini (2014a). Omar's (1973) longitudinal study examined the acquisition of different types of Arabic plurals by thirty-one children aged 6 months–15 years in an Egyptian village. The data obtained from conversations, elicitation tasks, and a twenty-item plural formation test showed that these children overgeneralized the use of the feminine sound plural marker *–aat* to contexts where the broken plural is expected (*kura* → *kuraat*; correct form is *kuwar*). Ravid and Farah (1999) investigated the acquisition of different types of plurals among Palestinian children (ages 2–6 years) using a Wug test (an elicited production task). The results showed that the sound feminine plural *–aat* was acquired and produced at ceiling by 3-year-old children whereas the two other types – sound masculine and broken plurals – were acquired gradually in later stages. Ravid and Farah argued that age plays a crucial role in the acquisition of the different plural forms, and that the ease of acquisition of feminine plural over masculine and broken plurals is due to semantic and structural factors characterizing the feminine plural, which would explain the 87% of broken plural targets being incorrectly formed as sound plurals using the feminine form.

Like the native Arabic-speaking children in these studies, the heritage speakers in Benmamoun *et al.* (2014) did better overall on the sound plurals, especially the feminine form, than on broken plurals, with accuracy rates of 91% for the Palestinian and 83% for the Egyptian heritage speakers. In addition to being relatively simpler than the broken plural because it does not entail isolating a root and mapping it onto a template, this mode of suffixation is familiar to heritage speakers whose dominant language is English, because plurality in English is achieved through the affixation of the suffix *–s*. However, this may not be a case of language transfer because not all sound plurals pattern the same way. Accuracy on masculine sound plurals was lower. For both L1 children and adult heritage speakers, the sound feminine plural acts as a type of default plural to be used as a last resort when learners cannot recall masculine sound plurals or broken plurals. At the same time, the concept of regularity is seriously challenged in Arabic morphology. Albirini (2014a), who studied older Jordanian Arabic children (ages 3–8) and discusses further similarities between adult heritage speakers and child learners of Arabic in the acquisition of plural morphology, noted that in both populations the patterns of errors are related to perceived distributions of the different plural forms in the adult native speaker input. Another study confirming that adult heritage speakers are like child L1 learners with morphological errors is Zobolou's (2011) study of Greek in Argentina, mentioned in Chapter 3. Many of the errors with irregular gender and plural forms produced by the Greek heritage speakers are similar to the errors produced by preschool children acquiring Greek in Greece before they completely master all these irregularities (Gavriilidou and Efthymiou 2003).

Larsson and Johannessen (2014) is another example of a study linking structural changes in heritage grammars to earlier stages of child L1 development of Scandinavian languages, this time with word order (syntax). Scandinavian languages are verb second (V2) languages. In declarative main clauses, the verb immediately follows the first constituent, which can be a subject, an adverbial, or some other fronted phrase, as in (7a) and (7b).

(7) a. Den tröjan   köpte han inte. (Swedish)
        that shirt.the bought he   not
        "He didn't buy that shirt."
     b. * Den tröjan   han köpte   inte.
          that   shirt.the he   bought not

Wh-questions also have the verb in second position, as in (8a) and (8b). In V2-contexts the verb is assumed to be in a higher position. Non-V2 languages do not have to move the verb to a higher position.

(8) a. Vad   köpte han? (Swedish)
        what bought he
        "What did he buy?"
     b. * Vad han köpte?
          what he   bought

Larsson and Johannessen show that Norwegian and Swedish as spoken in the American Midwest exhibit atypical verb–adverb word order in embedded clauses. They recorded oral production from 88 heritage speakers of Scandinavian and found a substantial amount of verb–adverb order in subordinate declaratives, embedded questions, and relative clauses. Although verb–adverb word order is ungrammatical in embedded questions and relative clauses in European Swedish and Norwegian, Larsson and Johannessen tell us that it is frequent in child Norwegian and Swedish. During the acquisition of V2, Scandinavian children assume V-to-I movement rather than V-to-C movement at an early stage, based on examples such as (9a) and (9b) (i.e., verb–subject order in nonsubject initial declaratives, wh-questions, and polarity questions) in the input. At the second stage children move the verb to C (depending on clause type). This yields a child grammar with both V-to-I movement and V-to-C movement, also found in heritage speakers.

> (9)   a. Hon läser inte den boken. (V-to-I or V-to-C)
>   she reads not that the.book
>   "She doesn't read that book."
>   b. Den boken läser hon inte. (V-to-C)
>   that the.book reads she not
>   "She doesn't read that book."

European Norwegian and Swedish L1 learners appear to retain a grammar with V-to-I movement, which is not surprising if the acquisition of embedded word order in Scandinavian languages appears to take longer than has sometimes been assumed. Waldmann (2008) studied 4 children during the ages of 2;3 and 4;00 who produced adverb–verb and nontarget verb–adverb order in embedded clauses throughout the investigated period. In another study, Westergaard and Bentzen (2007) showed that children older than 4;00 sometimes retain V-to-I movement. For example, a child named Iver (5;9.18) produced nontarget verb–adverb order in 7 out of 8 embedded questions during an elicitation task; as in (10) and never moved the verb across the subject.

> (10)   huske du koffer han Karsten **var ikke** i barnehagen?
>   remember you why he Karsten was not in the.kindergarten
>   "Do you remember why Karsten wasn't in kindergarten?"
>   (Iver 5;9.18, Northern Norwegian; from Westergaard and Bentzen 2007, p. 285)

According to Westergaard and Bentzen (2007), the frequency of embedded clauses with adverbs is considerably lower than the frequency of main clauses with subject-verb inversion in the input, and together with the complexity of the structures, this leads to their slower acquisition.

Compared to the child L1 acquisition situation, the evidence for adverb–verb order is even weaker in the input of the heritage speakers, Larsson and Johannessen (2014) argue. For one thing, relative clauses are less frequent in American Scandinavian than in European Scandinavian (Karstadt 2003) and examples with adverbs are also generally infrequent (Taranrød 2011). If frequency affects the rate of acquisition – but not the acquisitional path – heritage speakers are expected to retain V-to-I movement longer than children in

Norway and Sweden, and possibly even up until school age. At the age of 6, the heritage speakers start school and English quickly becomes the stronger language. It is therefore possible that the target grammar without V-to-I movement is never fully acquired, and that embedded clauses with verb–adverb order in adult heritage speakers are a consequence of incomplete acquisition. This would explain the differences between the fluent heritage speakers of Norwegian and Swedish and European Norwegian and Swedish speakers with respect to embedded word order, but not necessarily with respect to morphology and V2: morphology and V2 are acquired earlier in child language and have therefore been fully acquired in the heritage language.

A third example of a study finding striking parallels between adult heritage speakers and child L1 learners is Chung (2013). Chung conducted a series of experiments to investigate knowledge and acquisition of case drop or case ellipsis by Korean children in Korea and adult heritage speakers of Korean in the United States (in addition to other groups). Recall from Chapter 3 that subjects and objects are overtly case marked in Korean, yet case markers are frequently omitted in spoken Korean under a variety of syntactic and discourse-pragmatic conditions, such as topic, focus, definiteness, animacy, etc. Chung's is the first study investigating whether children know about when not to use case in Korean. In one of the experiments, Chung examined the factors of animacy, definiteness, and focus that constrained case ellipsis in adult native speakers of Korean in an elicited production task and in a written task. In another experiment, Chung administered the elicited oral production task to 23 child L1 learners of Korean, ages 5–7, to examine whether the children showed sensitivity to the factors that would lead to adult-like knowledge of Korean case ellipsis.

Chung found that the Korean children provided fewer case markers in both subject and object NPs. Chung found that Korean case ellipsis is acquired by children by age 5. At this age, Korean children in Korea produce case ellipsis in an adult-like manner and seem to have attained implicit knowledge of this apparently "optional" and abstract linguistic phenomenon. If Korean-speaking children acquire case ellipsis at a relatively young age one could assume that heritage speakers of Korean may also acquire this phenomenon fairly early, especially because case ellipsis is a conversational phenomenon. Chung conducted the same experiments with heritage speakers and L2 learners of Korean, to also understand the difference between the early and late acquisition of optional case marking in Korean. We will come back to the results of the L2 learners in this study in Chapter 8.

Chung found that the adult heritage speakers and the Korean L1 children were very similar in their performance. Both groups seemed capable of employing animacy, definiteness, and focus as factors in case ellipsis in an almost native-like manner but provided fewer case markers in subjects and objects than the adult Korean native speakers overall. They also showed greater ambivalence than the adult native speakers in group and individual results, and such quantitative differences seem to be characteristic of a developmental stage that both monolingual and early bilingual learners pass through. Group differences between Korean native speakers and the heritage speakers were more quantitative than qualitative in nature, and the heritage speakers seemed to have attained a certain degree of implicit knowledge of Korean case ellipsis.

In conclusion, comparing young adult heritage speakers with monolingual children acquiring the target language in a majority language environment allows us to trace developmental patterns typical of L1 development in heritage speakers. This comparative design affords us the opportunity to observe in another indirect manner the specific areas of grammatical knowledge that may or may not reach their full development in heritage speakers. While strengthening the links between L1 acquisition and heritage language acquisition, this research design also promotes the study and documentation of the linguistic development of relatively understudied languages, like Greek, Arabic, and Korean. This is a way in which the study of heritage languages enriches research on the monolingual acquisition of many other languages.

7.4   Child and adult heritage speakers

Because heritage speakers are bilinguals, it can reasonably be argued that their linguistic experience is different from that of the monolingual child. Hence, child heritage speakers (bilingual children) are another suitable population to compare to adult heritage speakers and examine the development of different aspects of language. In this case, the bilingual environment and potential amount of exposure to the two languages are controlled for, and the key variable is age at time of testing, which is a proxy for linguistic development and cognitive maturity. If the child heritage speaker exhibits errors in linguistic form or function x, and the adult heritage speaker does not produce form or function x, then we can assume that the adult heritage speaker never fully acquired the relevant features of x. If the child and adult heritage speakers produce the same types of errors, then we can conclude that what was not acquired at target-levels in childhood remained incompletely acquired into adulthood. If the child heritage speaker makes no errors and the adult heritage speaker does, then attrition of the heritage language may be assumed of the adult heritage speakers. O'Grady, Lee, and Lee (2011) investigated these possibilities with child and adult Korean heritage speakers, and the structure of interest was the scope of disjunction under negation.

In English, when the direct object of a negated verb contains *or*, the connective takes on a conjunctive "neither nor" interpretation (Chierchia *et al.* 2001).

(11)   John didn't eat [ice cream **or** cake].
        = "John ate neither ice cream nor cake."
        (conjunctive interpretation)

In contrast, the same type of construction in Japanese permits just a disjunctive "one or the other" interpretation (Goro and Akiba 2004).

(12)   John-wa [aisu **ka** keeki-o] tabe-nakat-ta.
        John-TOP ice cream or cake-ACC eat-not-PST
        "John didn't eat ice cream OR he didn't eat cake – one or the
        other." (disjunctive interpretation)

Korean differs from both English and Japanese in permitting either interpretation, although the "neither nor" interpretation appears to be dominant.

(13)   John-un [ice cream **ina** kheyik-ul] an mek-ess-ta.
        John-TOP ice cream or cake-ACC not eat-PST-DECL
        "John ate neither ice cream nor cake," *or*
        "John didn't eat ice cream OR he didn't eat cake – one or the
        other."

The meanings of negated constructions with *or* in Korean differ in very subtle ways, and the relevant sentences that provide evidence for this phenomenon (with an *or*-NP functioning as direct object of a negated verb) are relatively rare in the input. As such, they might present a special challenge for heritage learners. O'Grady, Lee, and Lee (2011) conducted an experiment to verify whether child heritage learners might manifest an understanding of disjunction. The study tested 11 children aged 3;11 to 8;0 (mean age, 5;5), who were students in Saturday morning *hangul hakkyo* (Korean language schools) in Honolulu. All the children were enrolled in English-language schools. The study also tested 11 adult Korean HL learners who were very fluent in Korean and had received similar exposure to Korean as the child heritage speakers they were compared to. Therefore, any sign of a deficit in the adult heritage speakers not present in the child heritage speakers could be plausibly attributed to attrition in the adult heritage speakers.

The experimental task was a Truth Value Judgment Task with stories and pictures. The test materials consisted of a series of ten illustrated stories, five of which were designed specifically to test for the "neither nor" versus the "one or the other" interpretation. A sample story in English is given in (14).

(14)   The teacher told a mouse, a pig, and a bear that they should
        eat all their food for good health. For lunch, there are noodles,

cucumber, and French fries. The teacher will give chocolate to any animal who eats all the different types of food. Let's see who got the chocolate. The bear ate only noodles. The mouse ate a cucumber, French fries, and noodles. However, the pig ate only the cucumber and noodles. Who do you think received the chocolate? [Answer: the mouse]

After each story, the child and adult Korean heritage speakers were asked to evaluate the truth of three sentences (some true and some false) as they looked at an accompanying picture that summarized who had eaten what.

(15) a. The bear ate noodles.
      b. The pig ate noodles. However, the pig did not eat French fries or cucumber
      c. The mouse did not eat cucumber.

The second question is the crucial one, since the answer reveals the interpretation of the *or*-phrase. A *yes* response indicates that the subject interprets the sentence to mean "The pig either didn't eat French fries or the pig didn't eat cucumber" (the disjunctive interpretation) – which is true since the pig didn't eat French fries. In contrast, a *no* response indicates that the subject takes the sentence to mean "The pig ate neither cucumber nor French fries" (the conjunctive interpretation) – which is false since the pig ate the cucumbers. Regardless of whether the answer was "yes" or "no," the children and the adults were asked to give a reason for their choice (e.g., "because the pig ate cucumbers").

The results showed that on the key test items containing *–ina* "or," such as (13), there was a preference for the "neither nor" interpretation – children selected it about two thirds of the time, compared to one third for the "one or the other" interpretation. Nonetheless, 8 of the 11 child subjects chose the "one or the other" interpretation at least once. Recall that all answers had to be justified by an appropriate explanation. Although most of the children permitted a "one or the other" interpretation, like Korean monolingual adults they tended to prefer the "neither nor" interpretation. The adult heritage speakers, by contrast, opted for the "neither nor" interpretation 100% of the time, without considering the "one or the other" interpretation. This specific finding suggests that the adults may have lost the possibility of the "one or the other" interpretation accepted by the children. Despite being quite fluent, attrition has presumably occurred in the absence of ongoing use and/or in the face of repeated exposure to the "neither nor" interpretation found in English.

Similar attrition effects along the lifespan in adult heritage speakers are documented by Polinsky (2011) in Russian as a heritage language. Polinsky (2011) investigated comprehension of subject and object relative clauses in four groups of Russian speakers: two monolingual control groups (15 children and 26 adults) and two experimental groups of heritage speakers (21

234 How native are heritage speakers?

children and 29 adults). The average age of the monolingual and bilingual children was 6;6 for the monolinguals and 6;2 for the heritage speakers. The average age of the monolingual adults was 32 and the average age of the Russian heritage speakers was 22. The child and adult monolingual Russian speakers were tested in Moscow; the child and adult heritage speakers came from the United States. All the heritage speakers were children of first generation immigrants. As a measure of proficiency, Polinsky elicited speech samples with the Frog Stories and calculated the speech rate for all speakers. All the child and adult heritage speakers had speech rates below one hundred words per minute.

Polinsky used a picture matching task, with reversible actions that could be performed by the two animate participants: a dog chasing a cat and a cat chasing a dog. The target sentences were presented in auditory form and included subject and object relative clauses with two possible word orders in Russian, as in (16)–(19). English and Russian subject relatives have the same word order when the Russian relative clause is V-O. English and Russian ORs have the same word order when the Russian relative clause is S-V. In the other two cases, the relative clauses do not match. The different word orders signal contrastiveness and focus (see Sekerina and Trueswell's 2011 study mentioned in Chapter 6).

(16) Gde koška [kotor-aja sobak-u dogonjaet]?
       where cat REL-NOM dog- ACC is_catching up
       "Where is the cat that is chasing the dog?"
(17) Gde koška [kotor-aja dogonjaet sobak-u]?
       where cat REL-NOM is_catching_up dog-ACC
       "Where is the cat that is chasing the dog?"
(18) Gde sobaka [kotoruju dogonjaet koška]?
       where dog REL-ACC is_catching up cat. NOM
       "Where is the dog that the cat is chasing?"
(19) Gde sobaka [kotoruju koška dogonjaet]?
       where dog REL-ACC cat. NOM is_catching up
       "Where is the dog that the cat is chasing?"

The participants heard questions with a relative clause (as in 16–19) and had to decide who was doing what by choosing the picture that depicted the correct action. Accuracy scores were entered into the statistical analysis. Table 7.2 summarizes the main results.

The child heritage speakers performed at ceiling, and their accuracy scores were not statistically significant from the age-matched monolingual Russian children and adult Russian native speakers. The adult heritage speakers were quite accurate with subject relative clauses, but they had significant problems comprehending object relative clauses as compared with the other three groups,

Table 7.2. *Mean accuracy on comprehension of Russian relative clauses (Polinsky 2011)*

		Subject relative clauses		Object relative clauses	
Groups	Mean age	Verb-object	Object-verb	Verb-subject	Subject-verb
Russian children	6.6	85.9	87.8	87.2	86.1
Russian adults	32	85	85	87.2	86.1
Child heritage speakers	6.2	99.4	99.4	98.9	99.4
Adult heritage speakers	22	87.8	92.2	43.9	52.2

with accuracy scores around and below chance. This result is an indication of attrition over the lifespan. Obviously, the children had adult-like grammatical knowledge of relative clauses, but the adult heritage speakers interpreted all relative clauses as subject relatives. It was not the case that the heritage speakers followed the word order of English with subject and object relatives in Russian, so dominant language transfer cannot be invoked in this case. Indeed, the results point to a significant bias in favor of subject relativization, which has been observed in other developing grammars crosslinguistically (Keenean and Comrie 1977) and in aphasic patients (Caplan 2000), a result that is consistent with a processing constraint (see O'Grady, Lee, and Choo 2001). However, Sánchez-Walker (2013), who tested Spanish heritage speakers on comprehension of similar relative clauses, found that the Spanish heritage speakers discriminated between subject and object relative clauses, probably because they were of higher proficiency in the heritage language than the heritage speakers of Russian tested by Polinsky (2011). In sum, both O'Grady, Lee, and Lee (2011) and Polinsky (2011) compared child and adult heritage speakers and found evidence of attrition over the lifespan for the adult heritage speakers. Lack of schooling and exposure to advanced language may perhaps underlie the level of language regression observed in the adults in these studies.

A third example of a study of child and adult heritage speakers indirectly testing attrition or incomplete acquisition of a given grammatical property is Montrul and Sánchez-Walker (2013). Montrul and Sánchez-Walker compared child and adult heritage speakers on their knowledge of differential object marking (DOM) in Spanish, and found evidence more consistent with incomplete acquisition rather than with attrition in the two age groups. DOM appears to be an early acquisition in child Spanish. According to a study by Rodríguez-Mondoñedo (2008) with 4 Spanish-speaking children (ages 0;9–2;11) from the CHILDES database, the children were 98.38% accurate before age 3;00 on their production of the *a* marker with animate and inanimate objects. Also using data available from the CHILDES database, Ticio (2015) examined the oral production of 6 simultaneous bilingual children between the ages of 1;00 and 3;00 (five Spanish-English and one Catalan-Spanish). She found that the children omitted obligatory DOM with animate objects 76.62% of the time, concluding that simultaneous bilingual children do not master DOM by age 3;00 like monolingual children.

Research on adult heritage speakers suggests that DOM is either not completely acquired or subject to attrition (Montrul 2004; Montrul and Bowles 2009). Montrul and Bowles (2009) found that even advanced heritage speakers are very inaccurate with DOM, not just low proficiency speakers. Montrul and Sánchez-Walker (2013) controlled for age of onset of bilingualism in child and adult heritage speakers, and tested heritage speakers who are simultaneous bilinguals exposed to Spanish and English before age 5, and heritage speakers who are sequential bilinguals, exposed to Spanish primarily in early childhood with acquisition of English after age 5. The 39 child heritage speakers and the 64 young adult heritage speakers who participated in the two studies were compared to age-matched monolingual speakers tested in Mexico (twenty children and twenty young adults). Controlling for age of onset of bilingualism in both studies allowed indirect assessment of whether quantity of early input in Spanish plays a role in incomplete acquisition or attrition of DOM. The children and the adults completed an oral narrative task. Prompted with pictures, they were asked to narrate the story of *Little Red Riding Hood*. They also completed an oral picture description task (see description and examples in Chapter 6).

Montrul and Sánchez-Walker (2013) found that both the child and adult heritage speakers omitted obligatory DOM with animate direct objects in the oral narrative task and in the picture description task, between 40% and 60% of the time for the children and about 20% of the time for the adults. By contrast, the two age-matched Mexican native speaker groups, both adults and children, showed accuracy rates well above 90% for the adults, and slightly lower for the children, 85%. If quantity of input matters, Montrul and Sánchez-Walker predicted that simultaneous bilinguals would omit DOM significantly more than sequential bilinguals. However, this hypothesis was not borne out with the children or the adult heritage speakers for this grammatical phenomenon (cf. Montrul and Sánchez-Walker 2015).

Figure 7.2 shows that the child bilinguals appear to show incomplete acquisition of DOM (close to 65% accuracy in the story retelling task) while young adult simultaneous bilinguals show about 80% accuracy. The child and adult native speakers are close to 98% accurate. Accuracy on the picture description task was much lower for adults and children, perhaps due to the more explicit nature of the task and the fact that they were required to use specific verbs.

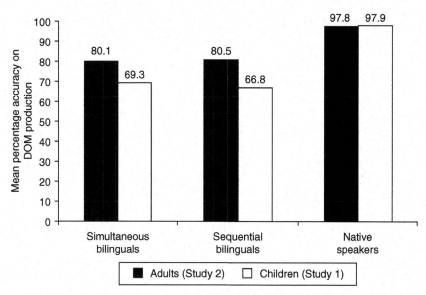

Figure 7.2. Accuracy on DOM with animate direct objects in the Story Retelling Task performed by the child (Study 1) and the adult heritage speakers (Study 2) (Montrul and Sánchez-Walker 2013).

If Ticio (2015) found that young bilingual children omitted DOM about 73% of the time, the trend in Figure 7.2 suggests that older bilingual children slowly continue their acquisition of DOM and it improves with age, but DOM is still not fully mastered by young adulthood. Although there seems to be some continuous development of DOM from childhood to adulthood in the heritage speakers, such development is the opposite of the adult-like accuracy that O'Grady, Lee, and Lee (2011) and Polinsky (2011) documented with child heritage speakers in Korean and in Russian. The trend found by Montrul and Sánchez-Walker is compatible with acquisition with incomplete mastery and not with L1 attrition.

To wrap up, I have shown that when carrying out longitudinal studies is not feasible, comparing young adult heritage speakers and child heritage speakers is another promising way to investigate which structures are mastered, which may be subject to attrition, and which ones may be subject to incomplete acquisition in the linguistic development of heritage speakers.

7.5   Different input?

So far, I have considered the hypothesis that quantity of input and frequency of use of the heritage language throughout the language development period is primarily responsible for many adult heritage speakers not developing mastery of several properties of the heritage language in different grammatical areas, but most notably in morphology. We saw that in many situations there are correlations between the proficiency of the heritage speakers and the degree of fluency and accuracy in different grammatical domains of the heritage language. We also saw that not all aspects of language are similarly vulnerable to reductions in input and use: some aspects of morphology and syntax are, while other aspects of syntax and semantics are not. But there is another possibility that could also account, perhaps to a lesser extent, for the structural changes observed in heritage speakers. This concerns the quality and characteristics of the input, which might also be structurally different in many respects from the assumed monolingual baseline, as brought up by Sorace (2004) and Rothman (2007).

The main sources of input to heritage speakers immersed in a community come from their parents, older relatives, and friends who speak the heritage language and live in the same bilingual environment. If the heritage speakers do not have contact with a wider heritage language speech community, the parents are usually the main providers of exposure to the heritage language and the main interlocutors, especially as they approach the teenage years (Oh and Fuligni 2010). Sorace (2004) has raised the possibility that the language of the speech community may be different from the language of recently arrived immigrants or native speakers in the country of origin, and this observation is particularly accurate with respect to the L2 of immigrants. When parents are L2 learners of the majority language, make L2 errors in their speech, and use the majority language instead of the heritage language with their children, they expose them to non-native patterns, as shown by Cornips and Hulk (2008) with Turkish speakers in the Netherlands and by Place and Hoff (2011) with Spanish-speaking children in Miami. The Dutch of Turkish-speaking children manifests many non-native features and delayed acquisition of aspects of Dutch, such as gender with definite and neuter determiners. Place and Hoff (2011) show that exposure to non-native input from the parents is detrimental to children learning the majority language because it does not provide good examples of the target language and, at the same time, takes time away from input in the heritage language. The implication of Place and Hoff's study is that parents should be encouraged to continue using the heritage language at home as much as possible.

The question is, as Sorace (2004) brought up, whether being exposed to structurally different input also occurs in the heritage language. After all, many of the interlocutors who are part of the social networks of heritage speakers may code-switch and show changes with respect to the monolingual baseline due to diachronic changes or attrition. Place and Hoff (2011) found that for the young children they studied in Miami the input in the heritage language was native. However, as parents' length of residence increases, some of them may experience attrition. But this, if it happens, would have to be demonstrated with parents of adult heritage speakers and not with parents of child heritage speakers, who would probably not exhibit attrition soon after arrival. In the next section we discuss studies showing potential diachronic change, differences in language varieties, and dialect leveling in heritage communities that may also affect the acquisition of the heritage language.

7.5.1   Potential diachronic change in the monolingual baseline

Kim, Montrul, and Yoon's (2009) study of three Korean anaphors *caki*, *casin*, and *caki-casin* by Korean heritage speakers in the United States addresses the possibility of changes in the assumed monolingual norm when accounting for the differences found between the interpretations of the young adult heritage speakers in the United States and the native speakers tested in Korea, who were between 40 and 50 years old. The study also included a group of late bilinguals: Koreans who have immigrated to the United States between the ages of 10 and 14. The results of a written Truth Value Judgment Task with pictures and stories (see examples in Chapter 5) showed that the Korean native speakers and the late bilinguals distinguished between the local and long-distance binding interpretations of the three anaphors, whereas the early bilingual heritage speakers had a two-anaphor system, and seemed to have collapsed *casin* and *caki* as a single anaphor, with local binding properties. Kim, Montrul, and Yoon (2009) entertained diachronic change and input frequency as a likely explanation, since the interpretation of *casin* as a long-distance anaphor is a relatively recent innovation in the Korean monolingual variety. In older stages, *casin* was primarily a local anaphor. *Caki* as a reflexive pronoun is much older than *casin*, attested in written records in the late sixteenth century (Kim 2001). The overall use of *casin* is rapidly expanding in contemporary Korean, and the rise of other *casin*-related forms, including *caki-casin*, is also under way. Although the diachronic development of *casin* has not been investigated systematically, Kim and Yoon (2008) documented a steady increase in the frequency of *casin* in later Bible translations, and with it, an increase in its usage as a long-distance anaphor. If this explanation holds, the grammars of early bilinguals as found in the Kim, Montrul, and Yoon study would be closer to the grammar of the earlier stages of Korean. This is hardly surprising in view of the fact that the language of an immigrant group tends to be more conservative than that of the native speakers in the home country (Aitchinson 1991), and the early bilinguals' primary source of Korean input before their dominant language shift is at home. In other words, it is likely that the parents may no longer speak the same variety of Korean as the monolingual generation tested in Korea, not because of attrition but because their language is isolated from the current diachronic changes it may be undergoing in the host country.

Those Korean monolinguals who either treated *casin* as a local anaphor or as an long-distance anaphor but without a strong long-distance binding preference were mostly in their 40s and 50s. In general, those Korean native speakers who treated *casin* as a long-distance anaphor with a strong long-distance binding preference were younger. The relative distribution of speakers in terms of age in the Kim, Montrul, and Yoon (2009) study seems consistent with the fact that the long-distance binding of *casin* is an innovation, and is also consistent with the evidence from the Bible translations. Given the recency of this change in the Korea variety of Korean and the overall conservative nature of immigrant grammars, it is easier to understand that the heritage speakers did not have sufficient exposure to the ongoing change, and the Korean they heard from their parents is qualitatively different from the current norm in Korea.

7.5.2   *Language varieties*

Rothman (2007) and Pires and Rothman (2009a,b) conducted studies of child Brazilian Portuguese, heritage speakers of Brazilian Portuguese, and heritage speakers of European Portuguese that also address the issue of different input as it relates to diachronic change. The focus of their studies was the morphological realization and the syntactic distribution and the interpretation of inflected infinitives (see Chapter 3 for description). Although, Brazilian Portuguese and European Portuguese are related, they are very different in many respects. Brazilian Portuguese, due to ongoing diachronic change, does not share many aspects of syntax and morphology in the colloquial, spoken variety. However, these have been preserved in the formal, written variety, which more resembles earlier stages of the language and has similarities with present-day European Portuguese. Three aspects that have changed in Brazilian Portuguese over the years with respect to the grammar of European Portuguese are verbal agreement paradigms and the instantiation of null/overt pronouns, the order and overt realization of object pronouns (or clitics), and inflected infinitives. Inflected infinitives, for example, are still very common in European Portuguese in both spoken and written registers, but mostly present in the written, formal register in Brazilian Portuguese. Inflected infinitives are inflected for person and number, as given in (20):

> (20)   nós saí+r+mos   vocês/ eles/elas saí+r+em
>   we to leave.AGR.1PL you.pl they   to leave.AGR.3PL

Like subjunctive forms, inflected infinitives must appear in embedded clauses, as in (21). Inflected infinitives have different referential properties from noninflected infinitives.

(21) Eu   esperei   um pouco para nós   saírmos
juntos.
1SG.NOM wait.PERF.1SG a little   for 1PL.NOM get out.INF.
1PL together.
"I waited a little for us to get out together."

In the L1 acquisition of Brazilian Portuguese, Pires and Rothman (2009b) showed that monolingual children between the ages of 9 and 12 did not know the syntax and semantics of inflected infinitives as tested with oral and written tasks, and claimed that because inflected infinitives are not part of the colloquial input young children are exposed to, they had not developed grammatical competence of this feature of the language. By contrast, the older learners (teenagers) tested in a written task had knowledge of the morphological, semantic, and syntactic distribution of inflected infinitives just like the monolingual adults. Because the teenagers and adults master the semantic and syntactic properties of inflected infinitives through schooling, this finding suggests that education and literacy contribute to the acquisition of grammatical knowledge that is restricted to a standard dialect. Similar findings are reported by Kato, Cyrino, and Corrêa (2009). Formal schooling, according to Kato, Cyrino, and Corrêa, can partially reverse important language change in vernacular varieties. Preschool children and adult individuals who were deprived at different rates from formal education will lack competence in many grammatical properties that are taken to be part of educated native dialects. Kato, Cyrino, and Corrêa show that preschool children and illiterate speakers do not have third person clitics in their grammars. But the speakers who participated in a written experiment at the end of the schooling period produced the same amount of third person clitics as manifested in eighteenth-century written texts. Literate speakers of Brazilian Portuguese control two dialects, one with clitics and one without third person clitics.

Following the same logic as Kato, Cyrino, and Corrêa (2009), Rothman (2007) used the same tasks Pires and Rothman (2009b) used with children, teenagers, and adults in Brazil to test heritage speakers of Brazilian Portuguese in the United States on their knowledge of inflected infinitives. Pires and Rothman (2009a) tested heritage speakers of European Portuguese in the United States. They found that the heritage speakers of European Portuguese demonstrated full competence of inflected infinitives, whereas the heritage speakers of Brazilian Portuguese, who did not receive schooling in Brazilian Portuguese, did not discriminate the morphological and semantic properties of inflected infinitives in different types of clauses. Heritage speakers of Brazilian Portuguese were simply exposed to a different dialectal variety (the vernacular), which does not exhibit many inflected infinitives. Therefore, what looks like incomplete acquisition in this case, Pires and Rothman argue, is full acquisition of their colloquial variety but not of the formal variety. This study underscores the importance of schooling in heritage language development, as also emphasized in the studies by Jia and Paradis (2014), Kupisch *et al.* (2013), and Kupisch, Akpinar, and Stöhr (2013) mentioned earlier. In this case, some properties of language are only available through the exposure to and mastery of the formal, written discourse, which many heritage speakers do not have experience with.

7.5.3   Dialect leveling in the heritage community

Otheguy, Zentella, and Livert (2007) conducted a study of pronominal subject use in New York City within the perspective of variationist sociolinguistics. Recall that in null subject languages like Spanish, Italian, Russian, Arabic, among others, both null and overt subjects are possible, but the distribution of one form over the other depends on discourse context. Overt subjects are used to introduce a new referent or as topics in discourse. Null subjects are usually required in topic continuation contexts, and the use of overt subjects in these situations is usually redundant, unless it is used to establish contrast. English is not a null subject language and requires that most subjects be overtly expressed through a pronoun or NP, except for contexts of a second conjunct in a coordinated sentence (e.g., *John came and brought me a present*).

The data come from groups of first, second, and third generation immigrants from Puerto Rico, the Dominican Republic, Cuba, Ecuador, Colombia, and Mexico living in New York City. These Spanish linguistic varieties differ in the rates of pronominal subject use: Caribbean dialects (Puerto Rico, Cuba, and the Dominican Republic) are known to exhibit higher percentages of overt subject pronouns than non-Caribbean varieties (Colombia, Ecuador, and Mexico). At the same time, the rate of pronominal subject use varies in Spanish and English, since Spanish is a prodrop language and English is not. Otheguy *et al.* were interested in issues of both dialect and language contact with respect to this particular linguistic variable. That is, contact between Spanish and English, and contact between different varieties of Spanish that differ on rates of overt subject pronouns.

In several hours of naturalistic speech, Otheguy *et al.* found that the longer the speakers had been in the United States, and especially those of the second generation (or heritage speakers), the higher the rate of overt subject pronoun production in Spanish. While the first generation speakers produced 30% overt pronouns, the Spanish speakers born in the United States produced 38%, a difference that was statistically significant. Unlike Silva-Corvalán (1994) and Flores Ferrán (2004), Otheguy *et al.* conclude that these changes in the second generation are primarily due to less use of Spanish and transfer from English, a language with overt pronouns.

In addition, when comparing first and second generation speakers from Caribbean and non-Caribbean dialects, Otheguy *et al.* found an increase of overt subject production in the two dialect zones in the second generation, giving rise to a new variety of US-Spanish where dialectal variation is also neutralized. That is, the heritage speakers of non-Caribbean varieties showed an increase in rate of overt pronouns with respect to the first generation, and all immigrants showed evidence of impact from English on their overt pronoun rates. Dialect leveling in the Spanish of New York City involves greater movement in the direction of Caribbean usage than in the direction of non-Caribbean usage due to influence from English, which only has overt subjects. In subsequent analyses of the same data, Shin and Otheguy (2013) found that these changes are correlated with social class and sex: affluent immigrant women are driving the increase in use of pronominal subjects in the Spanish of New York.

Montrul and Sánchez-Walker (2015) examined the distribution of null and overt subjects in child heritage speakers from Chicago and New York City and their findings support the observations made by Otheguy and Zentella (2012) on the Spanish spoken in New York. The children completed an oral narrative task. Montrul and Sánchez-Walker hypothesized that if child bilinguals produce higher rates of overt subjects and of pragmatically infelicitous subjects than age-matched monolinguals, it can be assumed that the bilinguals may not have had a chance to develop the pragmatic features of Spanish subjects fully (refer to the study by Silva-Corvalán 2014). They found that the simultaneous bilingual children used the highest rates of redundant lexical and pronominal subjects. Thus, their hypothesis stating that simultaneous bilinguals would produce more overt subjects and more pragmatic errors than sequential bilinguals was confirmed. As for infelicitous uses of null pronouns in switch reference contexts, they further hypothesized that if the bilingual children produce null subjects in switch reference contexts like monolingual children younger than twelve (Shin and Cairns 2012), this will also suggest that they have not fully mastered pronoun reference in Spanish. This hypothesis was also supported because the bilingual groups were comparable to the monolingual children from Mexico. The results are given in Table 7.3.

Montrul and Sánchez-Walker consider another potential explanation for the results of the simultaneous bilingual children, which has to do with where the children were living. Twenty of the children were recruited in Chicago: 19 were of Mexican heritage and one was from Colombia. Fifteen of these children were sequential bilinguals, and 5 were simultaneous bilinguals. The other 19 children who participated in the study were tested in New York City, and 10 of them were simultaneous bilinguals. Only 2 of the children tested in New York were of Mexican heritage. The rest were from Honduras, Ecuador, Colombia, and El Salvador. According to Otheguy and Zentella (2012), Spanish speakers of non-Caribbean varieties residing in New York produce higher rates of overt pronominal subjects than newcomers from the same regions due to contact with

Table 7.3. *Pragmatic distribution of subjects by context (# = pragmatically infelicitous) (Montrul and Sánchez-Walker 2015)*

		Switch reference context			Same reference context		
Child groups	N	Lexical (%)	Pron. (%)	#Null (%)	#Lexical (%)	#Pron. (%)	Null (%)
Mexican monolinguals	20	95.9	93.7	5.9	4.1	6.3	94.1
Simultaneous bilinguals	15	86.7	75.3	10.9	13.2	24.7	96.3
Sequential bilinguals	20	89.97	80.9	12.7	10.1	19.1	96.9

speakers of Caribbean Spanish (Puerto Rico, Cuba, and Dominican Republic). In addition to contact with English, all varieties of Spanish are converging on a higher use of overt subjects through dialect leveling.

Montrul and Sánchez-Walker considered this possibility and reanalyzed the results of the children by region – Mexico, Chicago, and New York City – and found significant differences in production of overt subjects and pronominal subjects between the three groups. The children from Mexico produced 5.8% null subjects in switch reference contexts. The Chicago bilinguals produced 20.1% but the children from New York hardly made these errors (1.7%). At the same time, the children from New York produced 72% of overt subjects, whereas the children from Chicago produced 61% and were not different from the children from Mexico, who produced 59%. The Mexican children produced 5.2% of overt pronominal subjects, the Mexican children from Chicago 8.1%, and the bilingual children from New York 29%. The highest rate was with redundant pronominal subjects in same reference contexts: the New York bilinguals produce a much higher rate of redundant subjects (30%) compared to the Chicago bilinguals (6.2%) and to Mexican children (8.9%). Taken together, the results suggest that the Chicago children, who were 95% from Mexican heritage and mostly sequential bilinguals, had problems establishing reference with null subjects in a discourse narrative, whereas the children from New York City did not have this problem but produced instead redundant overt pronominal subjects in same reference contexts.

To conclude, it seems that many factors contribute to the degree of indeterminacy of the pragmatic distribution of null and overt subjects in Spanish: strong pressure from English, structural complexity of overt subjects in Spanish, integration of syntactic and pragmatic features, contact with other dialects, and age of onset of bilingualism, among others. Together with the findings from

Silva-Corvalán (2014), Montrul and Sánchez-Walker's study shows that subject expression remains a vulnerable area in child bilingual grammars during the school-age period. The patterns found are also the same ones found in monolingual development, except that the magnitude of the effects is higher in Spanish speakers who live in a situation of language contact with English, as in the United States.

7.5.4   Attrition in the first generation

A final factor to consider when trying to understand the competence of heritage speakers is to look at first generation immigrants, since they are the main sources of input to the second generation. Although Nagy *et al.* (2014) found no differences in the first and second generation with respect to VOT (phonetics), there are several transgenerational studies showing that the linguistic abilities of the first generation are superior to those of the second and third generations in morphosyntax, semantics, pragmatics, and lexicon (Hulsen 2000; Schmidt 1985; Silva-Corvalán 1994). Although attrition in adults is generally uncommon, it happens, and it is also conceivable that some individuals of the first generation may undergo attrition in some grammatical areas and these areas are also incompletely acquired by the heritage speakers.

Montrul and Sánchez-Walker's (2013) study of DOM in Spanish mentioned earlier speaks to this possibility. Recall that this study included children and adults, and the adult heritage speakers were better than the children but still non-native because their accuracy scores reached 80% compared to above 90% for native speakers (see Figure 7.2 in Section 7.4). If monolingual Spanish-speaking children by age 3 show about 95% accuracy on DOM in Spanish, an important question is what prevents simultaneous and sequential bilingual heritage speakers from reaching much higher levels of accuracy, above 80%? The answer may be found in the results of the adult immigrants also tested in this study and compared to the heritage speakers, who showed similar proficiency scores in Spanish as the two adult heritage speaker groups and similar rates of DOM omission (20%) as the young adult heritage speakers. Many adult immigrants seem to be undergoing attrition of DOM, probably due to influence from English, which does not mark direct objects overtly. If adult heritage speakers use Spanish predominantly with their parents and older relatives, and their parents and older relatives also omit DOM to some extent, then the reason why heritage speakers who are university students do not produce DOM with an accuracy higher than 80% may be related to the "attrited" input they may be exposed to from parents and other heritage speakers. This would suggest that incomplete acquisition in childhood due to quantity of input and to qualitatively different input from their parents may also contribute to lack of development of DOM at age-appropriate levels in child

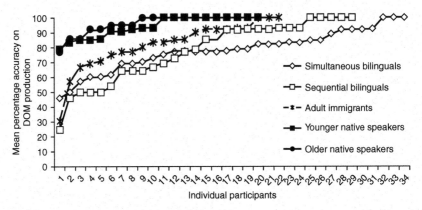

Figure 7.3. Accuracy on DOM in an oral narrative task by participants (Montrul and Sánchez-Walker 2013).

and adult heritage speakers. Figure 7.3 shows the rate of omission of DOM in an oral narrative task in the adults.

Of the 23 adult immigrants who participated in this study, 13 omitted DOM more than once. In general, those who omitted DOM were older than those who did not omit DOM at time of testing (48.3 versus 43.2), acquired English later in life (22 versus 20.2), and had resided in the United States longer (27.3 years versus 23.1 years). The 2 immigrants with the lowest accuracy on DOM (both 33%) had been in the United States for 33 and 37 years, respectively. These results suggest that DOM is also subject to attrition in adult Spanish speakers living in the United States for several years. The apparent incomplete acquisition manifested by child and adult heritage speakers is related to the amount of current input and use of Spanish and English. In the case of the young heritage speakers, rate of DOM omission may also be related to the non-native patterns of DOM they receive from their parents and relatives, some of whom may have undergone attrition.

Intergenerational language loss due to incomplete acquisition and attrition can lead to the emergence of a new dialectal feature in languages in contact. Whereas DOM with animate objects in monolingual varieties is not only obligatory but is also extending to inanimate objects, in US-Spanish the marker is on the verge of disappearing with animate objects. A similar situation is found with Spanish immigrants living in Switzerland (Grosjean and Py 1991), where Spanish is in contact with French, a language that does not mark DOM. Grosjean and Py (1991) reported that first and second generation Spanish immigrants in a French-speaking region of Switzerland also accepted ungrammatical sentences without DOM in Spanish, unlike Spanish speakers from Spain who were not living abroad. Therefore, in order to understand the precise source of these grammatical changes from one generation to the next, it is important to investigate the potential relationship between the grammars of different types of bilingual heritage speakers longitudinally and that of the first generation, who are the main interlocutors of the speakers of the second generation.

Even though Montrul and Sánchez-Walker (2013) documented what could be considered attrition in some individuals of the first generation, morphological attrition in the first generation does not happen that frequently and is not very widespread. And not all minority language communities show attrition to the same extent. For example, Montrul, Bhatt, and Girju (2015) compared the potential attrition and incomplete acquisition of DOM in Spanish, Hindi, and Romanian in the United States and found that the degree and extent of the erosion of DOM differs in the three languages. DOM turned out to be extensively more affected in Spanish than in Hindi and in Romanian, even when the Spanish language in the United States enjoys more presence in public life and education than Hindi, and Romanian, and heritage speakers appear to use their heritage language more than Hindi speakers, for example. That is, while some of the first generation immigrants in the Spanish study produced ungrammatical animate direct objects without DOM, none of the first generation Hindi and Romanian speakers did.

The study tested simultaneous and sequential heritage speakers, first generation adult immigrants, and young and older native speakers in the countries of origin (Mexico, India, and Romania) to test potential attrition effects in the first generation and incomplete acquisition in the second generation. The main task in each language was a bimodal grammaticality judgment task. Table 7.4 summarizes the overall patterns by counting how many participants in each group accepted ungrammatical sentences with DOM omission more than the native speaker baselines in a bimodal grammaticality judgment task in each language, as established by the higher end of their mean acceptability ranges (where 1 = totally unacceptable and 4 = perfectly acceptable). The mean acceptability range for native speakers from Mexico was between 1 for the lowest and 2.17 the highest, for the Hindi speakers in India it was between 1 and 2.16, and for native speakers of Romanian it was between 1 and 2.17.

Several heritage speakers within each group were affected and so were 62% of the first generation adult immigrants from Mexico. Overall, Spanish as a heritage language was more affected than Hindi and Romanian. Therefore, for *some* linguistic structures and for *some* populations, incomplete acquisition in heritage speakers may also relate to qualitatively different input provided by the parental generation. Although attrition in the first generation is possible, it cannot be directly linked to the changes observed in all heritage language grammars. This finding, at this point, cannot be generalized to other heritage languages and other structures.

Table 7.4. *Number and percentage of individuals in each group whose mean acceptability ratings for ungrammatical unmarked DOM in animate, specific direct objects was above the highest individual mean acceptability rating for native speakers of the languages in each country (Montrul, Bhatt, and Girju 2015)*

	Simultaneous bilingual heritage speakers	Sequential bilingual heritage speakers	Adult immigrants	Younger adult native speakers in the country	Older adult native speakers in the country
Spanish	25/32	15/24	13/21	0/20	0/21
	78%	62%	62%	0%	0%
Hindi	19/26	–	0/26	0/20	0/20
	73%		0%	0%	0%
Romanian	17/23	8/19	0/32	0/30	0/21
	74%	42%	0%	0%	0%

7.6   Summary

In this chapter we considered the inherent variability observed in heritage speakers with respect to native speakers, in order to assess whether the changes observed in heritage grammars are due to quantity and quality of input. Although it is possible to find heritage speakers with very high proficiency in the language, these do not appear to be in the majority. Heritage speakers with lower proficiency in the heritage language display grammatical patterns that are consistent with incomplete acquisition, with L1 attrition, and with changes in the input provided by the parental generation and other interlocutors. In general, however, most of the changes observed seem to be due to insufficient input leading to incomplete acquisition and attrition rather than to qualitative changes in the environment. The latter seem to be in the minority. This chapter also highlighted that many of the grammatical patterns attested in the grammars of adult heritage speakers share similarities with the developmental stages attested in L1 acquisition. But since heritage speakers are native speakers, or at least start as such, this is an expected finding.

8   Are heritage speakers like second language learners?

This book so far has traced the course of language development in heritage speakers. Heritage speakers are bilingual native speakers of their heritage language, except that the degree of ultimate attainment in the heritage language is variable, as we saw in previous chapters. When input and use of the heritage language are optimal in favorable sociolinguistic environments, heritage speakers are likely to become balanced bilinguals and develop native-like ability in some areas. But when input is restricted and insufficient for young adult heritage speakers, the development of the heritage language is delayed and interrupted, displaying properties typical of developmental stages of first language acquisition, as we saw in Chapter 7. Although heritage speakers start off as monolingual native speakers, they grow up in a bilingual environment and eventually undergo language shift. By the end of the language learning period (adolescence), the heritage language has become secondary, it feels to the heritage speakers like an L2, and in fact manifests many of the same characteristics of the interlanguage systems of L2 learners. Because this situation raises important theoretical and practical issues, this chapter focuses on the similarities and differences between heritage speakers and adult L2 speakers.

Knowledge of another language is what sets apart monolinguals from bilinguals. Just as many patterns found in L2 learners are due to persistent influence from the L1, many of the structural patterns observed in heritage speakers also arise from dominant language transfer. At the theoretical level, comparing how the dominant language influences the weaker language in heritage speakers and L2 learners informs how and why language transfer operates at the psycholinguistic level, and how it relates to age of acquisition of the second/ secondary weaker language. But there are other more practical reasons for comparing heritage speakers and L2 learners. As illustrated in the introductory chapter of this book, adult heritage speakers are very aware of their limitations in the heritage language, and those who want to improve seek to learn more about their heritage language in a formal classroom environment. When other options are not available, heritage speakers must enroll in programs conceived for L2 learners with no previous knowledge of the language and culture. When this practice started several years ago, it was found at the time that HL and L2 learners in the same classroom may not always benefit the HL learners and in recent years there have been efforts worldwide to create special language programs, curricula, and pedagogical materials to address the academic, communicative, and cultural needs of HL learners. Ideally, these programs must be based on empirical research evidence and informed by a thorough understanding of the key differences and similarities between heritage speakers, HL learners, and L2 learners revealed by research comparing all these groups.

This chapter presents examples of state-of-the art research on the linguistic knowledge of heritage speakers/learners and L2 learners. The first three parts focus on studies that address theoretical issues in L2 acquisition that are also relevant to understanding heritage language acquisition, such as transfer, fossilization, interface vulnerability, the role of experience, and age effects. The last part (Section 8.4) addresses directly the teaching of heritage languages in the classroom with an emphasis on how HL learners react to and benefit from instruction.

8.1   Differences and similarities between heritage speakers and second language learners

Heritage speakers and L2 learners are two types of bilingual individuals, and may share knowledge and use of the same two languages, as shown in Figure 8.1. Because heritage speakers acquired the heritage language and the majority language at birth (simultaneous bilinguals) or later in childhood as an L2 (sequential bilinguals) and before puberty, they are early bilinguals (see Figure 4.2 in Chapter 4). Like some heritage speakers, adult L2 learners are also sequential bilinguals, and because they learn the L2 after puberty another term applied to them is late bilinguals (see Figure 4.3 in Chapter 4). Heritage speakers and L2 learners share the same dominance pattern regardless of in what sequence the languages were acquired – Language B is the dominant language and Language A is the weaker language – but the level of proficiency in each language may differ. Furthermore, due to different age of acquisition (early in heritage speakers, late in L2 learners), their learning experience with the weaker language is very different. For L2 learners the weaker language is the L2 but for heritage speakers it is the L1 (or Language A if acquired simultaneously with Language B), as illustrated in Figure 8.1.

Suppose that we are comparing English-speaking L2 learners of Korean in the United States and heritage speakers of Korean with low-intermediate proficiency in Korean, as given in Table 8.1.

For both the L2 learners and the heritage speakers, English is the majority language and Korean is the minority language. For the two groups, English is primary and dominant and Korean is the secondary and weaker language. The main difference between the two groups is which language

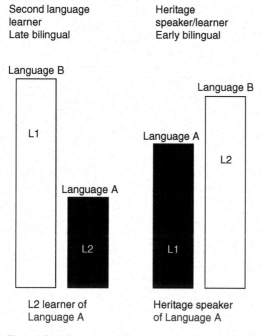

Figure 8.1. Patterns of language dominance in L2 learners and heritage speakers.

Table 8.1. *Profile of low to intermediate proficiency heritage speakers and L2 learners of Korean in the United States*

Relationship between the two languages		Heritage speakers	L2 learners
Order of acquisition	First language	*Korean*	*English*
	Second language	*English*	*Korean*
Sociopolitical status	Majority language	English	English
	Minority language	Korean	Korean
Functional dimension/ dominance pattern	Primary/dominant language	English	English
	Secondary/weaker language	Korean	Korean

they learned first. For the L2 learners, English is the L1 and Korean the L2; for the heritage speakers it is the reverse: Korean is the L1 and English the L2.

The order of acquisition of the two languages determines key differences between the two groups related to input and experience, as listed in Table 8.2.

Table 8.2. *Input differences between heritage speakers and L2 learners*

Input	Heritage speakers	L2 learners
Timing	Early (childhood)	Late (around puberty)
Setting	Naturalistic (home)	Instructed (classroom)/(naturalistic, study abroad)
Mode	Predominantly aural (literacy in some cases)	Written and aural (literacy)

Heritage speakers are exposed to their heritage language through the auditory medium and learn to speak the language through oral interaction with native speakers of the language in a culturally embedded context. Commonly, L2/FL learners in the United States start acquisition of the L2 in a classroom setting, instructed by a native or non-native teacher, and are exposed to written materials from the beginning. Opportunities to actually speak the L2 tend to be comparatively limited in most foreign language classrooms. Knowledge of the culture and target language community is another significant difference between the two groups. As we discussed in Chapter 2, heritage speakers are primary members of an ethnolinguistic community with deep knowledge of the cultural norms and appropriate ways of interaction within the community, whereas L2 learners may have partial knowledge of the community and may not be actually intimately connected to it. Differences in timing, frequency, and type of input carry significant theoretical implications for the role of age and ultimate attainment in bilingual acquisition, as well as for how quantity and quality of input contribute to language processing and eventual acquisition in adults. Together with the cultural component, these differences also have implications for materials development, curricula, and heritage language programs that seek to expand heritage speakers' knowledge and use of the heritage language.

8.2   Heritage speakers and second language research

Throughout this book, I have stressed that heritage language speakers and learners are very relevant to L1 acquisition, L2 acquisition, and linguistics more generally. This is because they afford these fields a unique opportunity to evaluate current claims about the complex nature of L1 and L2 competence acquired before and after the so-called critical period, the type of knowledge (implicit and explicit) acquired as a result of input and experience, the competence/performance dichotomy in formal linguistics, the specific innate and environmental ingredients for developing stable native speaker competence, the role of transfer, the role of schooling, and the limits and possibilities of bilingual competence in adulthood.

Valdés (2006, p. 242) called for a research agenda for heritage language development, with the objectives of (1) developing language evaluation assessment procedures that can identify key differences among heritage learners, (2) investigating the implicit systems of different types of heritage learners in their nondominant L1s, (3) determining the degree of restructuring of the linguistic system needed for heritage speakers at different levels of proficiency to carry out particular functions in particular settings using appropriate linguistic forms, and (4) identifying whether pedagogies used to bring about restructuring of the interlanguages of L2 learners can also be effective for heritage speakers. It merits stressing again that understanding key differences and similarities between heritage speakers and L2 learners at the level of linguistic knowledge is crucial for developing appropriate materials, pedagogical practices, and curricula. In Chapter 5, I made a case for extending existing mainstream theoretical approaches that are very relevant to the investigation and explanation of the nature of linguistic knowledge in both heritage speakers and L2 learners. In Montrul (2008), I argued that the non-native acquisition of heritage language speakers challenges many long-held notions about L2 acquisition.

For example, a profound question in cognitive and generative approaches to L2 acquisition is the explanation for observed differences in the outcome of L1 acquisition by children and L2 acquisition by adults. In fact, understanding the limits and possibilities of ultimate attainment motivates and guides the enduring comparison between L2 learners and monolingual children and adults. Like many heritage speakers, the level of ultimate attainment acquired by the vast majority of L2 learners is variable, also ranging from limited to near-native competence. It is common for L2 learners to stop developing specific grammatical aspects of their interlanguage system (some phonological contrasts, some morphology, collocations, etc.), a phenomenon known as fossilization (Han 2014; Selinker 1972), as we illustrated in Chapter 6 with Lardiere's (2007) case study of Patty. Fossilization does not happen in normally developing L1 acquisition in a monolingual setting.

A likely cause of L2 fossilization is amount of input: L2 learners receive much less input than children acquiring their native language, and the input is also different because child L1 learners and adult L2 learners use the language for different purposes and they use it in different contexts. Child L1 learners are more often exposed to native input from their caregivers, whereas L2 learners are more likely to be exposed to non-native input from non-native teachers and from their non-native peers. Another possibility for the different outcomes of the acquisition process in L2 learners and child L1 learners is the age of the learner and the language learning mechanisms that apply in childhood and those that apply after puberty. When children acquire language, they are primarily doing so implicitly, whereas adults learning a second language rely more on explicit knowledge than on implicit knowledge. Given that heritage language speakers combine characteristics of L1 learners and of L2 learners, they represent an ideal population to tease apart competing theoretical accounts. In what follows, I focus on the main theoretical issues that have been at the forefront of linguistic research on L2 acquisition and that are also relevant for heritage language acquisition, namely, age effects and linguistic modularity, dominant language transfer, and interface vulnerability. In Section 8.3, we consider the role of experience.

8.2.1   Age effects and linguistic modularity

The critical period hypothesis applied to language (Lenneberg 1967) states that there is a biologically determined propitious time in early childhood during which being exposed to language is crucial for developing language. This hypothesis has figured prominently in explanations of why adult L2 learners rarely reach the level of linguistic ability of native speakers (Bley-Vroman 1990; Clahsen and Muysken 1986; DeKeyser 2003; Granena and Long 2013; Hawkins and Hattori 2006; Hyltenstam 1992; Hyltenstam and Abrahamsson 2003; Johnson and Newport 1991; Long 1990; Meisel 2011; Paradis 2004; Schachter 1990; Selinker 1972; Tsimpli and Dimitrakopoulo 2007; among many others). Other researchers downplay the effects of age, maintaining that access to Universal Grammar – the Language Acquisition Device that guides language learning in childhood – is not subject to a critical period, remaining active after puberty (Birdsong and Molis 2001; Epstein, Flynn, and Martohardjono 1996; White and Genesee 1996). Others contend that age effects are not biologically related but are due instead to external factors that co-occur with age, such as education, cognitive maturity, and experience (Bialystok and Hakuta 1999; Marinova-Todd, Marshall, and Snow 2000). The existing literature on critical periods for language indicates that phonology is far more affected by age effects than syntax and morphology in L2 acquisition, although morphology is quite problematic as well.

Approaching the issue of age from cognitive and neurolinguistic perspectives, a similar and compatible position is maintained by DeKeyser (2000, 2003), Ullman (2001), Paradis (2004), and DeKeyser and Larson-Hall (2005). DeKeyser and Paradis, who do not believe that language ability is innate (see Chapter 5), distinguish instead between implicit and explicit memory systems and learning of language. The gist of this proposal is that young children learn language implicitly, without awareness. Implicit knowledge is stored in procedural memory (Ullman 2001). The specific linguistic content handled by this type of memory is grammar proper (i.e., productive rules and the computational system in generative terms (Pinker and Ullman 2002a,b; Ullman 2001)). However, the implicit learning mechanism becomes severely limited as children grow, due to both progressive loss of

Table 8.3. *Learning mechanisms available to children and adults*

	L1 acquisition by children	L2 acquisition by adults
The Fundamental Difference Hypothesis (Bley-Vroman 1990)	Universal grammar	L1 knowledge
	Specific linguistic mechanisms	General cognitive mechanisms
Neurocognitive approach (DeKeyser 2003; Paradis 2004)	Implicit learning (predominantly)	Implicit learning
	Explicit learning (at school age)	Explicit learning (predominantly)

neurological plasticity (recall discussion in Chapter 4) and the emergence of analysis and control of representational cognitive structures leading to meta-linguistic ability, awareness, and knowledge (Bialystok 2001, p. 131). As a result of this neurocognitive change, adults learn languages explicitly, with conscious effort and awareness. Explicit knowledge, which includes knowledge of words and of irregular morphological forms in addition to other nonlinguistic knowledge, is stored in declarative memory (Ullman 2001). As children age, they rely more and more on explicit learning than on implicit learning (Birdsong 1989). For Ullman (2001), reliance on procedural memory for language learning is subject to a critical period. This implies that inflectional morphology and productive computational morphological and syntactic rules are affected by age effects.

Note that the implicit learning mechanism stored in procedural memory may be akin to aspects of Universal Grammar acquired implicitly and without awareness, whereas according to DeKeyser (2000), the explicit mechanisms stored in declarative memory parallel the domain-general cognitive mechanisms discussed by Bley-Vroman (1990). My understanding of these positions is that both implicit and explicit learning mechanisms are available to children and adults, or at least to adults, but while children acquire their L1 predominantly with implicit mechanisms, adults acquire an L2 predominantly through explicit mechanisms. This is summarized in Table 8.3.

In recent years, explanations and predictions of developmental delays or inability to reach native-like attainment in specific areas of grammatical knowledge in different types of bilingual acquisition have been linked to the architecture of the language faculty (Slabakova 2008; Sorace 2011). The language faculty consists of a series of discrete modules (syntax, semantics, and phonology), each with their own structural and hierarchical organization, as well as connections between modules, or "interfaces" (Jackendoff 2002). The different modules and the interfaces appear to have different developmental schedules and possibilities for ultimate attainment.

If the linguistic and/or cognitive mechanisms assumed to operate for language acquisition in childhood are different from those deployed in adulthood, heritage speakers may have more native-like knowledge of the target language than L2 learners in many areas despite similar overall proficiency in the language. If timing of input is crucial for developing the essence of native speaker competence in some modules of the grammar (e.g., phonetics/phonology and phonological perception), heritage language learners should benefit from having received exposure to the heritage language, even if minimal, in early childhood. This means that heritage speakers may exhibit linguistic advantages (i.e., more native-like knowledge) over postpuberty L2 learners with early-acquired aspects of language, like some aspects of phonology and some aspects of morphosyntax and semantics that may not be highly dependent on input frequency. Alternatively, if the same learning mechanisms are accessible to the child and adult learner independently of age and cognitive development, L2 learners and heritage speakers should not differ in these areas.

Because heritage speakers do not typically receive schooling in the heritage language and because actual use (oral and written production, not just listening) of the heritage language decreases as they get older, even if they show advantages relative to L2 learners with some early-acquired aspects of language, it is possible that heritage speakers will not necessarily have advantages over L2 learners with structures and vocabulary that are more typical of later language development and may require high levels of literacy and metalinguistic awareness for their mastery (e.g., conditionals and counterfactuals, expressions of genericity). Therefore, linguistic advantages for heritage speakers over L2 learners are predicted for aspects of early language development (Montrul 2008), but not necessarily for aspects of later language development like complex syntax and semantics where the languages differ in some aspect of morphology or abstract formal feature (e.g., determiners and genericity: all languages express genericity but not all languages do it with determiners).

Age of acquisition seems to be particularly important for phonology. In very young infants, language-specific patterns in speech perception emerge prior to speech production (Imada *et al.* 2006; Kuhl *et al.* 2008). Native-like pronunciation by L2 learners is only achieved if language acquisition took place very early in childhood (Yeni-Komshian, Flege, and Liu 2000). Therefore, heritage language learners should have better pronunciation and perceptual discrimination than L2 learners.

Several studies have confirmed this hypothesis already. Au *et al.* (2002), Knightly *et al.* (2003), and Oh *et al.*'s (2003) studies of Korean and Spanish heritage speakers and L2 learners found that heritage speakers with very low proficiency in the language performed significantly better than L2 learners on perception and production of Voice Onset Time (VOTs) in the two languages and in their overall accent. Beyond VOTs and general measures of pronunciation, studies of segmental phonology have also found that heritage speakers have more native-like phonological perception and production of specific sounds than L2 learners. For example, Lukyanchenko and Gor (2011) found native-like perception by heritage speakers of the hard-soft /t-t'/ and /p-p'/ stop contrasts in Russian as opposed to L2 learners who were quite different from the native speakers. Chang *et al.* (2011) investigated the production of vowels, plosives, and postalveolar fricatives in Mandarin, and also found that the Mandarin heritage speakers tested were significantly better than the L2 learners.

Another recent study is Kim (2015), who examined Spanish heritage speakers' perception of word-level (lexical) stress – as in the difference between *paso* [páso] "I pass" and *pasó* [pasó] "He passed" in Spanish – and compared their patterns with those of native Spanish speakers and English-speaking L2 learners of Spanish. Heritage speakers were expected to show more native-like knowledge of lexical stress than L2 learners, who began acquisition of Spanish later in life.

Eleven heritage speakers of Spanish attending an American university, 47 English-speaking L2 learners of Spanish, and 25 Spanish native controls tested in Mexico participated in the study. The heritage speakers were of Mexican background and began exposure to English after age 5. As established by self-assessments and a background questionnaire, all the heritage speakers and the L2 learners were English dominant.

The perception task was a forced-choice identification task with minimal pairs of disyllabic Spanish regular –*ar* verbs that differ only in the position of lexical stress (i.e., *páso*-type words indicating first person singular of the present indicative and *pasó*-type words indicating third person singular of the simple past perfective tense). Target items and fillers (with verbs in present and past tense) were inserted in the second-to-last position of a meaningful sentence, followed by a subject (e.g., *Por la plaza "páso" yo*. "Through the plaza, I pass." *Por la plaza "pasó" él*. "Through the plaza he passed."). The sentences were presented in auditory form with the last words of each sentence removed (e.g., *Por la plaza "pasó"*…). The participants had to determine which of the two options was the subject of the incomplete sentences they heard. Participants' accuracy was automatically collected through the psycholinguistic software used. The results appear in Figure 8.2.

Although the heritage speakers and the L2 learners were statistically less accurate than the native speakers, the heritage speakers (HS) showed native-like patterns, and their performance was closer to that of the native speakers (NS) than that of the L2 learners (L2). The native speakers and the heritage speakers were both less accurate perceiving *páso* than *pasó* words, whereas the L2 learners showed the opposite pattern and were significantly less accurate with *pasó* than with *páso* words. In fact, the L2 learners performed below chance when perceiving *pasó*-type words, despite the noticeably large duration difference in

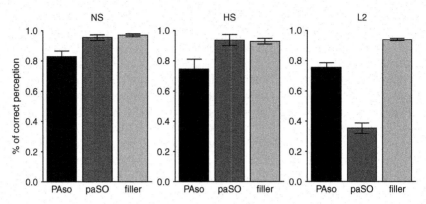

Figure 8.2. Accuracy rate of stress placement in native speakers (NS), heritage speakers (HS), and L2 learners (L2) of Spanish (Kim 2015).

this stress pattern. The L2 learners' accuracy rate of *páso*-type words did not differ from that of the native controls, even though the duration difference was close to zero. These results show that the heritage speakers retain native-like abilities in phonological perception: they are sensitive to acoustic cues (duration), whereas the L2 learners are not.

The perception of speech by non-native speakers is especially susceptible to adverse listening environments (Rogers *et al.* 2006; Simpson and Cooke 2005). Gor (2014) tested the abilities of high and low proficiency Russian heritage speakers and L2 learners of Russian to perceive Russian stimuli under high and low speech-babble noise. Gor (2014) asked whether heritage speakers are as efficient as L1 speakers under these conditions or whether they experience the same deficits as L2 learners. Gor also investigated the complex interaction of top-down and bottom-up processing in different groups of listeners. For example, consider the sentences in (1):

(1) a. Okolo doma stojala staraja *mashina*.
         near   house stood old   car.NOM.SG
         "An old car stood near the house."
     b. V sadu   rosla spelaja *malina*.
         in garden grew ripe   raspberry.NOM.SG
         "Ripe raspberries grew in the garden."

Under noisy conditions, the words *mashina* "car" in (1a) and *malina* "raspberry" in (1b) can be confused. If bottom-up acoustic phonetic information is not helpful to decode the meaning of the word, the listener has to rely on other top-down, contextual information in the sentence to recover the acoustically degraded signal. A speech under noise task was conducted with high and low noise levels and high and low predictability contexts. The results showed that the high proficiency heritage speakers did not differ from the monolingual Russian speakers tested as baseline. The high proficiency heritage speakers outperformed the high proficiency L2 learners: their increased phonological sensitivity interacted with their ability to rely on top-down processing in sentence integration, use contextual cues, and build expectancies in the high-noise/high-context condition. This experiment thus supports an early naturalistic advantage in the acquisition of phonology and phonological perception in heritage speakers. Because Gor did not find that the low proficiency heritage speakers had similar advantages over low proficiency L2 learners, her findings suggest that proficiency increases the ability to take advantage of the high predictability context (top-down processing) under adverse listening conditions.

Similar advantages for heritage speakers are confirmed by Saadah (2011), who investigated vowel production in heritage speakers of Palestinian Arabic and English-speaking L2 learners of Arabic. Arabic and English have different phonetic and phonological vowel systems in terms of the number of vowels and their acoustic realizations. Arabic is a six-vowel system consisting of /i, iː, u, uː, a, aː/, whereas English is a twelve-vowel system, excluding diphthongs. Saadah examined vowel arrangement in the acoustic space.

Stimuli of Modern Standard Arabic were elicited from 6 native Palestinian Arabic speakers who arrived in the United States after age 20, 12 heritage speakers of Palestinian Arabic who grew up in the United States, and 12 English-speaking learners of Arabic as L2. The heritage speakers and the L2 learners were between 18 and 35 years of age. The participants were asked to read a list of 114 Arabic words inserted in carrier phrases, such as *Say X twice*. The Arabic short vowels /i, u, a/ and their long counterparts /iː, uː, aː/ were tested in plain and pharyngealized forms.

Saadah hypothesized that the heritage language learners would show advantages in pronunciation over the L2 learners because they had established their Arabic vowel categories in childhood (Kuhl *et al.* 2008). At the same time, due to crosslinguistic phonetic interference between Arabic and English, the heritage speakers were also expected to differ from the monolingually raised Egyptian Arabic speakers. Figure 8.3 presents the Arabic vowel systems in the vowel space produced by the three groups.

Overall, the heritage speakers' values are closer to the values of the native speakers than those of the L2 learners. The Arabic heritage speakers were closer to the native speakers' values for high front vowels and to L2 learners for /uː/, whereas they fell in between for /u, a, aː/. This suggests that the heritage speakers of Arabic were more successful in achieving target-like categorical representation of some target vowels but not for others, thus demonstrating measurable native as well as non-native pronunciation of Arabic vowels. The

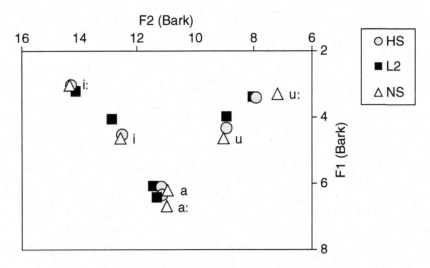

Figure 8.3. Production of Arabic vowels /a, aː, i, iː, u, uː/ by Palestinian native speakers, heritage speakers of Arabic, and L2 learners of Arabic (adapted from Saadah 2011).

native speakers and the L2 learners display an opposite pattern of more dispersed long vowels and more contracted short vowels. However, the heritage speakers' vowel triangles (for long and short vowels) were intermediate in the vowel space between the native speakers and the L2 learners.

In summary, the studies on phonology and pronunciation show that heritage speakers are more native-like than L2 learners. In perception, native speakers and heritage speakers do not differ under normal speech conditions. The heritage speakers tested in all these studies are also generally closer to the native speakers in pronunciation than the L2 learners, although they also show traces and features of non-native accents due to influence from the majority language. Therefore, the data from heritage speakers add strong support for the hypothesis that the acquisition and ultimate attainment of phonology is eminently affected by age of acquisition.

In the areas of morphosyntax, semantics, and pragmatics, by contrast, studies comparing heritage speakers and L2 learners do not always find an advantage (i.e., more native-like knowledge) for the heritage speakers due to age of acquisition. Au *et al.* (2002) and Knightly *et al.* (2003) were the first ones to report that low proficiency Spanish heritage speakers and L2 learners did not differ from each other on several aspects of the morphosyntax of Spanish. Both groups were significantly less accurate than the native speakers in production and grammaticality judgment tasks. Similarly, Bruhn de Garavito's (2002) study of verb movement in Spanish and O'Grady, Lee, and Choo's

(2001) study of case markers and relative clauses in Korean found no differences between L2 learners and heritage language learners.

However, other studies report different trends. Montrul's (2005) study of unaccusativity in Spanish detected advantages for heritage language learners over L2 learners of low proficiency. Yet, other studies report mixed results depending on structures. Håkansson (1995) found that heritage speakers of Swedish were significantly more native-like with word order (the Germanic V2 phenomenon) than L2 learners of Swedish, but the two groups were equally non-native on gender, number, and definiteness agreement in noun phrases. Montrul (2010, 2012) found no differences between Spanish heritage speakers and Spanish L2 learners with knowledge of object clitic placement in a written acceptability judgment task, but while the heritage speakers outperformed the L2 learners in their acceptance of sentences with alternative word order (topicalizations), the L2 learners were more native-like than the heritage speakers at rejecting ungrammatical sentences without differential object marking in Spanish. Albirini and Benmamoun (2014a) compared heritage speakers of Arabic and L2 learners of Arabic on knowledge of plural nouns. Their study shows that heritage speakers were overall more accurate than the L2 learners. The heritage speakers made errors similar to the developmental errors made by child learners of Arabic in their deployment of roots and patterns, while the L2 learners showed different error patterns. Therefore, it is not possible to generalize a specific pattern of performance for morphosyntax as we have been able to do for phonology so far. It looks like detecting advantages for heritage speakers on morphosyntax depends on the proficiency of the participants, on the area of grammar investigated (see Chapter 3), and the types of tasks used, as discussed in Chapter 6. Different areas of what is broadly described as morphosyntax involve a variety of structures with different degrees of frequency, complexity, saliency, form-meaning transparency, and in acquisition, developmental schedules and trajectories. It is no surprise, then, that the findings differ.

A study that offers a generally positive answer to the question of advantages for heritage speakers is Mikhaylova (2012), who compared L2 learners of Russian and heritage speakers of Russian on their knowledge of aspect. Compared to English, Russian's aspectual system is more complex and elaborated, since as we discussed in Chapter 3, aspect in Russian is calculated at the lexical, the syntactic, and the pragmatic level (recall Laleko 2010 in Chapter 3). In addition, verbs are encoded in the lexicon as perfective or imperfective and a complex system of suffixation marks overtly aspectual distinctions. The three questions motivating Mikhaylova's study were whether heritage speakers of Russian had an advantage over proficiency-matched L2 learners in their knowledge of aspect, whether telicity or boundedness presented greater difficulty for the two groups, and which morphological reflexes of Russian aspect (prefixation, suffixation, or a combination of both) posed greater difficulty in acquisition for each group. The participants were 30 native speakers of Russian tested in Russia, 22 high proficiency heritage speakers of Russian in the United States, and 11 high proficiency English-speaking L2 learners of Russian. They all scored above 80% in a written proficiency measure. The main task was a semantic interpretation task with different types of verbs. The participants had to interpret the event in each sentence as complete or incomplete and choose the appropriate continuation of the sentence. Without any contextual clues, the morphology on the verb was the only information available to arrive at the correct interpretation of the event, as in (2).

> (2)   Vladimir *pročital* detektiv...
>   "Vladimir read the detective story..."
>   a. ... i emu ne ponravilsja konec. correct choice
>   "and he didn't like the ending"
>   b. ... i on xotel uznat' konec
>   "... and he wanted to find out the ending"
>   c. Oba varianta vozmožny.
>   "Both variants are possible."

In this example, entailment (a) is the only possibility because the verb *pročital* has a perfective prefix and is interpreted as telic. Thus, in sentences like these, the first clause included verbs that manipulated telicity contrasts. Boundedness was tested using different types of predicates (states, activities, accomplishments, and achievements). Conditions 1 and 2 included structurally and morphologically complex predicates with lexically underspecified dynamic verbs; i.e., in these predicates both telicity and boundedness needed to be calculated for successful interpretation of the sentence. Condition 3, by contrast, included structurally simpler predicates with lexically specified [+telic] nondynamic verbs, so the processing task only involved calculation of the boundedness feature.

According to the results, the heritage speakers were statistically more accurate on aspectual distinctions in the sentence interpretation task: the native speakers' accuracy rate was 83%, the heritage speakers' 75%, and the L2 learners' 62%. The semantic contrast that posed greater difficulty for the L2 learners had to do with boundedness, and the morphological pattern of aspectual marking that presented more difficulty was prefixation combined with secondary imperfective suffixation, especially for the L2 group.

The results of this study show that despite scoring at a native speaker range of accuracy on the proficiency measure task, the heritage speakers and L2 learners do not display equally high proficiency in aspectual interpretations. Some aspectual contrasts pose greater difficulty than others, and heritage speakers' performance sometimes converges with L2 learners and sometimes with native speakers. Not surprisingly, the most morphologically simple or transparent verb types elicited more accurate interpretations than the prefixed–suffixed imperfective accomplishment verbs, which were the most difficult for the heritage speakers and the L2 learners. Mikhaylova concluded that morphology seems to be a stumbling block not only to L2 acquisition (following Slabakova 2008), but perhaps to heritage language acquisition as well. At the same time, there seems to be an advantage to early bilingualism versus late bilingualism, which is selective rather than categorical (Montrul 2008).

Other studies offer a more complex answer to whether and how heritage speakers have advantages compared to L2 learners, depending on several factors. Montrul and Perpiñán (2011) investigated whether heritage speakers and L2 learners of different proficiency levels have similar knowledge of tense-aspect and mood morphology; specifically, the morphology of preterit/imperfect and indicative/subjunctive and their semantic implications. Sixty L2 learners and 60 heritage speakers (ages 18–27) matched for proficiency on parts of the DELE test participated in the study. Most of the heritage speakers were enrolled in the same classes as the L2 learners, and had academic literacy in Spanish. That is, they were HL learners.

Knowledge of verbal morphology was tested with two cloze-type written tasks – one for tense and aspect and one for mood – where participants saw two passages and had to choose the correct form of the verb (preterite/imperfect or indicative/subjunctive). The semantic entailments of preterite/imperfect and indicative/subjunctive morphology were examined via two sentence conjunction judgment tasks (one for tense/aspect and one for mood), as in (3) and (4). The participants had to judge whether each sentence was logical or contradictory by choosing a number on the scale from -2 to 2 (-2 = contradictory, 2 = logical 0 = unable to decide).

(3) Example of preterite-imperfect with a stative predicate
La clase era a las 10:00 pero empezó a las 10:30.   IMPERFECT
(logical)
La clase fue a las 10:00 pero empezó a las 10:30.   PRETERIT
(contradictory)
"The class was at 10:00 but started at 10:30."

(4) Example of indicative-subjunctive with a relative clause
*Necesito un libro de cuentos para niños que tiene
ilustraciones de Miró, pero no sé si hay uno.   INDICATIVE
(contradictory)
Necesito un libro de cuentos para niños que tenga
ilustraciones de Miró pero no sé si hay uno.   SUBJUNCTIVE
(logical)
"I need a children's book that has illustrations by Miró, but I don't know if there is one."

Montrul and Perpiñán found some differences between L2 learners and HL learners, but these differences did not always entail an advantage for the HL learners. The HL learners were more accurate than the L2 learners with grammatical aspect but not with mood, a finding that is consistent with the developmental schedule of TAM in L1 acquisition. That is, in L1 acquisition, tense/aspect distinctions are acquired before mood distinctions, and therefore mood distinctions may never be acquired or may be lost by the heritage speakers before they receive sufficient support in the input (Blake 1983; Montrul 2004; Silva-Corvalán 1994, 2014). Furthermore, there was a task effect: the relative advantage of the HL learners over the L2 learners only showed up in the sentence conjunction judgment task testing sentences like (3) for tense-aspect but not in the same task testing mood, like the sentences in (4). By contrast, the L2 learners were overall more accurate than the HL learners in the two morphology recognition tasks across proficiency levels, as shown in Table 8.4. The morphological recognition tasks tested recognition of tense-aspect and mood morphology in obligatory contexts.

The results of the two sentence conjunction judgment tasks showed group by proficiency effects. The low and intermediate proficiency HL learners were more discriminating of the preterit/imperfect contrast with achievements and stative predicates than the L2 learners, but the differences between the two groups disappeared at the advanced level. A different pattern emerged with mood. The advanced L2 learners were more target-like at discriminating between subjunctive and indicative than advanced HL learners. Low and intermediate proficiency HL learners and L2 learners did not discriminate between subjunctive and indicative. Because tense and aspect are acquired before mood, the results of this study are consistent with developmental schedules reported in L1, L2, and bilingual acquisition. With respect to tasks, the morphology

Table 8.4. *Mean percentage accuracy scores in the morphology recognition tasks (Montrul and Perpiñán 2011)*

Group	N	Tense-aspect task		Mood task	
		Preterit	Imperfect	Indicative	Subjunctive
Native speakers	23	95.9	96.5	99.1	97.4
HL learners	60	89.2	73.1	92.3	64.8
Advanced	23	90.3	84.2	97.4	85.6
Intermediate	21	92.2	69.9	94.7	60.9
Low	16	83.5	61.3	81.8	40
L2 learners	60	89.3	88.9	92.8	78.3
Advanced	23	95.6	95.4	96.5	94.3
Intermediate	21	86.7	85.7	83.8	74.7
Low	16	83.5	83.9	99.4	60

recognition task tests explicit knowledge of morphology, whereas the sentence conjunction judgment task focuses on meaning, and supposedly taps more implicit knowledge of the relevant morphology. The L2 learners are usually more grammatically accurate in tasks that maximize explicit and metalinguistic knowledge (Montrul, Foote, and Perpiñán 2008a; Bowles 2011), whereas these tasks do not favor HL learners, who have poor metalinguistic awareness, as we discuss further in Section 8.4. Therefore, this study shows that early language experience brings advantages for *some*, but by no means all, aspects of morphosyntax.

Another study finding intriguing differences between L2 learners and HL learners is Laleko and Polinsky (2013). They examined syntactic and discourse-pragmatic knowledge of null and overt nominative case and topic markers in Japanese and Korean. Both languages use particles to encode the relevant contrasts: *–wa* (Japanese) and *–nun/–un* (Korean) attach to the noun phrase, which serves as the topic of the sentence, while *–ga* (Japanese) and *–i/–ka* (Korean) mark its grammatical subject. In both languages, topic markers can mark a generic expression, interpreted as referring to a general class of entities, an anaphoric noun phrase linked to prior discourse via linguistic or contextual antecedent, or a contrastive topic. Examples (5) and (6) from Japanese and Korean illustrate the phenomena:

(5) Sakana-wa tai-ga   oisii.   *Japanese*
    fish-TOP   red snapper-NOM delicious
    "Speaking of fish, red snapper is delicious."
(6) Sayngsen-un yene-ka   massiss-ta.   *Korean*
    fish-TOP   salmon-NOM delicious-DECL
    "Speaking of fish, salmon is delicious."

According to Laleko and Polinsky's review of the existing L1 acquisition literature on these phenomena in Korean and Japanese, the nominative marker begins to be used more consistently and earlier than the topic marker in the two languages. Laleko and Polinsky examined the interplay between syntactic and discourse-pragmatic factors in the knowledge of these markers to find out whether heritage speakers showed more native-like knowledge in this area as compared to L2 learners.

The participants were all adults: 29 Japanese and 35 Korean heritage speakers, 13 native speakers of Korean, 13 native speakers of Japanese, and 16 L2 learners of Korean and 31 L2 learners of Japanese. They all completed a written acceptability judgment task in Japanese or Korean with 56 grammatical and ungrammatical sentences, which the participants were asked to rate on a 1–5 scale. Ratings were elicited on a set of conditions, including appropriate use of the topic and subject markers; misuse of the markers, including use of the nominative particle in place of the topic particle and vice versa; and appropriate and inappropriate particle omissions.

Laleko and Polinsky found that discourse-level phenomena appear to present more difficulty to heritage speakers than sentence-level phenomena, an observation we already discussed in Chapter 3. The results showed that in the two languages, the heritage speakers were generally more accurate on conditions involving the nominative marker than on conditions involving the topic marker. But interesting differences between the groups obtained in the two languages. The heritage speakers of Korean were significantly closer to the native speakers than the L2 learners of Korean. In contrast, the heritage speakers of Japanese were closer to the L2 group, and both groups were significantly different from the group of Japanese native speakers, as shown in Figure 8.4.

While the native speakers of Japanese were sensitive to contrasts between acceptable and unacceptable sentences in all conditions, heritage speakers and L2 learners in the Japanese group exhibited nontarget knowledge of the linguistic functions of the topic and subject markers and principles that determine when these markers can be omitted.

In contrast to the Japanese group, the Korean heritage speakers were statistically indistinguishable from the Korean native speakers on all conditions except ungrammatical particle omissions, where heritage speakers were less accurate than the native speakers but still more accurate than L2 learners, who diverged from the native speakers to a greater extent. When compared with the L2 group, heritage speakers of Korean exhibited a number of advantages over L2 learners on conditions that required the nominative marker, but on conditions involving unacceptable omissions of the nominative marker, they employed the topic marker instead.

Despite similar ages, age of acquisition of English, and length of exposure to the heritage language, the level of proficiency of the Korean and Japanese heritage speakers in this study varied widely: the Korean speakers patterned more with native speakers of Korean, whereas the Japanese heritage speakers patterned more with the L2 learners of Japanese. All the heritage speakers of Korean had some proficiency in Korean, but many of the Japanese heritage speakers did not, and were like L2 learners, as discussed in Kondo-Brown's (2005) study mentioned in Chapter 2. For Laleko and Polinsky, the differences lie in the linguistic practices and the patterns of intergenerational transmission within the Korean and Japanese communities. Japanese immigration to the United States dates from the second half of the twentieth century, whereas the Korean immigration is much more recent. As reported by Carreira and Kagan (2011), Korean HL learners exhibit the highest rates of participation in community or church schools where they receive instruction in the heritage language. These

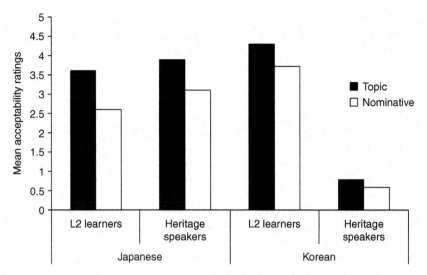

Figure 8.4. Mean acceptability ratings on topic and nominative markers in Japanese and Korean L2 learners and heritage speakers (adapted from Laleko and Polinsky 2013).

external factors could perhaps explain why Laleko and Polinsky found heritage speakers to have advantages over L2 learners in the Korean heritage group but not in the Japanese group. They would also underlie the fact that the availability and use of the heritage language contributes significantly to proficiency in the heritage language, perhaps more than potential early learning advantages.

In sum, heritage speakers show consistent advantages over L2 learners in speech perception and pronunciation, which can be due to age effects. However, aspects of morphosyntax, semantics, and pragmatics are subject to different developmental schedules in different languages and are affected by the structure of the languages, contextual, and experiential factors, in addition to maturational schedules. As a result, advantages for heritage speakers over L2 learners in these areas are not as robust or clear as they are in phonology, and we still do not understand why there is so much variability in these grammatical areas.

8.2.2   Dominant language transfer

Transfer or crosslinguistic influence is a linguistic and psycholinguistic process that characterizes several outcomes of bilingualism. In the language contact literature, Weinrich (1953, p. 7) defined transfer as "interlingual identifications," or the incorporation of linguistic features from one language into another with consequent restructuring. Transfer is very common in both developing and fossilized L2 grammars that have reached the end of development (Franceschina 2005; Han 2014; Lardiere 2007), and a feature of linguistic representations. A few documented cases of L1 attrition in adults at the level of phonetics (Major 1992), lexical semantics (Balcom 2003), and the syntax–discourse interface (Gürel 2002) can be easily characterized as L2 effects on the L1. Similarly, many patterns of incomplete acquisition in heritage speakers could be due to transfer from the dominant language. In fact, language transfer is one of the forms in which incomplete acquisition can be manifested, other forms being developmental errors like in L1 acquisition and structural simplification, as discussed in Chapter 7. In essence, and contrary to what Pascual y Cabo and Rothman (2012) argue, incomplete acquisition and dominant language transfer are not incompatible. Just like fossilization can often be linked to persistent L1 transfer in ultimate attainment in L2 acquisition (White 2003a), incomplete acquisition in early bilingual and heritage language acquisition can also manifest itself as dominant language transfer. However, it is worth emphasizing once more that not all the structural changes observed in heritage speakers are due to dominant language transfer. As in L2 acquisition, transfer and fossilization are localized and subject to modularity, manifesting themselves more readily in some grammatical areas than in others.

Montrul, Foote, and Perpiñán (2008b) investigated dominant language transfer in Spanish heritage speakers and L2 learners of Spanish whose L1 was English. The focus of the study was overt wh-movement in questions (and relative clauses). Questions in the two languages are formed by fronting a wh-phrase to clause-initial position. Spanish, however, exhibits obligatory subject-verb inversion in clauses where the wh-phrase has been extracted from an object position, as shown in (7). This inversion is similar, although not identical, to auxiliary verb inversion in English. Like in English, questioning an object from some constituents is ungrammatical, as shown in (8).

(7)   a. ¿Qué compró Juan en la tienda? *cf.* ¿*Qué Juan compró en la tienda?
       b. What did John buy at the store?
(8)   a. ¿*A quién habló José con María después de ver?
       b. *Who did Joe speak with Mary after seeing?

One difference between Spanish and English addressed in this study is the possibility of having (or not) an overtly expressed complementizer. In Spanish, the complementizer *que* is typically obligatory (9a), while in English the complementizer *that* is optional with some verbs in embedded complement clauses (9b).

(9)   a. María dijo que ella es de Colombia. *cf.* *Maria dijo ella es
         de Colombia.
       b. Maria said (that) she is from Colombia.

In Spanish, it is possible to form a question about a subject from an embedded clause following a complementizer, while English does not allow an overt complementizer in the same type of sentences, as the grammatical contrast in (10) shows.[1]

(10)   a. ¿Quién$_i$ piensa María que t_i es de Argentina?
       b. *Who$_i$ does Mary think that t_i is from Argentina?

If there is transfer in this grammatical domain, Spanish heritage speakers and L2 learners of Spanish with English as their stronger language may accept sentences with no complementizers and reject sentences with subject extraction due to the obligatory presence of the complementizer in Spanish. Participants were 22 native speakers of Spanish and 70 English-speaking L2 learners of Spanish ranging from low to advanced proficiency in Spanish. They completed a written grammaticality judgment task with a total of 50 sentences, each followed by a five-point Likert scale.

The results showed that L2 learners and heritage speakers knew that complementizers cannot be omitted in Spanish, and that subject questions with overt complementizers are grammatical. At the same time, the native speakers rated these sentences higher than the heritage speakers and the L2 learners, and there was evidence of transfer from English in the two experimental groups. Transfer from English, as measured by low ratings of grammatical sentences, was stronger in the speakers with lower proficiency in Spanish, regardless of whether they were L2 learners or heritage speakers.

In the area of semantics, Montrul and Ionin (2012) investigated the interpretation of definite plural articles in Spanish by L2 learners of Spanish and Spanish heritage speakers whose dominant language is English. Although both Spanish and English have definite and indefinite articles, the languages vary in the semantic interpretations of these. For example, genericity in English is expressed through bare plural noun phrases, as in (11a). With the definite article, as in (11b), the sentence refers to a specific group of tigers. In Spanish, bare plurals in subject position are typically ungrammatical, as in (12a), but the definite article can be used to express both a generic statement and a specific statement. So, sentence (12b) can be a generic statement about tigers (generic reading) or can also refer to a specific group of tigers (specific reading), depending on the context.

---

[1] This is known as the *that-t* effect (Chomsky 1986), which has been argued to be related to the different inflectional and null subject properties of the two languages.

(11) a. Tigers eat meat.   *generic*
       b. The tigers eat meat. *specific*
(12) a. *Tigres comen carne. *ungrammatical*
       b. Los tigres comen carne. *generic, specific*

Montrul and Ionin asked whether L2 learners of Spanish and heritage speakers would tend to interpret definite plural determiners as generic, very much like Spanish native speakers tend to interpret definite articles in Spanish, or as specific due to transfer from English. Results of an acceptability judgment task and a truth value judgment task administered to 22 native speakers of Spanish, 30 Spanish heritage speakers, and 30 L2 learners of Spanish matched for proficiency in Spanish showed significant differences between the native speakers and the two experimental groups. The L2 learners and the heritage speakers did not differ from each other, and unlike the native speakers who preferred a generic interpretation for plural definite articles, the L2 learners and the Spanish heritage speakers showed a preference for specific readings instead. Although Montrul and Ionin set up their hypothesis to examine the effects of age of acquisition for transfer, the results on definite plural articles in generic contexts confirmed that language dominance is more relevant than age of acquisition. Thus, in this regard, there were no advantages for the heritage speakers in terms of more native-like knowledge of semantics, and the two groups showed exactly the same patterns of dominant language transfer effects. The semantic interpretation of English definite determiners is imposed on the semantic interpretation of Spanish determiners. Montrul and Ionin (2010) tested some of the same heritage speakers in English (see Chapter 5) and showed that the heritage speakers had native interpretations of definite determiners in English. Therefore, it is clear that these participants transferred the semantic interpretations from the stronger language.

Kupisch (2012) tested Italian heritage speakers in Germany and German-speaking L2 learners of Italian. Like English and Spanish, German and Italian have definite and indefinite articles as well as contexts in which nouns can occur with or without articles. In both languages, bare noun phrases can occur in specific syntactic configurations, as shown in (13).

(13) a. Jeden Tag isst sie Kartoffeln.   German
       b. Ogni giorni mangia patate.   Italian
           "She eats potatoes every day."
(14) a. Katzen sind intelligent.   German
       b. *Gatti sono intelligenti.   Italian
       c. Il gatti sono intelligenti.
          "Cats are intelligent."

In Italian and German (and in English and Spanish), bare noun phrases can appear in object position, as in (13b). Bare nouns in German, as in English, have a generic meaning. In Italian (as in Spanish), bare plural nouns in subject position are ungrammatical (14b), and generic meanings are expressed with the definite article (14c). The participants were young adults recruited in Germany and Italy, and came from binational families (German-Italian parents). The 20 Italian heritage speakers grew up as simultaneous bilinguals, speaking Italian and Germany from birth, but 8 of them were dominant in Italian at the time of testing and the other 12 were dominant in German. The other group consisted of 15 advanced late L2 learners of Italian, with German as their L1. In the acceptability judgment task they completed, the three groups were very accurate (above 95%) with the grammatical sentences with and without articles. However, ratings on ungrammatical sentences with bare plurals in subject position were significantly different by group. The heritage speakers who were dominant in Italian performed at ceiling (97%), but the heritage speakers with Italian as the weaker language and the L2 learners were only 33% and 56% accurate, respectively, with bare NPs in specific and generic contexts, as in (14c).

The results of generic interpretations of sentences with definite plural articles tested in a truth value judgment task showed that the three groups imposed the interpretations of German onto Italian, showing preference for the specific more than the generic interpretation of definite articles in Italian. However, the heritage speakers who were dominant in Italian gave significantly fewer specific responses (and more generic responses) than the L2 learners of Italian. These results are given in Figure 8.5.

At least for this domain of the grammar, Kupisch (2012) agrees with Montrul and Ionin's conclusion (2012), claiming that when comparing L2 learners and heritage speakers, age of acquisition is overruled in this case by dominant language transfer. At the same time, Kupisch found that at the individual level, many Italian-dominant heritage speakers performed at ceiling suggesting, as stressed in Chapter 7, that it is possible to find advanced speakers with native command of the heritage language in Europe, depending on grammatical area.

In the three studies presented above, the heritage speakers were tested in their own native language, but Polinsky (2015) discusses the situations where heritage speakers are learners of a cognate heritage language, which in this case is like learning a third, different language: for example, a heritage speaker of Gujarati who is learning Hindi/Urdu in the classroom, or a speaker of Cantonese who is learning Mandarin Chinese. The issue of language transfer is particularly relevant in a situation of L3 acquisition, where previous knowledge of at least two other languages can influence the acquisition of a third language (Rothman 2015). The question these heritage speakers who are L3 learners raise is whether the previous linguistic knowledge of their heritage

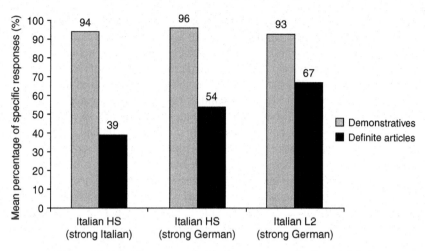

Figure 8.5. Specific responses with demonstrative plurals and definite articles in a TVJT in Italian (adapted from Kupisch 2012).

language transfers, and which of their languages influence the process. Does previous knowledge of a cognate heritage language facilitate or impede their progress in the instructed language? Through a review of existing studies that may contribute answers to these questions, Polinsky found the same general trend that has been found for L2 acquisition. In phonology, heritage speakers who are learning a cognate heritage language show significant advantages. That is, their heritage language (the L1) facilitates acquisition of the sound system of the cognate heritage language (the L3). However, in morphosyntax, the picture is much less clear as pointed out earlier. Heritage speakers show asymmetric transfer effects, relying heavily on their dominant language (English, in most cases) but not on their heritage language. Thus, the dominant language also plays a role in the acquisition of a cognate heritage language.

In conclusion, dominant language transfer is common in heritage speakers and in L2 learners and coexists with other processes. As in L2 acquisition, it is more prominent in heritage speakers of lower proficiency in the heritage language. As in L2 acquisition, it is sometimes possible to predict what transfers and when it is likely to happen, but not always. To this day, and despite the wealth of research it has generated, how transfer operates psycholinguistically is still an enigma.

8.2.3   Interface vulnerability

Not all structural changes observed in the grammars of heritage speakers that could be attributed to dominant language transfer are interpreted in this way. Sometimes, semantic, syntactic, and pragmatic complexity or frequency effects may converge on the same results. For example, the use of higher rates of overt subject pronouns in the Spanish of New York in topic continuation and focus contexts is seen by Otheguy and Zentella (2012) as transfer from English (a language that does not admit null pronouns) and dialect leveling. However, Silva-Corvalán (1994) and Sorace and colleagues (Belletti, Bennati, and Sorace 2007; Sorace 2011; Sorace and Filiaci 2006) see the same phenomenon in Spanish and Italian as related to difficulty with the syntax–discourse interface instead.

In recent years, explanations and predictions of developmental delays or inability to reach native-like attainment in specific areas of grammatical knowledge in different types of bilingual acquisition have been linked to the architecture of the language faculty (Slabakova 2008). A recurrent claim is that structures and grammatical properties at interfaces are inherently more "complex" than properties internal to a specific domain (syntax, phonology, and semantics) due to the integration of different levels of linguistic knowledge/ analysis. This is the Interface Hypothesis, proposed by Sorace and colleagues (see Sorace 2011 and commentaries). Intended as a theory to explain optionality in L2 grammars that have reached the end state of development, Sorace (2011) claimed that the Interface Hypothesis applies only to advanced stages of L2 acquisition and advanced stages of L1 attrition in adults and not to earlier stages of L2 acquisition and heritage language acquisition. Disagreeing on this restriction, White (2011) and Lardiere (2011) consider that that testing the Interface Hypothesis with lower proficiency learners would make the hypothesis stronger and richer, because nonconvergence problems in the end-state grammar do not just appear out of the blue. Testing interface knowledge in advanced L2 grammars or earlier, for example, may reveal how divergence in the near-native grammars comes into being. Montrul and Polinsky (2011) similarly argued that there is no reason not to think that whatever is already vulnerable to simplification and reduction during first generation language attrition will not be found in the second generation, that is, the heritage speakers. Thus, theoretical accounts that have been formulated to explain processes and outcomes of second language acquisition and L1 attrition can be profitably extended to predict and explain patterns in heritage language grammars, as I argued in Chapter 5. In fact, Leal Méndez, Rothman, and Slabakova's (2014) study on Spanish heritage speakers addresses this concern. Similarly, Mai (2012), described in more detail below, examined the explanatory power of the Interface Hypothesis with English-speaking learners of Mandarin Chinese as an L2 and Mandarin Chinese heritage speakers in the United Kingdom in the domain of grammatical focus.

In a sentence, the topic (usually the subject) is what the sentence is about, whereas the focus (the predicate) is the logical predicate or what is predicated about the topic. Grammatical focus is a product of multiple linguistic components, as phonology, morphology, syntax, semantics, and pragmatics all play a role, and languages differ in the devices they employ to encode and decode focus. Focus information may be encoded, for instance, by pitch accent (e.g., English), focus-marking particles (e.g., Japanese), word order manipulation (e.g., Hungarian, Italian, and Portuguese), cleft constructions (e.g., English and French), or by a combination of two or more of these devices (Lambrecht 2001). Mai investigated the *(shi)...de* focus construction in Mandarin, exemplified in (16), which includes several interface conditions related to the past at the level of semantic features, the verb phrase, the telicity of the verb phrase, and pragmatic notions related to the object and to focus.

(15) *Canonical sentence*
      Zhangsan zuotian   qu le   xuexiao.
      Zhangsan yesterday go PERF school
      "Zhangsan went to school yesterday."

(16) *Shi...de focus sentence*
      Zhangsan *shi* zuotian   qu xuexiao *de*.
      Zhangsan SHI yesterday go school DE
      "It was yesterday that Zhangsan went to school (rather than any other day)."

The element *shi* is commonly used as the copula in Mandarin, equivalent to "be" in English. In discourse, *shi* in the *(shi)...de* focus construction can be omitted under certain conditions. The other element *de* is a multifunctional category. In terms of meaning, the *shi...de* construction can convey an identificational focus meaning analogous to the meaning conveyed by the English *it-cleft* construction, as shown by the English translation in (16).

Mai used multiple experiments to test several semantic and discourse-syntactic properties (telicity, past event, and nonaffectedness) associated with this construction in Mandarin, in order to investigate whether the different properties presented different challenges to the two types of learners. The participants were sixteen monolingually raised native Chinese immigrants to English-speaking countries, 33 Chinese heritage speakers in English-speaking countries (fifteen were immigrant children and 18 were children of Chinese immigrants), and 118 English-speaking learners of Mandarin Chinese (lower levels) enrolled in Mandarin classes in the UK at the university level. A written cloze test was used to divide the HL and L2 learner participants into proficiency groups. To test all the meanings associated with the *shi ... de* structure, Mai used five written tasks: a sentence completion task, a multiple choice questionnaire, an acceptability judgment task, a contextualized acceptability judgment task, and a sentence ranking task.

According to the results, all the groups, except for the lower proficiency L2 learners, correctly interpreted *shi...de* focus sentences as past tense sentences at native levels. The heritage speakers and the advanced L2 learners exhibited native-like sensitivity to violations with future adverbs and violations of telicity, as tested in the acceptability judgment task. Thus, all groups showed no problems with the syntax–semantics interface as it relates to tense and aspect meanings associated with this structure. However, the L2 learners and the heritage speakers were less accurate than the adult Chinese immigrants with sentences that tested the "nonaffectee condition" on the focused element. Although both L2 learners and heritage speakers differed from the native speakers, the heritage speakers were more accurate than the L2 learners, including the advanced group. In general, the L2 learners and the HL learners were the most accurate in the tasks testing for the past and telic conditions, but displayed lower accuracy in the <+/– old-event> condition, and obtained the lowest accuracy in the nonaffectee condition. Overall, the HL learners outperformed proficiency-matched L2 learners across tasks. In general, Mai found a gradient, rather than a categorical distinction between different interfaces and between different types of learners.

In one of the semantic properties tested in this study, Mai found clear differences between prepuberty and postpuberty language acquisition with the nonaffectee condition, which was acquired (albeit vulnerable or missing in some learners) in heritage language acquisition, but largely not acquired by the L2 learners, as illustrated in Figure 8.6. This particular finding suggests that the acquisition of this semantic condition may be sensitive to the timing of Mandarin input.

The nonaffectee condition involves semantic computation and integration of other cognitive domains, as stated by the Interface Hypothesis. Mai argues convincingly that the concept of "affectee" cannot be missing in L1 English speakers' cognition, or that the L2 learners of Mandarin are unable to recognize the focused element in a *shi...de* focus sentence. The crucial difference between the L2 grammars and the monolinguals' grammar is that the linguistic link between these two concepts is missing. Mai concluded that prepuberty (heritage language) and postpuberty (L2) acquisition not only differ in the inventory of uninterpretable features, but also in the ability to create links between the syntactic, semantic, and cognition domains.

The heritage learners also performed better than proficiency-matched adult L2 learners in the other tasks included in the experiment. However, unlike what Mai found in the nonaffectee test, these HL and L2 learners only showed quantitative differences, rather than qualitative ones. Mai further acknowledged that most of the features/conditions tested are not discussed in formal L1/L2 instruction, and both groups have to rely on their implicit knowledge of the *(shi)...de* focus construction. As a result, the HL learners performed considerably better. Not only do the findings of this study show how the complexity

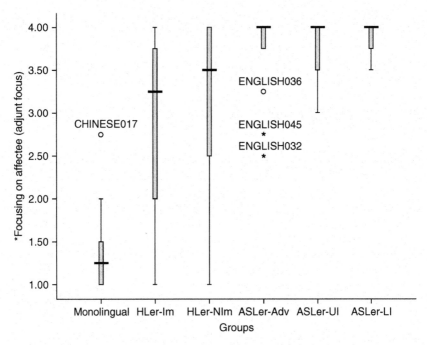

Figure 8.6. Boxplot of *Foc on Affectee Theme sentences (adjunct focus, all groups) (Mai 2012).

of different interfaces affects L2 learners and heritage speakers differently, but they also show that with noninstructed aspects of language, heritage speakers are superior to L2 learners.

Related to interfaces as well, Chung's (2013) study on semantic and discourse-pragmatic constraints on case ellipsis in Korean discussed in Chapter 7 also tested L2 learners. The study included an oral elicitation experiment with monolingual children in Korea and an experiment comparing heritage speakers and L2 learners of Korean. Recall from Chapter 7 that subjects and objects are overtly case-marked in Korean, yet case markers are frequently omitted in spoken Korean under a variety of syntactic and discourse-pragmatic conditions, such as topic, focus, definiteness, animacy, etc. Chung's study indicated that Korean case ellipsis is acquired by children by age 5, and the adult heritage speakers and the Korean L1 children were very similar in their performance. Chung also investigated whether L2 and HL learners can also successfully develop sensitivity to multiple cues that would lead them to acquire target-like competence in Korean. Participants completed a written elicited production task consisting of dialogues in informal speech and had to choose a case-marked or a bare NP within the context of a short conversation. The variables examined were contrastive focus, animacy, and definiteness, which have been identified as conditioning case ellipsis. The results displayed in Figure 8.7 showed that the heritage speakers and the L2 learners were different from the baseline group of Korean speakers, for whom the factors of contrastive focus, animacy, and definiteness determined the omission of case markers.

At the same time, the two bilingual groups differed from each other in significant ways. The heritage speakers were sensitive to multiple cues, behaving more like the Korean native speakers, and seemed to have attained a certain degree of implicit knowledge of Korean case ellipsis, whereas the L2 learners developed their own pattern of judgment, exclusively depending on animacy with almost no interaction with contrastive focus and definiteness. Because the higher proficiency heritage speakers appeared to have attained this subtle phenomenon while high proficiency L2 learners did not, one can assume that this difference may be due to age of acquisition (maturational effects), as discussed in the previous section.

If, according to the Interface Hypothesis bilinguals have difficulty integrating multiple sources of information, Chung's findings suggest that the L2 learners have acquired multiple types of information with respect to this phenomenon but do not know how to integrate context-inferred discourse-pragmatic cues in a native-like manner. Heritage speakers, by contrast, were more native-like in their performance, and still showed differences with respect to definiteness when dropping case in Korean. This is consistent with what Mai found in Chinese.

In conclusion, although originally conceived to explain non-native features in advanced stages of L2 acquisition and L1 attrition, the Interface Hypothesis can also successfully predict why some areas of grammar are robust while others are more vulnerable to attrition and incomplete acquisition in heritage language grammars and in earlier stages of L2 acquisition. It seems that phenomena that straddle different linguistic modules and extra-linguistic cognitive modules are vulnerable in all kinds of bilingual acquisition, and heritage language acquisition is no exception. This is an example of how existing theoretical approaches that have been conceived to explain phenomena in linguistic theory, in L2 acquisition, and in L1 attrition can also account for similar phenomena in heritage language acquisition, as discussed in Chapter 5.

8.3   The role of experience in heritage and second language development

As we have seen, although heritage speakers and L2 learners differ on age of acquisition of the heritage language and the L2, they sometimes make similar

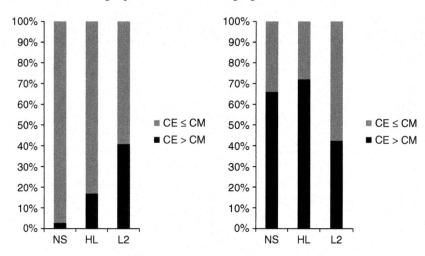

Figure 8.7. Percentage of individuals with an overall preference for CE or CM in subjects (left) and in objects (right) (Chung 2013).

types of errors in morphosyntax, semantics, and discourse, and both types of learners are affected by transfer from the dominant language, especially at lower levels of proficiency. At the same time, HL learners seem to have advantages over L2 learners in some areas, whereas L2 learners have advantages over HL learners in others. These differences appear to be related to the type of learning experience – specifically, type, modality, frequency, and amount of exposure to relevant input and use of the language, which in many ways is confounded with age.

As summarized in Table 8.2, heritage speakers were exposed to the language through the aural medium and their stronger skills are listening and speaking (see also Chapter 3). Many heritage speakers are illiterate in the heritage language, whereas others are functionally literate, but with little experience with academic language. In stark contrast, the vast majority of L2 learners, and especially those who start L2 acquisition after puberty and in the classroom, are exposed to spoken and written language from the beginning of instruction, and typically have more practice with the written modality than with speaking the language. A lot of language instruction in the classroom takes place through written tasks that present language in isolation and require metalinguistic reflection. If language experience plays a role in how L2 learners and heritage speakers perform on experimental tasks, this should be taken into account when drawing conclusions about the grammatical knowledge of the two types of language learners.

As mentioned in Section 8.2, cognitive and neurolinguistic approaches to second language acquisition and bilingualism consider that grammatical representations differ with respect to kinds of learning and storage in memory, distinguishing between implicit and explicit grammatical knowledge. Implicit knowledge is stored in procedural memory, where linguistic rules are typically stored, and is executed with automaticity and speed. Explicit knowledge is usually learned explicitly, with awareness of what is being learned and with conscious effort. It is stored in declarative memory and can be verbalized more often than not.

Research suggests that implicit knowledge of language develops in monolingual children during the critical period (Bialystok 1994), while metalinguistic ability and awareness of language emerges later, between ages 3 and 5 (Karmiloff-Smith 1979, 1986) when reading skills or preliteracy develops (Birdsong 1989). Especially in a classroom setting, explicit knowledge of the L2 develops first, and it is unclear to date whether or not it develops in tandem with implicit knowledge of the L2 system as well, or whether explicit knowledge becomes implicit, automatic, or integrated (Jiang 2007). As for early bilingual speakers of heritage languages, who received little or no schooling in the heritage language, they typically have limited academic literacy in their L1, developed through reading, writing, and spelling.

In addition to implicit/explicit grammatical knowledge, the tasks used in experiments to draw conclusions about linguistic knowledge can also be explicit or implicit in the presentation of the stimuli, the type of linguistic behavior they elicit, the automaticity of the responses, and the degree of awareness they require from the participants. Similarly related to input modality and experience is whether the tasks involve spoken or written language. Recall from Chapter 6 that different types of tasks used in L2 research and in the classroom (oral, written, production, comprehension, judgment, timed, untimed, etc.) tap and reveal different types of grammatical knowledge. Some tasks, especially written tasks, require high cognitive control and a high level of analyzed knowledge, whereas oral naturalistic production requires low control and a low level of analyzed knowledge (Bialystok and Ryan 1985). According to Ellis (2005), some tasks used to measure language ability maximize metalinguistic or explicit knowledge of language, while others minimize the opportunity to rely on metalinguistic, "studied," knowledge and allow the participant to use their more implicit grammatical knowledge. The variationist approach to L2 acquisition (Tarone 1979, 1983) described in Chapter 5 has long revealed the systematic variation demonstrated by L2 learners according to task and style. Recent research with heritage speakers supports these cognitive distinctions that have been advanced for L2 acquisition.

The first study to show this distinction with L2 learners and heritage speakers is Montrul, Foote, and Perpiñán (2008a), who investigated gender agreement in 72 L2 learners of Spanish and 70 heritage speakers of Spanish, ranging from low to advanced proficiency in the language. Knowledge of gender was assessed through a written picture identification task, a written elicited recognition task, and an oral picture description task. The oral production task was the most difficult of the three tasks because it included 50 high and low frequency nouns in five subconditions that varied the noun's gender and the gender transparency of the noun's ending. The two written tasks were untimed, whereas the oral task required spontaneous production. The overall results showed that the L2 learners were statistically more accurate with gender agreement in the two written tasks than in the oral production task. The heritage speakers showed exactly the opposite pattern – higher accuracy in oral production than in the written tasks. This study showed that error rates were quantitatively different in written comprehension and in oral production. Despite finding overall non-native mastery of gender in Spanish, this study showed that heritage speakers have an advantage over L2 learners when it comes to oral production and incidence of native-like knowledge and use. Alarcón (2011) partially replicated Montrul, Foote, and Perpiñán's (2008a) study with advanced proficiency L2 learners and heritage speakers. She also found that heritage speakers were accurate with gender and were better than the L2 learners in the oral task.

It is very likely that the patterns of results obtained by Montrul, Foote, and Perpiñán (2008a) and Alarcón's replication are a function of the tasks used, and the types of linguistic behavior and processing they elicit, rather than a reflection of how grammatical knowledge of Spanish gender agreement is represented and stored by L2 learners and heritage speakers. In other words, the two written tasks used were more metalinguistic, and required participants to make a choice out of two or three possible answers, leaving some room for reflection and guessing. The oral task used, on the other hand, required a spontaneous and fast response. In terms of difficulty, the two written tasks tested mostly canonical ending words, while the oral task included exceptional ending nouns as well. Two important questions that emerged from the results of the Montrul, Foote, and Perpiñán (2008a) study were first, whether in fact the type of task influences the type of linguistic knowledge elicited from heritage speakers and L2 learners and second, whether controlling for written and spoken modality and using more implicit measures of linguistic processing reveal differences between L2 learners and heritage speakers in gender and other areas of grammar.

The first question was pursued by Bowles (2011a), who investigated more directly whether L2 learners and heritage speakers performed differently on tests of grammatical ability depending on the degree of implicitness or explicitness of the task. Bowles asked whether L2 learners, who have more experience with classroom instruction than the HL learners, would score higher on tests of grammatical knowledge that maximize explicit knowledge, whereas HL learners would score lower on those measures because of their naturalistic language experience. The participants were Spanish native speakers, Spanish HL learners, and L2 learners of Spanish (the experimental groups had comparable proficiency in Spanish). The 5 tasks used tested aspects of Spanish morphosyntax (*ser/estar* "be," gender, *a* personal, preterit/imperfect, subjunctive, adjective placement, conditionals, and subject-verb agreement) and were an extension of the tasks proposed by Ellis (2005). An oral imitation test, oral narrative task, and a timed grammaticality judgment task were considered measures of implicit knowledge, whereas an untimed grammaticality judgment task and a metalinguistic knowledge test were the measures of explicit knowledge. The results showed that, as predicted, the L2 learners scored higher on the two tests that maximized reliance on explicit knowledge than on the three tests that minimized explicit knowledge. The HL learners showed exactly the opposite pattern, scoring much higher on the three tests of implicit knowledge and lower on the tests of explicit knowledge. As for direct comparisons between groups, the HL learners were more accurate than the L2 learners on the three implicit knowledge tasks. They scored as accurately as the L2 learners in the timed grammaticality judgment task. The only task in which the L2 learners scored statistically higher than the HL learners was, not surprisingly, the metalinguistic knowledge task. These results are summarized in Table 8.5.

Not only did Bowles's study confirm what Ellis found with L2 learners of English, but it also shows how explicitness of the task and modality matter for HL learners and should be taken into account when making comparisons between the two groups and drawing conclusions about their linguistic knowledge.

One potential problem with Ellis (2005) and Bowles's (2011a) replication and extension is that the issue of explicitness or implicitness of the task is confounded with modality. For example, two of the "implicit" tasks were oral, while the two "explicit" tasks were written. Were the HL learners better at the implicit tasks than the L2 learners because the tasks elicited oral production or because they were targeting implicit knowledge? Similarly, did the L2 learners do better in the more explicit tasks because they were written or because they were more explicit? The tasks that can actually answer this question are the timed (implicit) and untimed (explicit) GJTs. Comparison of these two tasks, which were both written, suggests that the more implicit the task, the better for the heritage speakers. The reverse holds for L2 learners; the more implicit the task, the more difficult for the L2 learners.

To bring more clarity to the issue of modality and explicitness of tasks, Montrul *et al.* (2013, 2014) followed up on the findings of Montrul, Foote, and Perpiñán's (2008a) study of gender agreement, focusing on the processing of spoken language exclusively. Montrul *et al.* (2014) implemented a different

Table 8.5. *Accuracy scores in the five tasks by groups (adapted from Bowles 2011)*

Test	Spanish native speakers (n = 10)	L2 learners of Spanish (n = 10)	HL learners of Spanish (n =10)
Oral imitation (IMPK)	99.7	46.7	78.8
Oral narration (IMPK)	100	47.9	95.9
Timed GJT (IMPK)	92.1	66.9	62.5
Untimed GJT (EXPK)	96.2	30.5	81.2
Metalinguistic knowledge (EXPK)	77.1	72.4	57.4

IMPK = implicit knowledge, EXPK = explicit knowledge.

set of tasks that might prove more efficient in tapping the participants' more automatic and implicit knowledge of grammatical gender than the written tasks used in previous studies (Alarcón 2011; Montrul, Foote, and Perpiñán 2008a). A group of Spanish native speakers, a group of L2 learners, and a group of heritage speakers of intermediate to advanced proficiency in Spanish completed three spoken word recognition experiments that varied on the degree of explicitness of the task: a gender monitoring task (GMT), a grammaticality judgment task (GJT), and a repetition task (RT). The GMT required participants to listen to grammatical and ungrammatical noun phrases containing a determiner, an adjective and a noun, and push one of two buttons on the keyboard (one for feminine and one for masculine), depending on the gender of the noun. In the GJT, participants listened to the noun phrases and pushed one of two buttons to indicate whether the phrase was grammatical or ungrammatical. In the RT, participants heard the noun phrases and were asked to repeat the last word in each phrase as quickly and accurately as possible. The GJT and the GMT focus on gender more explicitly than the RT. Reaction times and accuracy were measured.

The results showed that all the groups demonstrated sensitivity to gender agreement violations in Spanish noun phrases in general, but the heritage speakers displayed more native-like performance than the L2 learners depending on the implicitness of the task. That is, in the more explicit tasks, the GMT and the GJT, the heritage speakers and the L2 learners did not differ from each other nor did they differ from the native speakers, but in the more implicit task, the RT, the heritage speakers patterned with the native speakers, while the L2 learners showed the reverse response. We then have more evidence that when we control for modality, the explicitness of the task matters for these two types of learners. Therefore, the type of language learning experience early and later in life – naturalistic versus instructed – impacts how L2 learners and heritage speakers store, process, and retrieve linguistic knowledge in different experimental tasks.

Independent of task, the effect of language experience can also be evaluated from use and accuracy on different structures. As we know, some structures are very frequent in spoken language and other structures, like passives discussed in Chapter 4, for example, are more frequent in written language. Or, as we discussed next, some grammatical features are common in child language, but less common in adult language. Therefore, heritage language speakers are predicted to have better command of structures that are frequent in spoken language than L2 learners, independent of task, and in vocabulary and structures that are common in child language (see study on vocabulary by Montrul and Foote 2014 mentioned in Chapter 3).

Montrul (2010a,b) tested knowledge of object expression in Spanish heritage speakers and L2 learners of comparable proficiency in Spanish. Knowledge of direct object clitic placement with respect to verb finiteness, as in (17) and (18), the possibility of clitic climbing in restructuring constructions (19), and object topicalizations with obligatory clitic doubling (also called clitic left dislocations) (21) (cf. 20), were some of the structures tested via an oral narrative task and a visual acceptability judgment task.

(17)   Juan la vio. versus *Juan vio la.
       "Juan saw her."
(18)   Para leerlo. versus *Para lo leer.
       "To read it."
(19)   Juan la quiere comprar.
       *Juan quiere la comprar.
       Juan quiere comprarla.
       "Juan wants to buy it."
(20)   Juan llevó las carpetas a la oficina.
       "Juan took the folders to the office."
(21)   Las carpetas las llevó Juan a la oficina.
       "The folders, Juan took them to the office."

Although English (the primary language of the participants) does not have clitic pronouns, both L2 learners and heritage speakers demonstrated solid knowledge of clitics and did not differ from Spanish native speakers on their correct production of clitics with finite and nonfinite verbs. They were also able to correctly judge grammatical and ungrammatical sentences with clitic placement in the judgment task. However, significant differences between heritage speakers and L2 learners were evident in the production of clitic climbing and in the judgment of sentences with topicalizations (clitic left dislocations) in the judgment task. Unlike the L2 learners who only produced

14% of clitic climbing, the heritage speakers produced 65%, and the native speakers 60%. In the judgment task, the heritage speakers also accepted significantly more clitic climbing than the L2 learners. The oral narrative did not elicit spontaneous examples of topicalizations, but these were included in the judgment task. The heritage speakers were more accepting of topicalizations than the L2 learners. A possible explanation for these results could be related to experience and language use. Clitic climbing in Spanish occurs more often in spoken than in written registers (Davies 1995). Topicalizations in general, and clitic left dislocations in particular, are a feature of informal, spoken language. If these structures occur in written language at all, they typically occur under strict stylistic conditions. Since heritage speakers have more experience with spoken Spanish than L2 learners, the fact that they are more accepting of clitic climbing and of topicalizations than the L2 learners is not surprising. Leal Méndez, Rothman, and Slabakova (2014) and Leal Méndez, Slabakova, and Rothman (2015) found that heritage speakers were native-like with these structures.

Another example of studies showing that heritage speakers behave closer to native speakers than L2 learners with certain structures as a function of register comes from Chung's (2013) study of case ellipsis in Korean L2 learners and heritage speakers mentioned earlier. Since case ellipsis in Korean is a conversational phenomenon, and heritage speakers have more experience with spoken language than L2 learners, experience with the spoken register clearly explains why the heritage speakers were more similar to the L1 Korean children and the adult native speakers of Korean, whereas the L2 learners, even those with advanced proficiency in Korean, were different from the other groups. Chung's study also included a written task, which was administered to all the adult participants (native speakers, heritage speakers, and L2 learners). The task was similar to the oral production task. It presented a mini dialogue, and participants had to select a bare NP or case-marked NP, as shown in (22). The participants were asked to select one answer that sounded more natural in the context of the conversation as quickly as possible. The instructions also emphasized that there are no right or wrong answers for these questions.

(22)   ONII [Object, +CF, Inanimate, Indefinite], CM-Primed condition
       (Mina is getting a present for her niece)
       Mina: Mwe-l sacwu-ci?   Kulimchayk-**ul**   sacwu-l-kka?
                WH-ACC   buy?   picture book-**ACC**   buy-FUT-Q?
                "What should I get? Should I get her a picture book?"
       Youngsu: (pro)   acik   eli-nikka _____ sacwu-e.
                (s/he) still   young-CAUS _____ buy-DECL
                "Get her a _____ since she's still young."
       Answer options: cangnankam-ul (toy-ACC) versus cangnankam (toy)

According to the results, both L2 and HL learners were different from native speakers in their judgments of object and subject case ellipsis. However, there were similarities between the heritage speakers and the native speakers, while L2 learners were more variable and divergent, especially in the employment and integration of focus in their judgments. Although other studies found L2 learners to be more accurate than HL learners on untimed written tasks testing explicit metalinguistic knowledge, no such group advantage was found by Chung depending on task. In fact, the Korean HL learners showed an advantage over L2 learners in their acquisition of Korean case ellipsis in both task modes. This could be due to the nature of the case ellipsis phenomenon that primarily occurs in informal casual speech and thus requires access to implicit rather than explicit metalinguistic knowledge, even in the written mode.

These last two studies suggest that even when we rely on written tasks, heritage speakers perform more target-like than L2 learners with aspects of syntax, morphology, and discourse that are typical or more frequent in spoken language.

The last example of a recent study investigating the role of language experience in L2 learners and heritage speakers is Montrul *et al.* (2013). They examined the interaction of gender marking in nouns with diminutive formation to address whether the type of input received makes a difference in the acquisition in the two groups. Diminutives are a hallmark of child-directed speech in early language development and a highly productive morphological mechanism that facilitates the acquisition of declensional noun endings in many languages (Savickienė and Dressler 2007). In Spanish, diminutives regularize gender marking in nouns with a noncanonical ending. Gender learning is easier if the input contains fewer nontransparently gender-marked nouns (Kempe and Brooks 2001). In Spanish, the most common and frequent diminutive affix is *–it* or its variants *–cit*, *–ecit*, and with gender agreement it is *–ito*, *–cito*, *–ecito* (masculine) or *–ita*, *–cita*, *–ecita* (feminine) (Melzi and King 2003). The diminutive affix regularizes gender marking in nouns with noncanonical endings by making the canonical word marker on the noun explicit, as shown in Table 8.6.

Diminutives in Spanish are acquired and used productively between the ages of 1;9 and 1;10 (Marrero, Aguirre, and Albalá 2007). Spanish-acquiring children use thirteen times more diminutives than Spanish-speaking adults, and adults addressing children use them as much, if not more, than the children themselves (Marrero, Albalá, and Moreno 2007, p. 155). The hypothesis tested in this study was that Spanish heritage speakers should be more accurate at producing diminutives and at gender agreement with noncanonical nouns than L2 learners. Because the heritage speakers were exposed to Spanish since birth, they were potentially also exposed to many instances of diminutives through child-directed speech, whereas the L2 learners of Spanish were not exposed to such forms in early childhood. Although L2 learners of Spanish may have learned diminutives in the classroom as adults,

Table 8.6. *Gender agreement with canonical and noncanonical masculine and feminine nouns in simplex and diminutive forms (D stands for diminutive affix) (Montrul et al. 2013)*

	Canonical		Noncanonical	
	Simplex	Diminutive	Simplex	Diminutive
Masculine	el auto rojo the car red "the red car"	el aut*ito* rojo the car-D red "the little red car"	el coche negro the car black "the black car"	el coche*cito* negro the car-D black "the little black car"
			el lápiz amarillo the pencil yellow "the yellow pencil"	el lapic*ito* amarillo the pencil-D yellow "the little yellow pencil"
Feminine	la casa blanca the house white "the white house"	la cas*ita* blanca the house-D white "the little white house"	la nube blanca the cloud white "the white cloud"	la nube*cita* blanca the cloud-D white "the little white cloud"
			la nariz fría the nose cold "the cold nose"	la naric*ita* fría the nose-D cold "the little cold nose"

the frequency of diminutive use in adult speech is much lower than in the speech directed to children (Marrero, Aguirre, and Albalá 2007). Hearing noncanonical nouns in diminutive forms in early childhood may have helped the heritage speakers classify those nouns as feminine and masculine reliably in their mental lexicon as they were growing up, thereby reducing the likelihood of making agreement and assignment errors with those nouns later in adulthood.

The main task testing this hypothesis was an elicited production task with pictures. Participants saw 96 images, each with a big colored animal or object and a smaller version of the same colored animal or object placed on, under, to the right, or to the left of an image of a table. Participants heard four questions uttered by a female Mexican Spanish speaker: *¿Qué hay debajo de / encima de / a la derecha de / a la izquierda de la mesa?* "What is under / on top of / to the right of / to the left of the table?" Participants were asked to orally produce sentences like: *un elefante blanco* "a white elephant" or *un elefantito blanco* "a little white elephant." Both simplex and diminutive forms were requested. Responses were audio recorded, transcribed, and coded for analysis. The native speakers performed at ceiling (100% accuracy) on agreement. The L2 learners and the heritage speakers made gender errors, but the main finding was that the groups showed different accuracy scores depending on the canonical or noncanonical ending of the nouns, as displayed in Figure 8.8. Results showed

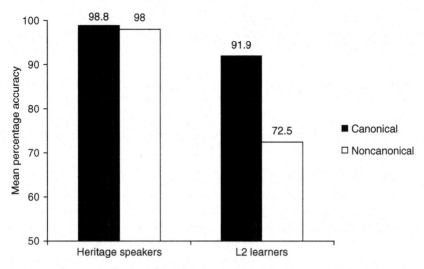

Figure 8.8. Accuracy on canonical and noncanonical ending nouns by group (adapted from Montrul *et al.* 2013).

that the heritage speakers were more accurate than the L2 learners with gender agreement in general, and with noncanonical ending nouns in particular.

At the same time, accuracy in general was uniform and was not affected by the form of the noun; that is, whether the nouns were in the simplex forms or in the diminutive, but the heritage speakers were more accurate with diminutive forms than the L2 learners (7% errors versus 18.5% errors), suggesting that they were more familiar with these morphemes than the L2 learners.

The most important result of this study was that none of the native speakers made gender agreement errors in this oral production task, and 19 of the 29 heritage speakers (65%) behaved like the native speakers and made no agreement errors. By contrast, none of the L2 learners showed this pattern as all of them made gender errors. This study confirms that early language experience and the type of input received confer some advantages to heritage speakers over L2 learners with early-acquired aspects of language, especially in oral production. There is a much higher incidence of native-like ability in the heritage speakers than in the L2 learners.

To summarize, the collective results from all these studies suggest that the role of language experience – as it relates to type of input and input modality – seems to affect the processing of language and linguistic performance of heritage speakers and L2 learners as measured by different tasks. Heritage speakers outperform L2 learners typically in tests that minimize metalinguistic knowledge and especially in oral production tasks. If linguistic knowledge elicited in this way is closer to grammatical competence than the knowledge elicited through reading and writing, then one may say that the heritage speakers have linguistic advantages not only on phonology, but on aspects of morphosyntax and syntax discourse as well. This is a topic that certainly deserves further research and discussion, but at this point we will focus on task modality because, as we will see in the next section, task modality is very relevant for instruction.

8.4   Classroom research

In many educational institutions throughout the world, but in North America in particular, traditional foreign language classes geared for second language learners have increasingly opened their doors to bilingual speakers of minority languages. It is fitting then that the field of heritage language acquisition would turn first to its sister field of second language acquisition to begin to understand what it needs. By investigating key linguistic differences between these two groups (L2 learners and heritage speakers), the findings obtained through linguistic and psycholinguistic research could eventually inform pedagogical practices that address their different linguistic and cultural needs.

Valdés *et al.* (2006, p. 119) dismissed the relevance of research on incipient or developing bilingualism in foreign or second languages to teachers of heritage students, claiming that views about L2 developmental sequences and L2 proficiency hierarchies can contribute little to the understanding of the instructional needs of the HL learner population. However, this view is not widespread these days, especially now that more research comparing the two groups of learners has been conducted in the last decade. Even if HL learners are in many ways different from typical L2 learners with no previous knowledge of the language, there are many parallels between HL and L2 acquisition and teaching that need to be investigated. Without proper understanding of how similar or different these two types of learners are it is difficult to tell whether the exact same methods applied to L2 learners in the classroom should also be applied to HL learners. A thorough comparison between HL and L2 learners is not only relevant but also urgent for language teaching in many countries.

HL learners need motivation to maintain and develop their heritage language beyond what they acquired at home. Many young adult heritage speakers seek to reacquire or improve their knowledge of the heritage language in the L2/FL classroom, and it is very common to find HL learners in several L2 and foreign language classes in North American and European universities (Håkansson 1995). The presence of these speakers in classes designed for L2 learners with no previous background in the language presents significant challenges. Many language practitioners have found it urgent to develop new programs, teacher handbooks, and pedagogical materials that could address the specific needs of heritage speakers (Beaudrie, Ducar, and Potowski 2014; Brinton, Kagan, and Bauckus 2008). Consequently, identifying how L2 learners and heritage speakers differ in their linguistic competence and processing abilities is a critical step toward developing efficient pedagogical solutions for language teaching.

In addition to learning about the nature of L2 knowledge, understanding how teaching helps learners restructure their grammars is of particular interest in instructed L2 acquisition. A central question in instructed acquisition is what types of linguistic input and learning environments are most beneficial for L2 learners, and whether explicit instruction helps learners restructure their linguistic systems. One main difference between acquisition by very young children, both monolingual and bilingual, and L2 acquisition by adults is that because child acquisition takes place primarily in a naturalistic setting, there is typically no explicit instruction or information about grammaticality. Many researchers argue that negative evidence – information regarding the impossibility of certain linguistic structures in the language being acquired – is not necessary and perhaps not even consistently available for bilingual and L1 acquisition (Pinker 1989). However, research on L2 acquisition, especially in immersion contexts, has suggested that positive evidence alone may not be sufficient for the acquisition of certain L1–L2 contrasts or structures that are not present in the L1 (Lightbown 1998; Long 1996; Trahey and White 1993; White 1991). That is, L2 learners may benefit from occasional form-focused instruction, which often involves providing learners with explicit information before or during exposure to L2 input, by means of either explicit grammatical explanations or corrective feedback (Sanz and Morgan-Short 2004). Much research investigating the role of explicit grammatical explanation in L2 acquisition has found form-focused instruction and feedback beneficial, especially for morphosyntax (Norris and Ortega 2000; Russell and Spada 2006). We need to know how heritage learners learn or relearn their heritage language in the classroom and the best methods to help them develop their language beyond what they acquired in childhood. If, as established by recent research, heritage speakers have less developed metalinguistic knowledge than L2 learners, and have less experience with explicit tasks, how do heritage language learners react to explicit instruction in general? Does form-focused instruction, in particular, help heritage language learners in the classroom?

The first study to address the role of explicit instruction in heritage language acquisition is Song et al.'s (1997) study of child heritage speakers of Korean in Hawaii. The study focused on knowledge of overt case markers in Korean. Having identified incomplete acquisition of case markers in the children tested, the next step in the study was to implement a teaching intervention with explicit explanations and examples of when to use case in Korean in S-O-V and O-S-V sentences. The children were pretested on comprehension of sentences with different word order and case markers. They then received explicit instructions and practiced recognizing case markers for two weeks, and they were tested again immediately after the instruction (immediate post-test) and nine weeks later (delayed post-test). The results showed noticeable improvements in accuracy at recognizing who was doing what in sentences with O-S-V order, from 25% accuracy in the pre-test to 66.3% accuracy on the immediate post-test, more than 100% improvement. The accuracy on the delayed post-test was retained (56%). Song *et al.* (1997) showed that explicit instruction had positive effects and produced improvement which was maintained nine weeks after the treatment. This study, however, did not include a group of L2 learners.

Bowles and Montrul (2009) investigated intermediate-level L2 learners' reactivity to instruction on differential object marking in Spanish and dative case marking with psychological verbs like *gustar* "like" (*A Juan le gusta el fútbol* "Juan likes soccer"), which are also problematic for L2 learners. Bowles and Montrul (2009) also used a pre-post-test research design to investigate the efficacy of an online instructional treatment on L2 learners' production and grammaticality judgments on structures requiring dative marking. The instructional treatment consisted of an explicit grammatical explanation of the uses of the preposition *a* followed by three practice exercises, for which participants received immediate, explicit feedback, including negative evidence. The results indicate that both recognition and production of *a*-marking (*Juan vio a María* versus **Juan vio María* "Juan saw Maria") improved significantly after the instruction, suggesting that at least in the short term explicit instruction facilitates classroom L2 acquisition. Montrul and Bowles (2010) extended the same research design to investigate reactivity to instruction in HL learners. They found that explicit instruction and feedback was very beneficial to HL learners as well. In fact, in terms of the magnitude of the gains on all the structures tested in the tasks (a written grammaticality judgment task and a written production task), it was higher in the HL learners studied by Montrul and Bowles (2010) than in the L2 learners in Bowles and Montrul (2009). Taken together, these two studies demonstrate that negative evidence plays a role in L2 acquisition and in HL relearning in a classroom setting, and that explicit form-focused instruction is beneficial for the two groups.

Potowski, Jegerski, and Morgan-Short (2009) asked whether the types of instruction mattered. They focused on the effectiveness of traditional output-based instruction as compared to input processing instruction (VanPatten 1996). In output-based instruction, learners are introduced to a rule and then asked to produce language with the rule. In input processing instruction, learners are guided to pay attention to critical pieces of language in comprehension only, with the aim of directing the way they process language. Language processing is a crucial step in learning, which precedes production. Six intact classes of Spanish for L2 learners and of Spanish for HL learners were randomly assigned to one type of instruction or the other. A production task, an interpretation task, and a grammaticality judgment task (all written tasks) were used to measure the learners' gains in accuracy on the Spanish imperfect subjunctive after each type of instruction. L2 learners and HL learners showed significant improvements in comprehension, production, and grammaticality judgments in the two types of instruction, although in this study the overall gains were greater for the L2 learners than for the HL learners. Interestingly, there were important task effects: the heritage speakers were more accurate on interpretation and production than on grammaticality judgments, the most metalinguistic task of the three. Only the L2 learners showed improvements in the grammaticality judgment, whereas the HL learners did not. Thus, this study also shows that the type of task matters when we are comparing the linguistic abilities of L2 learners and HL learners. L2 learners do better in metalinguistic tasks that tap explicit knowledge. The HL learners do better in tasks that tap more implicit knowledge of the language.

Moving away from form-focused instruction and onto other types of classroom activities, other studies have investigated linguistic gains through interaction in the classroom. A vast body of research in L2 acquisition summarized in Mackey and Goo (2007) supports the Interaction Hypothesis (Long 1996), demonstrating that adults learning an L2/FL language benefit from conversational interactions with native speakers. Following this tradition, Blake and Zyzik (2003) and Bowles (2011b) investigated the interactions between Spanish L2 learners and HL learners in the classroom, and showed that, while HL learners can provide useful lexical feedback to the L2 learners, they also face significant problems with respect to morphology and overall literacy. Bowles (2011b) analyzed interactions between HL and L2 learners of Spanish enrolled in the same classes at the university. Pairs consisting of a HL learner and an L2 learner completed two-way information gap communicative tasks in written and oral modality. Bowles asked whether one type of learner (L2 or HL) initiated more language-related episodes than the other; whether one learner's (L2 or HL) language-related episodes get resolved more often than the other's; whether one learner's (L2 or HL) language-related episodes get resolved in a more target-like way than the other's overall; and whether the modality of the task (oral versus written) plays a role in who initiates the language-related episodes and how they get resolved. Bowles found that both L2 and HL learners initiated a similar number of language-related episodes across oral and written tasks and that the language-related episodes initiated by both types of learners were resolved in equal proportions. Nevertheless, the data revealed different patterns by the two learner types on the written task: 47 of the 70 orthography-focused language-related episodes (67%) were initiated by HL learners, while the other 23 (33%) were initiated by L2 learners, a finding underscoring once again the heritage speakers' gaps with written language as a result of their language learning experience.

Bowles, Adams, and Toth (2014) analyzed the task-based interactions of 26 naturally occurring learner dyads in an intermediate-level, university Spanish language classroom, 13 of which were matched L2 learner dyads and 13 of which were mixed L2 learner-heritage learner (HL) dyads. Specifically, the study compared the two dyad types to determine whether they differed in their focus on form or in the amount of talk produced during interaction. Results revealed that the two types of dyads were largely similar, although instances of focus on form were more likely to be resolved in a target-like way by mixed L2–HL pairs than by matched L2–L2 pairs, and there was significantly more target language talk in mixed pairs. Interestingly, L2 learners used the target language significantly more with HL learners than they did with other L2 learners, suggesting that different conversational norms may be at play in the two pair types. Furthermore, post-task questionnaire data indicated that L2 and HL learners alike saw the interaction as a greater opportunity for the L2 learners' development than for the HL learners', calling into question whether classroom contexts like this one meet the needs of HL learners. Hence, if HLs take Spanish classes alongside adult L2 learners, these data suggest that greater care should be taken to provide tasks that address the needs and linguistic profile of both kinds of learners, so that classroom interactions will yield more mutual developmental benefits. Indeed, the laboratory study by Bowles (2011b) suggests that the two types of learners may be able to work together for mutual benefit, if oral and written tasks are balanced. Specifically, L2 learners may benefit from their HL partner's speaking ability in oral tasks, while HL learners benefit from their L2 partner's greater familiarity with written Spanish in writing tasks.

Finally, Warner (2014) examined 9 dyads that included 18 Spanish heritage learners paired according to the proficiency results of a DELE test. The dyads were given three collaborative tasks designed to spur communication, including one oral and two written activities. Transcripts of their interactions revealed 100 language-related episodes where a learner questioned the language in one of the following linguistic focus areas: grammar, pronunciation, vocabulary, and orthography. This number is significantly less than the episodes that occurred between HLs paired with L2s in previous research (Bowles 2011b). Significantly less language-related episodes were resolved between the dyads in the current study, and fewer results were target-like. The majority of the language-related episodes focused on orthography, a finding which supports earlier research attesting that HL learners struggle with issues such as spelling and accent placement (Montrul 2008). The greatest number of unresolved episodes also centered on orthography.

All in all, classroom research so far seems to suggest that HL learners, like L2 learners, benefit from form-focused instruction in the classroom. It is premature to say with certainty whether the teaching method itself matters (i.e., traditional versus input processing, for example), but the magnitude of gains on different aspects of morphosyntactic knowledge depends on type of structure and type of task. L2 learners do better in written, metalinguistic tasks that tap explicit knowledge. The heritage speakers do better in oral tasks and tasks that tap more implicit knowledge of the language. When it comes to interaction in the classroom, both types of learners benefit from and learn from each other, but differences again show up in task modality (written versus oral). All these results suggest, once again, that the type of language experience shapes the type of linguistic knowledge heritage speakers and L2 learners possess and how it is manifested in different language skills and modalities. Having L2 and HL learners working together in the classroom appears to benefit the two types of learners, at least in linguistic gains.

Other issues that languages like Arabic and Greek face when taught to HL learners is whether the colloquial varieties to which heritage speakers are exposed at home help them in learning the standard varieties of the language imparted in most college-level classrooms, as discussed by Albirini (2014). Modern Standard Arabic (MSA) is the official language of twenty-two countries of the Arab league. This variety is used in formal education, formal business transactions and documents, administration, Qur'anic schools, and print media. But Arabic people speak the colloquial varieties of Arabic, which differ in important ways from MSA and from each other (Egyptian, Palestinian, Jordanian, Moroccan, etc.). MSA and the colloquial varieties of Arabic coexist in a diglossic situation because the colloquial varieties are used in spoken language, at home, in informal business transactions, etc. MSA and the colloquial varieties differ in age of acquisition and in structures at the phonological, morphological, syntactic, and lexical levels. For example, syntactic negation is different in MSA and in the colloquial varieties, and so are agreement paradigms, modality markers, phonemes, and lexical items. While Arabic children learn the colloquial variety from birth, they begin exposure and acquisition of MSA when they enter school. Native speakers of Arabic control and use the two varieties. In general, heritage speakers of Arabic know the colloquial variety, although imperfectly, and may have heard some MSA on TV. Albirini (2014) conducted an experiment to test knowledge of sentential negation with 35 HL learners and 28 L2 learners of Arabic in an instructed setting. There were also 16 native speakers of Palestinian and Egyptian Arabic. One question was whether knowledge of the colloquial variety (Egyptian and Palestinian) provided an initial advantage for HL learners over L2 learners due to the overall similarities between the formal and informal Arabic varieties. In other words, is knowledge of the colloquial a source of transfer in the acquisition of MSA? Albirini tested

19 HL learners in elementary MSA classes and 16 HL learners in advanced MSA classes in order to answer whether the initial advantages that many HL learners may possess in elementary or even intermediate college classes carry over to more advanced levels.

The system of sentential negation used by the colloquial varieties of Arabic and MSA is different, at least on the surface (Benmamoun *et al.* 2013a). One basic difference discussed by Albirini (2014), for example, is that verbless clauses in MSA are negated with the particle *laysa* "not" and clauses with verbs use the negative particle *laa*, *lan*, or *maa*, depending on the tense and aspect of the verb. In the colloquial Arabic varieties tested (Egyptian and Palestinian), by contrast, the negative particles are *maa – š* and *miš*. The particle *maa – š* inserts the verb in between the *maa* and the *š* morphemes (e.g., *saafr-uu* "travel," "*maa-saafr-uu-š* "did not travel"), while the particle *miš* is a free morpheme used in verbless clauses. Tense and aspect also differentiate the use of the particles in these varieties in ways that is different from how tense and aspect regulate the use of particles in MSA.

All the participants completed 5 oral tasks that targeted negation in different types of clauses (with verbs and verbless) and with different verb tenses. The results showed that the HL learners in elementary MSA classes had an advantage over L2 learners because they already had some basic knowledge of MSA, whereas the L2 learners did not. When learning negation, their sentences were for the most part syntactically well-formed when compared to the sentences produced by the L2 learners. At the same time, overall accuracy on negation for the elementary level HL learners (23.55%) was lower than for lower proficiency L2 learners (69.73%). When the HL learners enrolled in beginners' classes made errors, 60% of their errors could be attributed to transfer from the colloquial varieties, whereas the majority of errors made by the L2 learners were due to misuse of the particles (38.1%). When the HL learners in the advanced classes were compared to L2 learners in the same classes, no significant advantage for the HL learners were found in sentential negation. About 25% of the errors made by the advanced HL learners were due to transfer, and like the L2 learners they also made about 24.3% errors with particles. Albirini (2014) concludes by proposing a different approach to teaching HL learners so that those at more advanced levels can continue to develop their heritage language further through differentiated instruction and activities.

Finally, questions that have not been asked very often, but that need to be answered are (1) whether heritage language education is beneficial for heritage language development and maintenance, (2) whether HL learners make progress in the areas targeted by instruction, and (3) whether the progress they make is integrated in their knowledge and eventually maintained long term. After all, the purpose of instruction is to bring about restructuring, change, and expansion of previous knowledge.

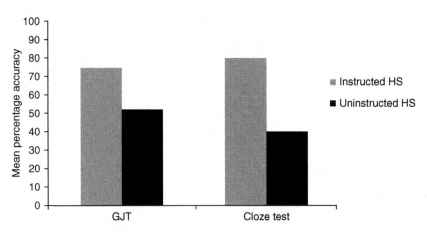

Figure 8.9. Mean percentage accuracy for instructed and noninstructed Spanish heritage speakers in Swedish High School in the two tests (adapted from Bylund and Díaz 2012).

Bylund and Díaz (2012) offer an answer to the first question. The study investigated the effects of weekly heritage language instruction on overall heritage language proficiency in two groups of Spanish heritage speakers in Sweden of high school age. One group (n = 28) was in twelfth grade and were receiving mother tongue instruction two times a week (two hours total), with a focus on literacy activities. The other group (n = 26) was also in twelfth grade, but had received instruction until the eleventh grade, and for scheduling conflict reasons were no longer attending heritage language classes in the twelfth grade. The Spanish speakers had arrived in Sweden between the ages of 1 and 12 (mean 7.1) and had received an average of 5 years of heritage language instruction at school. So, all things being equal (age of arrival in Sweden, length of residence in Sweden, amount of use of Swedish and Spanish, amount of previous HL instruction, etc.), the uninstructed group had not received instruction for 10 months. Overall proficiency was assessed with a written grammaticality judgment task testing several grammatical properties of Spanish (gender agreement, preterite and imperfect, and clitic pronouns) and with a written cloze test (a passage with missing blanks). Figure 8.9 gives the overall results.

The HL learners who were taking HL instruction at the time of testing outperformed the high school students who were not taking classes that year. Bylund and Díaz interpret these results as suggesting that continued HL instruction through literacy development contributes to language maintenance and prevents L1 attrition at a critical time for language development, following Bylund (2009) and Montrul's (2008) hypothesis of age effects in L1 loss. Naturally, because the two groups were not tested a year earlier, it is hard to tell from these findings whether the two groups were of similar proficiency before the year of interrupted instruction for one of the groups. Furthermore, as Bylund and Díaz acknowledge, the two measures used tested written proficiency and metalinguistic ability in some sense, and it is not clear whether the HL learners who were continuing with classes have also restructured their implicit system and knowledge of Spanish. Other types of implicit measures would have to be used to corroborate this possibility, including oral production. Because the L1 is being taught in the classroom explicitly, it could also be the case that what the HL learners are developing is their explicit knowledge. Post-tests would be needed to determine whether the knowledge acquired through classroom instruction is retained or undergoes attrition as well.

8.5   Summary

By now there are a good number of studies on heritage speakers and L2 learners. Three main themes that have received significant attention so far are (1) the resilience versus vulnerability of different aspects of grammatical knowledge as a function of age of acquisition, (2) how input and experience may shape heritage language grammars, and (3) the potential reacquisition of the heritage language in the classroom. In some areas, heritage speakers are like L2 learners and in other areas they are not. The collective results from all these studies to date suggest that phonology seems to be the most resilient area of grammar in heritage speakers, whereas syntax-discourse, semantics, and inflectional morphology are quite vulnerable and prone to attrition or incomplete acquisition. Early input seems to provide a clear advantage to heritage speakers in perception and production of phonology and in core aspects of syntax when compared to L2 learners.

Advantages for heritage speakers in vocabulary and inflectional morphology seem to be highly influenced by factors related to experience as they relate to type of input and input modality measured by different tasks. HL learners outperform L2 learners typically in tests that minimize metalinguistic knowledge and especially in oral production tasks. If linguistic knowledge elicited in this way is closer to grammatical competence than the knowledge elicited through reading and writing, then heritage speakers have linguistic advantages aspects of morphosyntax and syntax-discourse as well, and they bring all these advantages to the classroom.

Research investigating the role of explicit grammatical explanation in L2 acquisition has found instruction in general, and form-focused instruction and feedback in particular, beneficial especially for morphosyntax. Classroom research with HL learners is quite scant at the moment, but is certainly an area that deserves more detailed investigation. There are very few studies that have looked at the role of form-focused instruction on accuracy, type of instruction (traditional versus input processing), and interaction in the classroom in written and oral tasks. These studies have compared the performance of L2 learners and HL learners and have also found that, although the two groups react to the instruction, the types and magnitude of the gains differ in the two groups, once again as a function of previous linguistic knowledge and language learning experience. That is, L2 learners show more improvement in written and highly metalinguistic tasks than HL learners, and heritage speakers do better in oral tasks and have better command of vocabulary than L2 learners. While L2 learners struggle with grammatical accuracy and vocabulary knowledge, HL learners struggle with spelling and orthography in written language. More research on the development of HL learners in the classroom is needed, especially when dealing with mixed classrooms that include the two types of learners.

From the perspective of helping the HL learner, it seems that the initial advantages the HL learners bring to the classroom in phonology, aspects of the lexicon, conversational structures, and even slang (Au *et al.* 2002) can give HL learners a false sense of security and superiority over L2 learners that later gets in their way for further learning and restructuring of their linguistic systems. Relying on more implicit learning than explicit learning (compared to their L2 learner classmates), HL learners often overestimate their grammatical and lexical mastery in their HL because of their "feeling-of-knowing" without really knowing it. The result of this feeling is that the HL learners may not apply themselves that much when they have to actually study aspects of the HL grammar. By contrast, the L2 learners, who may feel inferior and insecure upon hearing the good oral language skills and facility with vocabulary of the HL learners, do study more and eventually obtain higher marks or grades in written tests and exams. In addition to training teachers to recognize the differences and similarities between the two types of learners (culturally, linguistically, and in terms of needs and goals) and to design differentiated instruction at the level of program, course offerings or class activities, another challenge of HL education is to help the HL become more aware of their weaknesses or strategies that get in the way of their learning. HL learners need to become aware that a lot of language learning happens through schooling in the classroom, and involves learning about grammar and about usage, just like they learn in the majority language at school. In addition to valuing their language variety and culture, raising this type of awareness on the part of the HL learners may eventually pave the way for more learning and improvement.

9   Some implications

The study of heritage language speakers, their patterns of language use, their linguistic varieties, as well as issues related to language policies that affect their language identity, have long been the realm of sociolinguistics (Fishman, 1966), although heritage language speakers and heritage languages have not always been called this way (Dorian 1981, 1989; Silva-Corvalán 1994; Zentella 1997). In the last decade, other fields of linguistics including formal linguistics, second language acquisition, psycholinguistics, and language teaching, have seen increasing interest and unprecedented value in understanding how the heritage language may have been acquired in childhood, how it develops (or fails to fully develop) in comparison to the other language and to a second language; how it is represented, accessed and processed in the mind of these speakers; how it is used; and how it is learned or reacquired in a formal language environment. Heritage language acquisition has moved from the periphery to the center of converging interests within linguistics and many related fields. Among the factors that have contributed to this interest are the most recent demographic changes and immigration patterns, and the pressing practical considerations they entail for national education and language policies.

   Throughout this book I have described the characteristics of heritage languages and heritage speakers, with special emphasis on their language and their language learning process. The main arguments I advanced are (1) that heritage languages are native languages that develop in a specific bilingual environment, (2) not all heritage languages develop in the same way by early adulthood, (3) different properties of the grammar (vocabulary, phonology, morphology, syntax, and interfaces) show different developmental profiles across languages and within individuals, and (4) due to changing environmental circumstances, heritage languages show different degrees of stability after the age of basic grammatical development. The sociopolitical status of the heritage language as a minority language plays a fundamental role in the degree of language acquisition, maintenance, and loss of the heritage language throughout early childhood, middle childhood, and adolescence; that is, the entire span of the language learning period. For languages that have a written tradition, academic support of the language and development of literacy and metalinguistic skills during the school-age period can contribute significantly to language maintenance and the degree of linguistic competence acquired in the heritage language in early adulthood. All in all, the age at which intense exposure to the majority language begins plays a fundamental role in the degree of heritage language acquisition.

The last few years has seen a wealth of empirical studies on the linguistic abilities of heritage speakers of different languages, and before these developments, the field of heritage language acquisition was portrayed as atheoretical. Given this perception, another goal of this book has been to show that the study of heritage languages and of the acquisition of heritage languages today is hardly atheoretical. Indeed, it has been embraced by mainstream theoretical approaches to language and language acquisition within linguistics like sociolinguistics, formal linguistics, and psycholinguistics, among others. If heritage language acquisition is another instance of language acquisition, the study of heritage grammars intersects naturally with research on contact linguistics, first language acquisition, bilingual acquisition in childhood, child and adult second language acquisition, and first language attrition. In this way, heritage language acquisition is not an isolated phenomenon, but is central to the language sciences and related disciplines like communication studies. As we saw in Chapters 7 and 8, much needs to be discovered about how heritage language speakers are similar to and different from child and adult monolingual native speakers, bilingual children, fully fluent bilingual adults, and second language learners. These comparisons yield crucial information about the nature of language and language development as a function of age and cognitive development (children versus adults) and the linguistic environment (monolingual versus bilingual). Methods and empirical tools from sister disciplines can be easily adapted, and have been extended, to study the heritage language acquisition situation. As stressed in Chapter 6, the particular characteristics of heritage speakers need to be taken into account when choosing appropriate methods to elicit their linguistic behavior.

Understanding heritage language acquisition has implications for theoretical claims about language and bilingualism, for language education and for language policies.

9.1   Language sciences

One of the goals of the language sciences is to understand the nature of the language faculty as represented in adult native speaker knowledge and how that knowledge develops in children. As such, psycholinguistically oriented experimental studies rely heavily on the notion of the native speaker and the predominant focus has been on understanding the monolingual native speaker, even though the majority of the world's population is bilingual and multilingual. It is also often assumed that once acquired, linguistic knowledge is stable, at least in adults, and it does not erode easily in situations of reduced exposure and language disuse, especially in areas of morphosyntax. However, we have seen throughout this book that language development and native speaker knowledge can be profoundly shaped by their environment, and this is especially significant in bilingualism where context of use and amount of input in each language vary. The study of heritage speakers raises critical questions about current understanding of language development in a dual language context and the role of input and experience in both learning and maintaining a language. It also leads us to question what aspects of language develop fully and which ones end up incompletely mastered, as well as how reduced input and use interact with the age of the bilingual speaker in determining patterns of acquisition and language loss. Variability in language development under these conditions also raises fundamental questions about the nature of language. For example, which aspects of grammatical competence are specifically vulnerable and prone to simplification and erosion under limited input conditions in heritage grammars and which others are more resilient, and why? These are the questions that many recent studies have addressed, and that we are still in the process of answering. But the picture that emerges so far is that phonology is very well-preserved and to some extent basic syntax (like word order) and universal aspects of semantics are as well. However, morphology, and interface areas (morphosyntax, syntax-semantics, syntax-discourse) remain vulnerable to incomplete acquisition, attrition, and eventual simplification.

In this book, I have characterized heritage speakers as a type of native speaker, but many may find the characterization of heritage speakers as native speakers unconvincing. When one thinks about a native speaker, what usually comes to mind is a monolingual person, or a person who grew up in a monolingual environment and was educated in the native language. One can certainly find numerous native speakers of many standard languages like English, French, Spanish, Japanese, among many others, who are truly monolingual, but the reality is that the majority of the world's population knows and speaks another language. In fact, bilingual native speakers of one or more languages outnumber monolingual native speakers, who speak only one language. Furthermore, not all languages have monolingual native speakers, so it should not be assumed that a native speaker is only a monolingual person. All native speakers of Euskera and Catalan speak Spanish as well, the majority language in Spain, and there are practically no exclusively monolingual speakers of these languages alive. The purpose of this book has been to show that acquiring a heritage language is like acquiring a native language, except that its acquisition happens in a sociopolitically bilingual environment, where access to the heritage language and opportunities to use the heritage language waxes and wanes during the entire language development period, which I argued in this book goes well beyond the preliteracy age, extending until after puberty, when linguistic maturity is reached.

A central issue in contemporary studies of heritage language acquisition has been a proper characterization of the linguistic profiles of heritage speakers and the type of linguistic ability they possess in their heritage language. For more than a decade now, we have been describing heritage speakers as bilingual individuals with stronger command of the majority language than of the heritage language learned at home in childhood. In fact, one of the most distinctive features of heritage speakers is the wide range of overall proficiency and specific proficiencies they exhibit in their heritage language, ranging from minimal to superior, depending on the language and on their lifelong experience with it. The fact that heritage speakers undergo language shift with the onset of schooling in the majority language, if not earlier, contributes significantly to reduction in input and opportunities to use the language at a critical time during language development. Amount and quality of input and frequent and consistent use of the language are of course fundamental to successful linguistic outcomes, but so is exposure to the language since birth and in early childhood (age of acquisition or timing of input). In fact, some specific aspects of language, like phonology, for example, develop very early in life, and even when input and exposure to the language is reduced later on, it is possible to retain native-like ability in some specific areas, like acoustic perception. At the same time, some heritage speakers are able to overcome these odds and develop very high levels of proficiency in the heritage language overall, and/or in specific domains of their linguistic competence, including morphosyntax, syntax, semantics, and discourse pragmatics.

In the last decade, there has been a considerable body of research on the linguistic characteristics of heritage speakers, and the psycholinguistic and sociolinguistic underpinnings of the nature of their grammatical knowledge. Significant emphasis has also been placed on the process and circumstances of the language acquisition process in these speakers, and the interaction of age and the nature of input. This book has featured the most recent research on heritage speakers from different parts of the world, and the majority of studies have been concerned with individuals at the lower end of the proficiency spectrum, characterizing the nontarget-like linguistic abilities of heritage speakers as resulting from incomplete acquisition and/or attrition. Because many heritage speakers do not control many grammatical features of the heritage language at native levels, they resemble second language learners in many respects. Therefore, the vast majority of studies to date have been invested in understanding the nature of the grammatical deficits observed in heritage speakers and their theoretical, social, and educational implications. This focus has been important to advance knowledge in this field in general, because by understanding how heritage speakers differ from monolingual children, from second language learners, from their own parents, and from native speakers who do not live in a bilingual situation, we can identify what specific properties of the language need to be targeted, emphasized, and developed when heritage speakers come to the classroom. These comparisons also allow us to elucidate the difference between the normal process and outcome of bilingualism and monolingual acquisition, and the range of variation that is normal in bilingual acquisition. It is by looking at the nonconvergent cases that we often begin to understand the role of input, both oral and through literacy instruction at school, as a function of age in the developing child, as this interaction would be impossible to see clearly in a monolingual situation, unless it is done in the context of case studies of abnormal circumstances.

But more needs to be done to understand the possibilities of heritage language acquisition, and I hope that this book leaves the door open for further advances. Documenting and characterizing the high end of the proficiency spectrum in heritage speakers, for example, has not been the focus of much research in heritage speakers, but it is certainly an area that deserves attention. We know that truly balanced bilingualism is not as typical as one may think, but it does happen. Can heritage speakers be fluent speakers of the two languages? If so, what are the personal and environmental circumstances that lead to that outcome? And what is the incidence of that outcome in the general population of heritage speakers? For example, in the foundational essay on interlanguage grammars, Selinker (1972) hypothesized than less than 5% of second language learners could reach native-like ability in a second language, given the right environmental circumstances. Assuming that the "success" rate set arbitrarily by Selinker (and supported by many others subsequently) was relatively accurate, would a similar 5% of fully fluent and balanced bilingualism in adulthood be expected of heritage speakers? Or could the rate be much higher in this population? Perhaps it depends on context: in societies where multilingualism is seen as an asset (Canada and many countries in Europe), higher levels of heritage language development and maintenance may be found than in countries where bilingualism is often perceived as a handicap and an obstacle to be overcome (United States). Studies on heritage languages in Europe suggest that high levels of competence in the heritage language and in the majority language are documented, but this is an area of research that certainly deserves more attention, especially if we are to derive implications for language education and for language policies at a national level, where there is a need for professionals with high levels of proficiency and professional competence in critical languages.

9.2   Language education

Regardless of the answers to these highly important theoretical questions, the fact is that many heritage speakers feel a need in early adulthood to reconnect with their culture and learn more about the language, especially to regain some of the skills that come from schooling. The most pressing concern is how to help heritage speakers who want to improve their level of proficiency and expand the linguistic repertoire of their current knowledge of the heritage language. Let me share the following example of a message I received as I was finishing this book. (I have replaced the actual name by heritage speaker of Twi.)

From: Heritage speaker of African language
Sent: Sunday, June 08, 2014 1:27 PM
To: Montrul, Silvina Andrea
Subject: Relearning as a Heritage Speaker

Dear Dr. Montrul,
My name is XX, and I recently read one of your articles online. I was absolutely fascinated by your findings, as I found myself able to relate to the evidence displayed through your research. I am a heritage speaker of a Ghanaian language called Twi, also known as Akan, and I was raised in the United States. I speak English, Spanish, and basic French. I believe that rejecting the language (Twi) became psychological – as you stated often occurs with the minority language.
I am getting ready to take my first trip to Ghana and I am interested in relearning my first language. Do you have any advice/suggestions as to what I should avoid? I have applied to study the language at the college level because I would like to improve my Twi writing and reading skills.

Thank you in advance,
Heritage speaker of Twi.

How can we answer questions like this one? What is the right advice to give? How do we encourage heritage speakers to embrace the relearning of their heritage language? What is realistic for them to expect in terms of gains when they take a class?

The language teaching profession has been struggling for years to find answers and solutions to the pedagogical challenges that heritage speakers pose. What are the goals of heritage language classes and programs these days? Are these goals being met? How can HL and L2 learners learn and work together in the same classroom?

The teaching of Spanish to heritage speakers of Spanish may date back to the 1930s in the United States, according to Carreira (2012), but the first official recognition of the field of heritage language teaching dates back to 1972, when the American Association of Teachers of Spanish and Portuguese (AATSP) issued a statement in support of specialized Spanish classes for Latino students. The goal of instruction at the time was to develop literacy and reinforce other levels of the curriculum at all levels of instruction. Because bilingualism at that time was seen as a problem to be overcome (Martínez 2013), the teaching approaches in vogue then were highly prescriptive and normative, and the heritage language was seen as an imperfect language that needed to be replaced and polished by learning the standard Spanish language. As a result, this approach contributed to heritage language learners' linguistic insecurities and low linguistic self-esteem. In the 1980s, when the focus changed to seeing the acquisition of the heritage language as a right (Martínez 2013), Guadalupe Valdés proposed a more comprehensive pedagogical approach where the heritage language is placed within its cultural and sociolinguistic context as another variety of Spanish. The goals of instruction since then have been to respect the local varieties spoken by heritage speakers and expand their linguistic repertoire through literacy instruction (reading and writing). In addition to addressing linguistic needs and goals, current approaches are also more sensitive to attending to heritage language learners' cultural and socio-affective needs by approaching the teaching of the language through cultural, social, and political themes that are relevant to heritage language learners (social justice, immigration, bilingualism, biculturalism, etc.). Today, heritage languages are seen as a valuable resource in many arenas, something worth nurturing and preserving, so attitudes toward heritage languages and bilingualism are seemingly more positive than before (Martínez 2013). As we continue to learn more about heritage languages and heritage language learners, the field has been evolving toward a more positive and comprehensive approach that takes into account all the needs of the learner. Today we understand more about how the heritage language learners feel about their language, how they perceive their language, and what they want to get out of the heritage language classroom. What is not abundantly clear is the extent to which our methods are meeting these needs.

As far as the classroom is concerned, linguistic assessment tools have also allowed us to assess more precisely the specific areas of language (vocabulary, grammar, and language skills) that need development within curricula and that bring together content-based, task-based, and project-based approaches. Kagan and Dillon (2009) suggested a matrix for the HL-learner curriculum that incorporates proper placement and stresses the significant amount of time that HL learners need to relearn and expand their language. The matrix includes programmatic rigor, HL specific instructional materials, community-based curriculum, and instructors trained in HL teaching methodologies and approaches.

However, the reality in many institutions is that heritage language learners must share the classroom with second language learners, and the question of how best to support heritage learners' linguistic development in these situations is an important one. It is undeniably the case that heritage language learners tend to have stronger speaking and pronunciation skills and a broader vocabulary than the L2 learners, owing largely to the differences between the contexts in which the two groups learned their language, as discussed at length in this book and elsewhere (Montrul 2008). It is just as undeniable that both groups of learners are often placed in the same course, either because they had just completed one of the requirements or because their scores on a written placement test routed them there. Language placement tests are not 100% reliable even in L2 learners (Brown, Hudson, and Clark 2004) and when the same tests are applied to HL learners, the results are even less satisfying. Progress is being made toward reliable and valid assessments of language proficiency for HL learners, and this will undoubtedly result in better instructional outcomes for students in the long term. The largest base of research related to heritage language placement has been conducted with Spanish as a heritage language (Beaudrie 2012), likely because it is the language with the greatest number of heritage speakers in the United States. But regardless of how placement is achieved in classrooms, it is important to conduct more classroom studies because they have ecological validity and are more representative of what actually happens in language classrooms on a regular basis.

There are other important areas of heritage language teaching and learning that deserve more attention in future research. Continuing to focus on differences and similarities between L2 learners and heritage speakers is fundamental to understand what these two types of learners have in common and how they differ. This information is key to developing specific programs and materials to address the particular needs of heritage speakers. And if the two groups need to share the same classroom, as is the case in many institutions, then we need to know which activities enhance learning in the heritage speakers while these students interact with each other and with L2 learners. There has not been much research on heritage speakers' knowledge of vocabulary in general, and since vocabulary knowledge is related to literacy and academic achievement in the language, this is an area of significant interest.

What is the linguistic capacity for learning and relearning in the heritage language in the classroom? In Chapter 8, we saw that the very few studies that have identified grammatical gaps in heritage speakers and have developed form-focused interventions to address them in the classroom reported high reactivity and learning on the part of the heritage speakers. But due to the nature of the studies and the limitations of the post-test designs, how long lasting after the courses are over those gains are is hard to tell. Some studies have shown that child and adult heritage speakers are responsive to form-focused instruction and practice in the classroom: Song et al.'s (1997) study of case markers in Korean heritage children and Montrul and Bowles (2010) study of differential object marking in Spanish heritage speakers. Are these gains retained beyond the classroom, say, a year later, forever? Did the instruction actually change the linguistic competence of the HL learner? These questions are still awaiting answers, and call for more longitudinal studies of instructed heritage speakers when they leave the classroom.

We also need to see studies that look at the linguistic knowledge of heritage speakers who are heritage language learners in the classroom and heritage speakers who do not attend or have never attended formal classes in the heritage language, that is, the difference between heritage speakers and heritage language learners discussed in Chapter 2. An example with young school children who speak Mandarin as a heritage language is Jia and Paradis (2014). This type of research would allow us to understand indirectly whether some sort of formal exposure to the heritage language makes a difference in heritage language speakers' linguistic development, and the overall assessment of Jia and Paradis is that the children who are enrolled in a dual immersion English-Mandarin school are more proficient in Mandarin than the children who are enrolled in English-only schools. Will the advantages for the children receiving schooling in Mandarin prevail when these Mandarin heritage speakers are young adults? Finally, we need to understand how heritage speakers develop metalinguistic awareness in their heritage language, which seems to be very important for advancing in the language in a formal environment.

Unlike L1 learners, heritage speakers need motivation to develop the heritage language beyond what they learned at home in childhood. Beyond grammatical development, few studies have analyzed the role of attitudes and motivation in the acquisition and development of the heritage language, and especially the fact that these change over time in heritage speakers (Ducar 2012). Although both L2 learners and heritage speakers need motivation and a positive attitude to learn their language successfully, the type of motivation and attitude toward the language can vary widely in the two groups. What also sets L2 learners and HL learners apart is identity. Heritage speakers are part of a heritage community and may look at the language and the culture from inside, whereas L2 learners do not have cultural ties to the community and look at the language and the culture from outside. Studies that have addressed this issue have adopted Gardner's socioeducational definition and methods for studying motivation as developed for L2 acquisition in Canada. More studies are needed where issues of identity and integrative motivation are also taken into account in evaluating heritage speakers' needs in the classroom. Furthermore, there may be important differences in attitudes and motivation depending on the heritage language and the vitality of the language. For example Chinese heritage speakers in the United States want to learn their heritage language because they see career advantages and professional opportunities (Wen 2011), but heritage speakers of Romanian in the United States may not see similar career advantages for studying Romanian. Learning the language better would be only for the purpose of communicating with the family, perhaps. But if the heritage speaker wants to communicate better with the family, do they have to learn the formal variety of the language? In addition to identity, another fruitful line of inquiry to pursue is how the heritage speakers perceive their own language and culture and how they position themselves in their culture.

The findings on heritage language acquisition also need to reach the teachers who work with heritage language learners because their attitudes and perceptions of the pedagogical challenges heritage language learners present are crucial for the success of their teaching. More and more, the professional development of language teachers needs to include discussion of the heritage language learners, their characteristics, their linguistic goals, and their needs. Teachers need to keep learning about language learning, the impact of age and experience on acquisition, and sociolinguistic diversity in languages in general. Teachers need to understand the process of language acquisition under suboptimal input conditions, as in the case of heritage speakers, as well as all the factors that lead to that type of linguistic development. Because it is largely the result of global geopolitical and economic trends and developments that determine specific migration patterns, the field of heritage language acquisition/learning/teaching will always be in constant flux, and it may not be possible to develop everything for every language. Having a network of heritage language teachers of different languages can help share knowledge and best practices for current and future heritage languages. Finally, as much as possible, teachers would seek to work closely to the heritage language communities to assess their needs. Transformations that happen from the bottom up, where initiatives for changes or innovation come from the stakeholders, are more effective and long lasting in the long run than innovations that are imposed top down, from policy makers or researchers who are not in actual contact with the people whose lives will be affected by the innovation or change. The teaching of heritage languages in the classroom can succeed when it connects students to their communities of residence through their home language as it also promotes the learning of the standard variety of the language, especially if the language has professional currency in the global economy. This applies to middle and high school levels as well. Given the complexity of the heritage language acquisition process and the diversity among heritage languages, heritage language speakers, and learners of a given language, the field of heritage language teaching must continue to develop learner-centered approaches, where the linguistic, cultural, and affective characteristics and needs of the learners are the main elements that drive the curriculum for the learner or a particular class. Although the job is challenging, heritage language teachers will eventually become the experts in teaching multilevel classrooms.

9.3   Language policies

Throughout this book, I have also emphasized that the period of later language development, which coincides with schooling, is crucial for heritage language growth and maintenance, and it is often rich input during this crucial time that is missing in heritage speakers. Education in the heritage language is important to provide access to the heritage language beyond the home, to learn to use the language in more advanced communicative contexts that require more diversified vocabulary and a wider range of grammatical expressions, and to also promote the stability and the value of the language. Heritage languages all over the world differ significantly in the degree of governmental support they receive and whether the languages are imparted at school in any way.

Education has been a major component in efforts to revitalize endangered heritage languages all over the world. The Basque country and Catalonia in Spain have been very successful in adopting national educational programs that incorporate Euskera and Catalan as languages of instruction in immersion programs from kindergarten to university in their education system, and since the new constitution of 1978 bilingualism in the younger generations has increased significantly, and so have increased the positive attitudes toward using these languages in these regions in everyday life. But not all countries with similar linguistic situations have been as successful in revitalizing and maintaining their language. According to Bale (2010), in wealthy nations and developing ones alike, in rural contexts as in urban ones, researchers have consistently cited similar key factors impacting the success of heritage language education policies. These factors include linguistically and pedagogically competent teachers for heritage language programs, curricular materials in the target heritage language that are age and culturally appropriate, issues of language standardization and corpus planning, heritage language assessment, and finding ways to integrate multiple venues for heritage language education into existing administrative and accreditation systems. While there is consensus that school-based factors impact the development and acquisition of heritage languages, school cannot be the only site for heritage language revitalization, maintenance, and growth.

Nowhere is perhaps the need to use the language beyond what the education system offers in terms of heritage language education more clear than in Ireland. The Republic of Ireland has recently conducted large-scale research to develop a 20-year official language strategy for the revitalization of Irish (Ó Flatharta *et al.* 2008). The reason for this strategy is due to the current perception that despite efforts to protect and revitalize the Irish language through education since the inception of the Irish Free State in 1922, focusing on teaching Irish in schools has not been sufficient. The focus of much of this language planning has been in the Gaeltacht region in western Ireland, where the majority of the population is Irish-speaking (from 67% to 93% depending on region, Ó Giollagáin 2011). According to Laoire (2005), immersion approaches to Irish education in the Gaeltacht date back to the 1930s, and the number of immersion programs began to rise again in the 1980s and 1990s.

However, the majority of students across the Republic now study Irish as a school subject. Despite improvements in how Irish is taught – for example, the use of communicative syllabi focusing on everyday rather than "school" Irish and the fact that Irish has gained in prestige since becoming a working language of the European Union – Laoire (2005, p. 276) notes the language still faces important challenges. For example, immigration to Ireland, which has led to an increase in students in school who speak neither English nor Irish, has further complicated the efforts to meet the needs of all its students while developing proficiency in Irish. In Ireland, it seems that the school has been the primary site of Irish acquisition, not the home. Many Irish speakers prefer to use English in their daily lives, and their preference seems to undermine the government effort to promote the use of Irish. The emergence of majority language social networks also undermines efforts of family-based language transmission by transforming the language dynamics of the young (Ó Giollagáin 2011). This is an example of how imposing the study of a language through a national policy to re create the sociolinguistic conditions for socialization in Irish may not work entirely if the speakers and their families do not see the value of the language and use it at home or beyond the school. There is a simple discrepancy between formal policy and actual language practice, and education programs cannot compensate for language attitudes and practice in society more broadly. The full development of the heritage language seems to require the full support of the home, the school, and the community. And because different heritage languages and the territories where those languages are spoken differ not only in number of speakers but also in perceived value and attitudes toward the language by the speakers and the rest of the society, they differ in the degree the accessibility to the language at home, at school, and in the broader society. All these external attitudinal and sociopolitical factors contribute as well to differential levels of success in the acquisition of the heritage language at the individual, psycholinguistic level. More comparative research of heritage languages in different parts of the world is needed to understand how these sociopolitical factors impact the development of the heritage language at the individual level.

9.4   Conclusion

In sum, the last decade has made tremendous strides in promoting the study of heritage languages and heritage speakers from diverse fields within linguistics that converge on the common interest in understanding this specific type of acquisition situation and the sociopolitical factors that play a role in the outcome of acquisition. The intense and ever-improving research in the last two decades has advanced our state of knowledge in significant ways. Today we understand more the conditions under which heritage language grammars are acquired and develop, the nature of the grammatical system as it develops, and the factors that contribute to their different degrees of ultimate attainment. At the same time, many fundamental questions about the potential for heritage language relearning and development beyond what was acquired in childhood remain unanswered. Hopefully, the synthesis of the latest research presented in this volume, and the copious amount of research that is currently being produced but that did not make it to these pages, will inspire others to continue our search for answers to these tantalizing questions.

References

Aarsen, J., de Ruiter, J. and Verhoeven, L. (1993), 'Summative assessment of ethnic group language proficiency' in G. Extra and L. Verhoeven (eds.), *Immigrant Languages in Europe* (Clevedon: Multilingual Matters), 285–296.

Abrahamsson, N. and Hyltenstam, K. (2008), 'The robustness of aptitude effects in near-native second language acquisition', *Studies in Second Language Acquisition* 30, 481–509.

(2009), 'Age of onset and nativelikeness in a second language: listener perception versus linguistic scrutiny', *Language Learning* 59, 249–306.

Aitchinson, J. (1991), *Language Change: Progress or Decay?* (Cambridge, UK: Cambridge University Press).

Alarcón, I. (2011), 'Spanish gender agreement under complete and incomplete acquisition: early and late bilinguals' linguistic behavior within the noun phrase', *Bilingualism: Language and Cognition* 14, 332–350.

Albirini, A. (2013), 'Toward understanding the variability in the language proficiencies of Arabic heritage speakers', *International Journal of Bilingualism*. doi: 10.1177/1367006912472404.

(2014a), 'Factors affecting the acquisition of plural morphology in Jordanian Arabic', *Journal of Child Language*, First View Article, August 2014, 1–29. doi: 10.1017/S0305000914000270.

(2014b), 'The role of the colloquial varieties in the acquisition of the Standard Variety: the case of Arabic heritage speakers', *Foreign Language Annals* 47, 447–463. doi: 10.1111/flan.12087.

Albirini, A. and Benmamoun, E. (2014a), 'Aspects of second language transfer in the oral production of Egyptian and Palestinian heritage speakers', *International Journal of Bilingualism* 18, 3, 244–273. doi: 10.1177/1367006912441729.

(2014b), 'Factors affecting the retention of sentential negation in heritage Egyptian Arabic', *Bilingualism: Language and Cognition*. Epub ahead of print June 4, doi:10.1017/S1366728914000066.

Albirini, A., Benmamoun, E. and Chakrani, I. (2013), 'Gender and number agreement in the oral production of Arabic heritage speakers', *Bilingualism: Language and Cognition* 16, 1–18.

Albirini, A., Benmamoun, E. and Saadah, E. (2011), 'Grammatical features of Egyptian and Palestinian Arabic heritage speakers' oral production', *Studies in Second Language Acquisition* 33, 273–304.

Allen, S. (2007), 'The future of Inuktitut in the face of majority languages: bilingualism or language shift?', *Applied Psycholinguistics* 28, 515–536.

Allen, S., Crago, M. and Presco, D. (2006), 'The effect of majority language exposure on minority language skills: the case of Inuktitut', *International Journal of Bilingual Education and Bilingualism* 9, 578–596.

Amaral, L. and Roeper, T. (2014), 'Multiple grammars and second language representations', *Second Language Research* 30, 3–36.

Anderson, R. (1999), 'Noun phrase gender agreement in language attrition. Preliminary results', *Bilingual Research Journal* 23, 318–337.

Aoun, J., Benmamoun, E. and Choueiri, L. (2010), *The Syntax of Arabic* (New York, NY: Cambridge University Press).

Armon-Lotem, S., Joffe, S., Abutbul-Oz, H., Altman, C. and Walters, J. (2014), 'Language exposure, ethnolinguistic identity and attitudes in the acquisition of Hebrew as a second language among bilingual preschool children from Russian- and English-speaking backgrounds' in T. Grüter and. J. Paradis (eds.), *Input and Experience in Bilingual Development* (Amsterdam: John Benjamins), 77–98.

Au, T., Knightly, L., Jun, S.-A., and Oh, J. (2002), 'Overhearing a language during childhood', *Psychological Science* 13, 238–243.

Austin, J. (2007), 'Grammatical interference and the acquisition of ergative case in bilingual children learning Basque and Spanish', *Bilingualism: Language and Cognition* 10, 315–331.

Bachman, L. F. (1985), 'Performance on cloze tests with fixed ratio and rational deletions', *TESOL Quarterly* 16, 61–70.

Balcom, P. (2003), 'Crosslinguistic influence of L2 English on middle constructions in L1 French' in V. Cook (ed.), *Effects of the Second Language on the First* (Clarendon: Multilingual Matters), 168–192.

Baldwin, D. and Meyer M. (2009), 'How inherently social is language?' in E. Hoff and M. Shatz (eds.), *The Blackwell Handbook of Language Development* (Malden, MA: Blackwell), 87–106.

Bale, J. (2010), 'International comparative perspectives on heritage language education policy research', *Annual Review of Applied Linguistics* 30, 42–65.

Barreña, A. (1995), *Gramatikaren Jabekuntzagarapena eta Haur Euskaldunak* (Bilbao: Servicio Editorial de la Universidad del País Vasco).

(1997), 'Desarrollo diferenciado de sistemas gramaticales en un niño vasco-español bilingüe' in A. T. Pérez-Leroux and W. Glass (eds.), *Contemporary Perspectives on the Acquisition of Spanish* (Sommerville, MA: Cascadilla Press), 55–74.

Barriga Villanueva, R. (2004), *Estudios Sobre el Habla Infantil en los Años Escolares. "Un Solecito Calientote."* (México, DF: El Colegio de México).

(2008), 'Miradas a la interculturalidad', *Revista Mexicana de Investigación Educativa* 13, 39, 1229–1254.

Baten, K. (2011), 'Processability theory and German case acquisition', *Language Learning* 61, 455–505.

Bates, E. (1976), *Language and Context: The Acquisition of Pragmatics* (New York, NY: Academic Press).

Bavin, E. (1989), 'Some lexical and morphological changes in Warlpiri' in N. Dorian (ed.), *Investigating Obsolescence. Studies in Language Contraction and Death* (Cambridge, UK: Cambridge University Press), 267–286.

Bayley, R. and Tarone, E. (2011), 'Variationist perspectives' in A. Mackey and S. Gass (eds.), *Routledge Handbook of Second Language Acquisition* (New York, NY: Routledge), 41–56.

Bayram, F. (2013), 'Acquisition of Turkish by heritage speakers: a processability Approach', Unpublished doctoral dissertation, University of Newcastle, UK.

Beaudrie, S. (2012), 'Introduction: developments in Spanish heritage language placement', *The Heritage Language Journal* 9, i–xi.

Beaudrie, S., Ducar, C. and Potowski, K. (2014), *Heritage Language Teaching: Research and Practice* (New York, NY: McGraw-Hill).

Beaudrie, S. and Fairclough, M. (2012), *Spanish as a Heritage Language in the United States* (Washington, DC: Georgetown University Press).

Beebe, L. (1980), 'Sociolinguistic variation and style shifting in second language acquisition', *Language Learning* 30, 433–447.

Belletti, A., Bennati, E. and Sorace, A. (2007), 'Theoretical and developmental issues in the syntax of subjects. Evidence from near-native Italian', *Natural Language and Linguistic Theory* 25, 657–689.

Benmamoun, A., Albirini, A. Montrul, S. and Saadah, E. (2014), 'Arabic plurals and root and pattern morphology in Palestinian and Egyptian heritage speakers', *Linguistic Approaches to Bilingualism* 4, 89–123.

Benmamoun, E., Montrul, S. and Polinsky, M. (2013a), 'Keynote article. Heritage languages and their speakers: opportunities and challenges for linguistics', *Theoretical Linguistics* 39, 129–181.

(2013b), 'Defining an "ideal" heritage speaker: theoretical and methodological challenges. Reply to peer commentaries', *Theoretical Linguistics* 39, 259–294.

Berman, R. (1987), 'A developmental route: learning the form and function of complex nominal', *Linguistics* 25, 1057–1085.

(1988), 'Word class distinctions in developing grammars' in Y. Levy, I. Schlesinger and M. Braine (eds.), *Categories and Processes in Language Acquisition* (Hillsdale, NJ: Lawrence Erlbaum), 45–72.

(2001), 'Crosslinguistic aspects of later language development' in S. Strömqvist (ed.), *The Diversity of Language and Language Learning* (Lund: Lund University), 25–44.

(2004), 'Between emergence and mastery: the long developmental route of language acquisition' in R. Berman (ed.), *Language Development across Childhood and Adolescence* (Amsterdam: John Benjamins), 9–34.

Berman, R. and Slobin, D. (1994), *Relating Events in Narrative: a Crosslinguistic Developmental Study* (Hillsdale, NJ: Lawrence Erlbaum).

Bhatt, R. (2002), 'Experts, dialects, and discourse', *International Journal of Applied Linguistics* 12, 74–109.

Bialystok, E. (1994), 'Analysis and control in the development of second language proficiency', *Studies in Second Language Acquisition* 16, 157–168.

(2001), *Bilingualism in Development: Language, Literacy and Cognition* (Cambridge: Cambridge University Press).

Bialystok, E. and Hakuta, K. (1999), 'Confounded age: linguistic and cognitive factors in age differences for second language acquisition' in D. Birdsong (ed.), *Second Language Acquisition and the Critical Period Hypothesis* (Mahwah, NJ: Lawrence Erlbaum), 161–181.

Bialystok, E. and Ryan, E. (1985), 'A metacognitive framework for the development of first and second language skills' in D. L. Forrester-Pressley, G. E. MacKinnon and T. G. Waller (eds.), *Metacognition, Cognition, and Human Performance* (Orlando, FL: Academic Press), 207–252.

Bianchi, G. (2013), 'Gender in Italian-German bilinguals: a comparison with German L2 learners of Italian', *Bilingualism: Language and Cognition* 16, 538–557.

Birdsong, D. (1989), *Metalinguistic Performance and Interlinguistic Competence* (Berlin: Springer-Verlag).

(1992), 'Ultimate attainment in second language acquisition', *Language* 68, 706–755.

(ed.), (1999), *Second Language Acquisition and the Critical Period Hypothesis* (Mahwah, NJ: Lawrence Erlbaum).

Birdsong, D. and Molis, M. (2001), 'On the evidence for maturational constraints in second language acquisition', *Journal of Memory and Language* 44, 235–249.

Bishop, D. and Adams, C. (1990), 'A prospective study of the relationship between specific language impairment, phonological disorders and reading retardation', *Journal of Child Psychology and Psychiatry* 31, 1027–1050.

Blake, R. (1983), 'Mood selection among Spanish-speaking children, ages 4 to 12', *The Bilingual Review* 10, 21–32.

Blake, R. and Zyzik, E. (2003), 'Who's helping whom?: learner/heritage-speakers' networked discussions in Spanish', *Applied Linguistics* 24, 519–544.

Bley-Vroman, R. (1989), 'The logical problem of second language learning' in S. Gass and J. Schachter (eds.), *Linguistic Perspectives on Second Language Acquisition* (Cambridge: Cambridge University Press), 41–68.

(1990), 'The logical problem of foreign language learning', *Linguistic Analysis* 20, 3–49.

Bley-Vroman, R. (2009), 'The evolving context of the fundamental difference hypothesis', *Studies in Second Language Acquisition* 31, 2, 175–198.

Blom, E. and Unsworth, S. (eds.), (2010), *Experimental Methods in Language Acquisition Research* (Amsterdam: John Benjamins).

Bloom, P. (1990), 'Syntactic distinctions in child language', *Journal of Child Language* 17, 343–355.

Bolonyai, A. (1998), 'In between languages: language shift/ maintenance in childhood bilingualism. *The International Journal of Bilingualism* 2, 21–43.

(2007), '(In)vulnerable agreement in incomplete bilingual L1 learners', *The International Journal of Bilingualism* 11, 3–21.

Bonilla, C. (2015), 'From number agreement to the subjunctive: evidence for processability theory in L2 Spanish', *Second Language Research* 15, 1, 53–74.

Bonvillian, J. and Folven, R. (1993), 'Sign language acquisition: developmental aspects' in M. Marschark and D. Clark (eds.), *Psychological Perspectives on Deafness* (New York, NY: Oxford University Press), 229–265.

Bowles, M. (2011a), 'Measuring implicit and explicit linguistic knowledge: what can heritage language learners contribute?', *Studies in Second Language Acquisition* 33, 247–272.

(2011b), 'Exploring the role of modality: L2–heritage learner interactions in the Spanish language classroom', *The Heritage Language Journal* 8, 30–65.

Bowles, M., Adams, R. and Toth, P. (2014), 'A comparison of L2-L2 and L2-heritage learner interactions in Spanish language classrooms', *The Modern Language Journal* 98, 2, 497–517.

Bowles, M. and Montrul, S. (2009), 'Instructed L2 acquisition of differential object marking in Spanish' in R. Leow, H. Campos and D. Lardiere (eds.), *Little Words: Their History, Phonology, Syntax, Semantics, Pragmatics and Acquisition* (Georgetown, TX: Georgetown University Press), 199–210.

Boyd, S. (1985), 'Language survival: a study of language contact, language shift and language choice in Sweden', Unpublished doctoral dissertation, University of Gothenburg, Sweden.

Braine, M. (1987), 'What is learned in acquiring word classes – a step toward an acquisition theory' in B. MacWhinney (ed.), *Mechanisms of Language Acquisition* (Hillsdale, NJ: Lawrence Erlbaum), 65–87.

Brehmer, B. and Czachór, A. (2012), 'The formation and distribution of the analytic future tense in Polish-German bilinguals' in K. Braunmüller and C. Gabriel (eds.), *Multilingual Individuals and Multilingual Societies* (Amsterdam: John Benjamins), 297–314.

Bresnan, J. (2001), *Lexical-functional Syntax* (Malden, MA: Blackwell).

Brinton, D., Kagan, O. and Bauckus, S. (eds.), (2008), *Heritage Language Education: A New Field Emerging* (New York, NY: Routledge).

Brooks, M. and Nagy, N. (2012), 'Speech rates across generations in two Toronto heritage languages', Paper presented at the *Workshop on Heritage Languages: The Road Less Travelled*, University of Toronto, October 26–27.

Brown, J. D. (1983), 'A closer look at cloze: validity and reliability' in J. W. Oller, Jr. (ed.), *Issues in Language Testing Research* (Rowley, MA: Newbury House), 237–250.

Brown, J. D., Hudson, T. and Clark, M. (2004), 'Issues in language placement' (Manoa, Hawai'i: National Foreign Language Resource Center), Retrieved 14 June 2014 from http://nflrc.hawaii.edu/NetWorks/NW41.pdf

Brown, R. (1958), *Words and Things* (New York, NY: The Free Press).

(1973), *A First Language: The Early Stages* (Cambridge, MA: Harvard University Press).

Bruhn de Garavito, J. (2002), 'Verb raising in Spanish: a comparison of early and late bilinguals', *Proceedings of the 26th Annual Boston University Conference on Language Development* (Sommerville, MA: Cascadilla Press), 84–94.

Burzio, L. (1986), *Italian Syntax: A Government and Binding Approach* (Dordrecht: Reidel).

Butt, M. (2006), *Theories of Case* (Cambridge University Press).

Bybee, J. (1985), *Morphology: A Study of the Relation between Meaning and Form.* (Amsterdam: John Benjamins).

(1995), 'Regular morphology and the lexicon', *Language and Cognitive Processes* 10, 425–455.

(2002), 'Phonological evidence for exemplar storage of multiword sequences', *Studies in Second Language Acquisition* 24, 215–221.

(2008), 'Usage-based grammar and second language acquisition' in P. Robinson and N. Ellis (eds), *Handbook of Cognitive Linguistics and Second Language Acquisition* (New York, NY: Routledge), 216–236.

Bybee, J. and Hopper, P. (eds.), (2001), *Frequency and the Emergence of Linguistic Structure* (Amsterdam: John Benjamins).

Bylund, E. (2009a), 'Effects of age of L2 acquisition on L1 event conceptualization patterns', *Bilingualism: Language and Cognition* 12, 305–322.

(2009b), 'Maturational constraints and first language attrition', *Language Learning* 59, 687–715.

Bylund, E., Abrahamsson, N. and Hyltenstam, K. (2012), 'Does first language maintenance hamper nativelikeness in a second language? A study of ultimate attainment in early bilinguals', *Studies in Second Language Acquisition* 34, 215–241.

Bylund, E. and Díaz, M. (2012), 'The effects of heritage language instruction on first language proficiency: a psycholinguistic perspective', *International Journal of Bilingual Education and Bilingualism* 15, 5, 593–609. doi: 10.1080/13670050.2 012.676620.

Caldas, S. and Caron-Caldas, S. (2000), 'The influence of family, school and community on bilingual preference: results from a Louisiana/Québec case study', *Applied Psycholinguistics* 21, 365–381.

Caplan, D. (2000), 'Positron emission tomographic studies of syntactic processing' in Y. Grozinsky, L. Shapiro and D. Swinney (eds.), *Language and the Brain: Representation and Processing* (San Diego, CA: Academic Press), 315–325.

Carey, S. (1978), 'The child as a word learner' in M. Halle, J. Bresnan and G. Miller (eds.), *Linguistic Theory and Psychological Reality* (Cambridge, MA: MIT Press).

Carreira, M. (2003), 'Profiles of SNS students in the 21st century: pedagogical implications of the changing demographics and social status of US Hispanics' in A. Roca and C. Colombi (eds.), *Mi Lengua: Spanish as a Heritage Language in the United States, Research and Practice* (Washington, DC: Georgetown University Press), 51–77.

(2004), 'Seeking explanatory adequacy: a dual approach to understanding the term "heritage language learner"', *The Heritage Language Journal* 2, 25 pages.

(2012), 'Spanish as a heritage language' in J. I. Hualde, A. Olarrea and E. O'Rourke (eds.), *The Handbook of Hispanic Linguistics* (Malden, MA: Wiley-Blackwell), 765–782.

Carreira, M. and Kagan, O. (2011), 'The results of the national heritage language survey: implications for teaching, curriculum design, and professional development', *Foreign Language Annals* 44, 40–64.

Carreira, M. and Potowski, K. (2011), 'Pedagogical implications of experimental SNS research', *The Heritage Language Journal* 8, 134–151.

Cenoz, J. and Gorter, D. (2008), 'Applied linguistics and the use of minority languages in education', *AILA Review* 21, 5–12.

Chang, C., Yao, Y., Haynes, E. and Rhodes, R. (2011), 'Production of phonetic and phonological constrast by heritage speakers of Mandarin', *Journal of the Acoustic Society of America* 129, 3964–3980.

Chierchia, G., Crain, S., Guasti, M. T., Gualmini, A. and Meroni, L. (2001), 'The acquisition of disjunction: evidence for a grammatical view of scalar implicatures', *Proceedings of the 25th Boston University Conference on Language Development* (Somerville, MA: Cascadilla Press), 157–168.

Cho, S.-W. (1982), 'The acquisition of word order in Korean', Unpublished doctoral dissertation, The University of Calgary.

(1989), 'Parameter, subset principle, and the acquisition of the Korean reflexive pronoun', *Proceedings for the Cognitive Science Conference* (Seoul, Korea), 296–301.

(1992), 'The syntax and acquisition of 'kyay' ('s/he') and 'caki' ('self')', *Studies in Generative Grammar*, 361–392.

Chomsky, C. (1969), *The Acquisition of Syntax in Children from 5 to 10.* (Cambridge, MA: MIT Press).

Chomsky, N. (1965), *Aspects of the Theory of Syntax* (Cambridge, MA: MIT Press).

(1980), *Rules and Representations.* (New York, NY: Columbia University Press; Oxford: Basil Blackwell Publishers).

(1981), *Lectures on Government and Binding* (Dordrecht: Foris).

(1986), *Knowledge of Language: Its Nature, Origin and Use* (New York, NY: Praeger).

Chung, E.-S. (2013), 'Exploring the degree of native-likeness in bilingual acquisition: first, second and heritage language acquisition of Korean case ellipsis', Unpublished doctoral dissertation, University of Illinois at Urbana-Champaign.

Clahsen, H. and Muysken, P. (1986), 'The availability of universal grammar to adult and child learners: a study of the acquisition of German word order', *Second Language Research* 5, 93–119.

Clark, E. (1971), 'On the acquisition of the meaning of *before* and *after*', *Journal of Verbal Learning and Verbal Behavior* 10, 266–275.

Clyne, M. (1991), *Community Languages: The Australian Experience* (Cambridge, UK: Cambridge University Press).

Colombi, C. and Alarcón, F. (eds.), (1997), *La enseñanza del español a hispano-hablantes: praxis y teoría* (Boston, MA: Houghton Mifflin).

Comrie, B. (1976), *Aspect* (Cambridge, UK: Cambridge University Press).

Cook, V. and Newson, M. (2007), *Chomsky's Universal Grammar: An Introduction* (Malden, NJ: Blackwell).

Cornips, L. and Hulk, A. (2008), 'Factors of success and failure in the acquisition of grammatical gender in Dutch', *Second Language Research* 24, 267–295.

Correa, M. (2011), 'Heritage language learners of Spanish: what role does metalinguistic knowledge play in their acquisition of the subjunctive?', *Selected Proceedings of the 13th Hispanic Linguistics Symposium* (Somerville, MA: Cascadilla Proceedings Project), 128–138.

Coulmas, F. (ed.), (1991), *A Language Policy for the European Community* (Berlin: Mouton de Gruyter).

Cowart, W. (1997), *Experimental Syntax* (Thousand Oaks, CA: Sage Publications).

Crain, S. (1991), 'Language acquisition in the absence of experience', *Behavioral and Brain Science* 14, 597–650.

Crain, S. and Lillo-Martin, D. (1999), *An Introduction to Linguistic Theory and Language Acquisition* (Oxford: Blackwell).

Crain, S. and McKee, C. (1985), 'The acquisition of structural restrictions on anaphora', *Proceedings of NELS 15* (Amherst: University of Massachusetts, GLSA), 94–110.

Crain, S. and Thornton, R. (1998), *Investigations in Universal Grammar: A Guide to Experiments on the Acquisition of Syntax and Semantics* (Cambridge, MA: MIT Press).

Cummins, J. (2005), 'A proposal for action: strategies for recognizing heritage language competence as a learning resource within the mainstream classroom', *The Modern Language Journal* 89, 585–592.

Curtiss, S. (1977), *Genie: A Linguistic Study of a Modern Day "Wild" Child* (New York, NY: Academic Press).

(1989), 'The case of Chelsea: a new case test of the critical period for language acquisition', Unpublished manuscript. University of California, Los Angeles.

Cuza, A. and Frank, J. (2011), 'Transfer effects in the syntax-semantics interface: the case of double-que questions in heritage Spanish', *The Heritage Language Journal* 8, 66–89.

Dąbrowska, E. (1997). 'The LAD goes to school: a cautionary tale for nativists', *Linguistics* 35, 735–766.

(2012), 'Different speakers, different grammars: individual differences in native language attainment', *Linguistic Approaches to Bilingualism* 2, 219–253.

Daller, M., Yıldız, C., de Jong, N., Kan, S. and Başbaği, R. (2011), 'Language dominance in Turkish-German bilinguals: methodological aspects of measurements in structurally different languages', *The International Journal of Bilingualism* 15, 215–236.

Davies, M. (1995), 'Analyzing syntactic variation with computer-based corpora: the case of modern Spanish clitic climbing', *Hispania* 78, 370–380.

de Bot, K. and Gorter, D. (2005), 'A European perspective on heritage languages', *The Modern Language Journal* 89, 612–616.

DeGraff, M. (1999), *Language Creation and Language Change: Creolization, Diachrony and Development* (Cambridge, MA: MIT Press).

De Groot, C. (2005), 'The grammars of Hungarian outside Hungary from a linguistic-typological perspective' in A. Fenyvesi (ed.), *Hungarian Language Contact Outside Hungary* (Amsterdam: John Benjamins), 351–370.

De Houwer, A. (2003), 'Home language spoken in officially monolingual Flanders: a survey', *Plurilingua* 24, 71–87.

(2009), *Bilingual First Language Acquisition* (Bristol: Multilingual Matters).

DeKeyser, R. (2000), 'The robustness of critical period effects in second language acquisition', *Studies in Second Language Acquisition* 22, 499–534.

(2003), 'Implicit and explicit learning' in C. Doughty and M. Long (eds.), *The Handbook of Second Language Acquisition* (Malden, MA: Blackwell), 313–348.

DeKeyser, R. and Larson-Hall, J. (2005), 'What does the critical period really mean?' in J. Kroll and A. de Groot (eds.), *The Handbook of Bilingualism: Psycholinguistic Approaches* (Oxford University Press), 88–108.

de Prada Pérez, A. and Pascual y Cabo, D. (2011), 'Invariable gusta in the Spanish of heritage speakers in the U.S' in J. Hershenschon and D. Tanner (eds.), *Proceedings of the 11th Generative Approaches to Second Language Acquisition (GASLA)* (Somerville, MA: Cascadilla Proceedings Project) 110–120.

De Swart, P. (2013), 'A (single) case for heritage speakers?', *Theoretical Linguistics* 39, 251–258.

Deuchar, M. and Quay, S. (2000), *Bilingual Acquisition: Theoretical Implications of a Case Study* (Oxford: Oxford University Press).

Di Biase, B. and Kawaguchi, S. (2002), 'Exploring the typological plausibility of processability theory: language development in Italian second language and Japanese second language', *Second Language Research* 18, 274–302.

Di Gregorio, D. (2005), 'The phenomenon of international adoption with a focus on second language acquisition: a case study of internationally adopted children and adolescents from Russia', Unpublished doctoral dissertation, Indiana University of Pennsylvania.

Dickinson, D., McCabe, A., Anastasopoulos, L., Peisner-Feinberg, E. and Poe, M. (2003), 'The comprehensive language approach to early literacy: the interrelationships among vocabulary, phonological sensitivity, and print knowledge among preschool-aged children', *Journal of Educational Psychology* 95, 465–481.

Diessel, H. (2004), *The Acquisition of Complex Sentences* (Cambridge, UK: Cambridge University Press).

Dixon, R. and Blake, B. (1979), *Handbook of Australian Languages*, vol. 1 (Canberra: A. N. U. Press and Amsterdam: John Benjamins).

Doherty, M. and Perner, J. (1998), 'Metalinguistic awareness and theory of mind: just two words for the same thing?', *Cognitive Development* 13, 279–305.

Döpke, S. (1992), *One Parent, One Language: An Interactional Approach* (Amsterdam: John Benjamins).

— (1998), 'Competing language structures: the acquisition of verb placement by bilingual German-English children', *Journal of Child Language* 25, 555–584.

Dorian, N. (1981), *Language Death* (Philadelphia, PA: University of Pennsylvania Press).

— (ed.), (1989), *Investigating Obsolescence* (Cambridge, UK: Cambridge University Press).

Dowty, D. (1986), 'The effects of aspectual class on the temporal structure of discourse: semantics or pragmatics?', *Linguistics and Philosophy* 9, 37–61.

Ducar, C. (2012), 'SHL learners' attitudes and motivations' in S. Beaudrie and M. Fairclough (eds.), *Spanish as a Heritage Language in the United States* (Washington, DC: Georgetown University Press), 161–178.

Duff, P. (2007), 'Second language socialization and sociocultural theory: insights and issues', *Language Teaching* 40, 309–319.

— (2008a), 'Heritage language education in Canada' in D. Brinton, O. Kagan and S. Bauckus (eds.), *Heritage Language Education: A New Field Emerging* (New York, NY: Routledge), 71–90.

Duff. P. (2008b), *Case Study Research in Applied Linguistics* (New York, NY: Erlbaum).

Dunn, L. and Dunn, D. (2007), *Peabody Picture Vocabulary Test*, 4th Edition (Minneapolis, MN: Pearson).

Dunn, L., Padilla, E., Lugo, D. and Dunn, L. (1986), *Test de Vocabulario en Imágenes Peabody: Adaptación Hispanoamericana* (Minneapolis, MN: Pearson).

Ebert, K. H. (1971), *Referenz, Spreechsituation und die Bestimmten Artikel in Einem Nordfriesischen Dialekt (Fering)* (Bredstedt: Nordfriisk Instituut).

Eckert, P. (1989), *Jocks and Burnouts: Social Categories and Identity in the High School* (New York, NY: Teachers College Press).

El Aissati, A. (1997), 'Language loss among native speakers of Moroccan-Arabic in the Netherlands' in G. Extra and T. Verhoeven (eds.), *Bilingualism and Migration* (Studies in Multilingualism, 6) (Tilburg: Tilburg University Press).

Ellis, A. and Morrison, C. (1998), 'Real age of acquisition effects in lexical retrieval', *Journal of Experimental Psychology: Learning, Memory and Cognition* 24, 515–523.

Ellis, N. (1966), 'Sequencing in SLA: phonological memory, chunking and points of order', *Studies in Second Language Acquisition* 18, 91–126.

Ellis, N. C. (2002), 'Frequency effects in language processing: a review with implications for theories of implicit and explicit learning', *Studies in Second Language Acquisition* 23, 143–188.

Ellis, R. (2005), 'Measuring implicit and explicit knowledge of a second language: a psychometric study', *Studies in Second Language Acquisition* 27, 141–172.

Elman, J., Bates, E., Johnson, M., Karmiloff-Smith, A., Parisi, D. and Plunkett, K. (1998), *Rethinking Innateness* (Cambridge, MA: MIT Press).

Epstein, S., Flynn, S. and Martohardjono, G. (1996), 'Second language acquisition: theoretical and experimental issues in contemporary research', *Behavioral and Brain Sciences* 19, 677–758.

Erickson, F. and Shultz, J. (1982), *The Counselor as Gatekeeper: Social Interactions in Interviews* (New York, NY: Academic Press).

Escobar, A. M. (2004), 'Bilingualism in Latin America' in T. Bhatia and W. Ritchie (eds.), *Handbook of Bilingualism* (Malden, MA: Blackwell), 642–661.

Extra, G. and Gorter, D. (2001), *The Other Languages of Europe* (Clevedon: Multilingual Matters).

Extra, G. and Verhoeven, L. (1993), *Immigrant Languages in Europe* (Clevedon: Multilingual Matters).

Ezeizabarrena Segurola, M. J. (1996), *Adquisición de la morfología verbal en esukera y español por niños bilingües.* (Bilbao: Servicio de Publicaciones de la Universidad del País Vasco).

(2001), 'Dos tipos de morfología verbal, dos modos de adquisición en bilingües vasco-españoles' in C. Rojas Nieto and L. de León Pasquel (eds.), *La adquisición de la lengua materna: español, lenguas maya, euskera* (México: Universidad Nacional Autónoma de México), 237–263.

(2011), 'The (in)consistent ergative marking of early Basque: L1 vs. child L2', *Lingua* 122, 303–317.

Fairclough, M. (2005), *Spanish and Heritage Language Education in the United States. Struggling with Hypotheticals* (Frankfurt: Verveurt Iberoamericana).

(2011), 'Testing the lexical recognition task with Spanish/English bilinguals in the United States', *Language Testing* 28, 273–297.

Fedzechkina, M., Jaeger, T. F. and Newport, E. (2012), 'Language learners restructure their input to facilitate efficient communication', *Proceedings of the National Academy of Sciences* 109, 44, 17897–17902, doi:10.1073/pnas.1215776109.

(2013), 'Communicative biases shape structures of newly acquired languages' in M. Knauff, M. Pauen, N. Sebanz and I. Wachsmuth (eds.), *Proceedings of the 35th Annual Conference of the Cognitive Science Society* (Austin, TX: Cognitive Science Society), 430–435.

Fedzechkina, M., Newport, E. and Jaeger, T. F. (2014), 'Trading off information transmission against effort in language learning and language structure', *Poster presented at the 39th Annual Boston University Conference on Language Development*, November 6–9.

Fenson, L., Bates, E., Dale, O., Goodman, J., Reznick, J. and Thal, D. (2000), 'Measuring variability in early child language: don't shoot the messenger', Comments on Feldman *et al. Child Development* 71, 323–328.

Fenson, L., Dale, P., Reznick, S., Bates, E., Thal, D. and Pethick, S. (1994), 'Variability in early communicative development', *Monographs of the Society for Research in Child Development*, Serial number 242, 59, 5, 1–173.

Fenyvesi, A. (2000), 'The affectedness of the verbal complex in American Hungarian' in A. Fenyvesi and K. Sándor (eds.), *Language Contact and the Verbal Complex of Dutch and Hungarian: Working Papers from the 1st Bilingual Language Use Theme Meeting of the Study Centre on Language Contact*, November 11–13, 1999, Szeged, Hungary (Szeged: JGyTF Press), 94–107.

Ferguson, C. (1959). 'Diglossia', *Word* 15, 325–340.

Ferjan Ramírez, N., Leonard, M. K., Torres, C., Hatrak, M., Halgren, E. and Mayberry, R. I. (2013), 'Neural language processing in adolescent first-language learners', *Cerebral Cortex.* (Epub ahead of print). doi: 10.1.1093/cercor/bht137.

Fernández Martínez, A. (1994), 'El aprendizaje de los morfemas verbales: datos de un estudio longitudinal' in S. López Ornat (ed.), *La adquisición de la lengua española* (Madrid: Siglo XXI), 29–45.

Fishman, J. (1966), *Language Loyalty in the United States: The Maintenance and Perpetuation of Non-English Mother Tongues by American Ethnic and Religious Groups* (The Hague: Mouton).

(1972), *The Sociology of Language: An Interdisciplinary Social Science Approach to Language in Society* (New York, NY: Newbury House Publishers).

(2001), *Can Threatened Languages be Saved?* (Clevedon: Multilingual Matters).

(2006), 'Three-hundred plus years of heritage language education in the United States' in G. Valdés, J. Fishman, R. Chávez and W. Pérez, *Developing Minority Language Resources: The Case of Spanish in California* (Clevedon: Multilingual Matters), 12–23.

Flores, C. (2010), 'The effect of age on language attrition: evidence from bilingual returnees', *Bilingualism: Language and Cognition* 13, 533–546.

(2012), 'Differential effects of language attrition in the domain of verb placement and object expression', *Bilingualism: Language and Cognition* 15, 550–567.

Flores Ferrán, N. (2004), 'Spanish subject personal pronoun use in New York City Puerto Ricans: can we rest the case of English contact?', *Language Variation and Change* 16, 49–73.

Franceschina, F. (2005), *Fossilized Second Language Grammars: The Acquisition of Grammatical Gender* (Amsterdam: John Benjamins).

Freudenthal, D., Pine, J. M. and Gobet, F. (2006), 'Modelling the development of children's use of optional infinitives in Dutch and English using MOSAIC', *Cognitive Science* 30, 277–310.

Friedman, D. and Kagan, O. (2008), 'Academic writing proficiency of Russian heritage speakers: a comparative study' in D. Brinton, O. Kagan and S. Bauckus (eds.), *Heritage Language Education: A New Field Emerging* (New York, NY: Routledge), 181–198.

Gábor, B. and Lukács, A. (2012), 'Early morphological productivity in Hungarian: evidence from sentence repetition and elicited production', *Journal of Child Language* 39, 411–442.

Gal, S. (1989), 'Lexical innovation and loss: the use and value of restricted Hungarian' in N. Dorian (ed.), *Investigating Obsolescence: Studies in Language Contraction and Death* (Cambridge, UK: Cambridge University Press), 313–331.

Gambhir, S. and Gambhir, V. (2013), 'The maintenance and vitality of Hindi in the United States', *The Heritage Language Journal* 10, 35–42.

Guasti, M. T. (2004). *Language Acquisition: The Growth of Grammar*. Cambridge, MA: MIT Press.

Gavriilidou, Z. and Efthymiou, A. (2003), 'The acquisition of Greek gender by preschool children: a pilot study' in A. Anastasiadi-Simeonidi, A. Ralli and D. Chila-Markopoulou (eds.), *Gender* (Athens: Patakis), 190–207.

Genesee, F. (1989), 'Early bilingual development: one language or two?', *Journal of Child Language* 6, 161–179.

Genesee, F. and Nicoladis, E. (2009). 'Bilingual first language acquisition' in E. Hoff and M. Shatz (eds.), *Handbook of Language Development* (Oxford, UK: Blackwell), 324–342.

Genesee, F., Nicoladis, E. and Paradis, J. (1995), 'Language differentiation in early bilingual development', *Journal of Child Language* 22, 611–631.

Gerken, L. A. and Shady, M. (1996), 'The picture selection task' in D. McDaniel, C. McKee and H. Smith Cairns (eds.), *Methods for Assessing Children's Syntax* (Cambridge, MA: MIT Press), 125–146.

Gillis, S. and De Houwer, A. (eds.), (2001), *The Acquisition of Dutch* (Amsterdam: John Benjamins).

Gleitman, L. and Newport, E. (1995), 'The invention of language by children: environmental and biological influences on the acquisition of language' in L. Gleitman and M. Liberman (eds.), *Language: An Invitation to Cognitive Science*, 2nd Edition vol. 1 (Cambridge, MA: MIT Press), 1–24.

Glennen, S. (2005), 'New arrivals, speech and language assessment for internationally adopted infants and toddlers within the first months at home', *Seminars in Speech and Language* 26, 10–21.

Godson, L. (2004), 'Vowel production in the speech of Western Armenian heritage speakers', *The Heritage Language Journal* 2, 1–26.

Goldberg, A. (1995), *Constructions: A Construction Grammar Approach to Argument Structure* (Chicago, IL: University of Chicago Press).

(1999), 'The emergence of the semantics of argument structures' in B. MacWhinney (ed.), *The Emergence of Language* (Mahwah, NJ: Erlbaum), 197–212.

Gollan, T. H., Starr, J. and Ferreira, V. S. (in press), 'More than use it or lose it: the number of speakers effect on heritage language proficiency', *Psychonomic Bulletin and Review* 22, 1, 147–155. doi: 10.3758/s13423-014-0649-7.

Goodluck, H. (2009), 'Formal and computational constraints on language development' in E. Hoff and M. Shatz (eds.), *The Blackwell Handbook of Language Development* (Malden, MA: Blackwell), 46–67.

Gor, K. (2014), 'Raspberry, not a car: context predictability and a phonological advantage in early and late learners' processing of speech in noise', *Frontiers in Psychology* 5, 1449, 1–15. doi: 10.3389/fpsyg.2014.01449.

Gordon, P. (1996), 'The truth value judgment task' in D. McDaniel, C. McKee and H. Smith Cairns (eds.), *Methods for Assessing Children's Syntax* (Cambridge, MA: MIT Press), 211–232.

Goro, T. and Akiba, S. (2004), 'The acquisition of disjunction and positive polarity in Japanese' in G. Garding and M. Tsujimura (eds.), *Proceedings of the 23rd West Coast Conference on Formal Linguistics* (Somerville, MA: Cascadilla Press), 101–114.

Granena, G. and Long, M. (2013), 'Age of onset, length of residence, language aptitude, and ultimate attainment in three linguistic domains', *Second Language Research* 29, 311–343.

Grosjean, F. (1997), 'The bilingual individual', *Interpreting* 2, 163–187.

(1998), 'Studying bilinguals: methodological and conceptual issues', *Bilingualism: Language and Cognition* 1, 131–149.

(2008), *Studying Bilinguals* (Oxford: Oxford University Press).

(2010), *Bilingual: Life and Reality* (Cambridge, MA: Harvard University Press).

Grosjean, F. and Py, B. (1991), 'La restructuration d'une première langue: l'intégration de variantes de contact dans la compétence de migrants bilingues', *La Linguistique* 27, 35–60.

Guasti, M. T. (2002), *Language Acquisition: The Growth of Grammar* (Cambridge, MA: MIT Press).

Gürel, A. (2002), 'Linguistic characteristics of second language acquisition and first language attrition: Turkish overt versus null pronouns', Unpublished doctoral dissertation, McGill University, Montreal.

(2004), 'Selectivity in L2 induced L1 attrition: a psycholinguistic account', *Journal of Neurolinguistics* 17, 53–78.

Gürel, A. and Yılmaz, G. (2013), 'Restructuring in the L1 Turkish grammar: effects of L2 English and L2 Dutch' in M. Schmid and B. Köpke (eds.), *First Language Attrition* (Amsterdam: John Benjamins), 37–66.

Gutiérrez, M. (1996), 'Tendencias y alternancia en la expresión de condicionalidad en el español hablado en Houston', *Hispania* 79, 568–577.

Håkansson, G. (1995), 'Syntax and morphology in language attrition: a study of five bilingual expatriate Swedes', *International Journal of Applied Linguistics* 5, 153–171.

Han, C., Lidz, J. and Musolino, J. (2007), 'Verb-raising and grammar competition in Korean: evidence from negation and quantifier scope', *Linguistic Inquiry* 38, 1–47.

Han. Z. H. (2014), 'From Julie to Wes to Alberto: revisiting the construct of fossilization' in Z. H Han and E. Tarone (eds.), *Interlanguage: Forty Years Later* (Amsterdam: John Benjamins), 47–74.

Harris, J. (1991), 'The exponence of gender in Spanish', *Linguistic Inquiry* 22, 27–62.

(2008), 'The declining role of primary schools in the revitalization of Irish', *AILA Review* 21, 49–68.

Hawkins, J. A. (1999), 'Processing complexity and filler-gap dependencies across grammars', *Language* 75, 244–285.

(2004), *Efficiency and Complexity in Grammars* (Oxford: Oxford University Press).

Hawkins, R. and Hattori, H. (2006), 'Interpretation of English multiple wh-questions by Japanese speakers: a missing uninterpretable feature account', *Second Language Research* 22, 269–301.

He, A. W. (2006), 'Toward an identity theory of the development of Chinese as a heritage language', *The Heritage Language Journal* 4, 1–28.

(2010), 'The heart of heritage: sociocultural dimensions of heritage language learning', *Annual Review of Applied Linguistics* 30, 66–82.

Henshaw, F. (2013), 'Learning opportunities and outcomes of L2-L2 and L2-HL learner interaction during a collaborative writing task', Unpublished doctoral dissertation, University of Illinois at Urbana-Champaign.

Hernández Pina, F. (1984). *Teorías psicosociolingüísticas y su aplicación a la adquisición del español como lengua materna* (Madrid: Siglo XXI).

Herschensohn, J. (2007), Language Development and Age (Cambridge, UK: Cambridge University Press).

Hindley, R. (1990), *The Death of the Irish Language* (New York, NY: Routledge).

Hirakawa, M. (1990), 'A study of the L2 acquisition of English reflexives', *Second Language Research* 6, 60–85.

Hoekstra, T. and Hyams, N. (1998), 'Aspects of root infinitives', *Lingua* 106, 81–112.

Hoff, E. (2006), 'How social contexts support and shape language development', *Developmental Review* 26, 55–88.

Hoff, E., Core, C., Place, S., Rumiche, R., Señor, M. and Parra, M. (2011), 'Dual language exposure and early bilingual development', *Journal of Child Language* 39, 1–27.

Hoff, E., Welsh, D., Place, S. and Ribot, K. (2014), 'Properties of dual language input that shape bilingual development and properties of environment that shape dual language input' in T. Grüter and J. Paradis (eds.), *Input and Experience in Bilingual Development* (Amsterdam: John Benjamins), 119–140.

Hopp, H. and Schmid, M. (2013), 'Perceived foreign accent in L1 attrition and L2 acquisition: the impact of age of acquisition and bilingualism', *Applied Psycholinguistics* 34, 361–394.

Hornberger, N. (1988), *Bilingual Education and Language Maintenance: A Southern Peruvian Quechua Case* (Berlin: Mouton).

Hornberger, N. and Wang, S. (2008), 'Who are our heritage language learners? Identity and biliteracy in heritage language education in the United States' in D. Brinton, O. Kagan and S. Bauckus (eds.), *Heritage Language Education: A New Field Emerging* (New York, NY: Routledge), 3–38.

Hróarsdóttir, T. (2001), *Word Order Change in Icelandic* (Amsterdam: John Benjamins).

Hrycyna, M., Lapinskaya, N., Kochetov, A. and Nagy, N. (2011), 'VOT drift in 3 generations of heritage language speakers in Toronto', *Canadian Acoustics* 39, 166–167.

Huffines, M. (1989), 'Case usage among the Pennsylvania German sectarian and non-sectarians' in N. Dorian (ed.), *Investigating Obsolescence: Studies in Language Contraction and Death* (Cambridge, UK: Cambridge University Press), 211–226.

Hulsen, M. (2000), 'Language loss and language processing: three generations of Dutch migrants in New Zealand', Doctoral dissertation, University of Nijmegen, The Netherlands.

Hulstijn, J. (2011), 'Language proficiency in native and nonnative speakers: an agenda for research and suggestions for second language assessment', *Language Assessment Quarterly* 8, 3, 229–249. doi: 10.1080/15434303.2011.565844.

(2015). *Language Proficiency in Native and Non-native Speakers: Theory and Research* (Amsterdam: John Benjamins).

Huttenlocher, J. and Smiley, P. (1987), 'Early word meanings: the case of object names', *Cognitive Psychology* 19, 63–89.

Hutz, M. (2007), 'Is there a natural process of decay? A longitudinal study of language attrition' in M. Schmid, B. Köpke, M. Keijer and L. Weilmar (eds.), *First Language Attrition* (Amsterdam: John Benjamins), 189–206.

Hyltenstam, K. (1992), 'Non-native features of near-native speakers: on ultimate attainment of childhood L2 learners' in R. Harris (ed.) *Cognitive Processing in Bilinguals* (Amsterdam: Elsevier), 351–368.

Hyltenstam, K. and Abrahamsson, N. (2003), 'Maturational constraints in SLA' in C. Doughty and M. Long (eds.), *The Handbook of Second Language Acquisition* (Oxford: Blackwell), 539–588.

Hyltenstam, K., Bylund, E., Abrahamsson, N. and Park, H. S. (2009), 'Dominant language replacement: the case of international adoptees', *Bilingualism: Language and Cognition* 12, 121–140.

Ibrahim, Z. and Allam, J. (2006), 'Arabic learners and heritage students redefined: present and future' in K. Wahba, A. Taha and L. England (eds.), *Handbook for Arabic Language Teaching Professionals in the 21st Century* (Mahwah, NJ: Lawrence Erlbaum), 437–446.

Imada, T., Zhang, Y., Cheour, M., Taulu, S., Ahonen, A. and Kuhl, P. (2006), 'Infant speech perception activates Broca's area: a developmental magnetoencephalography study', *NeuroReport* 17, 957–962.

Ionin, T. (2013), 'Recent publications on research methods in second language acquisition', *Second Language Research* 29, 119–128.

Ionin, T. and Zyzick, E. (in press), 'Judgment and interpretation tasks', *Annual Review of Applied Linguistics*.

Isurin, L. (2000), 'Deserted island or a child's first language forgetting', *Bilingualism: Language and Cognition* 3, 151–166.

Itard, J.-M. G. (1801), *De l'éducation d'un homme sauvage ou des premiers développements physiques et moraux du jeune sauvage de l'aveyron* (Paris: Gouyon).

Iverson, M. (2012), 'Advanced language attrition of Spanish in contact with Brazilian Portuguese', Unpublished doctoral dissertation, University of Iowa.

Jackendoff, R. (2002), *Foundations of Language: Brain, Meaning, Grammar, Evolution* (Oxford: Oxford University Press).

Jia, G. (2008), 'Heritage language development, maintenance, and attrition among recent Chinese immigrants in New York City' in A. W. He and Y. Xiao (eds.), *Chinese as a Heritage Language* (Honolulu, HI: National Foreign Language Resource Center/University of Hawaii Press), 189–203.

Jia, G. and Aaronson, D. (2003), 'A longitudinal study of Chinese children and adolescents learning English in the United States', *Applied Psycholinguistics* 24, 131–161.

Jia, G., Aaronson, D., Young, D., Chen, S. and Wagner, J. (2005), 'Bilingual Mandarin-, Russian- and Spanish-English speakers' grammatical proficiency in their two languages' in M. Minami, H. Kobayashi, M. Nakayama, and H. Sirai (eds.), *Studies in Language Sciences* (Tokyo: Kurosio), 160–171.

Jia, R. and Paradis, J. (2014), 'The use of referring expressions in narratives by Mandarin heritage language children and the roles of language environment factors in predicting individual differences', *Bilingualism: Language and Cognition*, First View Article, December 2014, pp. 1–16. doi: 10.1017/S1366728914000728.

Jiang, N. (2007), 'Selective integration of linguistic knowledge in adult second language learning', *Language Learning* 57, 1–33.

Jisa, H. (2004), 'Growing into academic French' in R. Berman (ed.), *Language Development across Childhood and Adolescence* (Amsterdam: John Benjamins), 135–162.

Johns, A. and Mazurkewich, I. (2001), 'The role of the university in the training of native language teachers: Labrador' in L. Hilton and K. Hale (eds.), *The Green Book of Language Revitalization in Practice* (San Diego, CA: Academic Press), 355–366.

Johnson, J. and Newport, E. (1989), 'Critical period effects in second language learning: the influence of maturational state on the acquisition of English as a second language', *Cognitive Psychology* 21, 60–99.

(1991), 'Critical period effects on universal principles of language: the status of subjacency in the acquisition of a second language', *Cognition* 39, 215–258.

Johnson, V., de Villiers, J. and Seymour, H. (2005), 'Agreement without understanding? The case of third person singular /s/', *First Language* 25, 317–330.

Kagan, O. and Dillon, K. (2003), 'Heritage speakers' potential for high level language proficiency' in H. Byrnes and H. Maxim (eds.), *Advanced Foreign Language Learning: A Challenge to College Programs* (Boston, MA: Heinle/Thomson), 99–112.

(2009), 'Russian in the United States' in K. Potowski (ed), *Language Diversity in the United States* (Cambridge: Cambridge University Press), 179–194.

Kageyama, T. (1996), *Dooshi imi-ron [Semantics of Verbs]*. (Tokyo: Kuroshio Shuppan).

Kang, B.-M. (1998), 'Mwunpep-kwa ene sayong: Khophes-ey kipanhan caykwisa 'caki', 'casin', 'caki-casin'-uy kinung pwunsek-ul cwungsim-ulo [Grammar and the use of language: Korean reflexives 'caki, 'casin', and caki-casin]', *Kwuk-e-hak* 31, 165–204.

Kang, Y. and Nagy, N. (2012), 'VOT merger in heritage Korean in Toronto' *Actes du congrès annuel de l'Association canadienne de linguistique 2012. [Proceedings of the 2012 Annual Conference of the Canadian Linguistic Association]*, (Toronto), 1–15.

Kanno, K., Hasegawa, T., Ikeda, K., Ito, Y. and Long, M. (2008), 'Relationships between prior language-learning experience and variation in the linguistic profiles of advanced English-speaking learners of Japanese' in D. Brinton, O. Kagan and S. Bauckus (eds.), *Heritage Language Education: A New Field Emerging* (New York, NY: Routledge), 165–180.

Karmiloff-Smith, A. (1979), 'Micro- and macrodevelopmental changes in language acquisition and other representational systems', *Cognitive Science* 3, 91–117.

(1986), 'Some fundamental aspects of language development after age 5' in P. Fletcher and M. Garman (eds.), *Language Acquisition: Studies in First Language Development* (Cambridge, UK: Cambridge University Press), 455–474.

Karstadt, A. (2003), *Tracking Swedish-American English: A Longitudinal Study of Linguistic Variation and Identity* (Uppsala: University of Uppsala).

Kato, M., Cyrino, S. and Corrêa, V. (2009), 'Brazilian Portuguese and the recovery of lost clitics through schooling' in A. Pires and J. Rothman (eds.), *Minimalist Inquiries into Child and Adult Language Acquisition: Case Studies across Portuguese* (Berlin and New York: Mouton DeGruyter), 245–272.

Kaufman, D. and Aronoff, M. (1991), 'Morphological disintegration and reconstruction in first language attrition' in H. Seliger and R. Vago (eds.), *First Language Attrition* (Amsterdam: John Benjamins), 175–188.

Kazanina, N. and Phillips, C. (2001), 'Coreference in child Russian: distinguishing syntactic and discourse constraints', *Proceedings of the 25th Annual Boston University Conference on Language Development* (Sommerville, MA: Cascadilla Press), 413–424.

Keating, G., VanPatten, B. and Jegerski, J. (2011), 'Who was walking on the beach? Anaphora resolution in Spanish heritage speakers and adult second language learners', *Studies in Second Language Acquisition* 33, 193–222.

Keel, W. (2015), 'Noun phrase case shift in Volga German varieties on the Great Plains of Kansas' in R. Page and M. Putnam (eds.), *Moribund Germanic Heritage Languages in the Americas: Theoretical Perspectives and Empirical Findings* (Leiden: Brill), 133–152.

Keenean, E. and Comrie, B. (1977), 'Noun phrase accessibility and universal grammar', *Linguistic Inquiry* 8, 63–99.

Keijzer, M. (2007), *Last in First Out? An Investigation of the Regression Hypothesis in Dutch Emigrants in Anglophone Canada* (Vrije Universiteit Amsterdam; LOT, Netherlands Graduate School of Linguistics).

Kempe, V. and Brookes, P. (2001), 'The role of diminutives in the acquisition of Russian gender: can elements of child directed speech aid in learning morphology?', *Language Learning* 51, 221–256.

Kenrick, D. (1993), 'Romani at the crossroads' in G. Extra and L. Verhoeven (eds.), *Immigrant Languages in Europe* (Clevedon: Multilingual Matters), 285–296.

Kerswill, P. (1996), 'Children, adolescents and language change', *Language Variation and Change* 8, 177–202.

Kim, J. Y. (2012), 'Discrepancy between the perception and production of stop consonants by Spanish heritage speakers in the United States', Paper presented at *CASPSLaP [Current Approaches to Spanish and Portuguese Second Language Phonology]*, Columbia, South Carolina.

(2015), 'Perception and production of prominence in Spanish by heritage speakers and English L2 learners of Spanish' Selected Proceedings of the 6th Conference on Laboratory Approaches to Romance Phonology in E. W. Willis, P. M. Butragueño and E. H. Zendejas. Cascadilla Proceedings Project, Sommerville, MA, 106–128.

Kim, J.-H. and Yoon, J. (2008), 'An experimental syntactic study of the binding of multiple anaphors in Korean', *Journal of Cognitive Science* 9, 1–30.

Kim, J.-H., Montrul, S. and Yoon, J. (2009), 'Binding interpretation of anaphors in Korean heritage speakers', *Language Acquisition* 16, 3–35.

(2010), 'Dominant language influence in acquisition and attrition of binding: interpretation of the Korean reflexive caki', *Bilingualism: Language and Cognition* 13, 73–84.

Kim, M.-H. (2001), 'Kwuke taymyengsa-uy ehwisa [A study on the diachronic change of Korean pronouns]', *Korean Semantics* 9, 1–48.

Kim, M. Y., Kim, E., Montrul, S. and Yoon, J. (2014), 'On-line and off-line binding properties of Korean reflexives by heritage Korean speakers', Paper presented at the *2nd East Asian Psycholinguistics Colloquium*, University of Chicago, March 7–8.

King, K. and Ennser-Kananen, J. (2013), 'Heritage languages and language policy' in C. Chapelle (ed.), *The Encyclopedia of Applied Linguistics* (Malden, NJ: Blackwell), 1–4.

Knightly, L., Jun, S., Oh, J. and Au, T. (2003), 'Production benefits of childhood overhearing', *Journal of the Acoustic Society of America* 114, 465–474.

Kohnert, K., Bates, E. and Hernández, A. (1999), 'Balancing bilinguals, lexical-semantic production and cognitive processing in children learning Spanish and English', *Journal of Speech, Language and Hearing Research* 42, 1400–1413.

Kondo-Brown, K. (2005), 'Differences in language skills: heritage language learner subgroups and foreign language learners', *The Modern Language Journal* 89, 563–581.

(ed.), (2006), *Heritage Language Development: Focus on East Asian Immigrants* (Amsterdam: John Benjamins).

(2010), 'Curriculum development for advancing heritage language competence: recent research, current practices and a future agenda', *Annual Review of Applied Linguistics* 30, 24–41.

Köpke, B. (2007), 'Language attrition at the crossroads of brain, mind, and society' in B. Köpke, M. Schmid, M. Keijzer and S. Dosterst (eds.), *Language Attrition: Theoretical Perspectives* (Amsterdam: John Benjamins), 9–37.

Köpke, B. and Schmid, M. (2003), 'Language attrition: the next phase' in M. Schmid, B. Köpke, M. Keijzer and L. Weilemar (eds.), *First Language Attrition: Interdisciplinary Perspectives on Methodological Issues* (Amsterdam: John Benjamins), 1–143.

Kovács, A. M. and Mehler, J. (2009), 'Flexible learning of multiple speech structures in bilingual infants', *Science* 325, 611–612. doi: 10.1126/science.1173947.

Kuhl, P., Conboy, B., Coffey-Corina, S., Padden, D., Rivera-Gaxiola, M. and Nelson, T. (2008), 'Phonetic learning as a pathway to language: new data and native language magnet theory expanded (NLM-e)', *Philosophical Transactions of the Royal Society B* 363, 979–1000.

Kupisch, T. (2012), 'Generic subjects in the Italian of early German-Italian bilinguals and German learners of Italian as second language', *Bilingualism: Language and Cognition* 15, 736–756.

(2013), 'A new term for a better distinction? A view from the higher end of the proficiency scale', *Theoretical Linguistics* 39, 203–214.

Kupisch, T., Akpinar, D. and Stöhr, A. (2013), 'Gender assignment and gender agreement in adult bilinguals and second language learners of French', *Linguistic Approaches to Bilingualism* 3, 150–189.

Kupisch, T. and Barton, D. (2013), 'Generic reference in adult German bilinguals: how bilinguals deal with variation', *Studia Linguistica* 67, 1–27.

Kupisch, T., Belikova, A., Özçelik, Ö., Stangen, I. and White, L. (in press), 'On complete acquisition in heritage speakers: the definiteness effect in German-Turkish bilinguals', *Linguistic Approaches to Bilingualism*.

Kupisch, T., Lein, T., Barton, D., Schröder, D., Stangen, I. and Stoehr, A. (2014), 'Acquisition outcomes across domains in adult simultaneous bilinguals with French as weaker and stronger language', *Journal of French Language Studies* 24, 347–376.

Kwon, N., Kluender, R., Kutas, M. and Polinsky, M.(2013), 'Subject/object processing asymmetries in Korean relative clauses: evidence from ERP data', *Language* 89, 3, 537–585.

Labov, W. (1966), *The Social Stratification of English in New York City* (New York, NY: Cambridge University Press).

(1970), 'The study of language in its social context', *Studium Generale* 23, 30–87.

(1972), *Sociolinguistic Patterns* (Philadelphia, PA: University of Pennsylvania Press).

(1989), 'The child as linguistic historian', *Language Variation and Change* 1, 85–97.

(2001), *Principles of Linguistic Change: Social Factors* (Cambridge, MA: Blackwell).

(2006), *The Social Stratification of English in New York City*, 2nd Edition (New York, NY: Cambridge University Press).

(2007), 'Transmission and diffusion', *Language* 83, 2, 344–387.

Lainio, J. (1987), 'Language use of Finns in Sweden: implicational patterns in four domains', *Scandinavian Working Papers in Bilingualism* 7, 11–28.

(1993), 'Sweden Finnish' in G. Extra and L. Verhoeven (eds.), *Immigrant Languages in Europe* (Clevedon: Multilingual Matters), 21–54.

Laleko, O. (2008), 'Compositional telicity and heritage Russian aspect' in M. Grosvald and D. Soares (eds.), *Proceedings of the Thirty-Eighth Western Conference on Linguistics (WECOL) 19* (UC Davis, Davis, CA), 150–160.

(2010), 'The syntax-pragmatics interface in language loss: covert restructuring of aspect in heritage Russian', Unpublished doctoral dissertation, University of Minnesota.

Laleko, O. and Polinsky, M. (2013), 'Marking topic or marking case: a comparative investigation of heritage Japanese and heritage Korean', *The Heritage Language Journal* 10, 40–64.

Lambrecht, K. (2001), 'A framework for the analysis of cleft constructions', *Linguistics* 39, 3, 463–516.

Lantolf, J. and Appel, G. (eds.), (1994), *Vygotskian Approaches to Second Language Research* (Norwwod, NJ: Ablex).

Lantolf, J. and Thorne, S. (2006), *Sociocultural Theory and the Genesis of Second Language Development* (New York, NY: Oxford University Press).

Lanza, E. (2004), *Language Mixing in Infant Bilingualism: A Sociolinguistic Perspective* (New York, NY: Oxford University Press).

Laoire, M. (2005), 'The language planning situation in Ireland', *Current Issues in Language Planning* 6, 251–314.

Lardiere, D. (2007), *Ultimate Attainment in Second Language Acquisition: A Case Study* (Mahwah, NJ: Erlbaum).

(2009), 'Some thoughts on the contrastive analysis of features in second language acquisition', *Second Language Research* 25, 173–227.

(2011), 'Who is the interface hypothesis about?', *Linguistic Approaches to Bilingualism* 1, 48–53.

Larmouth, D. (1974), 'Differential interference in American Finnish cases', *Language* 50, 356–366.

Larsson, I. and Johannessen, J. (2014), 'Embedded word order in heritage Scandinavian' in M. Hilpert, J.-O. Östman, C. Mertzlufft, M. Rießler and J. Duke (eds.), *New Trends in Nordic and General Linguistics* (Berlin: De Gruyter), 239–264.

(2015), 'Incomplete acquisition and verb placement in heritage Scandinavian' in R. Page and M. Putnam (ed.), *Moribund Germanic Heritage Languages in the Americas: Theoretical Perspectives and Empirical Findings* (Leiden: Brill), 153–189.

Leal Méndez, T., Rothman, J. and Slabakova, R. (2014), 'A rare structure at the syntax-discourse interface: heritage and Spanish-dominant native speakers weigh in', *Language Acquisition* 21, 4, 411–429. doi: 10.1080/10489223.2014.892946.

Leal Méndez, T., Slabakova, R. and Rothman, J. (2015), 'Discourse-sensitive clitic-doubled dislocations in heritage Spanish', *Lingua* 155, 85–97.

Lee, H. (1990), 'Logical relations in the child's grammar: relative scope, bound variables, and long-distance binding in Korean', Unpublished doctoral dissertation, University of California, Irvine.

Lee, H. and Wexler, K. (1987), 'The acquisition of reflexives and pronouns in Korean: from a cross-linguistic perspective', Paper presented at the *12th Annual Boston University Conference on Language Development*, November 3–4.

Lee, S.-B. (2006), 'A pragmatic analysis of accusative case-marker deletion', *Discourse and Cognition* 13, 69–89.

Lee, T. (2011), 'Grammatical knowledge of Korean heritage speakers: early vs. late bilinguals', *Linguistic Approaches to Bilingualism* 1, 149–174.

Legate, J. and Yang, C. (2007), 'Morphosyntactic learning and the development of tense', *Language Acquisition* 14, 315–344.

Lenneberg, E. (1967), *Biological Foundations of Language* (New York, NY: Wiley).

Leopold, W. F. (1939–1949), *Speech Development of a Bilingual Child: A Linguist's Record*, 4 vols. (Evanston, IL: Northwestern University Press).

Levelt, W. (1989), *Speaking: From Intention to Articulation* (Cambridge, MA: MIT Press).

Lewis, G. (2008), 'Current challenges in bilingual education in Wales', *AILA Review* 21, 87–103.

Li, M.-C. (2012), 'The acquisition of tense and agreement by early child second language learners', Unpublished doctoral dissertation, University of Illinois at Urbana-Champaign.

Li, W. (1994), *Three Generations, Two Languages, One Family* (Clevedon: Multilingual Matters).

Lidz, J. (2009), 'The abstract nature of syntactic representations' in E. Hoff and M. Shatz (eds.), *The Blackwell Handbook of Language Development* (Malden, MA: Blackwell), 277–303.

Lidz, J., Waxman, S. and Freedman, J. (2003), 'What infants know about syntax but couldn't have learned: experimental evidence for syntactic structure at 18-months', *Cognition* 89, B65–B73.

Lieven, E. and Tomasello, M. (2008), 'Children's first language acquisition from a usage-based perspective' in P. Robinson and N. Ellis (eds.), *Handbook of Cognitive Linguistics and Second Language Acquisition* (New York, NY: Routledge), 216–236.

Lightbown, P. M. (1998), 'The importance of timing in focus on form' in C. Doughty and J. Williams (eds.), *Focus on Form in Classroom Second Language Acquisition* (New York, NY: Cambridge University Press), 177–196.

Lightfoot, D. (in press), 'Imperfect transmission and discontinuity' in A. Ledgway and I. Roberts (eds.), *Cambridge Handbook of Historical Syntax* (Cambridge, UK: Cambridge University Press).

Lipski, J. (1994), *Latin American Spanish* (New York, NY: Longman).

Lo Bianco, J. (2008), 'Policy activity for heritage language connections with representation and citizenship' in D. Brinton, O. Kagan and S. Bauckus (eds.), *Heritage Language Education: A New Field Emerging* (New York, NY: Routledge), 53–70.

Long, M. (1990), 'Maturational constraints on language development', *Studies in Second Language Acquisition* 12, 251–285.

  (1996), 'The role of the linguistic environment in second language acquisition' in W. Ritchie and T. Bhatia (eds.), *Handbook of Second Language Acquisition* (San Diego, CA: Academic Press), 413–468.

  (2003), 'Stabilization and fossilization in interlanguage development' in C. Doughty and M. Long (eds.), *The Handbook of Second Language Acquisition* (Malden, MA: Blackwell), 487–536.

  (2007), *Problems in SLA* (Mahwah, NJ: Lawrence Erlbaum).

López, D. (1996), 'Language: diversity and assimilation' in R. Waldinger and M. Bozorgmehr (eds.), *Ethnic Los Angeles* (New York, NY: Russell Sage Foundation), 139–163.

Lukyanchenko, A. and Gor, K. (2011), 'Perceptual correlates of phonological representations in heritage speakers and L2 learners', *Proceedings of the 35th Annual Boston University Conference on Language Development* (Somerville, MA: Cascadilla Press), 414–426.

Lynch, A. (1999), 'The subjunctive in Miami Cuban Spanish: bilingualism, contact and language variability', Unpublished doctoral dissertation, University of Minnesota.

(2003), 'Toward a theory of heritage language acquisition: Spanish in the United States' in A. Roca and M. C. Colombi (eds.), *Mi Lengua: Spanish as a Heritage Language in the United States* (Washington, DC: Georgetown University Press), 25–50.

Maandi, K. (1989), 'Estonian among immigrants in Sweden' in N. Dorian (ed.), *Investigating Obsolescence: Studies in Language Contraction and Death* (Cambridge, UK: Cambridge University Press), 227–242.

Mackey, A. and Gass, S. (eds.), (2012), *Research Methods in Second Language Acquisition: A Practical Guide* (Oxford: Wiley-Blackwell).

Mackey, A. and Goo, J. (2007), 'Interaction research in SLA: a meta-analysis and research synthesis' in A. Mackey (ed.), *Conversational Interaction in Second Language Acquisition* (Oxford: Oxford University Press), 407–452.

Mackey, W. (1962), 'The description of bilingualism', *Canadian Journal of Linguistics* 7, 51–85.

MacWhinney, B. (1987), 'The competition model' in B. MacWhinney (ed.), *Mechanisms of Language Acquisition* (Hillsdale, NJ: Lawrence Erlbaum), 249–308.

(1992), 'Transfer and competition in second language learning' in R. Harris (ed.), *Cognitive Processing in Bilinguals* (Amsterdam: Elsevier), 371–390.

(2006), 'Emergentism – use often and with care', *Applied Linguistics* 27, 729–740.

Mahajan, G. (2009), 'Ongoing deficits in heritage Hindi', Paper presented at the *Third Annual Heritage Language Institute,* Urbana Champaign, June 12–20.

Mai, Z. (2012), 'Properties of the (*Shi*) . . .*de* focus construction in adult L2 acquisition and heritage language acquisition of Mandarin Chinese', Unpublished doctoral dissertation, University of Cambridge.

Major, R. (1992), 'Losing English as a first language', *The Modern Language Journal* 76, 190–209.

Mansouri, F. (2005), 'Agreement morphology in Arabic as a second language: typological features and their processing implications' in M. Pienemann (ed.), *Cross-linguistic Aspects of Processability Theory* (Philadelphia, PA: John Benjamins), 117–54.

Maratsos, M. (1988), 'The acquisition of formal word classes' in Y. Levy, I. Schlesinger, M. Braine (eds.), *Categories and Processes in Language Acquisition* (Hillsdale, NJ: Lawrence Erlbaum), 31–44.

Marinova-Todd, S., Marshall, D. and Snow, C. (2000), 'Three misconceptions about age and L2 learning', *TESOL Quarterly* 34, 9–34.

Marrero, V., Aguirre, C. and Albalá, M. J. (2007), 'The acquisition of diminutives in Spanish' in I. Savickienė and W. Dressler (eds.), *The Acquisition of Diminutives: A Crosslinguistic Perspective* (Amsterdam: John Benjamins), 155–184.

Martin, C. (2013), 'Assessing the oral proficiency of heritage speakers according to the ACTFL Proficiency guidelines 2012 – Speaking', *The Heritage Language Journal* 10, 73–87.

Martínez, G. (2013), 'Policy and planning research for Spanish as a heritage language: from language rights to linguistic resource' in S. Beaudrie and M. Fairclough (eds.), *Spanish as a Heritage Language in the United States* (Washington, DC: Georgetown University Press), 61–78.

Mason, M. (1942), 'Learning to speak after six and one half years of silence', *Journal of Speech Disorders* 7, 295–304.

Mayberry, R. (1993), 'First language acquisition after childhood differs from second language acquisition: the case of American sign language', *Journal of Speech and Hearing Research* 36, 1258–1270.

(2010), 'Early language acquisition and adult language ability: what sign language reveals about the critical period for language' in M. Marschark and P. Spencer (eds.), *Oxford Handbook of Deaf Studies, Language, and Education*, vol. 2 (New York, NY: Oxford University Press), 281–291.

Mayberry, R. and Fischer, S. D. (1989), 'Looking through phonological shape to lexical meaning: the bottleneck of non-native sign language processing', *Memory and Cognition* 1, 740–754.

Mayberry, R. and Lock, E. (2003), 'Age constraints on first versus second language acquisition: evidence for linguistic plasticity and epigenesis', *Brain and Language* 87, 369–383.

Mayberry, R. and Squires, B. (2006), 'Sign language acquisition' in E. Lieven (ed.), *Language Acquisition: Encyclopedia of Language and Linguistics*, 2nd Edition (Oxford: Elsevier), 291–296.

Mayberry, R. I., Chen, J.-K., Witcher, P. and Klein, D. (2011), 'Age of acquisition effects on the functional organization of language in the adult brain', *Brain and Language* 119, 16–29.

Mayer, M. (1969), *Frog, Where are You?* (New York, NY: Dial Books for Young Readers).

McCarthy, C. (2008), 'Morphological variability in the comprehension of agreement: an argument for representation over computation', *Second Language Research* 24, 459–486.

McCarthy, J. and Prince, A. (1990), 'Foot and word in prosodic morphology: the Arabic broken plural', *Natural Language and Linguistic Theory* 8, 209–283.

McDaniel, D., McKee, C. and Smith Cairns, H. (eds.) (1996). *Methods for Assessing Children's Syntax* (Boston, MA: MIT Press).

McDonough, K. and Trofimovich, P. (2008), *Using Priming Methods in Second Language Research* (New York, NY: Routledge).

McWhorter, J. (2007), *Language Interrupted: Signs of Non-native Acquisition in Standard Language Grammars* (New York, NY: Oxford University Press).

Meara, P. and Buxton, B. (1987), 'An alternative to multiple choice vocabulary tests', *Language Testing* 4, 142–154.

Meara, P. and Jones, G. (1988), 'Vocabulary size as placement indicator' in P. Grunwell (ed.), *Applied Linguistics in Society* (London: CILT), 80–87.

Meisel, J. (ed.), (1990), *Two First Languages* (Dordrecht: Foris).

(ed.), (1994), *Bilingual First Language Acquisition: French and German Grammatical Development* (Amsterdam: John Benjamins).

(2001), 'The simultaneous acquisition of two first languages' in J. Cenoz and F. Genesee (eds.), *Trends in Bilingual Acquisition* (Amsterdam: John Benjamins), 11–41.

(2007), 'The weaker language in early child bilingualism: acquiring a first language like a second language?', *Applied Psycholinguistics* 28, 495–514.

(2011), First and Second Language Acquisition (Cambridge, UK: Cambridge University Press).

(2013), 'Heritage language learners: unprecedented opportunities for the study of grammars and their development?', *Theoretical Linguistics* 39, 225–236.

Melzi, G. and King, K. (2003), 'Spanish diminutives in mother-child conversations', *The Journal of Child Language* 30, 281–304.

Menyuk, P. and Brisk, M. E. (2005), *Language Development and Education: Children with Varying Language Experience* (New York, NY: Palgrave).

Merino, B. (1983), 'Language loss in bilingual Chicano children', *Journal of Applied Developmental Psychology* 4, 277–294.

Mikhaylova, A. (2012), 'Aspectual knowledge of high proficiency L2 and heritage speakers of Russian', *The Heritage Language Journal* 9, 50–69.

Miller, K. (2007), 'Variable input and the acquisition of plurality in two varieties of Spanish', Unpublished doctoral dissertation, Michigan State University.

(2013), 'Acquisition of variable rules: /s/ lenition in the speech of Chilean Spanish-speaking children and their caregivers', *Language Variation and Change* 25, 311–340.

Miller, K. and Schmitt, C. (2012), 'Variable input and the acquisition of plural morphology', *Language Acquisition*, 19, 3, 223–261.

Moag, R. (1995), 'Semi-native speakers: how to hold and mold them' in V. Gambhir (ed.), *The Teaching and Acquisition of South Asian Languages* (Philadelphia, PA: University of Pennsylvania Press), 168–181.

Montrul, S. (2002), 'Incomplete acquisition and attrition of Spanish tense/aspect distinctions in adult bilinguals', *Bilingualism: Language and Cognition* 5, 39–68.

(2004a), *The Acquisition of Spanish* (Amsterdam: John Benjamins).

(2004b), 'Subject and object expression in Spanish heritage speakers: a case of morpho-syntactic convergence', *Bilingualism: Language and Cognition* 7, 125–142.

(2005), 'Second language acquisition and first language loss in adult early bilinguals: exploring some differences and similarities', *Second Language Research* 21, 199–249.

(2006a), 'Incomplete acquisition as a feature of L2 and bilingual grammars' in R. Slabakova, S. Montrul and P. Prévost (eds.), *Inquiries in Language Development: Studies in Honor of Lydia White* (Amsterdam: John Benjamins), 335–359.

(2006b), 'On the bilingual competence of Spanish heritage speakers: syntax, lexical-semantics and processing', *International Journal of Bilingualism* 10, 37–69.

(2007), 'Interpreting mood distinctions in Spanish as a heritage language' in K. Potowski and R. Cameron (eds.), *Spanish in Contact: Policy, Social and Linguistic Inquiries* (Amsterdam: John Benjamins), 23–40.

(2008), *Incomplete Acquisition in Bilingualism: Re-examining the Age Factor* (Amsterdam: John Benjamins).

(2009), 'Heritage language programs' in C. Doughty and M. Long (eds.), *The Handbook of Second and Foreign Language Teaching* (Malden, MA: Blackwell), 182–200.

(2010a), 'How similar are L2 learners and heritage speakers? Spanish clitics and word order', *Applied Psycholinguistics* 31, 167–207.

(2010b), 'Dominant language transfer in Spanish L2 learners and heritage speakers', *Second Language Research* 26, 293–327.

(2011), 'First language retention and attrition in an adult Guatemalan adoptee', *Language, Interaction and Acquisition* 2, 276–311.

(2012), 'Is the heritage language like a second language?' *EUROSLA Yearbook* 12, 1–29.

(2013), *El bilingüismo en el mundo hispanohablante* (Malden, MA: Wiley-Blackwell).

(2016), 'Dominance and proficiency in early and late bilinguals' in C. Silva-Corvalán and J. Treffers-Daller (eds.), *Language Dominance in Bilinguals: Issues of Measurement and Operationalization* (Cambridge, UK: Cambridge University Press), 15–35.

Montrul, S. and Bowles, M. (2009), 'Back to basics: differential object marking under incomplete acquisition in Spanish heritage speakers', *Bilingualism: Language and Cognition* 12, 363–383.

(2010), 'Is grammar instruction beneficial for heritage language learners? Dative case marking in Spanish', *The Heritage Language Journal* 7, 47–73.

Montrul, S. and Foote, R. (2014), 'Age of acquisition interactions in bilingual lexical access: a study of the weaker language in L2 learners and heritage speakers', *The International Journal of Bilingualism* 18, 274–303.

Montrul, S. and Ionin, T. (2010), 'Transfer effects in the interpretation of definite articles by Spanish heritage speakers', *Bilingualism: Language and Cognition* 13, 449–473.

(2012), 'Dominant language transfer in Spanish heritage speakers and L2 learners in the interpretation of definite articles', *The Modern Language Journal* 96, 70–94.

Montrul, S. and Perpiñán, S. (2011). 'Assessing differences and similarities between instructed L2 learners and heritage language learners in their knowledge of Spanish Tense-Aspect and Mood (TAM) Morphology', *The Heritage Language Journal* 8, 1, 90–133.

Montrul, S. and Potowski, P. (2007), 'Command of gender agreement in school-age Spanish bilingual children', *International Journal of Bilingualism* 11, 301–328.

Montrul, S. and Polinsky, M. (2011), 'Why not heritage speakers?', *Linguistic Approaches to Bilingualism* 1, 58–62.

Montrul, S. and Sánchez-Walker, N. (2013), 'Differential object marking in child and adult Spanish heritage speakers', *Language Acquisition* 20, 109–132.

(2015), 'Subject expression in school-age Spanish-English bilingual children' in A. Carvalho, R. Orozco and N. Shin (eds.), *Subject Pronoun Expression in Spanish: A Crossdialectal Perspective* (Washington, DC: Georgetown University Press) 231–248.

Montrul, S. and Slabakova, R. (2003), 'Competence similarities between native and near-native speakers: an investigation of the preterite/imperfect contrast in Spanish', *Studies in Second Language Acquisition* 25, 351–398.

Montrul, S., Bhatt, R. and Bhatia, A. (2012), 'Erosion of case and agreement in Hindi heritage speakers', *Linguistic Approaches to Bilingualism* 2, 141–176.

Montrul, S., Bhatt, R. and Girju, R. (2015), 'Differential object marking in Spanish, Hindi and Romanian as heritage languages', *Language*, 91: 3, 564–610.

Montrul, S., de la Fuente, I., Davidson, J. and Foote, R. (2013). 'The role of experience in the acquisition and production of diminutives and gender in Spanish: evidence from L2 learners and heritage speakers', *Second Language Research* 29, 1, 87–118.

Montrul, S., Davidson, J., de la Fuente, I. and Foote, R. (2014), 'Early language experience facilitates gender agreement processing in Spanish heritage speakers', *Bilingualism: Language and Cognition* 17, 118–138.

Montrul, S., Foote, R. and Perpiñán, S. (2008a), 'Gender agreement in adult second language learners and Spanish heritage speakers: the effects of age and context of acquisition', *Language Learning* 58, 503–553.

(2008b), 'Knowledge of wh-movement in Spanish L2 learners and heritage speakers' in J. Bruhn de Garavito and E. Valenzuela (eds.), *Selected Papers from the 8th Hispanic Linguistics Symposium* (Somerville, MA: Cascadilla Press), 93–106.

Morford, J. (2003), 'Grammatical development in adolescent first language learners', *Linguistics* 41, 681–721.

Mueller-Gathercole, V. and Hoff, E. (2009), 'Input and the acquisition of language: three questions' in E. Hoff and M. Shatz (eds.), *The Blackwell Handbook on Language Development* (Malden, MA: Blackwell), 107–127.

Mueller-Gathercole, V. and Thomas, E. (2009), 'Bilingual first-language development: dominant language takeover, threatened minority language take-up', *Bilingualism: Language and Cognition* 12, 213–237.

Mueller-Gathercole, V., Sebastián, E. and Soto, P. (2002), 'The emergence of linguistic person in Spanish-speaking children', *Language Learning* 52, 679–722.

Müller, N. and Hulk, A. (2001), 'Crosslinguistic influence in bilingual language acquisition: Italian and French as recipient languages', *Bilingualism: Language and Cognition* 4, 1–21.

Murasugi, K. (2012), 'Ergative and antipassive structures in bilingual Inuktitut speakers' Poster presented at the *Conference on Formal Approaches to Heritage Language*, University of Massachusetts, Amherst, April 21–22.

Nagy, N., Aghdasi, N., Denis, D. and Motut, A. (2011), 'Null subjects in heritage languages: contact effects in a crosslinguistic context', *University of Pennsylvania Working Papers in Linguistics* 17, 135–144.

Nagy, N., Aghdasi, N., Kang, Y., Kochetov, A., Denis, D., Motut, A. and Walker, J. (2014), 'Heritage Russian variation and change in Toronto', *Международного междисциплинарного научного совещания билингвизм и бикультурализм [Proceedings of the International Interdisciplinary Scientific meeting: Bilingualism and Biculturalism, Perm State National Research University]*, (Tomsk, Russia), 53–68.

Newport, E. (1981), 'Constraints on structure: evidence from American Sign Language and language learning', in W. A. Collins (ed.), *Aspects of the Development of Competence :Minnesota Symposium on Child Psychology* (Hillsdale, NJ: Lawrence Erlbaum Associates).

Newport, E. (1990), 'Maturational constraints on language learning', *Cognitive Science* 14, 11–28.

Nicoladis, E. and Grabois, H. (2002), 'Learning English and losing Chinese: a case study of a child adopted from China', *International Journal of Bilingualism* 6, 441–454.

Nippold, M. (1998), *Later Language Development: The School-age and Adolescent Years* (Austin, TX: Pro-ed).

(2004), 'Research on later language development: international perspectives' in R. Berman (ed.), *Language Development across Childhood and Adolescence* (Amsterdam: John Benjamins), 1–8.

Norris, J. and Ortega, L. (2000), 'Effectiveness of L2 instruction: a research synthesis and quantitative meta-analysis', *Language Learning* 50, 417–528.

Ó Flatharta, P., NicPháidín, C., Williams, C. Grin, F. and Lo Bianco, J. (2008), *20 Year Strategy for Irish* (Fiontar, Dublin: Dublin City University).

Ó Giollagáin, C. (2011), 'Speaker diversity in the majority-minority linguistic context', *Annales Series historia et sociologia* 21, 1, 101–112.

O'Grady, W. (2005), *Syntactic Carpentry: An Emergentist Approach to Syntax* (Mahwah, NJ: Erlbaum).

(2008), 'The emergentist program', *Lingua* 118, 447–464.

(2013), 'The illusion of language acquisition', *Linguistic Approaches to Bilingualism* 3, 253–285.

O'Grady, W., Kwak, H. Y., Lee, O.-S. and Lee, M. (2011), 'An emergentist perspective on heritage language acquisition', *Studies in Second Language Acquisition* 33, 223–246.

O'Grady, W., Lee, M. and Choo, M. (2001), 'The acquisition of relative clauses by heritage and non-heritage learners of Korean as a second language, a comparative study', *Journal of Korean Language Education* 12, 283–294.

O'Grady, W., Lee, O.-S. and Lee, J.-H. (2011), 'Practical and theoretical issues in the study of heritage language acquisition', *The Heritage Language Journal* 8, 23–40.

O'Grady, W., Schafer, A. Perla, J., Lee, O.-S. and Wieting, J. (2009), 'A psycholinguistic tool for the assessment of language loss: the HALA project', *Language Documentation and Conservation* 3, 100–112.

Oh, J. S. and Fuligni, A. J. (2010), 'The role of heritage language development in the ethnic identity and family relationships of adolescents from immigrant backgrounds', *Social Development* 19, 1, 202–220.

Oh, J., Au, T. and Jun, S.-A. (2010), 'Early childhood language memory in the speech perception of international adoptees', *The Journal of Child Language* 37, 1123–1132.

Oh, J., Jun, S. A., Knightly, L. and Au, T. (2003), 'Holding on to childhood language memory', *Cognition* 86, B53–B64.

Oller, K. and Jarmulowicz, L. (2009), 'Language and literacy in bilingual children in the early school years' in E. Hoff and M. Shatz (eds.), Blackwell Handbook of *Language Development* (Malden, MA: Wiley-Blackwell), 368–387.

Olshtain, E. and Barzilay, M. (1991), 'Lexical retrieval difficulties in adult language attrition' in H. Seliger and R. Vago (eds.), *First Language Attrition* (Cambridge, UK: University Press), 139–150.

Omar, M. (1973), *The Acquisition of Egyptian Arabic as a Native Language* (The Hague: Mouton).

Ortega, L. (2013), 'SLA for the 21st century: disciplinary progress, transdisciplinary relevance, and the bi/multilingual turn', *Language Learning* 63, Supplement 1, 1–24.

Otheguy, R. and Zentella, A. C. (2012), *Spanish in New York* (New York, NY: Oxford University Press).

Otheguy, R., Zentella, A. C. and Livert, D. (2007), 'Language and dialect contact in Spanish in New York: towards the formation of a speech community', *Language* 83, 770–802.

Pakulak, E. (2012), 'Individual differences in native speakers and the broader picture: socioeconomic status and neuroplasticity', *Linguistic Approaches to Bilingualism* 2, 277–280.

Pakulak, E. and Neville, H. J. (2010), 'Proficiency differences in syntactic processing of native speakers indexed by event-related potentials', *Journal of Cognitive Neuroscience* 23, 2752–2765.

Pallier, C. (2007), 'Critical periods in language acquisition and language attrition' in B. Köpke, M. Schmid, M. Keijzer and S. Dosterst (eds.), *Language Attrition: Theoretical Perspectives* (Amsterdam: John Benjamins), 99–120.

Pallier, C., Dehaene, S., Poline, J. B., LeBihan, D., Argenti, A. M., Dupoux, E. and Mehler, J. (2003), 'Brain imaging of language plasticity in adopted adults: can a second language replace the first?', *Cerebral Cortex* 13, 155–161.

Paradis, J. (2001), 'Do bilingual two-year olds have independent phonological systems?', *International Journal of Bilingualism* 5, 19–38.

Paradis, J. and Genesee, F. (1996), 'Syntactic acquisition in bilingual children, autonomous or interdependent?', *Studies in Second Language Acquisition* 18, 1–25.

Paradis, J., Genesee, F. and Crago, M. (2011), *Dual Language Development & Disorders: A Handbook on Bilingualism & Second Language Learning*, 2nd edn. (Baltimore, MD: Paul H. Brookes).

Paradis, J. and Navarro, S. (2003), 'The use of subjects by a Spanish-English bilingual child: crosslinguistic influence or the influence of the input?', *The Journal of Child Language* 30, 371–393.

Paradis, J., Nicoladis, E., Crago, M. and Genesee, F. (2010), 'Bilingual children's acquisition of the past tense: a usage-based approach', *Journal of Child Language* 37, 1–25.

Paradis, M. (2004), *A Neurolinguistic Theory of Bilingualism* (Amsterdam: John Benjamins).

(2009), *Declarative and Procedural Determinants of Second Languages* (Amsterdam: John Benjamins).

Parodi, C. (2008), 'Stigmatized Spanish inside the classroom and out: a model of language teaching to heritage speakers' in D. Brinton, O. Kagan and S. Bauckus (eds.), *Heritage Language Education: A New Field Emerging* (New York, NY: Routledge), 199–214.

Pascual y Cabo, D. (2013), 'Agreement reflexes of emerging optionality in heritage speaker Spanish', Unpublished doctoral dissertation, University of Florida.

Pascual y Cabo, D. and Rothman, J. (2012), 'The (il)logical problem of heritage speaker bilingualism and incomplete acquisition', *Applied Linguistics* 33, 1–7.

Penfield, W. (1953), 'A consideration of the neurophysiological mechanisms of speech and some educational consequences', *Proceedings of the American Academy of Arts and Sciences* 82, 199–214.

Penfield, W. and Roberts, L. (1959), *Speech and Brain Mechanisms* (Princeton, NJ: Princeton University Press).

Pénicaud, S., Klein, D., Zatorre, R. J., Chen, J.-K., Witcher, P., Hyde, K. and Mayberry, R. I. (2013), 'Structural brain changes linked to delayed first language acquisition in congenitally deaf individuals', *Neuroimage* 66, 42–49.

Perdue, C. and Bowerman, M. (1990), 'The structure of the simple clause in language acquisition: introduction', *Linguistics* 28, 1131–1133.

Pérez Núñez, A. (under review), 'The effects of implicit writing instruction on the writing development of heritage and L2 learners of Spanish', *Journal of Second Language Writing*.

Perpiñán, S. (2013), 'Optionality in bilingual native grammars' in M. Schmid and B. Köpke (eds.), *First Language Attrition* (Amsterdam: John Benjamins), 127–156.

Pérez Pereira, M. (1991). ' The acquisition of gender: what Spanish children tell us', *Journal of Child Language* 18, 571–590.

Petitto, L. A., Katerelos, M., Levy, B., Gauna, K., Tétrault, K. and Ferraro, V. (2001), 'Bilingual signed and spoken language acquisition from birth: implications for mechanisms underlying early bilingual language acquisition', *Journal of Child Language* 28, 2, 453–496.

Pfaff, C. (1991), 'Turkish in contact with German: language maintenance and loss among immigrant children in West Berlin', *International Journal of the Sociology of Language* 90, 77–129.

(1994), 'Early bilingual development of Turkish children in Berlin' in G. Extra and L. Verhoeven (eds.), *The Crosslinguistic Study of Bilingual Development* (Amsterdam: North Holland), 76–97.

Phillips, C. (1995), 'Syntax at age two: cross-linguistic differences' in C. Schütze, J. Ganger and K. Broihier (eds.), *Papers on Language Processing and Acquisition. MITWPL #26*, 225–282 (reprinted in *Language Acquisition*, 2010).

Pienemann, M. (1998), Language Processing and Language Development: Processability Theory (Amsterdam: John Benjamins).

(2005), 'Discussing PT' in M. Pienemann (ed.), *Cross-linguistic Aspects of Processability Theory* (Amsterdam: John Benjamins).

Pienemann, M. and Håkansson, G. (1999), 'A unified approach toward the development of Swedish as L2: a processability account', *Studies in Second Language Acquisition* 21, 383–420.

Pierce, L., Klein, D., Chen, J.-K., Delcenserie, A. and Genesee, F. (2014), 'Mapping the unconscious maintenance of a first language', *Proceedings of the National Academy of Sciences of the United States*, 111, 48, 17314–17319. doi: 10.1073/pnas.1409411111.

Pinker, S. (1984), *Language Learnability and Language Development* (Cambridge, MA: Harvard University Press).

(1989), *Learnability and Cognition: The Acquisition of Argument Structure* (Cambridge, MA: The MIT Press).

(1999), *Words and Rules* (New York, NY: Harper Books).

Pinker, S. and Ullman, M. (2002a), 'The past and future of the past tense', *Trends in Cognitive Sciences* 6, 456–463.

(2002b), 'Combination and structure, not gradedness, is the issue', *Trends in Cognitive Sciences* 6, 472–474.

Pires, A. and Rothman, J. (2009a), 'Disentangling contributing variables to incomplete acquisition competence outcomes: what differences across Brazilian and European Portuguese heritage speakers tell us', *International Journal of Bilingualism* 13, 211–238.

(2009b), 'Acquisition of Brazilian Portuguese in late childhood: implications for syntactic theory and language change' in A. Pires and J. Rothman (eds.), Minimalist Inquiries into Child and Adult Language Acquisition: Case Studies across Portuguese (Berlin and New York: Mouton DeGruyter), 129–154.

Place, S. and Hoff, E. (2011), 'Properties of dual language exposure that influence two-year-olds' bilingual proficiency', *Child Development* 82, 1834–1849.

Polinsky, M. (1995), 'Cross-linguistic parallels in language loss', *Southwest Journal of Linguistics* 14, 88–123.

(1997), 'American Russian: language loss meets language acquisition', *Proceedings of the Annual Workshop on Formal Approaches to Slavic Linguistics (The Cornell Meeting 1995)* (Ann Arbor, MI: Michigan Slavic Publications), 370–406.

12333

(2000), 'A composite linguistic profile of a speaker of Russian in the U.S' in O. Kagan and B. Rifkin (eds.), *The Learning and Teaching of Slavic Languages and Cultures* (Bloomington, IN: Slavica), 437–465.

(2004), 'Word class distinctions in an incomplete grammar' in D. Diskin and H. Bat-Zeev (eds.), *Perspectives on Language and Language Development* (Dordrecht: Kluwer), 419–436.

(2006), 'Incomplete acquisition: American Russian', *Journal of Slavic Linguistics* 14, 191–262.

(2008a), 'Russian gender under incomplete acquisition', *The Heritage Language Journal* 6, 40–71.

(2008b), 'Heritage language narratives' in D. Brinton, O. Kagan and S. Bauckus (eds.), *Heritage Language Education: A New Field Emerging* (New York, NY: Routledge), 149–164.

(2008c), 'Without aspect' in G. Corbett and M. Noonan (eds.), *Case and Grammatical Relations* (Amsterdam: John Benjamins), 263–282.

(2009), 'What breaks in A- and A-bar chains under incomplete acquisition', Paper presented at *22nd Annual CUNY Conference on Human Sentence Processing*, University of California, Davis.

(2011), 'Reanalysis in adult heritage language: a case for attrition', *Studies in Second Language Acquisition* 33, 305–328.

(2015). 'When L1 becomes an L3: do heritage speakers make better L3 learners?,' *Bilingualism, Language and Cognition* 18, 163–178.

Polinsky, M. and Kagan, O. (2007), 'Heritage languages: in the "wild" and in the classroom', *Language and Linguistics Compass* 1, 368–395.

Polio, C. (2001), 'Research methodology in second language writing research: the case of text based studies' in T. Silva and P. K. Matsuda (eds.), *On Second Language Writing* (Mahwah, NJ: Lawrence Erlbaum), 91–116.

Poplack, S. (1980), 'The notion of the plural in Puerto Rican Spanish: competing constraints on (s) deletion' in W. Labov (ed.), *Locating Language in Time and Space* (New York, NY: Academic Press), 55–67.

Portes, A. and Rumbaut, R. (1996), *Immigrant America: A Portrait* (Berkeley, CA: University of California Press).

Potowski, K. (ed.), (2010), *Language Diversity in the United States* (Cambridge, UK: Cambridge University Press).

(2012), 'Identity and heritage learners: moving beyond essentializations' in S. Beaudrie and M. Fairclough (eds.), *Spanish as a Heritage Language in the United States* (Washington, DC: Georgetown University Press), 179–202.

(2013), '"Transnational" youth: (re)integration into Mexican schools', Talk given at Stanford University, January 15.

Potowski, K., Jegerski, J. and Morgan-Short, K. (2009), 'The effects of instruction on linguistic development in Spanish heritage language speakers', *Language Learning* 59, 537–579.

Putnam, M. and Salmons, J. (2013), 'Losing their (passive) voice: syntactic neutralization in heritage German', *Linguistic Approaches to Bilingualism* 2, 233–252.

Radford, A. (1990), *Syntactic Theory and the Acquisition of English Syntax* (Oxford: Blackwell).

Ramsey, S. (1987), *The Languages of China.* (Princeton, NJ: Princeton University Press).

Rao, R. (2013), 'Allophonic variation in the voiced stop phonemes of heritage speakers of Spanish', Paper presented at the *7th Heritage Language Summer Institute*, University of Illinois at Chicago, June 18.

Ravid, D. (2004), 'Derivational morphology revisited: later lexical development in Hebrew' in R. Berman (ed.), *Language Development across Childhood and Adolescence* (Amsterdam: John Benjamins), 53–82.

Ravid, D. and Farah, R. (1999), 'Learning about noun plurals in early Palestinian Arabic', *First Language* 19, 187–206.

Ravid, D. and Tolschinsky, L. (2002), 'Developing linguistic literacy: a comprehensive model', *Journal of Child Language* 29, 417–447.

Reetz-Kurashige, A. (1999), 'Japanese returnees' retention of English-speaking skills: changes in verb usage over time' in L. Hansen (ed.), *Second Language Attrition in Japanese Contexts* (New York, NY: Oxford University Press), 21–58.

Reilly, J., Zamora, A. and McGivern, R. (2005), 'Acquiring perspective in English: the development of stance', *Journal of Pragmatics* 37, 185–208.

Rice, M. (2010), 'Mean length of utterance levels in 6-month intervals for children 3 to 9 years with and without language impairment', *Journal of Speech, Language and Hearing Research* 53, 333–349.

Rizzi, L. (1994), 'Early null subject and root null subjects' in B. Lust, G. Hermon and J. Kornfilt (eds.), *Syntactic Theory and First Language Acquisition: Cross-linguistic Perspectives. Volume 2: Binding Dependencies and Learnability* (Hillsdale, NJ: Erlbaum), 249–272.

Roberts, J. (1997), 'Acquisition of variable rules: a study of (-t,d) deletion in preschool children', *Journal of Child Language* 24, 351–372.

Rodina, Y. and Westergaard, M. (2012), 'A cue-based approach to the acquisition of grammatical gender in Russian', *Journal of Child Language* 39, 1077–1106.

Rodríguez-Mondoñedo, M. (2008), 'The acquisition of differential object marking in Spanish', *Probus* 20, 111–145.

Roeper, T. (1999), 'Universal bilingualism', *Bilingualism, Language and Cognition* 2, 169–186.

(2009), *The Prism of Grammar* (Cambridge, MA: MIT Press).

Rogers, C. L., Lister, J. J., Febo, D. M., Besing, J. M. and Abrams, H. B. (2006), 'Effects of bilingualism, noise, and reverberation on speech perception by listeners with normal hearing', *Applied Psycholinguistics* 27, 465–485.

Rothman, J. (2007), 'Heritage speaker competence differences, language change, and input type: inflected infinitives in heritage Brazilian Portuguese', *The International Journal of Bilingualism* 11, 359–389.

(2015), 'Linguistic and cognitive motivations for the Typological Primacy Model (TPM) of third language (L3) transfer: timing of acquisition and proficiency considered', *Bilingualism: Language and Cognition* 18, 179–190.

Russell, J. and Spada, N. (2006), 'The effectiveness of corrective feedback for the acquisition of L2 grammar: a meta-analysis of the research' in J. Norris and L. Ortega (eds.), *Synthesizing Research on Language Learning and Teaching* (Amsterdam: John Benjamins), 133–164.

Saadah, E. (2011), 'The production of Arabic vowels by English L2 learners and Heritage speakers of Arabic', Unpublished doctoral dissertation, University of Illinois at Urbana-Champaign.

Sánchez, L. (2003), *Quechua-Spanish Bilingualism: Interference and Convergence in Functional Categories* (Amsterdam: John Benjamins).

Sánchez, R. (1983), *Chicano Discourse: Socio-historic Perspectives* (Rowley, MA: Newbury House).

Sánchez-Walker, N. (2013), 'Comprehension of subject and object relative clauses in Spanish heritage speakers and L2 learners of Spanish', Qualifying doctoral paper, University of Illinois at Urbana-Champaign.

Sanz, C. and Morgan-Short, K. (2004), 'Positive evidence vs. explicit rule presentation and explicit negative feedback: a computer-assisted study', *Language Learning* 54, 35–78.

Savickiené, I. and Dressler, W. (2007), *The Acquisition of Diminutives: A Crosslinguistic Perspective* (Amsterdam: John Bejamins).

Schachter, J. (1990), 'On the issue of completeness in second language acquisition', *Second Language Research* 6, 93–124.

Scheele, A., Leseman, P. and Mayo, A. (2010), 'The home language environment of monolingual and bilingual children and their language proficiency', *Applied Psycholinguistics* 31, 117–140.

Schmid, M. (2002), *First Language Attrition, Use and Maintenance: The Case of German Jews in Anglophone Countries* (Amsterdam: John Benjamins).

(2007), 'The role of L1 use for L1 attrition' in B. Köpke, M. Schmid, M. Keijzer and S. Dosterst (eds.), *Language Attrition: Theoretical Perspectives* (Amsterdam: John Benjamins), 135–154.

(2011), *Language Attrition* (New York, NY: Cambridge University Press).

(2014), 'The debate on maturational constraints in bilingual development: a perspective from first language attrition', *Language Acquisition* 21, 4, 386–410. doi: 10.1 080/10489223.2014.892947.

Schmid, M. and Jarvis, S. (2014), 'Lexical first language attrition', *Bilingualism: Language and Cognition* 17, 729–748. doi: 10.1017/S1366728913000771.

Schmidt, A. (1985), *Young People's Dyirbal: An Example of Language Death from Australia* (Cambridge, UK: Cambridge University Press).

Schmitt, C. and Miller, K. (2010), 'Using comprehension methods in language acquisition research' in S. Unsworth and E. Blom (eds.), *Experimental Methods in Language Acquisition Research* (Amsterdam: John Benjamins), 35–56.

Schwartz, B. and Sprouse, R. (1996), 'L2 cognitive states and the full transfer/full access hypothesis', *Second Language Research* 12, 40–72.

Scott, C. (2004), 'Syntactic contributions to literacy' in A. Stone, E. Silliman, B. Ehren and K. Apel (eds.), *Handbook of Language and Literacy* (New York, NY: Guilford), 340–362.

Sebastián-Gallés, N. (2010), 'Bilingual language acquisition: where does the difference lie?', *Human Development* 53, 245–255.

Sekerina, I., Fernández, E. and Clahsen, H. (eds.), (2008), *Developmental Psycholinguistics: On-line Methods in Children's Language Processing* (Amsterdam: John Benjamins).

Sekerina, I. and Trueswell, J. (2011), 'Processing of contrastiveness by heritage Russian bilinguals', *Bilingualism: Language and Cognition* 14, 280–300.

Seliger, H. (1978), 'Implications of a multiple critical periods hypothesis for second language learning' in W. Ritchie (ed.), *Second Language Acquisition Research: Issues and Implications* (New York, NY: Academic Press), 11–19.

(1991), 'Language attrition, reduced redundancy, and creativity' in H. Seliger and R. Vago (eds.), *First Language Attrition* (Cambridge, UK: Cambridge University Press), 173–184.

(1996), 'Primary language attrition in the context of bilingualism' in W. Ritchie and T. Bhatia (eds.), *Handbook of Second Language Acquisition* (New York, NY: Academic Press), 605–625.

Selinker, L. (1972), 'Interlanguage', *International Review of Applied Linguistics* 10, 209–231.

Serratrice, L. (2001), 'The emergence of verbal morphology and the lead-lag pattern issue in bilingual acquisition' in J. Cenoz and F. Genesee (eds.), *Trends in Bilingual Acquisition* (Amsterdam: John Benjamins), 43–70.

(2002), 'Overt subjects in English: evidence for the marking of person in an English-Italian bilingual child', *Journal of Child Language* 29, 327–355.

Serratrice, L. Sorace, A. Filiaci, F. and Baldo, M. (2009), 'Bilingual children's sensitivity to specificity and genericity: evidence from metalinguistic awareness', *Bilingualism: Language and Cognition* 12, 239–257.

Sharma, D. (2005a), 'Dialect stabilization and speaker awareness in non-native varieties of English', *Journal of Sociolinguistics* 9, 194–224.

(2005b), 'Language transfer and discourse universals in Indian English article use', *Studies in Second Language Acquisition* 27, 535–566.

Shatz, M. (2009), 'On the development of the field of language development' in E. Hoff and M. Shatz (eds.), *Blackwell Handbook of Language Development* (Malden, MA: Wiley-Blackwell), 368–387.

Sheldon, A. (1974), 'The role of parallel function in the acquisition of relative clauses in English', *Journal of Verbal Learning and Verbal Behavior* 13, 272–281.

Sherkina-Lieber, M. (2011), 'Comprehension of Labrador Inuttitut functional morphology by receptive bilinguals', Unpublished doctoral dissertation, University of Toronto.

Sherkina-Lieber, M., Pérez-Leroux, A. T. and Jones, A. (2011), 'Grammar without speech production: the case of Inuttitut heritage receptive bilinguals', *Bilingualism: Language and Cognition* 14, 301–317.

Shin, N. (2014), 'Grammatical complexification in Spanish in New York: 3sg pronoun expression and verbal morphology', *Language Variation and Change* 26, 303–330. doi: 10.1017/S095439451400012X.

Shin, N. and Cairns, H. (2012), 'The development of NP selection in school-age children: reference and Spanish subject pronouns', *Language Acquisition* 19, 3–38.

Shin, N. and Otheguy, R. (2013), 'Social class and gender impacting change in bilingual settings: Spanish subject pronoun use in New York', *Language in Society* 42, 429–452.

Shin, S. (2002), 'Birth order and the language experience of bilingual children', *TESOL Quarterly* 36, 103–113.

(2005), *Developing in Two Languages: Korean Children in America* (Clevedon: Multilingual Matters).

Shiri, S. (2010), 'Arabic in the United States' in K. Potowski (ed.), *Language Diversity in the United States* (Cambridge, UK: Cambridge University Press), 206–222.

Silva-Corvalán, C. (1994), *Language Contact and Change: Spanish in Los Angeles* (Oxford: Clarendon).

(2001), *Sociolingüística y pragmática del español* (Washington, DC: Georgetown University Press).

(2003), 'Linguistic consequences of reduced input in bilingual first language acquisition' in S. Montrul and F. Ordóñez (eds.), *Linguistic Theory and Language Development in Hispanic Languages* (Somerville: Cascadilla Press), 375–397.

(2014), *Bilingual Language Acquisition: Spanish and English in the First Six Years* (Cambridge, UK: Cambridge University Press).

Silva-Corvalán, C. and Treffers-Daller, J. (eds.), (2016), *Language Dominance in Bilinguals: Issues of Measurement and Operationalization* (Cambridge, UK: Cambridge University Press).

Simpson, S. A. and Cooke, M. P. (2005), 'Consonant identification in N-talker babble is a nonmonotonic function of N', *Journal of the Acoustical Society of America* 118, 2775–2778.

Slabakova, R. (2008), *Meaning in the Second Language* (Berlin: Mouton de Gruyter).

Slobin, D. (1973), 'Cognitive prerequisites for the development of grammar' in C. Ferguson and D. Slobin (eds.), *Studies of Child Language Development* (New York, NY: Hold Reinhart and Winston), 175–208.

Smith, C. (1991), *The Parameter of Aspect* (Dordrecht: Kluwer Academic Press).

Smith, J., Durham, M. and Fortune, L. (2007), 'Mam, my trousers is fa'in doon!: community, caregiver, and child in the acquisition of variation in a Scottish dialect', *Language Variation and Change* 19, 63–99.

Snyder, W. (2007), *Child Language: The Parametric Approach* (Oxford: Oxford University Press).

Song, M., O'Grady, W., Cho, S. and Lee, M. (1997), 'The learning and teaching of Korean in community schools' in Y.-H. Kim (ed.), *Korean Language in America 2* (Honolulu, HI: American Association of Teachers of Korean), 111–127.

Sorace, A. (2000), 'Differential effects of attrition in the L1 syntax of near-native L2 speakers', *Proceedings of the 24th Boston University Conference on Language Development* (Sommerville, MA: Cascadilla Press), 719–725.

(2004), 'Native language attrition and developmental instability at the syntax-discourse interface: data, interpretations and methods', *Bilingualism: Language and Cognition* 7, 143–145.

(2011), 'Pinning down the concept of "interface" in bilingualism', *Linguistic Approaches to Bilingualism* 1, 1–34.

Sorace, A. and Filiaci, F. (2006), 'Anaphora resolution in near native speakers of Italian', *Second Language Research* 22, 339–368.

Spolsky, B. and Shohamy, E. (1999), *The Languages of Israel: Policy, Ideology and Practice* (Clevedon: Multilingual Matters).

Sprouse, J. and Almeida, D. (2012), 'Assessing the reliability of textbook data in syntax: Adger's Core Syntax', *Journal of Linguistics* 48, 609–652.

Stern, C. and Stern, W. (1907), *Die Kindersprache: Eine Psychologische und Sprachtheorische Untersuchung* (Leipzig: Barth).

Stölten, K. (2013), 'The effects of age of onset on VOT in L2 acquisition and L2 attrition', *Dissertations in Bilingualism* 23, Stockholm University.

Swain, M. (2000), 'The output hypothesis and beyond: mediating acquisition through collaborative dialogue' in J. Lantolf (ed.), *Sociocultural Theory and Second Language Learning* (New York, NY: Oxford University Press), 97–114.

Tagliamonte, S. and Denis, D. (2010), 'The stuff of change: general extenders in Toronto, Canada', *Journal of English Linguistics* 38, 355–367.

Taranrød, B. (2011), 'Leddstillingen i relativsetninger i amerikansknorsk', Master's thesis, Department of Linguistics and Nordic Studies, University of Oslo, Oslo.

Tarone, E. (1979), 'Interlanguage as chameleon', *Language Learning* 29, 181–191.

(1983), 'On the variability of interlanguage systems', *Applied Linguistics* 4, 143–163.

Tarone, E. and Han, H. Z. (eds.) (2014), *Interlanguage: 40 Years Later: In Honor of Larry Selinker*. (Amsterdam: John Benjamins).

Tarone, E. and Liu, G.-Q. (1995), 'Situational context, variation and SLA theory' in G. Cook and B. Seidlhofer (eds.), *Principles and Practice in Applied Linguistics: Studies in Honor of H. G. Widdowson* (Oxford University Press), 125–144.

Tavakolian, S. (1977), 'Structural principles in the acquisition of complex sentences', Doctoral dissertation, University of Massachusetts, Amherst.

Thal, D., Bates, E., Goodman, J. and Jahn-Samilo, J. (1997), 'Continuity of language abilities in late and early-talking toddlers', *Developmental Neurospychology* 13, 239–273.

Thomas, M. (1995), 'Acquisition of the Japanese reflexive zibun and movement of anaphors in logical form', *Second Language Research* 11, 206–234.

(2013), 'History of the study of second language acquisition' in J. Herschensohn and M. Young-Scholten (eds.), *The Cambridge Handbook of Second Language Acquisition* (Cambridge, UK: Cambridge University Press), 26–45.

Thomason, S. (2001), *Language Contact* (Washington, DC: Georgetown University Press).

Thomason, S. and Kaufman, T. (1988), *Language Contact, Creolization, and Genetic Linguistics* (Berkeley, CA: University of California Press).

Thordardottir, E. (2013), 'The effect of amount of input on simultaneous and sequential bilingual acquisition', Plenary talk, *International Conference on Multilingualism*, McGill University, Montreal, October 24–25.

Ticio, E. (2015), 'The acquisition of differential object marking in Spanish-English early bilinguals', *Linguistic Approaches to Bilingualism* 5, 62–90.

Tolchinsky, L. (2004), 'The nature and scope of later language development' in R. Berman (ed.), *Language Development across Childhood and Adolescence* (Amsterdam: John Benjamins), 233–248.

Tomasello, M. (2001), 'The item-based nature of children's early syntactic development' in M. Tomasello and E. Bates (eds.), *Language Development: The Essential Readings* (Malden, MA: Blackwell), 169–186.

(2003), *Constructing a Language: A Usage-Based Theory of Language Acquisition* (Cambridge, MA: Harvard University Press).

Tomasello, M. and Farrar, J. (1986), 'Joint attention and early language', *Child Development* 57, 1454–1463.

Tomiyama, M. (1999), 'The first stage of second language attrition: a case study of a Japanese returnee' in L. Hansen (ed.), *Second Language Attrition in Japanese Contexts* (New York, NY: Oxford University Press), 59–79.

(2008), 'Age and proficiency in L2 attrition: data from two siblings', *Applied Linguistics* 30, 253–275.

Toribio, A. J. (2003), 'The social significance of language loyalty among black and white Dominicans in New York', *Bilingual Review/La Revista Bilingüe* 27, 3–11.

Torres Cacoullos, R. and Travis, C. (2015), 'Subject pronoun realization in Spanish and English: assessing inter-linguistic functional equivalence via intra-linguistic inherent variability' in A. M. Carvalho, R. Orozco and N. L. Shin (eds.), *Subject Pronoun Expression in Spanish: A Cross-dialectal Perspective* (Washington, DC: Georgetown University Press) 81–100.

Trahey, M. and White, L. (1993), 'Positive evidence and preemption in the second language classroom', *Studies in Second Language Acquisition* 15, 181–204.

Treffers-Daller, J. (2011), 'Operationalizing and measuring language dominance', *International Journal of Bilingualism*, 15, 147–163.

Treffers-Daller, J. and Korybski, T. (2016), 'Using lexical diversity measures to operationalise language dominance in bilinguals' in C. Silva-Corvalán and J. Treffers-Daller (eds.), *Language Dominance in Bilinguals: Issues of Measurement and Operationalization* (Cambridge, UK: Cambridge University Press).

Tremblay, A. (2011), 'Proficiency assessment standards in second language acquisition research: closing the "gap"', *Studies in Second Language Acquisition* 33, 339–372.

Trudgill, P. (1976–1977), 'Creolization in reverse: reduction and simplification in the Albanian dialects of Greece', *Transactions of the Philological Society* 75, 32–50.

Tse, L. (1998), 'Affecting affect: the impact of heritage language programs on student attitudes' in S. Krashen, L. Tse and J. Mcquillan (eds.), *Heritage Language Development* (Culver City, CA: Language Education Associates) 51–72.

(2001a), *Why don't They Learn English? Separating Fact from Fallacy in the U.S. Language Debate* (New York and London: Teachers College Press).

(2001b), 'Resisting and reversing language shift: heritage-language resilience among U.S. native biliterates', *Harvard Educational Review* 71, 676–708.

Tseng, V. and Fuligni, A. J. (2000), 'Parent-adolescent language use and relationships among immigrant families with East Asian, Filipino, and Latin American backgrounds', *Journal of Marriage and Family* 62, 2, 465–476.

Tsimpli, I. (2007), 'First language attrition from a minimalist perspective: interface vulnerability and processing effects' in B. Köpke, M. Schmid, M. Keijzer and S. Dosterst (eds.), *Language Attrition. Theoretical Perspectives* (Amsterdam: John Benjamins), 83–98.

Tsimpli, I. and Dimitrakopoulou, M. (2007), 'The interpretability hypothesis: evidence from wh-interrogatives in second language acquisition', *Second Language Language Research* 23, 215–242.

Tsimpli, I., Sorace, A., Heycock, C. and Filiaci, F. (2004), 'First language attrition and syntactic subjects: a study of Greek and Italian near-native speakers of English', *International Journal of Bilingualism* 8, 157–177.

Turian, D. and Altenberg, E. (1991), 'Compensatory strategies of child first language attrition' in H. Seliger and R. Vago (eds.), *First Language Attrition* (Cambridge, UK: Cambridge University Press), 207–227.

Ullman, M. (2001), 'The neural basis of lexicon and grammar in first and second language: the declarative/procedural model', *Bilingualism: Language and Cognition* 4, 105–122.

Unsworth, S. (2005), 'Child L2, adult L2, child L1: differences and similarities. A study on the acquisition of direct object scrambling in Dutch', Doctoral dissertation, Utrecht University, the Netherlands.

Unsworth, S. and Hulk, A. (2010), '*L1 acquisition of neuter gender in Dutch: production and judgement*', *Proceedings of GALA 09* (Cambridge: Cambridge Scholars Publishing) 1–10.

Vago, R. (1991), 'Paradigmatic regularity in first language attrition' in H. Seliger and R. Vago (eds.), *First Language Attrition* (Cambridge, UK: Cambridge University Press), 241–252.

Valdés, G. (1989), 'Teaching Spanish to Hispanic bilinguals: a look at oral proficiency testing and the proficiency movement', *Hispania* 73, 392–401.

(1995), 'The teaching of minority languages as 'foreign' languages: pedagogical and theoretical challenges', *The Modern Language Journal* 79, 299–328.

(2000), 'Introduction' in *Spanish for Native Speakers, Volume I. AATSP Professional Development Series Handbook for Teachers K-16* (New York, NY: Harcourt College) 1–20.

(2001), 'Heritage language students: profiles and possibilities' in J. Peyton, D. Renard and S. McGinnis (eds.), *Heritage Languages in America: Preserving a National Resource* (Washington, DC: Center for Applied Linguistics), 37–77.

(2005), 'Bilingualism, heritage learners, and SLA research: opportunities lost or seized?', *Modern Language Journal* 89, 410–426.

(2006), 'The Spanish language in California' in G. Valdés, J. Fishman, R. Chávez and W. Pérez (eds.), *Developing Minority Language Resources. The Case of Spanish in California* (Clevedon: Multilingual Matters), 24–53.

Valdés, G., Fishman, J., Chávez, R. and Pérez, W. (2006), *Developing Minority Language Resources. The Case of Spanish in California* (Clevedon: Multilingual Matters).

Valenzuela, E., Faure, A., Ramírez-Trujillo, A., Barski, E., Pangtay, Y. and Diez, A. (2012), 'Gender and heritage Spanish bilingual grammars: a study of code-mixed determiner phrases and copula constructions', *Hispania* 95, 481–494.

Valian, V. (2009), 'Innateness and learnability' in E. Bavin (ed.), *Handbook of Child Language* (Cambridge, UK: Cambridge University Press), 15–34.

Van Deusen-Scholl, N. (2003), 'Toward a definition of heritage language: sociopolitical and pedagogical considerations', *Journal of Language, Identity and Education* 2, 211–230.

VanPatten, B. (1996), *Input Processing and Grammar Instruction. Theory and Research* (Norwood, NJ: Ablex).

VanPatten, B. and Jegerski, J. (eds.), (2010), *Research on Second Language Processing and Parsing* (Amsterdam: John Benjamins).

Ventureyra, V. (2005), 'A la recherche de la langue perdue: etude psycholinguistique de l'attrition de la première langue chez des coréens adoptés en France', Unpublished doctoral dissertation, Ecole des Hautes Etudes en Sciences Sociales.

Ventureyra, V. and Pallier, C. (2007), 'In search of the lost language' in M. Schmid, B. Köpke, M. Keijer and L. Weilmar (eds.), *First Language Attrition* (Amsterdam: John Benjamins), 207–221.

Verkuyl, H. (1994), *A Theory of Aspectuality: The Interaction between Temporal and Atemporal Structure* (Cambridge University Press).

Viswanath, A. (2013), 'Heritage English in Israeli children', Undergraduate Honors thesis, Harvard University.

Volterra, V. and Taeschner, T. (1978), 'The acquisition and development of language by bilingual children', *The Journal of Child Language* 5, 311–326.

Von Raffler-Engel, W. (1965), 'Del bilinguismo infantile', *Archivio Glottologico Italiano* 50, 175–180.

Waldmann, C. (2008), 'Input och output: ordföljd i svenska barns huvudsatser och Bisatser', Unpublished doctoral dissertation, University of Lund, Lund.

Warner, S. (2014), 'Task-based interactions between Spanish-speaking heritage learners', Unpublished undergraduate senior thesis, University of Illinois, Urbana-Champaign.

Watson, S. (1989), 'Scottish and Irish Gaelic: the giant's bed-fellows' in N. Dorian (ed.), *Investigating Obsolescence. Studies in Language Contraction and Death* (Cambridge, UK: Cambridge, UK: Cambridge University Press), 41–59.

Weinrich, U. (1953), *Languages in Contact* (New York, NY: The Linguistic Circle).

Wen, X. (2011), 'Chinese language learning motivation: a comparative study of heritage and non-heritage learners', *The Heritage Language Journal* 8, 41–66.

Westergaard, M. and Bentzen, K. (2007), 'The (non-)effect of input frequency on the acquisition of word order in Norwegian embedded clauses' in I. Gülzow and N. Gagarina (eds.), *Frequency Effects in Language Acquisition: Defining the Limits of Frequency as an Explanatory Concept* (Berlin: Mouton de Gruyter), 271–306.

Wexler, K. (1994), 'Optional infinitives, head movement and the economy of derivations' in D. Lightfoot and N. Hornstein (eds.), *Verb Movement* (Cambridge, UK: Cambridge University Press), 305–363.

Wexler, K. and Chien, Y.-C. (1985), 'The development of lexical anaphors and pronouns', *Papers and Reports on Child Language Development* 24, 138–149.

White, L. (1989), *Universal Grammar and Second Language Acquisition* (Amsterdam: John Benjamins).

(1991), 'Adverb placement in second language acquisition: some positive and negative evidence in the classroom', *Second Language Research* 7, 133–161.

(2003a), 'Fossilization in steady state L2 grammars: persistent problems with inflectional morphology', *Bilingualism: Language and Cognition* 6, 129–141.

(2003b), *Second Language Acquisition and Universal Grammar* (Cambridge, UK: Cambridge University Press).

(2008), 'Definiteness effects in the L2 English of Mandarin and Turkish speakers', *Proceedings of the 32nd Annual Boston University Conference on Language Development* (Somerville, MA: Cascadilla Press), 550–561.

(2011), 'The interface hypothesis: how far does it extend?', Linguistic Approaches to Bilingualism 1, 108–110.

White, L., Belikova, A., Hagström, P., Kupisch, T. and Özcelik, Ö. (2012), 'Restrictions on definiteness in second language acquisition', *Linguistic Approaches to Bilingualism* 2, 54–89.

White, L., Bruhn-Garavito, J., Kawasaki, T., Pater, J. and Prévost, P. (1997), 'The researcher gave the subject a test about himself: problems of ambiguity and preference in the investigation of reflexive binding', *Language Learning* 47, 1, 145–172.

White, L and Genesee, F. (1996), 'How native is near-native? The issue of ultimate attainment in adult second language acquisition', *Second Language Research* 12, 238–265.

White, L., Hirakawa, M. and Kawasaki, T. (1996), 'Effect of instruction on second language acquisition of the Japanese long-distance reflexive zibun', *Canadian Journal of Linguistics/Revue canadienne de linguistique* 41, 135–154.

348   References

White, L., Valenzuela, E., Kozlowska-Macgregor, M. and Leung, Y.-K. I. (2004), 'Gender agreement in nonnative Spanish: evidence against failed features', *Applied Psycholinguistics* 25, 105–133.

Wiley, T. (2008), 'Chinese "dialect" speakers as heritage language learners: a case study' in D. Brinton, O. Kagan and S. Bauckus (eds.), *Heritage Language Education: A New Field Emerging* (New York, NY: Routledge), 91–106.

Wong-Fillmore, L. (1991), 'When learning a second language means losing the first', *Early Childhood Research Quarterly* 6, 323–346.

(2000), 'Loss of family languages: should educators be concerned?', Theory into Practice 39, 203–210.

Yeatman, J. D., Dougherty, R. F., Ben-Shachar, M. and Wandell, B. (2012), 'The development of white matter and reading skills', *Proceedings of the National Academic Sciences USA* 109, 44, E3045–E3053.

Yeni-Komshian, G., Flege, J. and Liu S. (2000), 'Pronunciation proficiency in the first and second languages of Korean-English bilinguals', *Bilingualism: Language and Cognition* 3, 131–149.

Yılmaz, G. (2013), 'Complex embedding in free speech production among late Turkish-Dutch bilinguals' in M. Schmid and B. Köpke (eds.), *First Language Attrition* (Amsterdam: John Benjamins), 67–90.

Yip, V. and Mathews, S. (2006), 'Assessing language dominance in bilingual acquisition: a case for mean length utterance differentials', *Language Assessment Quarterly* 3, 97–116.

Yip, V. and Matthews, S. (2007), *The Bilingual Child: Early Development and Language Contact* (Cambridge, UK: Cambridge University Press).

Yoshitomi, A. (1999), 'On the loss of English as a second language by Japanese returnee children' in L. Hansen (ed.), *Second Language Attrition in Japanese Contexts* (New York, NY: Oxford University Press), 80–111.

Yuan, B. (1998), 'Interpretation of binding and orientation of the Chinese reflexive ziji by English and Japanese speakers', *Second Language Research* 14, 324–340.

Zaretsky, E. and Bar-Shalom, E. (2010), 'Does reading in shallow L1 orthography slow attrition of language-specific morphological structures?', *Clinical Linguistics and Phonetics* 24, 401–415.

Zatorre, R., Fields, D. and Johansen-Berg, H. (2012), 'Plasticity in grey and white: neuroimaging changes in brain structure during learning', *Nature Neuroscience* 15, 528–536.

Zentella, A. C. (1990), 'Returned migration, language, and identity: Puerto Rican bilinguals in dos worlds/two mundos', *International Journal of the Sociology of Language* 84, 81–100.

(1997), *Growing Up Bilingual: Puerto Rican Children in New York* (Malden, MA: Blackwell).

Zhang, Y. (2005), 'Processing and formal instruction in the L2 acquisition of five Chinese grammatical morphemes' in M. Pienemann (ed.), *Cross-linguistic Aspects of Processability Theory* (Philadelphia, PA: John Benjamins), 155–178.

Zobolou, K. (2011), 'Attrition in Greek Diaspora: grammars in contact or incomplete acquisition?' in K. Ihemere (ed.), *Language Contact and Language Shift: Grammatical and Sociolinguistic Perspectives*, Chapter 3, *LINCOM Studies in Language Typology* 17 (Munich, Germany).

Index

aboriginal language(s), *see* indigenous language(s)
abstract grammatical/linguistic knowledge, 134, 139
abstract language, 106
accusative, 58, 59, 159, 205
Acceptability Judgment Tasks (AJT), 79, 193, 197, 203, 209, 213, 221, 261, 265, 271, 274, 283
acquisition, 90, 104, 117, 123
ACTFL, 183
adjectives, 210
adult L2 learners, 96, 143
adult second language learners, 129
age effects, 98, 110, 113, 177, 217, 250, 254, 267, 296
Age of Acquisition (AoA), 51, 52, 90, 93, 112, 113, 129, 177, 256, 260, 266, 270, 271, 277, 296
age of exposure, 45
age of onset of bilingualism, 6
agreement, 56, 104, 124, 170, 191
  nominal, verbal, 53
AJT, 198, 200, 214
Amelioration Hypothesis, 161
America, 33
American Association of Teachers of Spanish and Portuguese (AATSP), 303
American Russian, 155
American Scandinavian, 229
American Sign Language, 111, 116
amount of input, 253
anaphora, 137
anaphors, 158
Arabic, 27, 28, 30, 54, 56, 74, 81, 84, 174, 184, 226, 227, 231, 259, 261, 293, 294
Argentina, 56, 228
Arizona, 120
Armenian, 184
articles, 78
  definite articles, 78

artificial language, 88
Arvanitika, 70
Asian languages, 6
ASL, *see* American Sign Language
aspect, 53, 63, 64, 65, 68, 124, 218, 261, 263, 275
  grammatical aspect, 65, 68
  imperfective, 63
  imperfective aspect, 63
  lexical aspect, 63
  perfective aspect, 63, 152
  viewpoint aspect, 63
aspectual interpretations, 262
aspectual morphology, 63
attitudes, 120, 306, 307, 308, 309
attrition, 37, 38, 68, 90, 112, 113, 114, 115, 119, 126, 151, 156, 160, 173, 184, 189, 206, 216, 217, 218, 231, 233, 235, 245, 246, 247, 296, 300, 301, *see* language loss, forgetting
aural acceptability judgment tasks, 196
aural grammaticality judgment tasks, 197
Australia, 33, 34, 49
Austria, 49
Aymará, 31, 33

balanced bilinguals, 42, 93, 99, 249
bare nouns, 271
baseline, 123, 125, 165, 167, 169, 171, 172, 173, 174, 175, 178, 181, 204, 207, 219, 238, 259
Basque, 32, *see* Euskera
Basque Country, 31, 32, 96, 120, 308
Berber, 29
bilingual acquisition, 132
bilingual approach, 177, 213
bilingual children, 35, 36, 38, 40, 81, 94, 101, 114, 118, 127, 168, 174, 231
bilingual design, 177, 178
bilingual education, 30
bilingual families, 34, 35

Author index

Printed by Printforce, United Kingdom